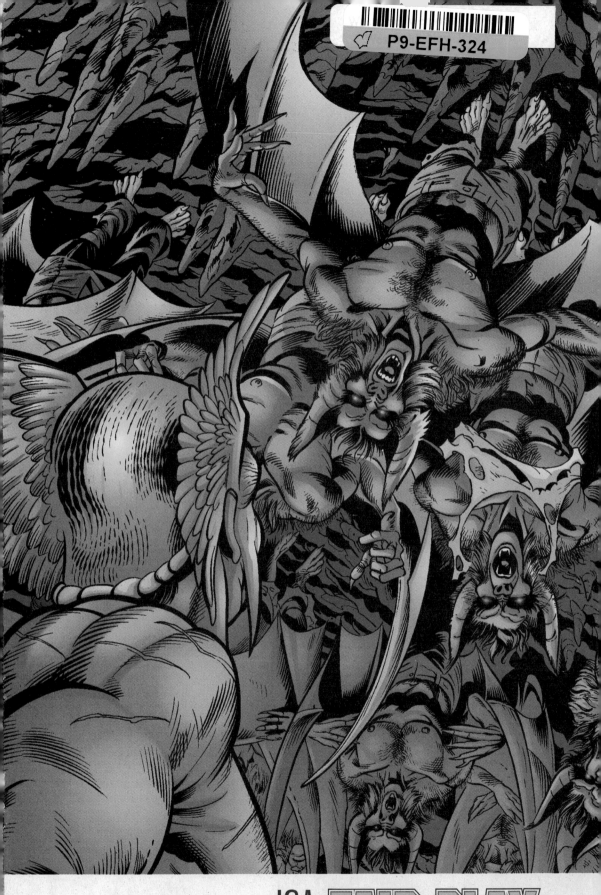

JSA FAIR PLAY

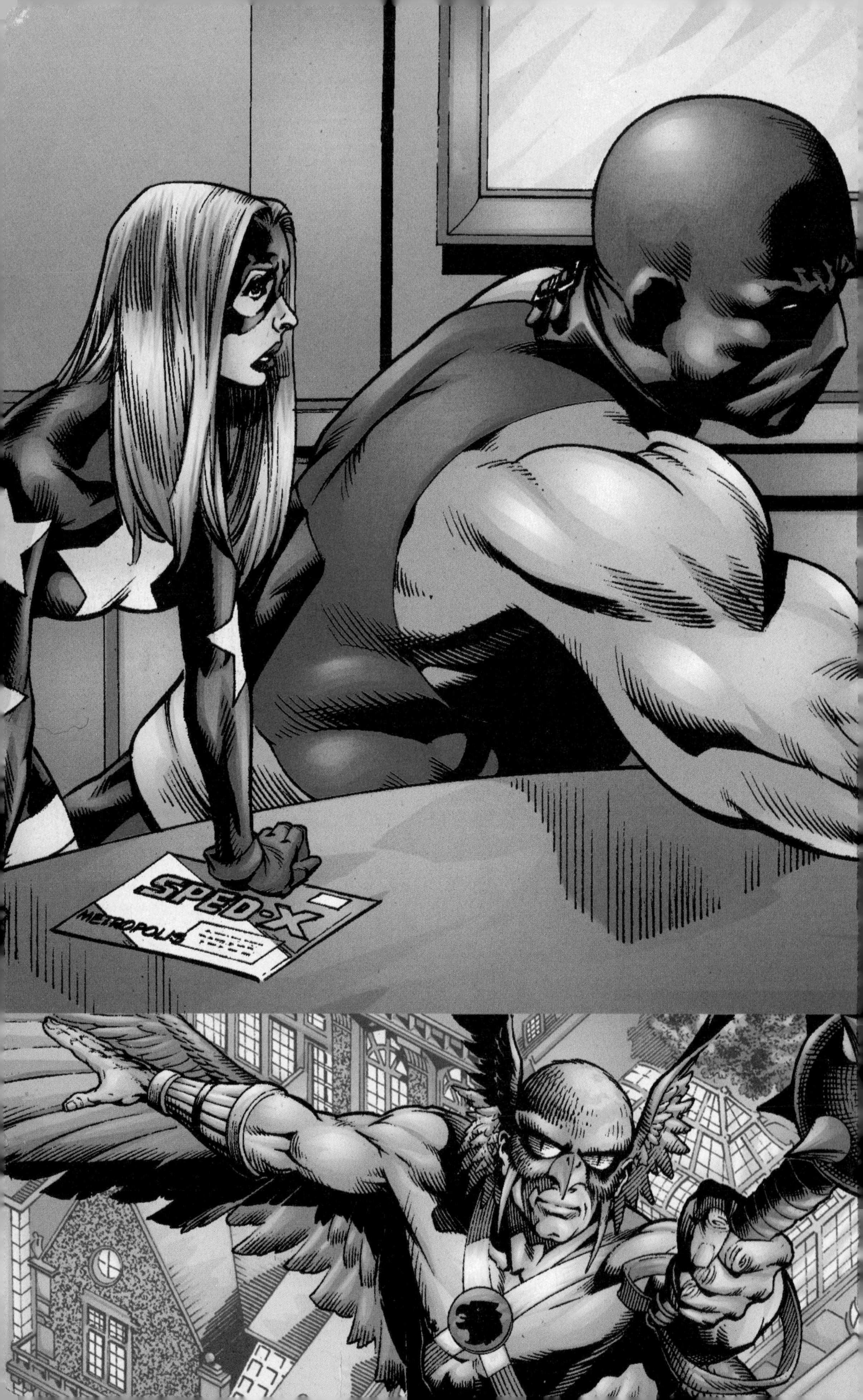
SPED-X
METROPOLIS

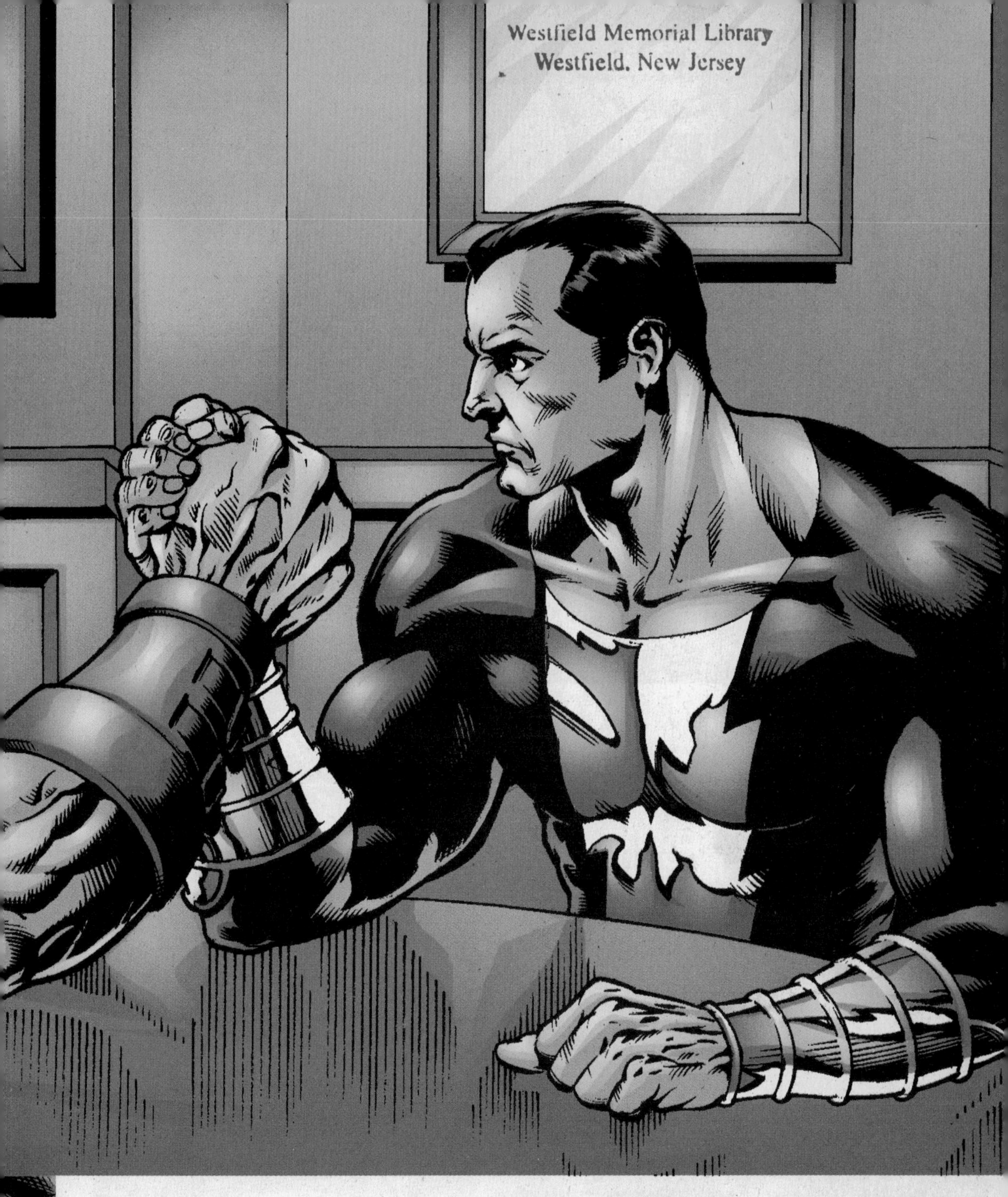

JSA FAIR PLAY

GEOFF JOHNS **WRITER** RAGS MORALES STEPHEN SADOWSKI PETER SNEJBJERG JAVIER SALTARES DEREC AUCOIN **PENCILLERS** MICHAEL BAIR KEITH CHAMPAGNE PETER SNEJBJERG RAY KRYSSING DAVID MEIKIS CHRISTIAN ALAMY **INKERS** JOHN KALISZ TOM MCCRAW **COLORISTS** KEN LOPEZ KURT HATHAWAY **LETTERERS**

Mike Carlin — VP-Executive Editor

Peter Tomasi — Editor-original series

Bob Greenberger — Senior Editor-collected edition

Robbin Brosterman — Senior Art Director

Paul Levitz — President & Publisher

Georg Brewer — VP-Design & Retail Product Development

Richard Bruning — VP-Creative Director

Patrick Caldon — Senior VP-Finance & Operations

Chris Caramalis — VP-Finance

Terri Cunningham — VP-Managing Editor

Dan DiDio — VP-Editorial

Joel Ehrlich — Senior VP-Advertising & Promotions

Alison Gill — VP-Manufacturing

Lillian Laserson — Senior VP & General Counsel

David McKillips — VP-Advertising

John Nee — VP-Business Development

Cheryl Rubin — VP-Licensing & Merchandising

Bob Wayne — VP-Sales & Marketing

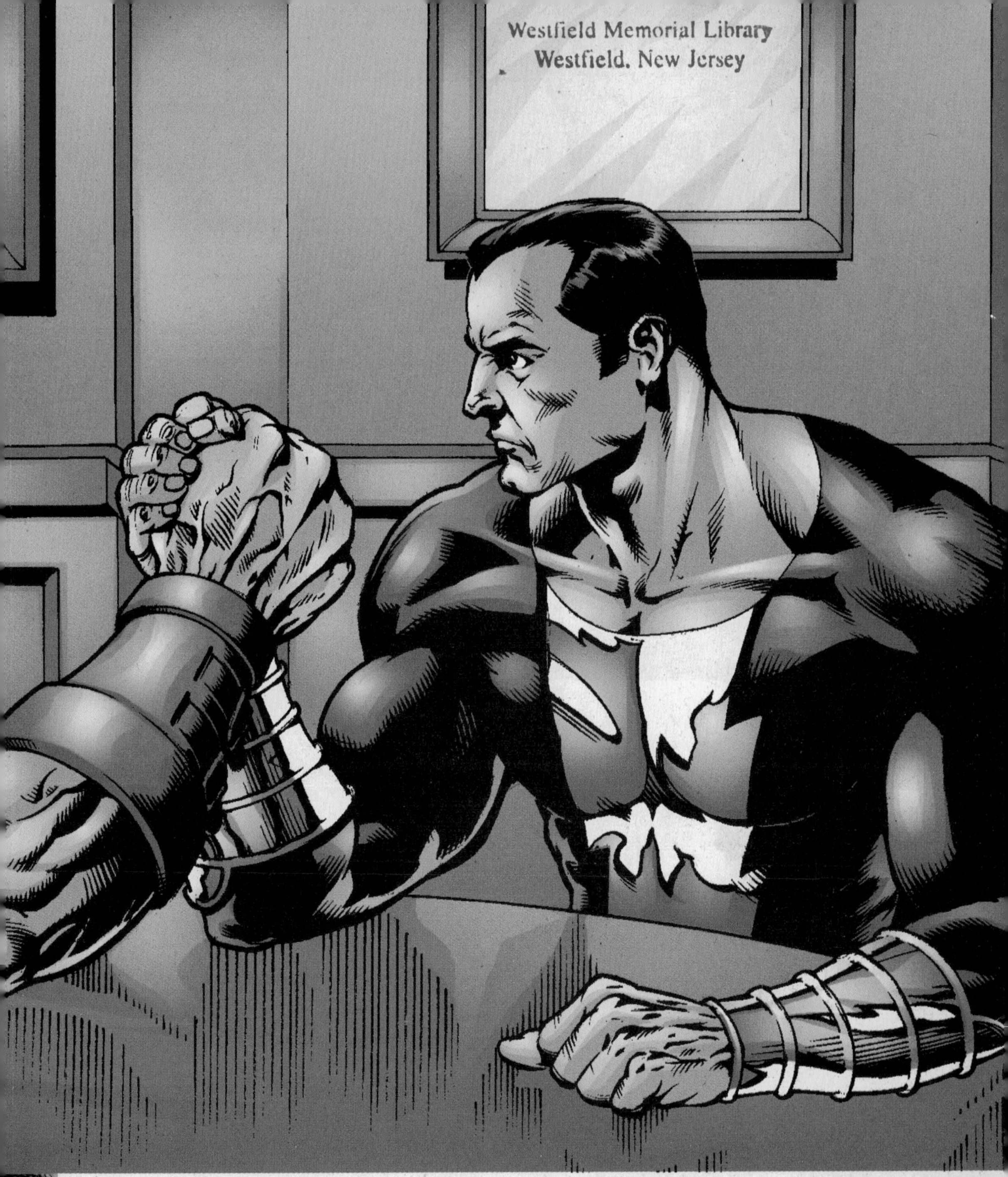

JSA FAIR PLAY

GEOFF JOHNS WRITER RAGS MORALES STEPHEN SADOWSKI PETER SNEJBJERG JAVIER SALTARES DEREC AUCOIN PENCILLERS MICHAEL BAIR KEITH CHAMPAGNE PETER SNEJBJERG RAY KRYSSING DAVID MEIKIS CHRISTIAN ALAMY INKERS JOHN KALISZ TOM MCCRAW COLORISTS KEN LOPEZ KURT HATHAWAY LETTERERS

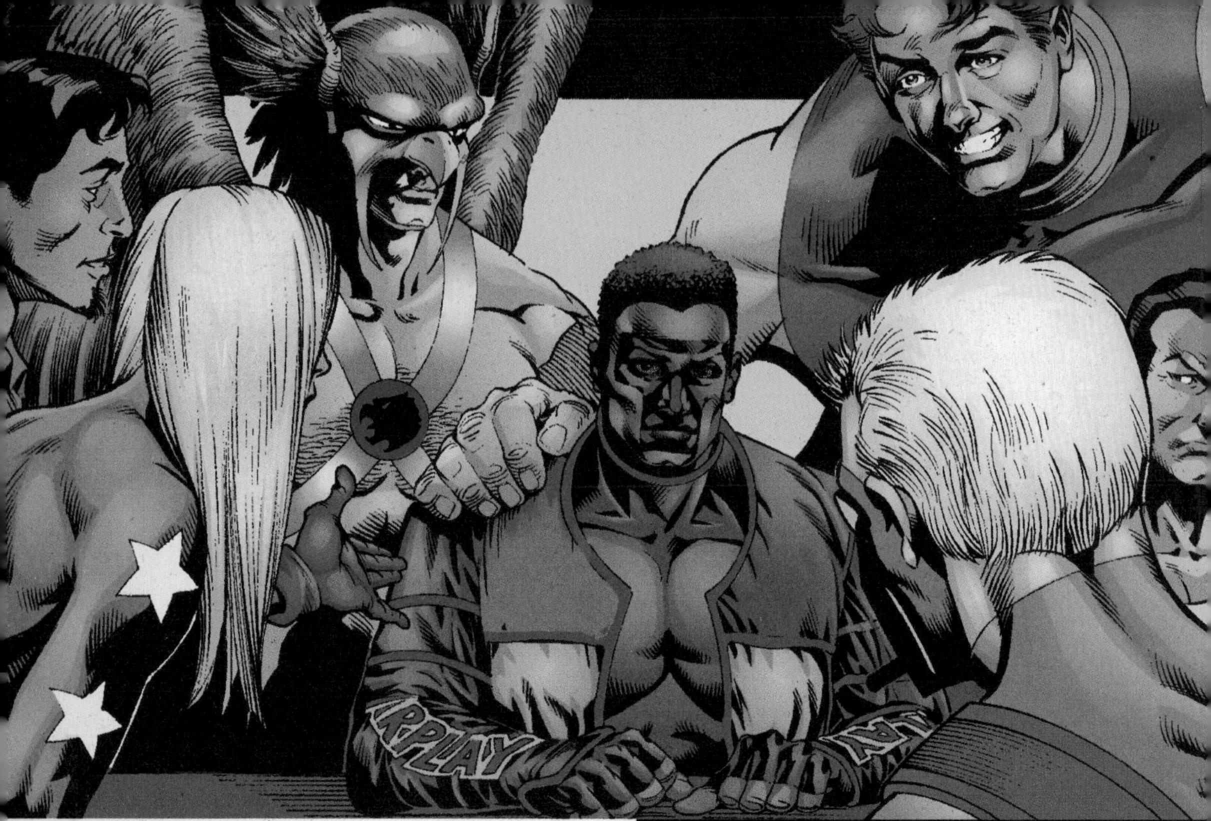

Mike Carlin	VP-Executive Editor
Peter Tomasi	Editor-original series
Bob Greenberger	Senior Editor-collected edition
Robbin Brosterman	Senior Art Director
Paul Levitz	President & Publisher
Georg Brewer	VP-Design & Retail Product Development
Richard Bruning	VP-Creative Director
Patrick Caldon	Senior VP-Finance & Operations
Chris Caramalis	VP-Finance
Terri Cunningham	VP-Managing Editor
Dan DiDio	VP-Editorial
Joel Ehrlich	Senior VP-Advertising & Promotions
Alison Gill	VP-Manufacturing
Lillian Laserson	Senior VP & General Counsel
David McKillips	VP-Advertising
John Nee	VP-Business Development
Cheryl Rubin	VP-Licensing & Merchandising
Bob Wayne	VP-Sales & Marketing

JSA: FAIR PLAY Published by DC Comics. Cover and compilation copyright © 2003 DC Comics. All Rights Reserved. Originally published in single magazine form in JSA 26-31 and JSA SECRET FILES 2. Copyright © 2001, 2002 DC Comics. All Rights Reserved. All characters, their distinctive likenesses and related indicia featured in this publication are trademarks of DC Comics. The stories, characters, and incidents featured in this publication are entirely fictional. DC Comics does not read or accept unsolicited submissions of ideas, stories, or artwork. DC Comics, 1700 Broadway, New York, NY 10019 A division of Warner Bros. - An AOL Time Warner Company. Printed in Canada. First Printing. ISBN: 1-56389-959-0. Cover illustration by Michael Bair. Cover color by John Kalisz.

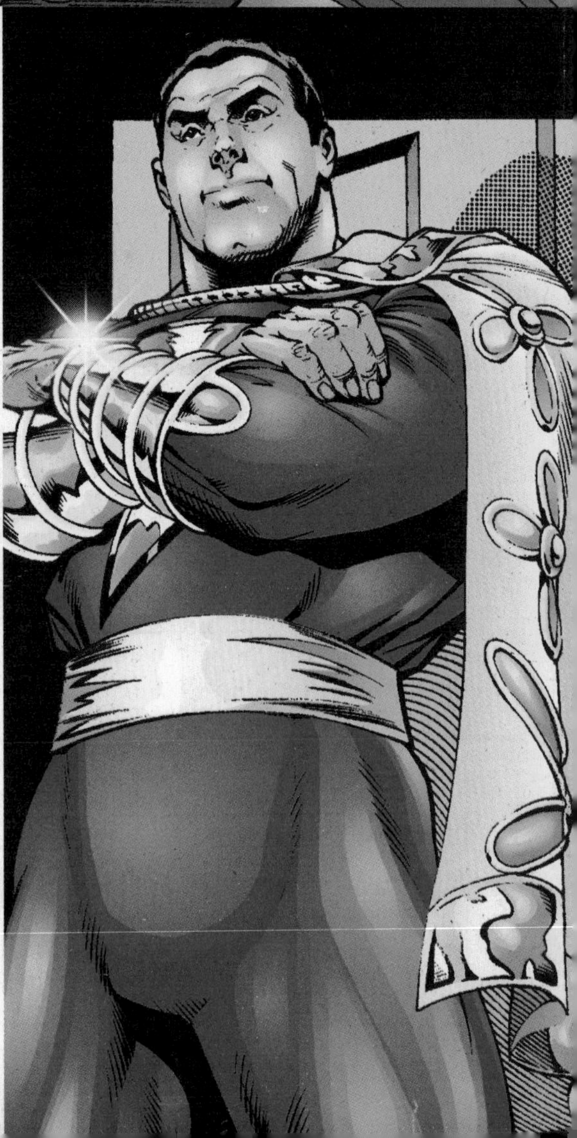

There has always been a need for heroes. In the dawning days of World War II, America produced a generation of heroes the likes of which had never been seen before. The mightiest of them banded together to protect the innocent as the Justice Society of America. For a decade they fought the good fight, retiring from the public spotlight when their day had passed.

But the need for heroes has never been greater. So the JSA lives once more, led by the survivors of the original team who now train a new generation of crime-fighters. Under their elders' guidance, these younger heroes not only learn how to harness their power but also come to understand who paved their way and the tremendous legacy they have inherited.

Since the JSA's re-formation, they have rediscovered old friends, fought familiar enemies, and buried some of their own members. The team has also reestablished its roots in Gotham City, with their headquarters doubling as meeting place and museum for the general public.

As we begin, the JSA is...

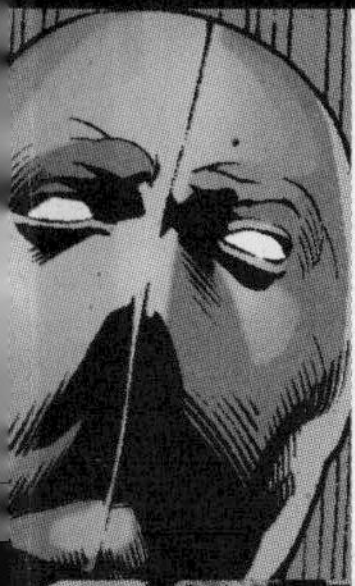

ATOM SMASHER

Al Rothstein never wanted anything more than to become a member of the Justice Society of America. Although his grandfather was the super-villain known as Cyclotron, Al is trying to live up to the legacy of a hero — his godfather, the original Atom. Al inherited his superhuman strength and the ability to increase his mass from his grandfather's atomic-powered physiology.

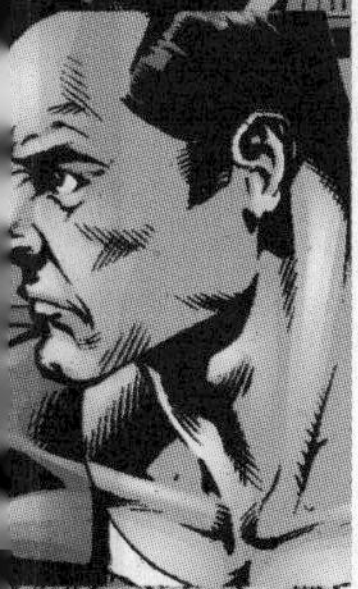

BLACK ADAM

Teth-Adam was the first to wield the mystical powers bestowed by the wizard Shazam. As Mighty Adam, he battled evil during Egypt's 15th Dynasty until the power ultimately corrupted him. Shazam imprisoned Adam within a scarab that was lost for centuries. A few years ago, two archaeologists, C.C. and Mary Batson, unearthed the scarab. Teth-Adam's powers and soul took root in the body of his descendant, Theo Adam, a thief and murderer. He now struggles for redemption.

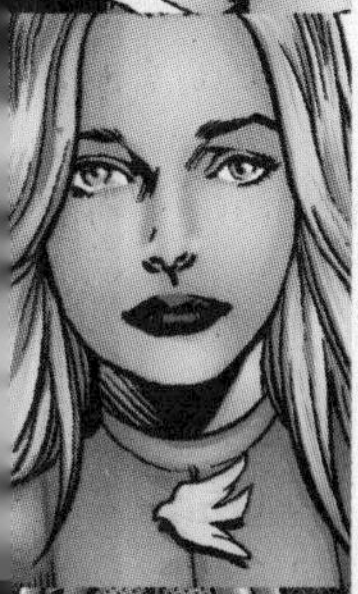

BLACK CANARY

A skilled detective and martial artist, Dinah Lance has idolized her mother — the original Black Canary — and her JSA teammates all her life. Currently, she is partnered with the mysterious Oracle and travels the globe as a troubleshooter.

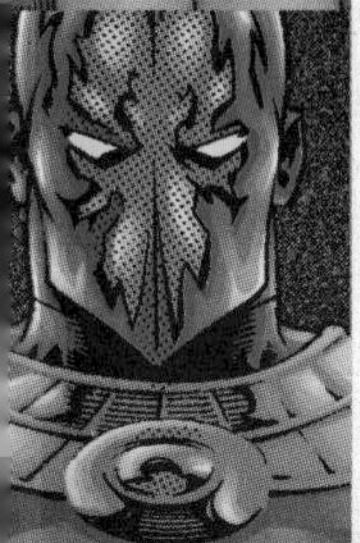

DR. FATE

Nabu, a Lord of Order, was exiled to Earth in 3500 B.C. There he took the guise of an Egyptian sorcerer and served as advisor to Prince Khufu. Later, his essence and powers were entombed in a golden helmet and amulet. In 1940, Kent Nelson assumed the golden armaments and became the first Dr. Fate. Several others have worn the mantle since then. Its current possessor is Hector Hall, the son of Hawkman.

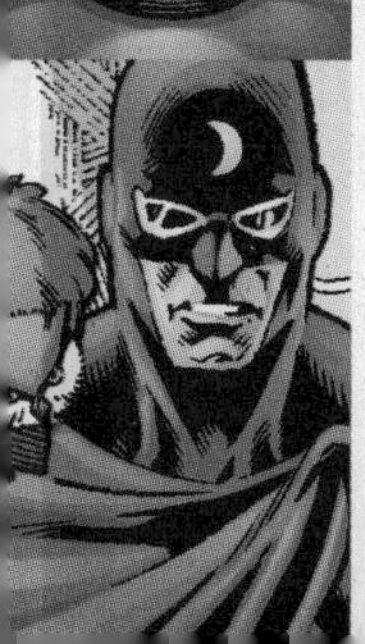

DR. MID-NITE

A medical prodigy, Pieter Anton Cross refused to work within the system. Treating people on his own, he came into contact with a dangerous drug that altered his body chemistry, letting him see light in the infrared spectrum. Although he was blinded in an explosion, he continues to protect the weak in the assumed identity of Dr. Mid-Nite.

HAWKMAN and HAWKGIRL

Thousands of years ago, in ancient Egypt, Prince Khufu and his Princess Chay-Ara discovered an alien spacecraft from the planet Thanagar. The ship was powered by a mysterious antigravity element which they called Nth metal. The unearthly energies of the Nth metal, enhanced by the strength of their love, transformed the souls of the Prince and Princess. For centuries, they were reincarnated, life after life, destined to meet one another and rekindle their love... until today. Today, he is Carter Hall, archaeologist and adventurer. She is Kendra Saunders, trained to inherit the mantle of Hawkgirl. But, Kendra has no recollection of her past lives or her past love with Carter, nor any interest whatsoever in renewing that love.

JAKEEM THUNDER

Keystone City's Jakeem Williams was raised by his aunt after his mother died and his father disappeared. He grew a large attitude and did poorly in school but, secretly, he wasn't happy about it. Asking the Flash for his autograph, Jakeem came into possession of a pen that was actually the vessel for a 5th-Dimensional being known as Thunderbolt. Jakeem became his new partner and is now learning how to use this power.

MR. TERRIFIC

Haunted by the death of his wife, Olympic gold medal-winning decathlete Michael Holt was ready to take his own life. Instead, inspired by the Spectre's story of the original Mr. Terrific, he rededicated himself to ensuring fair play among the street youth using his wealth and technical skills.

SAND

The ward of original Sandman Wesley Dodds, and the nephew of Dodds's lifelong partner Dian Belmont, Sandy Hawkins was transformed through a bizarre experiment into a crazed silicon monster. Revived from a state of suspended animation and cured of his condition some years ago, Sandy now serves as JSA chairman. He has become a geomorph, able to transform his body into sand and to control silicon to a limited degree.

THE STAR-SPANGLED KID

When Courtney Whitmore first discovered the cosmic converter belt once worn by the JSA's original Star-Spangled Kid, she saw it as an opportunity to cut class and kick some butt. Now, she is slowly — very slowly — beginning to learn about the awesome legacy she has become a part of.

WILDCAT

A former heavyweight boxing champ, Ted Grant, a.k.a. Wildcat, prowls the mean streets defending the helpless. One of the world's foremost hand-to-hand combatants, he has trained many of today's best fighters — including Black Canary, Catwoman, and the Batman.

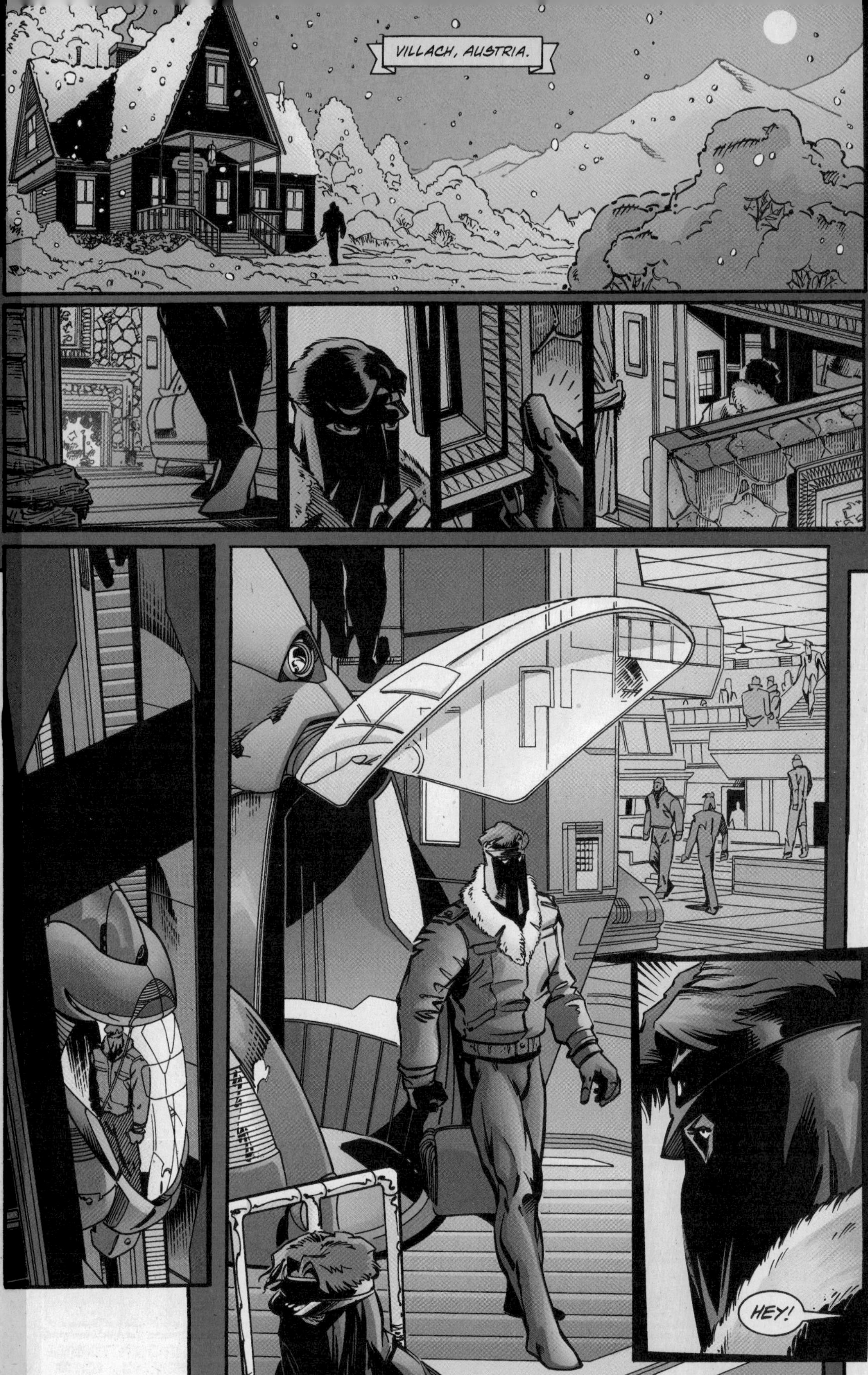
VILLACH, AUSTRIA.
HEY!

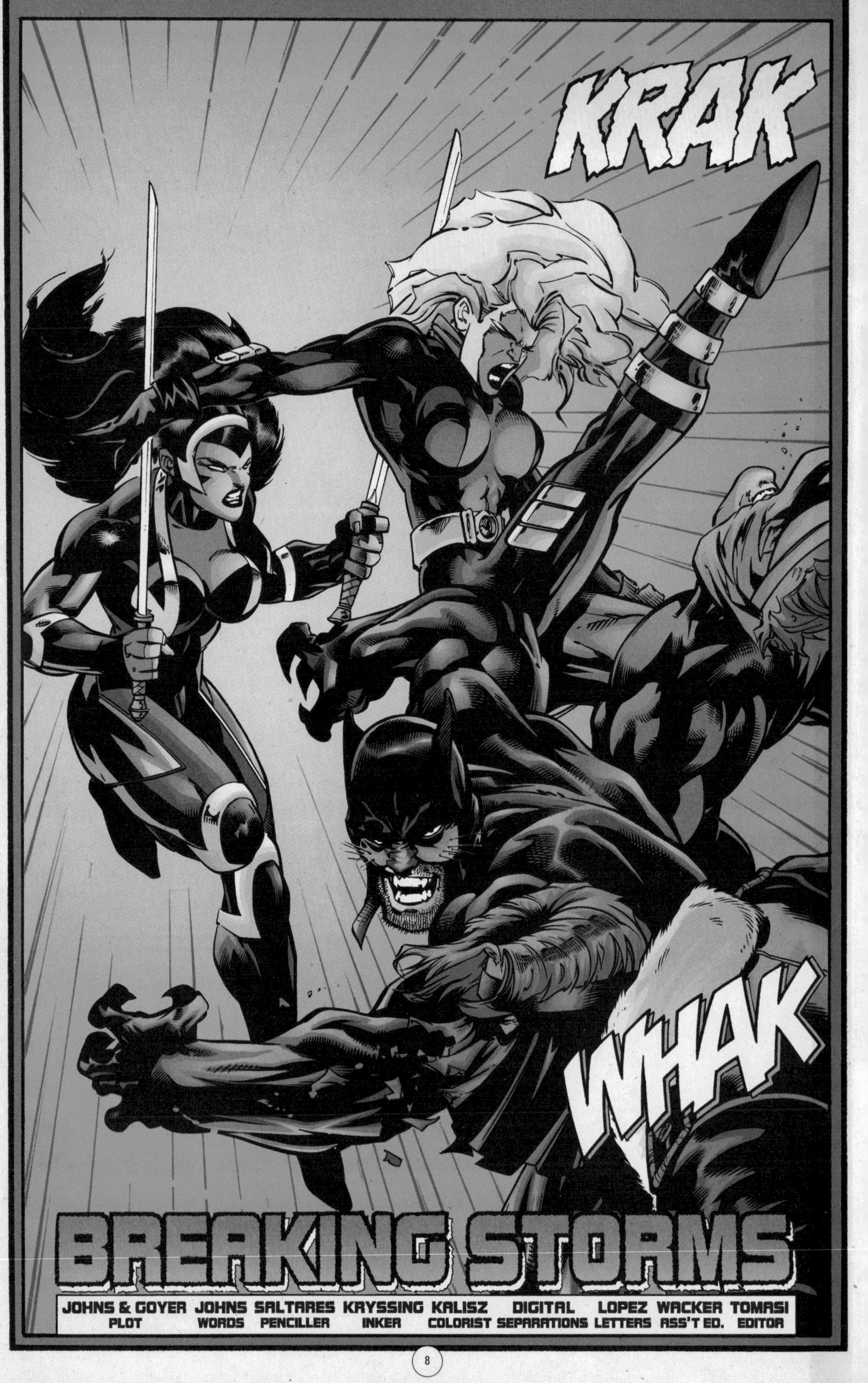
KRAK
WHAK
BREAKING STORMS
JOHNS & GOYER PLOT
JOHNS WORDS
SALTARES PENCILLER
KRYSSING INKER
KALISZ COLORIST
DIGITAL SEPARATIONS
LOPEZ LETTERS
WACKER ASS'T ED.
TOMASI EDITOR

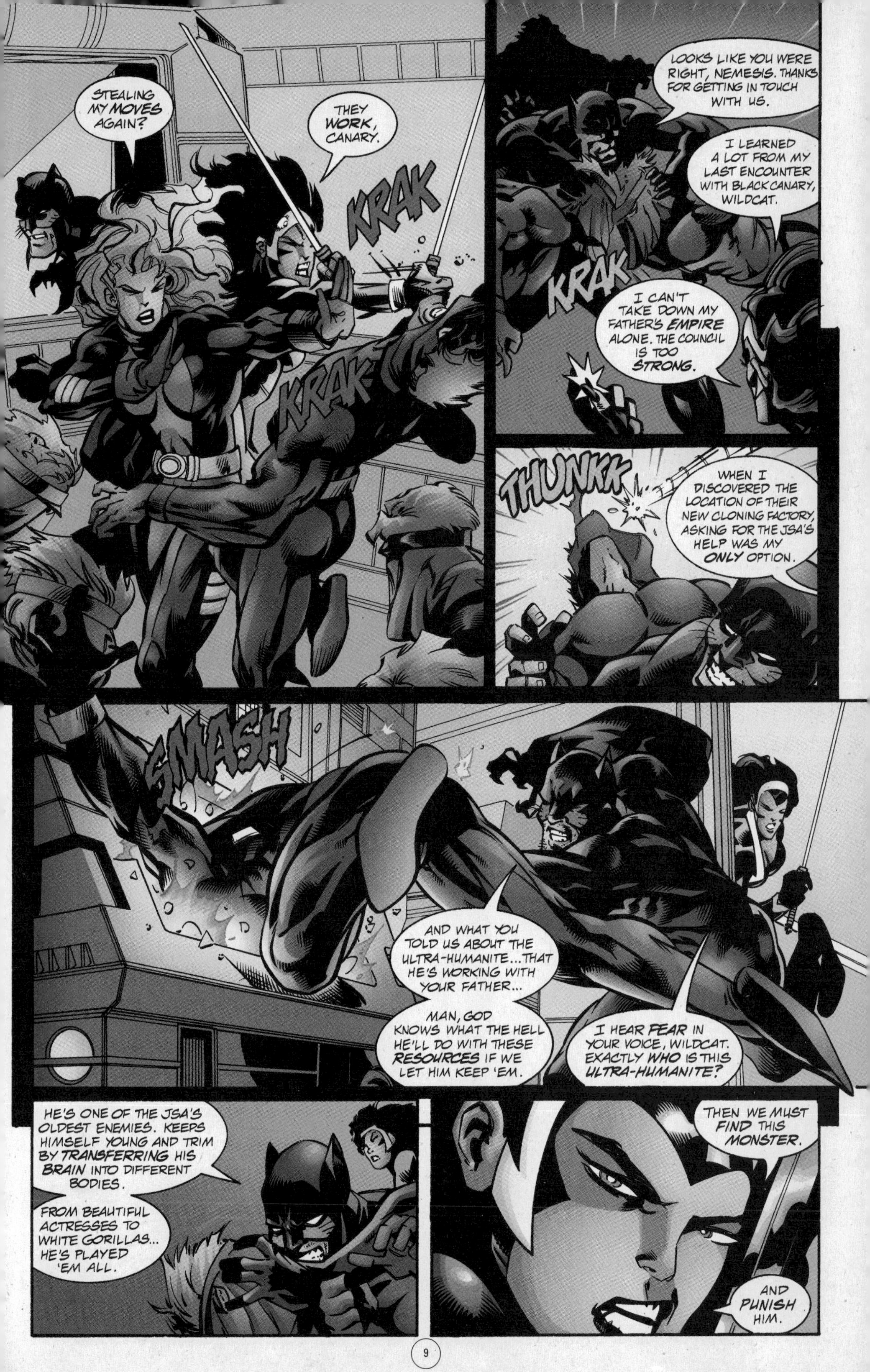
STEALING MY MOVES AGAIN?
THEY WORK, CANARY.
KRAK
KRAK
LOOKS LIKE YOU WERE RIGHT, NEMESIS. THANKS FOR GETTING IN TOUCH WITH US.
I LEARNED A LOT FROM MY LAST ENCOUNTER WITH BLACK CANARY, WILDCAT.
KRAK
I CAN'T TAKE DOWN MY FATHER'S EMPIRE ALONE. THE COUNCIL IS TOO STRONG.
THUNKK
WHEN I DISCOVERED THE LOCATION OF THEIR NEW CLONING FACTORY, ASKING FOR THE JSA'S HELP WAS MY ONLY OPTION.
SMASH
AND WHAT YOU TOLD US ABOUT THE ULTRA-HUMANITE... THAT HE'S WORKING WITH YOUR FATHER...
MAN, GOD KNOWS WHAT THE HELL HE'LL DO WITH THESE RESOURCES IF WE LET HIM KEEP 'EM.
I HEAR FEAR IN YOUR VOICE, WILDCAT. EXACTLY WHO IS THIS ULTRA-HUMANITE?
HE'S ONE OF THE JSA'S OLDEST ENEMIES. KEEPS HIMSELF YOUNG AND TRIM BY TRANSFERRING HIS BRAIN INTO DIFFERENT BODIES.
FROM BEAUTIFUL ACTRESSES TO WHITE GORILLAS... HE'S PLAYED 'EM ALL.
THEN WE MUST FIND THIS MONSTER.
AND PUNISH HIM.

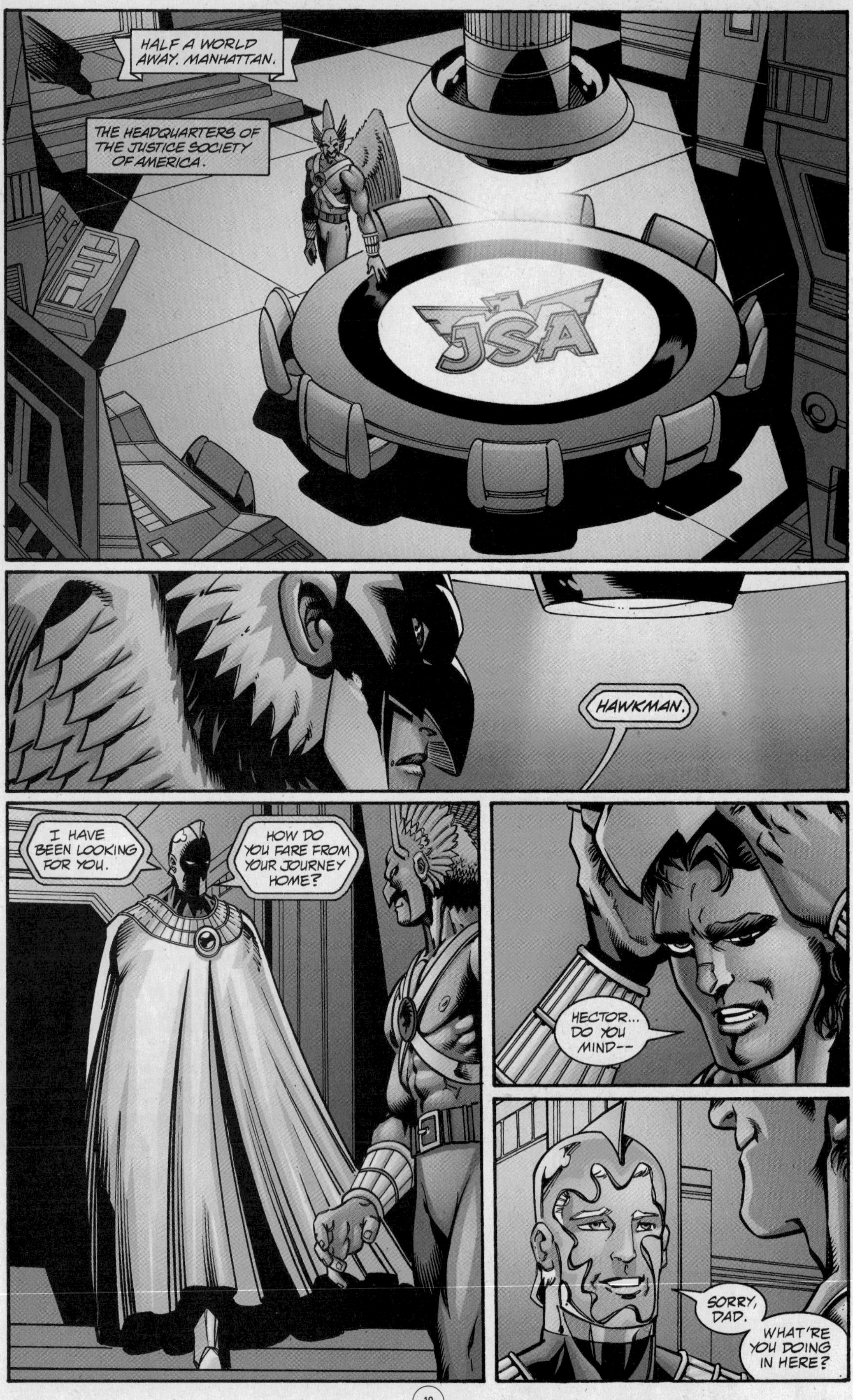
HALF A WORLD AWAY. MANHATTAN.
THE HEADQUARTERS OF THE JUSTICE SOCIETY OF AMERICA.
JSA
HAWKMAN.
I HAVE BEEN LOOKING FOR YOU.
HOW DO YOU FARE FROM YOUR JOURNEY HOME?
HECTOR... DO YOU MIND--
SORRY, DAD.
WHAT'RE YOU DOING IN HERE?

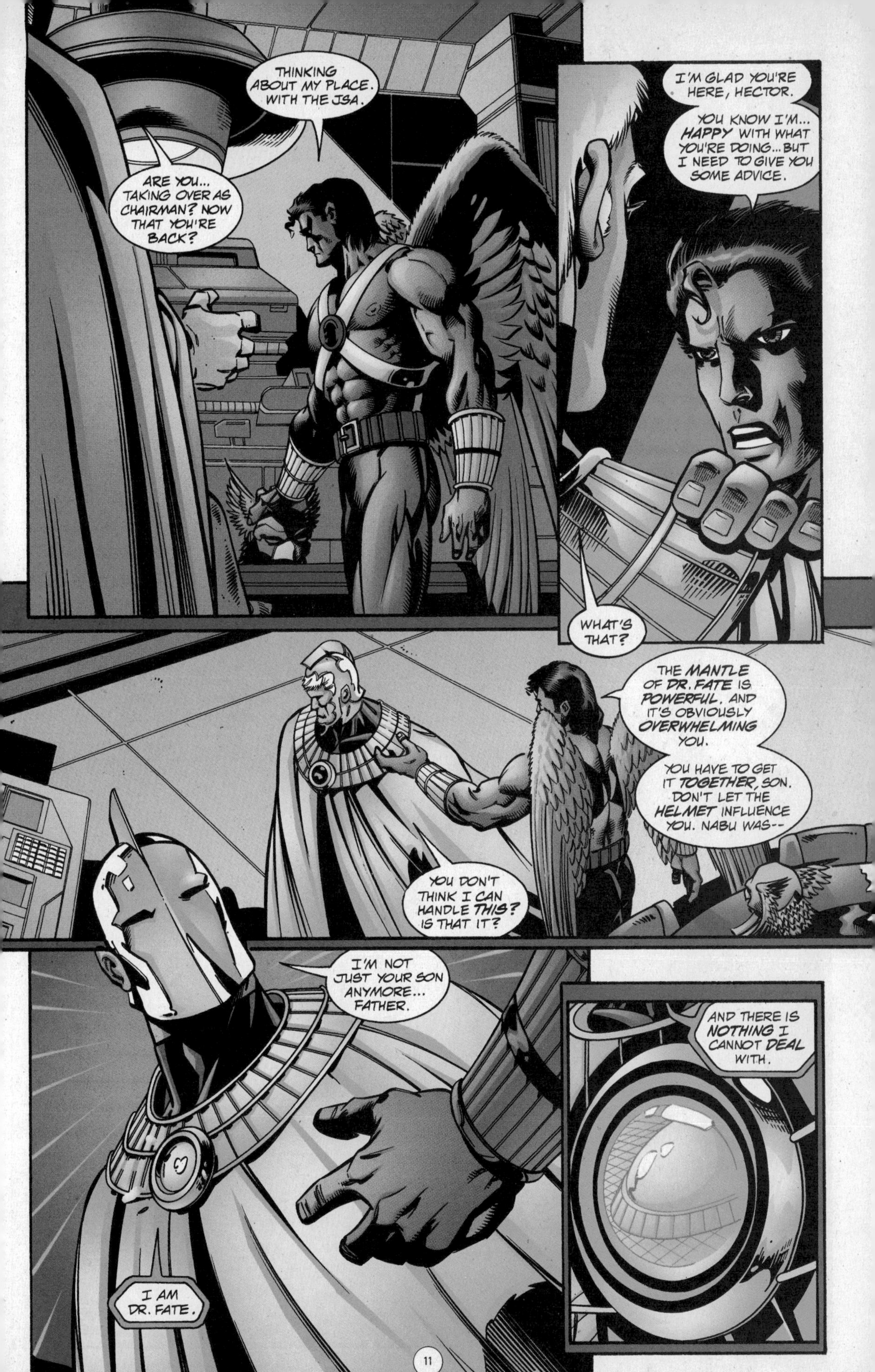

THINKING ABOUT MY PLACE. WITH THE JSA.
ARE YOU... TAKING OVER AS CHAIRMAN? NOW THAT YOU'RE BACK?
I'M GLAD YOU'RE HERE, HECTOR.
YOU KNOW I'M... HAPPY WITH WHAT YOU'RE DOING... BUT I NEED TO GIVE YOU SOME ADVICE.
WHAT'S THAT?
THE MANTLE OF DR. FATE IS POWERFUL. AND IT'S OBVIOUSLY OVERWHELMING YOU.
YOU HAVE TO GET IT TOGETHER, SON. DON'T LET THE HELMET INFLUENCE YOU. NABU WAS--
YOU DON'T THINK I CAN HANDLE THIS? IS THAT IT?
I'M NOT JUST YOUR SON ANYMORE... FATHER.
I AM DR. FATE.
AND THERE IS NOTHING I CANNOT DEAL WITH.

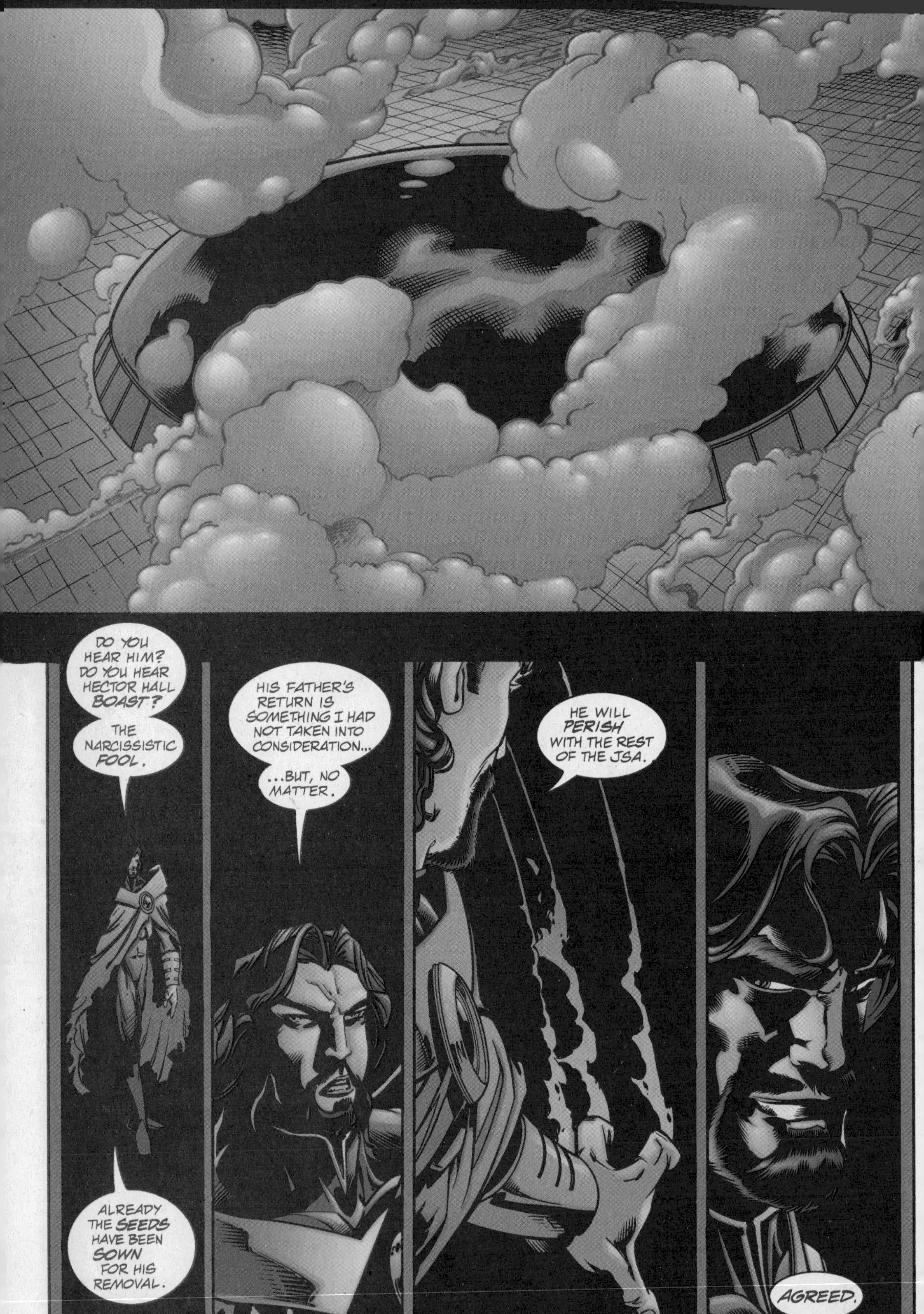
DO YOU HEAR HIM? DO YOU HEAR HECTOR HALL BOAST?
THE NARCISSISTIC FOOL.
ALREADY THE SEEDS HAVE BEEN SOWN FOR HIS REMOVAL.
HIS FATHER'S RETURN IS SOMETHING I HAD NOT TAKEN INTO CONSIDERATION...
...BUT, NO MATTER.
HE WILL PERISH WITH THE REST OF THE JSA.
AGREED.

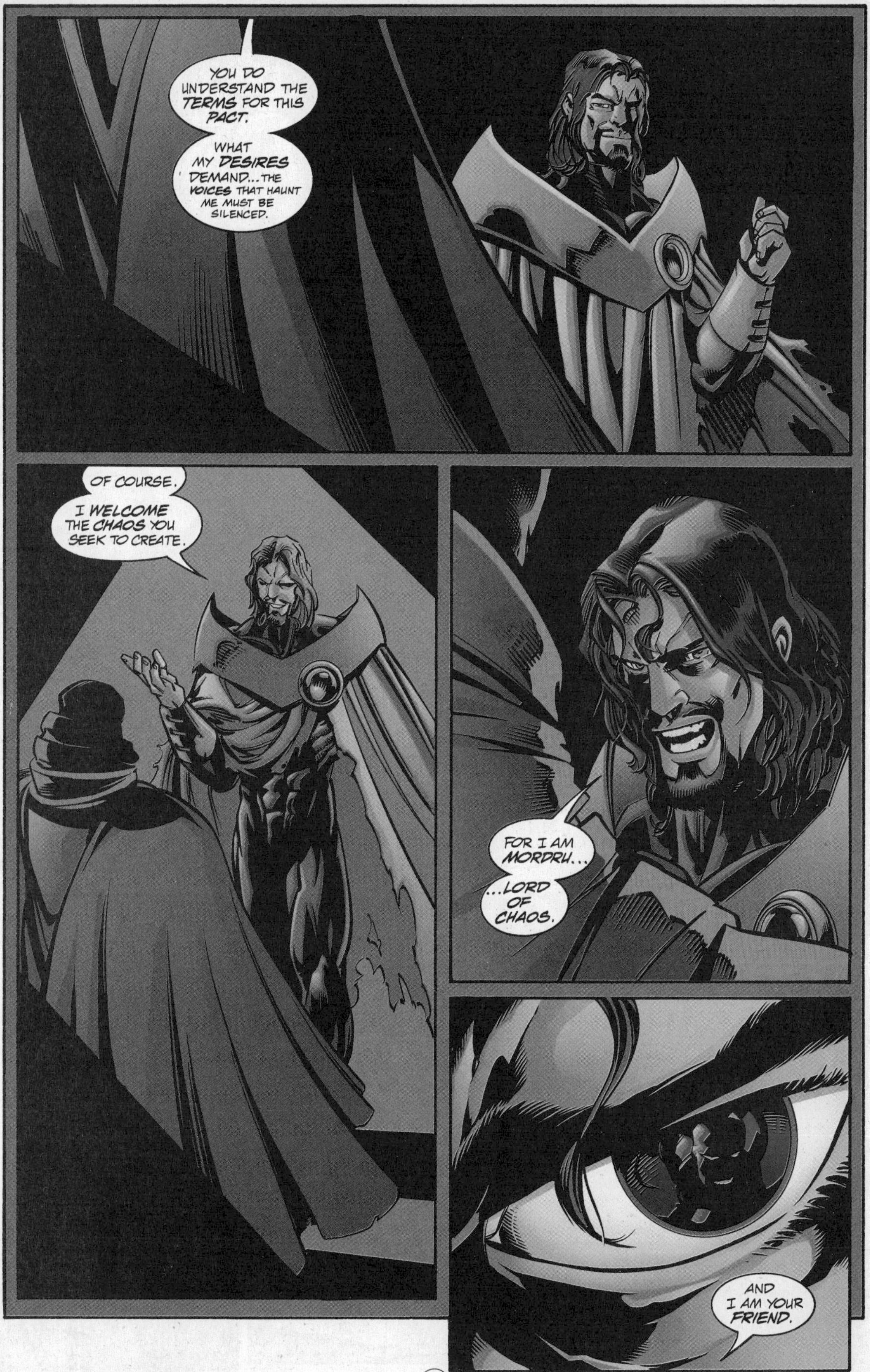
YOU DO UNDERSTAND THE TERMS FOR THIS PACT.
WHAT MY DESIRES DEMAND... THE VOICES THAT HAUNT ME MUST BE SILENCED.
OF COURSE.
I WELCOME THE CHAOS YOU SEEK TO CREATE.
FOR I AM MORDRU...
...LORD OF CHAOS.
AND I AM YOUR FRIEND.

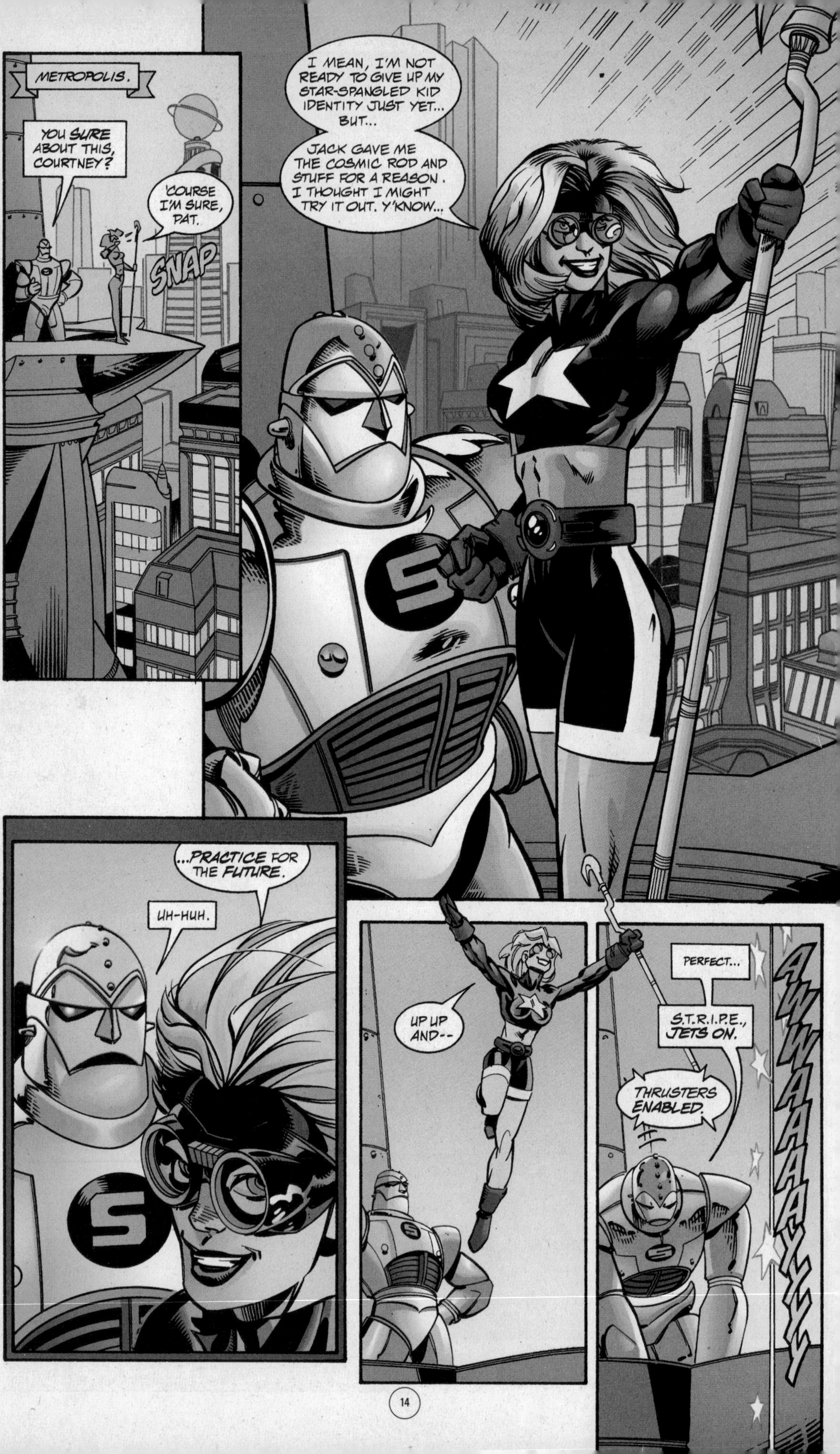

METROPOLIS.
YOU SURE ABOUT THIS, COURTNEY?
'COURSE I'M SURE, PAT.
SNAP
I MEAN, I'M NOT READY TO GIVE UP MY STAR-SPANGLED KID IDENTITY JUST YET... BUT...
JACK GAVE ME THE COSMIC ROD AND STUFF FOR A REASON. I THOUGHT I MIGHT TRY IT OUT. Y'KNOW...
...PRACTICE FOR THE FUTURE.
UH-HUH.
UP UP AND--
PERFECT...
S.T.R.I.P.E., JETS ON.
THRUSTERS ENABLED.
AWWAAAAAYYY

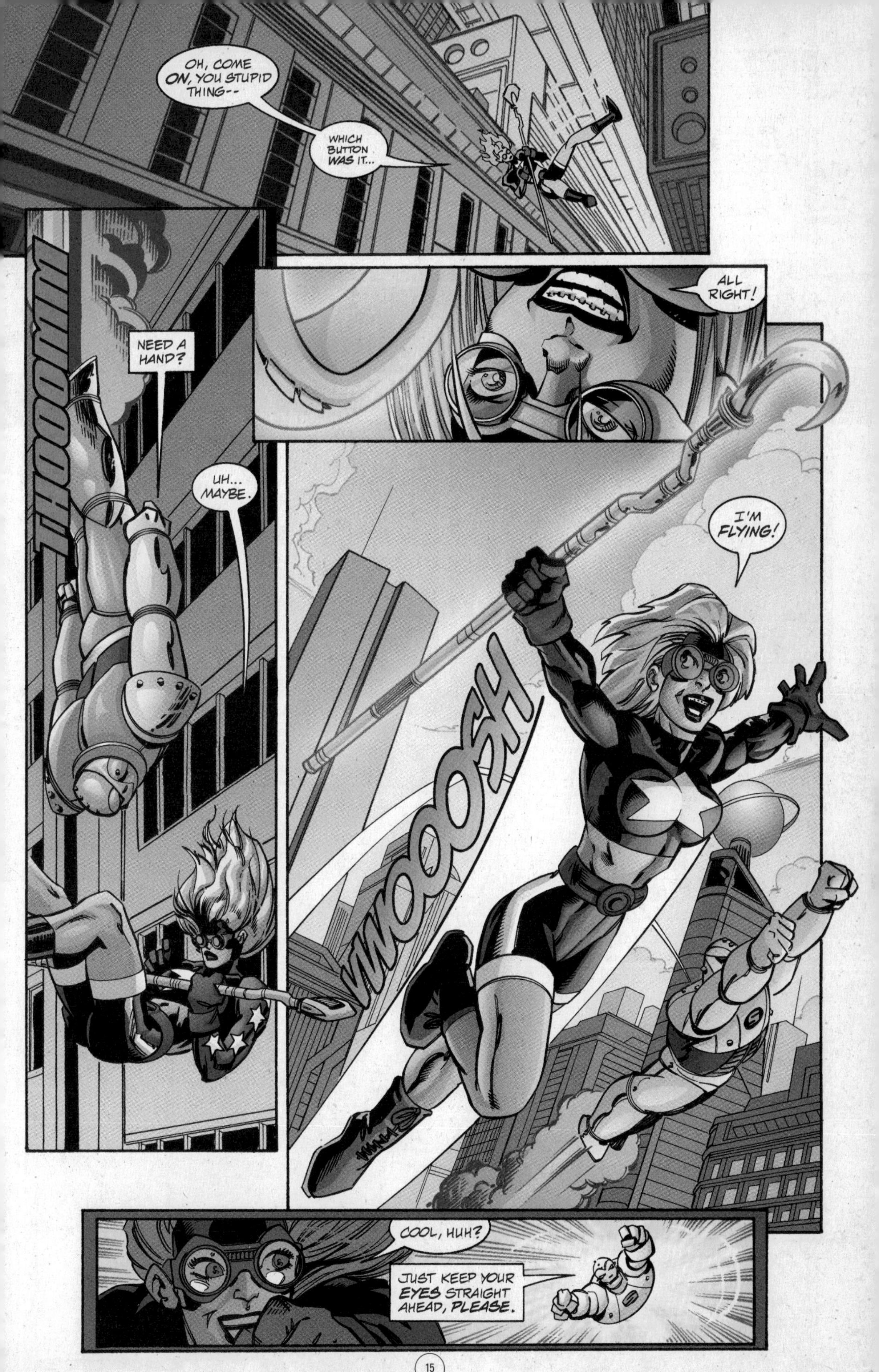
OH, COME ON, YOU STUPID THING--
WHICH BUTTON WAS IT...
WHOOOSH!
NEED A HAND?
UH... MAYBE.
ALL RIGHT!
I'M FLYING!
WHOOOSH
COOL, HUH?
JUST KEEP YOUR EYES STRAIGHT AHEAD, PLEASE.

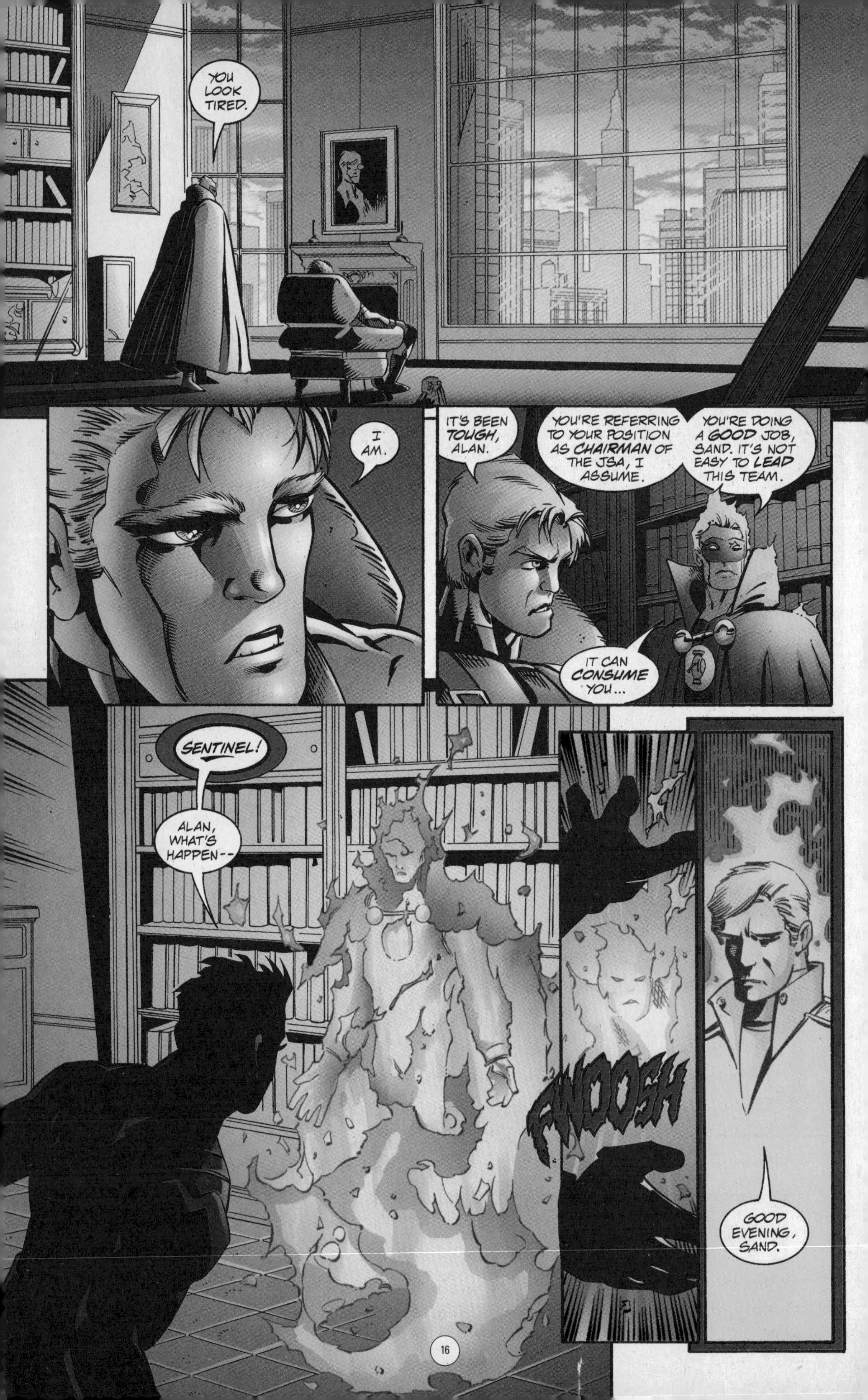
YOU LOOK TIRED.
I AM.
IT'S BEEN TOUGH, ALAN.
YOU'RE REFERRING TO YOUR POSITION AS CHAIRMAN OF THE JSA, I ASSUME.
YOU'RE DOING A GOOD JOB, SAND. IT'S NOT EASY TO LEAD THIS TEAM.
IT CAN CONSUME YOU...
SENTINEL!
ALAN, WHAT'S HAPPEN--
FWOOSH
GOOD EVENING, SAND.

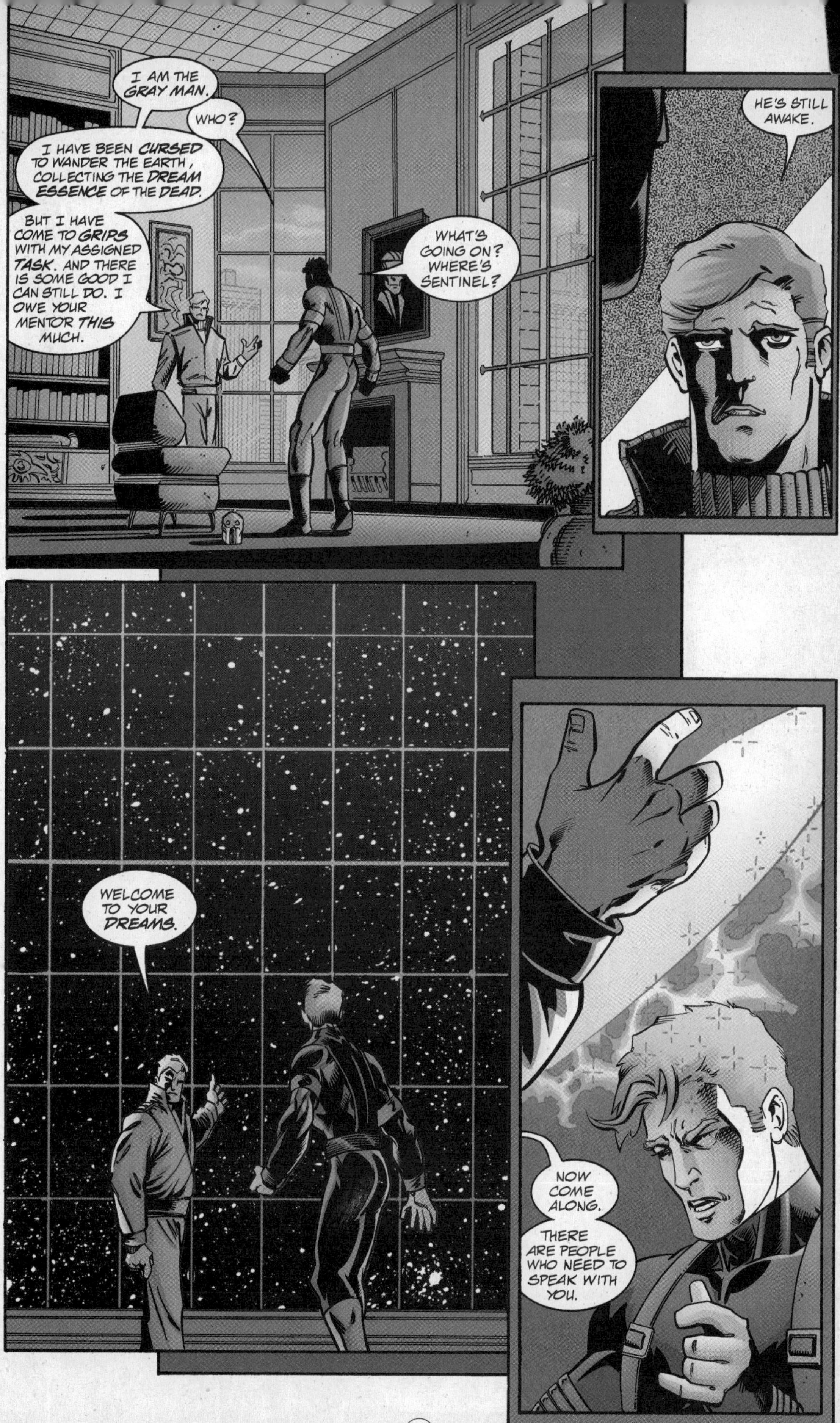
I AM THE GRAY MAN.
WHO?
I HAVE BEEN CURSED TO WANDER THE EARTH, COLLECTING THE DREAM ESSENCE OF THE DEAD.
BUT I HAVE COME TO GRIPS WITH MY ASSIGNED TASK. AND THERE IS SOME GOOD I CAN STILL DO. I OWE YOUR MENTOR THIS MUCH.
WHAT'S GOING ON? WHERE'S SENTINEL?
HE'S STILL AWAKE.
WELCOME TO YOUR DREAMS.
NOW COME ALONG.
THERE ARE PEOPLE WHO NEED TO SPEAK WITH YOU.

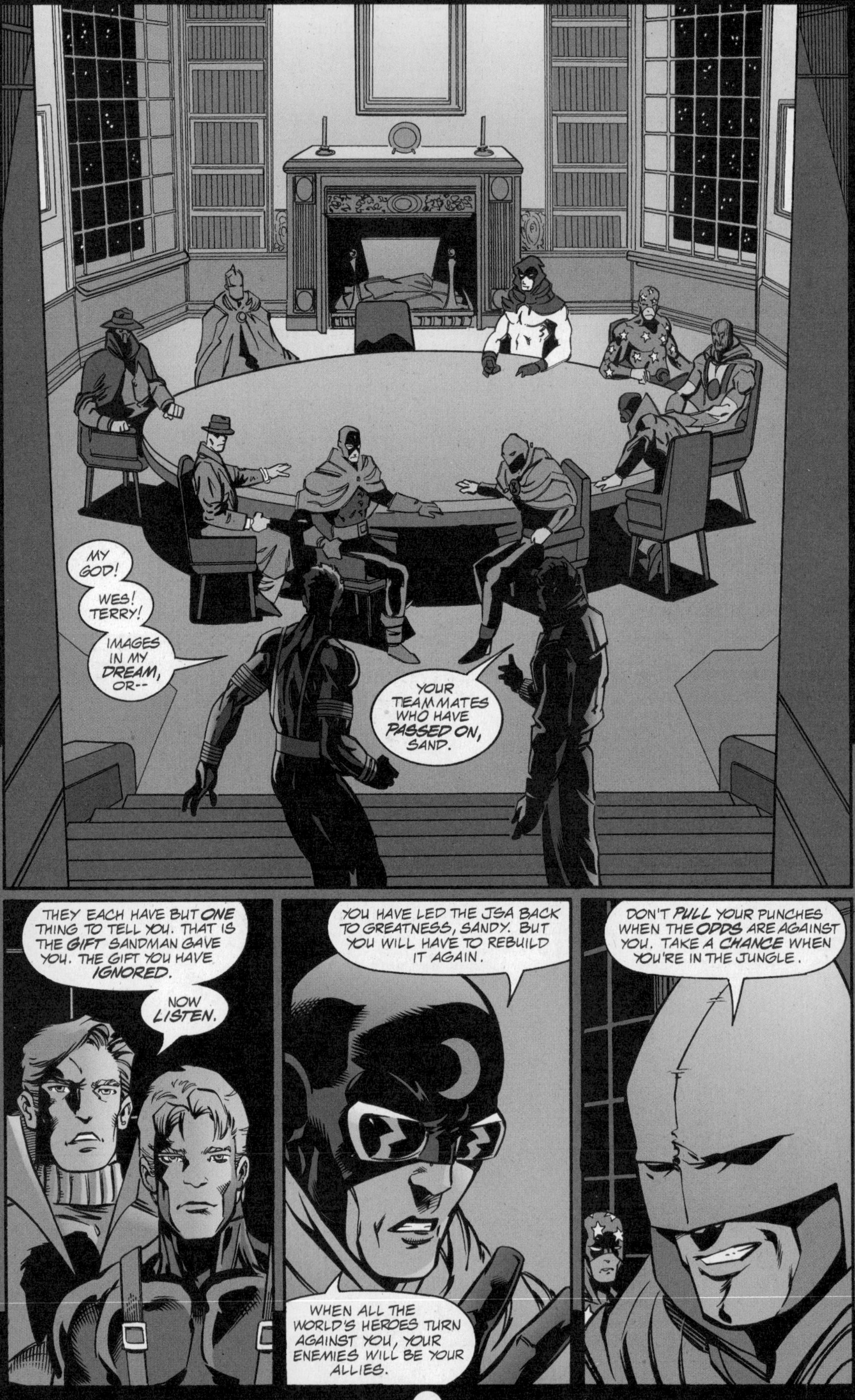
MY GOD! WES! TERRY! IMAGES IN MY DREAM, OR--
YOUR TEAMMATES WHO HAVE PASSED ON, SAND.
THEY EACH HAVE BUT ONE THING TO TELL YOU. THAT IS THE GIFT SANDMAN GAVE YOU. THE GIFT YOU HAVE IGNORED.
NOW LISTEN.
YOU HAVE LED THE JSA BACK TO GREATNESS, SANDY. BUT YOU WILL HAVE TO REBUILD IT AGAIN.
WHEN ALL THE WORLD'S HEROES TURN AGAINST YOU, YOUR ENEMIES WILL BE YOUR ALLIES.
DON'T PULL YOUR PUNCHES WHEN THE ODDS ARE AGAINST YOU. TAKE A CHANCE WHEN YOU'RE IN THE JUNGLE.

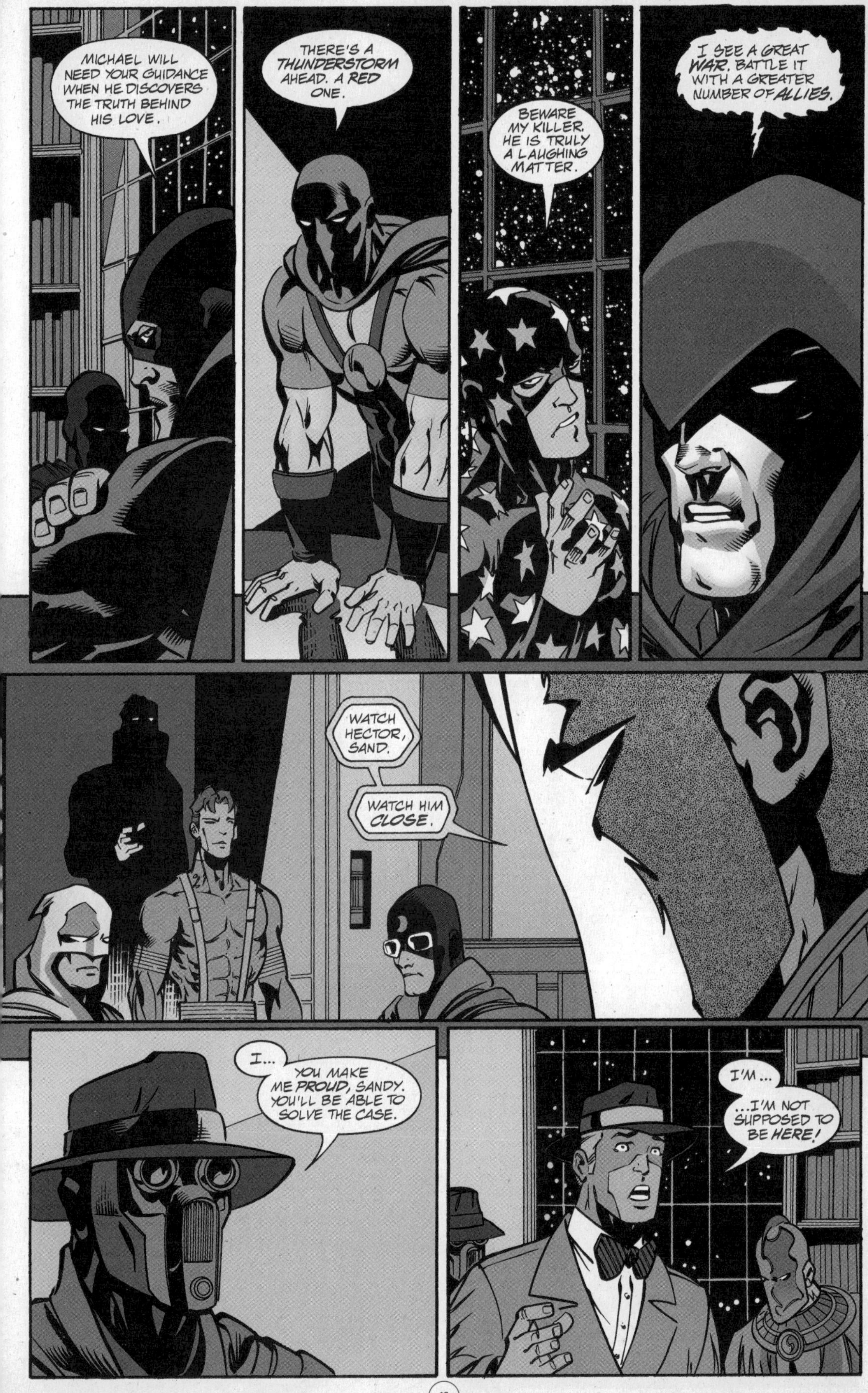
MICHAEL WILL NEED YOUR GUIDANCE WHEN HE DISCOVERS THE TRUTH BEHIND HIS LOVE.
THERE'S A THUNDERSTORM AHEAD. A RED ONE.
BEWARE MY KILLER. HE IS TRULY A LAUGHING MATTER.
I SEE A GREAT WAR. BATTLE IT WITH A GREATER NUMBER OF ALLIES.
WATCH HECTOR, SAND.
WATCH HIM CLOSE.
I...
YOU MAKE ME PROUD, SANDY. YOU'LL BE ABLE TO SOLVE THE CASE.
I'M ...
...I'M NOT SUPPOSED TO BE HERE!

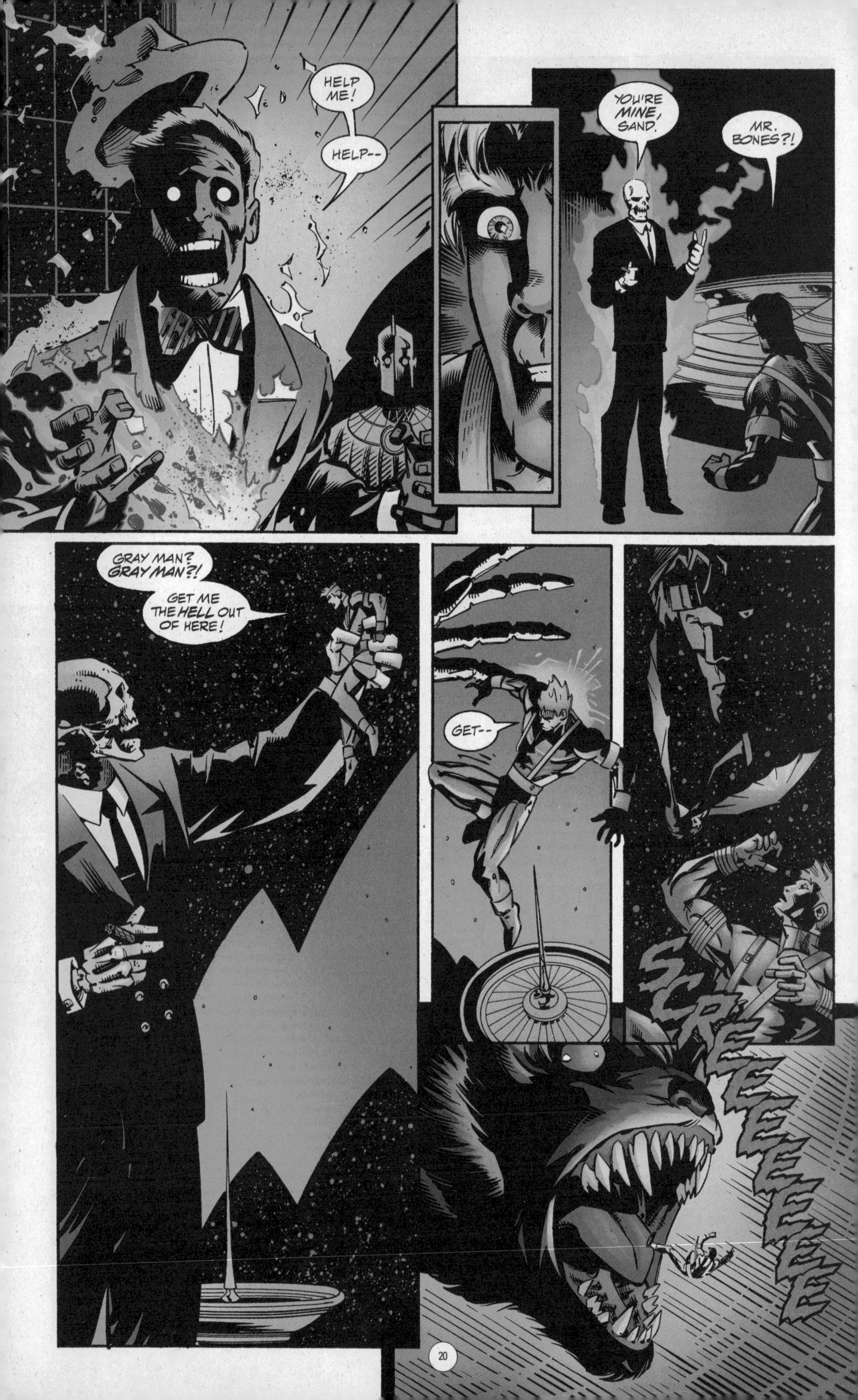
HELP ME!
HELP--
YOU'RE MINE, SAND.
MR. BONES?!
GRAY MAN? GRAY MAN?!
GET ME THE HELL OUT OF HERE!
GET--
SCREEEEEEEEEE

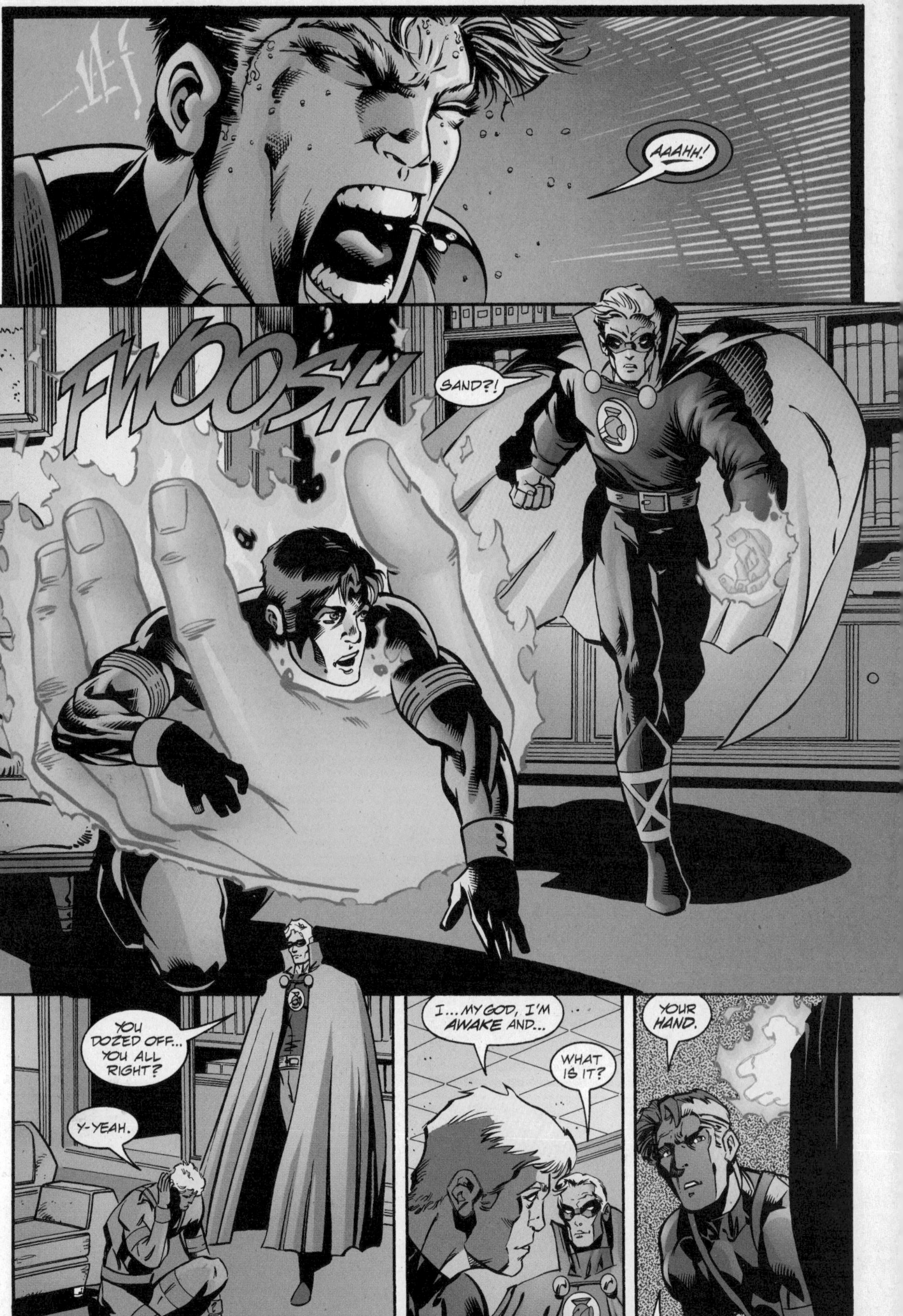
AAAHH!
FWOOSH
SAND?!
YOU DOZED OFF... YOU ALL RIGHT?
Y-YEAH.
I... MY GOD, I'M AWAKE AND...
WHAT IS IT?
YOUR HAND.
WHAT'S WRONG WITH YOUR HAND?

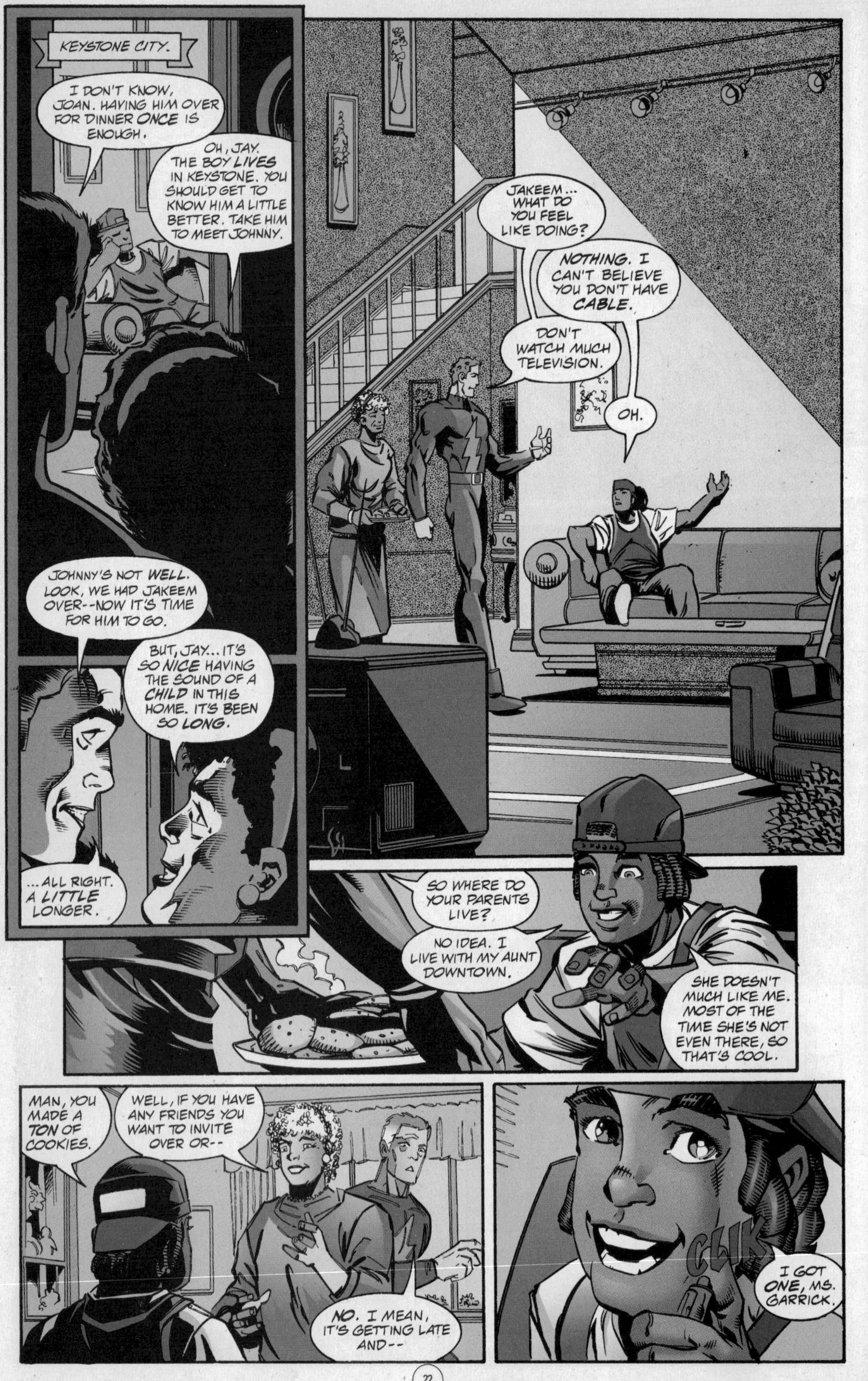
KEYSTONE CITY.
I DON'T KNOW, JOAN. HAVING HIM OVER FOR DINNER ONCE IS ENOUGH.
OH, JAY. THE BOY LIVES IN KEYSTONE. YOU SHOULD GET TO KNOW HIM A LITTLE BETTER. TAKE HIM TO MEET JOHNNY.
JAKEEM... WHAT DO YOU FEEL LIKE DOING?
NOTHING. I CAN'T BELIEVE YOU DON'T HAVE CABLE.
DON'T WATCH MUCH TELEVISION.
OH.
JOHNNY'S NOT WELL. LOOK, WE HAD JAKEEM OVER--NOW IT'S TIME FOR HIM TO GO.
BUT, JAY... IT'S SO NICE HAVING THE SOUND OF A CHILD IN THIS HOME. IT'S BEEN SO LONG.
...ALL RIGHT. A LITTLE LONGER.
SO WHERE DO YOUR PARENTS LIVE?
NO IDEA. I LIVE WITH MY AUNT DOWNTOWN.
SHE DOESN'T MUCH LIKE ME. MOST OF THE TIME SHE'S NOT EVEN THERE, SO THAT'S COOL.
MAN, YOU MADE A TON OF COOKIES.
WELL, IF YOU HAVE ANY FRIENDS YOU WANT TO INVITE OVER OR--
NO. I MEAN, IT'S GETTING LATE AND--
CLIK
I GOT ONE, MS. GARRICK.

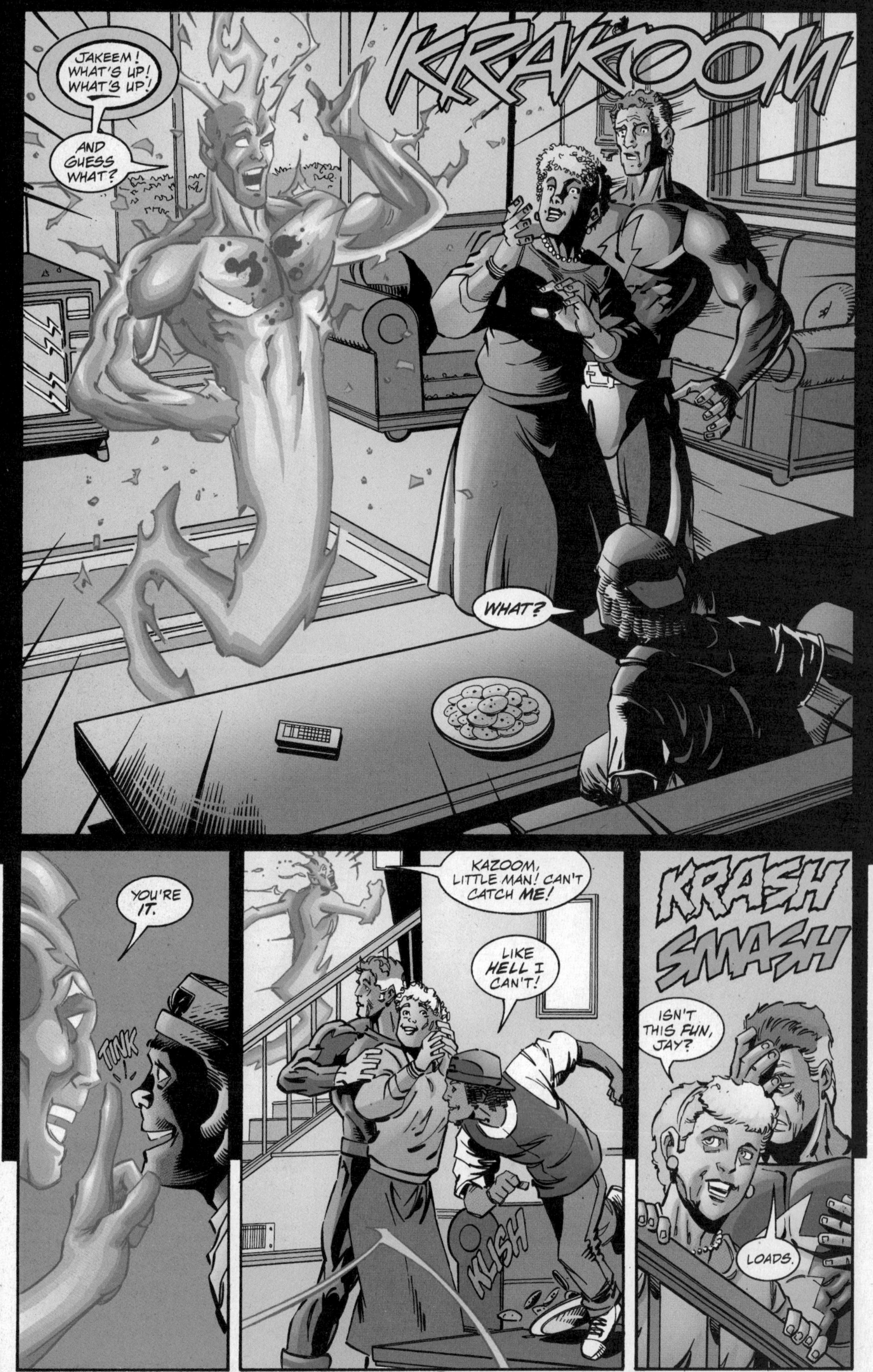
KRAKOOM
JAKEEM! WHAT'S UP! WHAT'S UP!
AND GUESS WHAT?
WHAT?
YOU'RE IT.
TINK
KAZOOM, LITTLE MAN! CAN'T CATCH ME!
LIKE HELL I CAN'T!
KLISH
KRASH
SMASH
ISN'T THIS FUN, JAY?
LOADS.

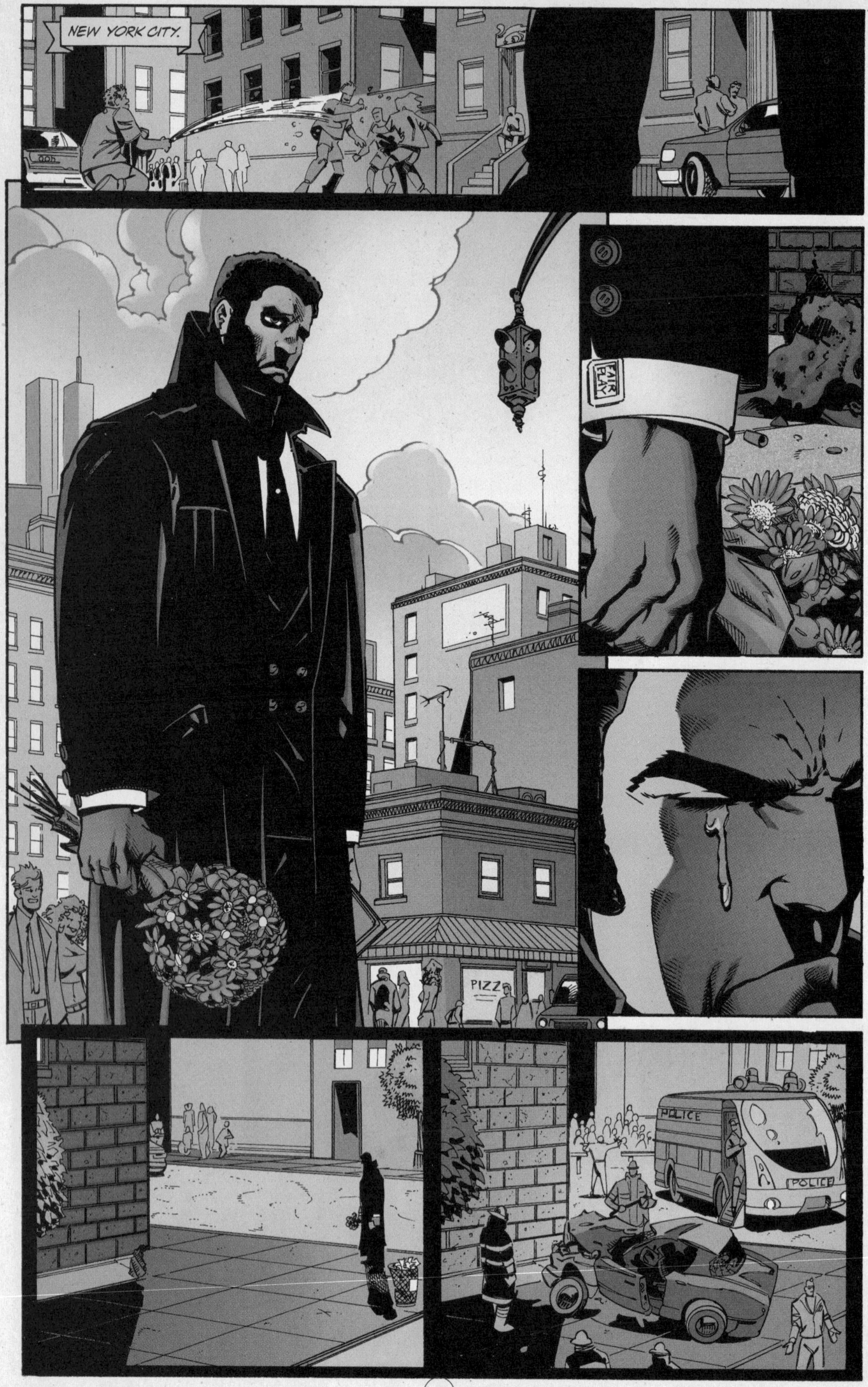
NEW YORK CITY.
FAIR PLAY
PIZZ
POLICE
POLICE

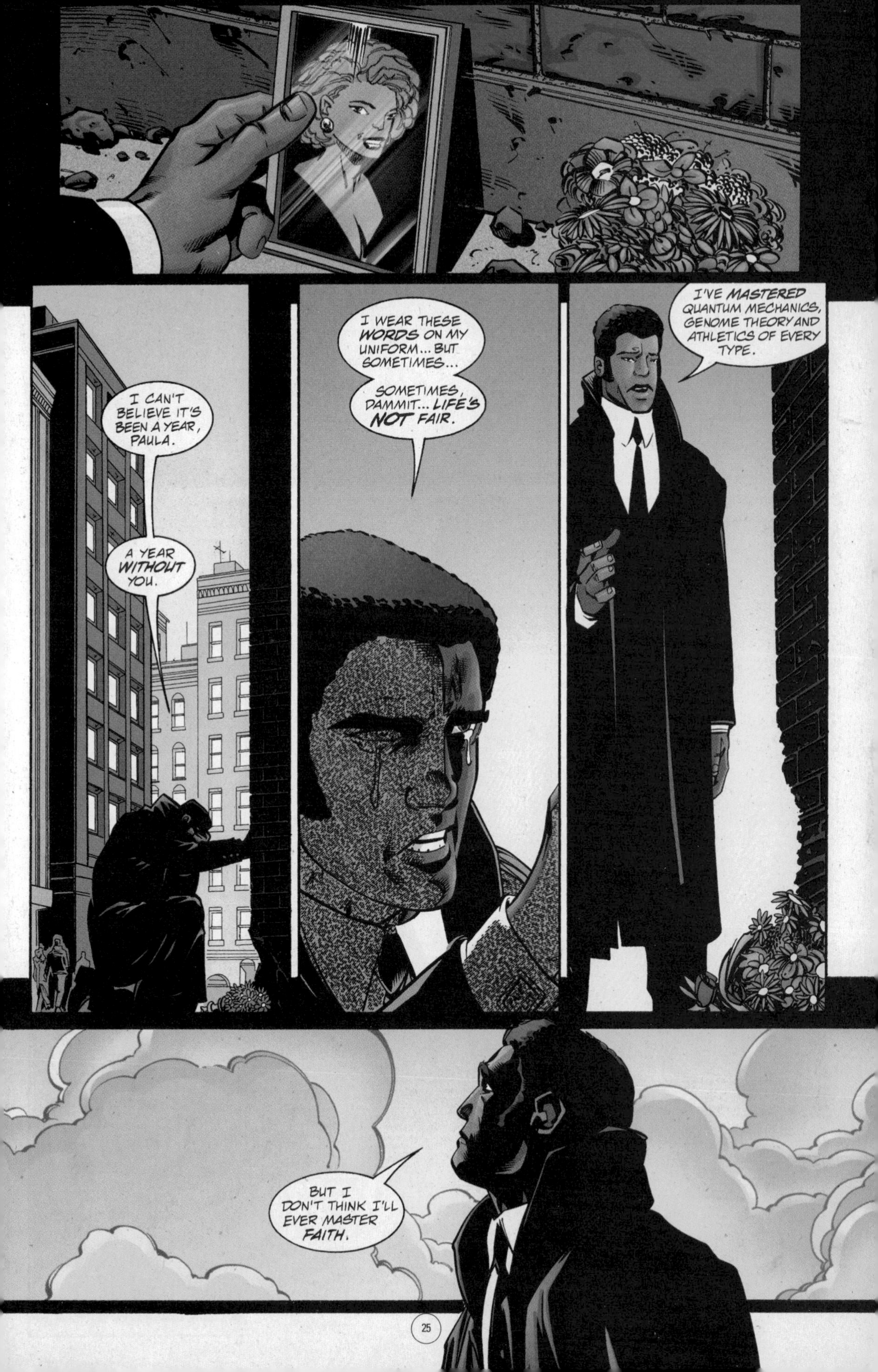
I CAN'T BELIEVE IT'S BEEN A YEAR, PAULA.
A YEAR WITHOUT YOU.
I WEAR THESE WORDS ON MY UNIFORM... BUT SOMETIMES...
SOMETIMES, DAMMIT... LIFE'S NOT FAIR.
I'VE MASTERED QUANTUM MECHANICS, GENOME THEORY AND ATHLETICS OF EVERY TYPE.
BUT I DON'T THINK I'LL EVER MASTER FAITH.

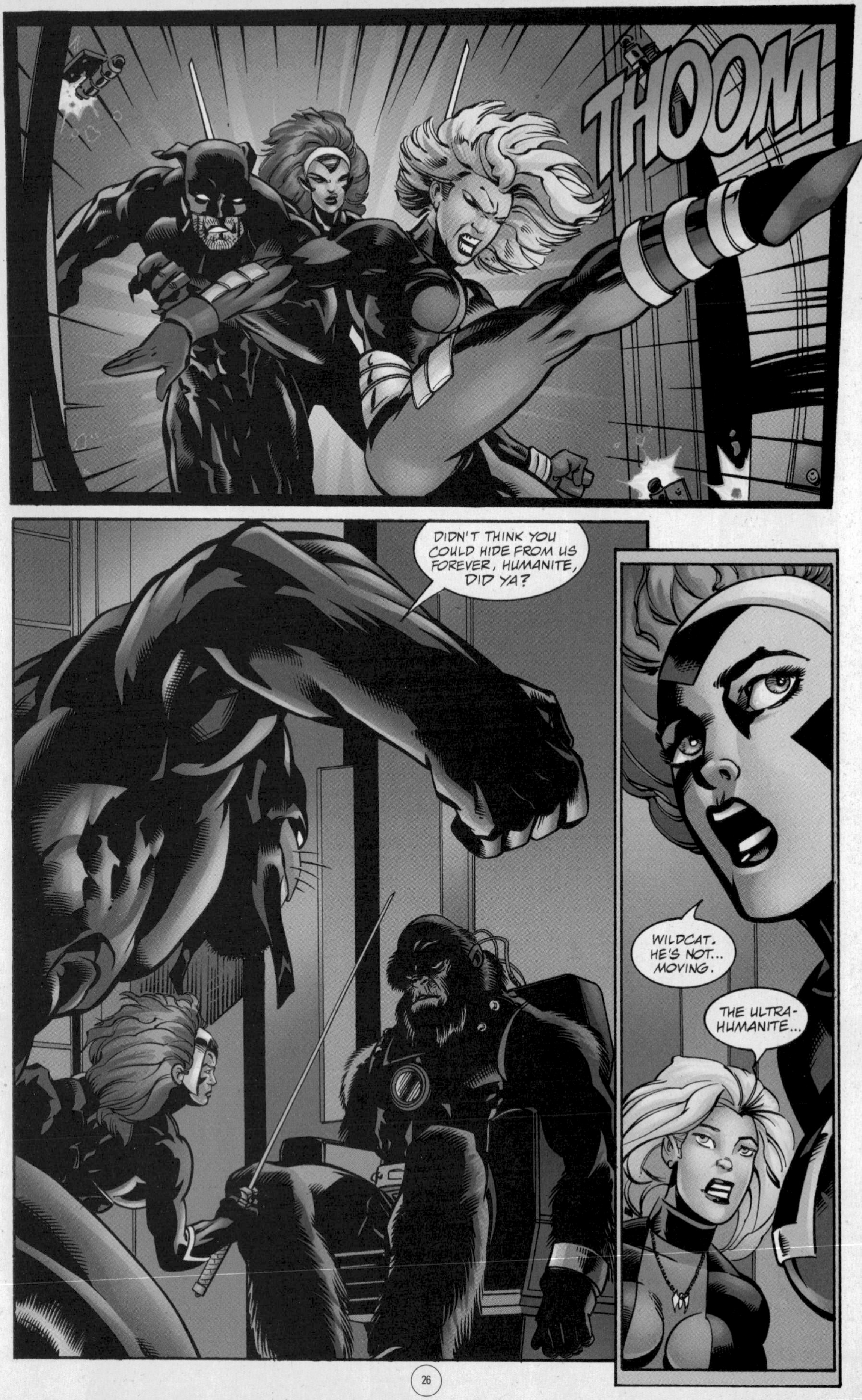
THOOM
DIDN'T THINK YOU COULD HIDE FROM US FOREVER, HUMANITE, DID YA?
WILDCAT. HE'S NOT... MOVING.
THE ULTRA-HUMANITE...

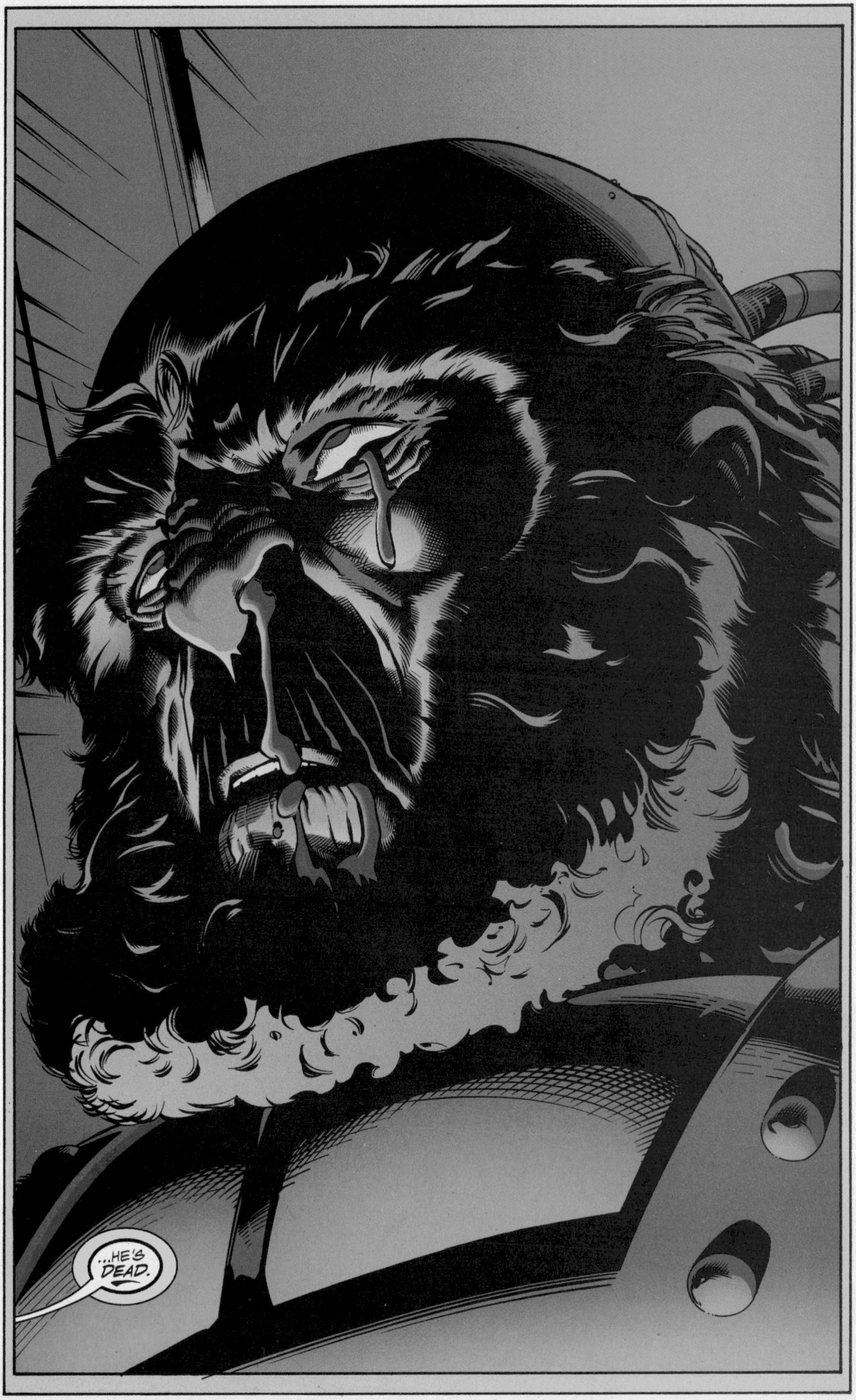
...HE'S DEAD.

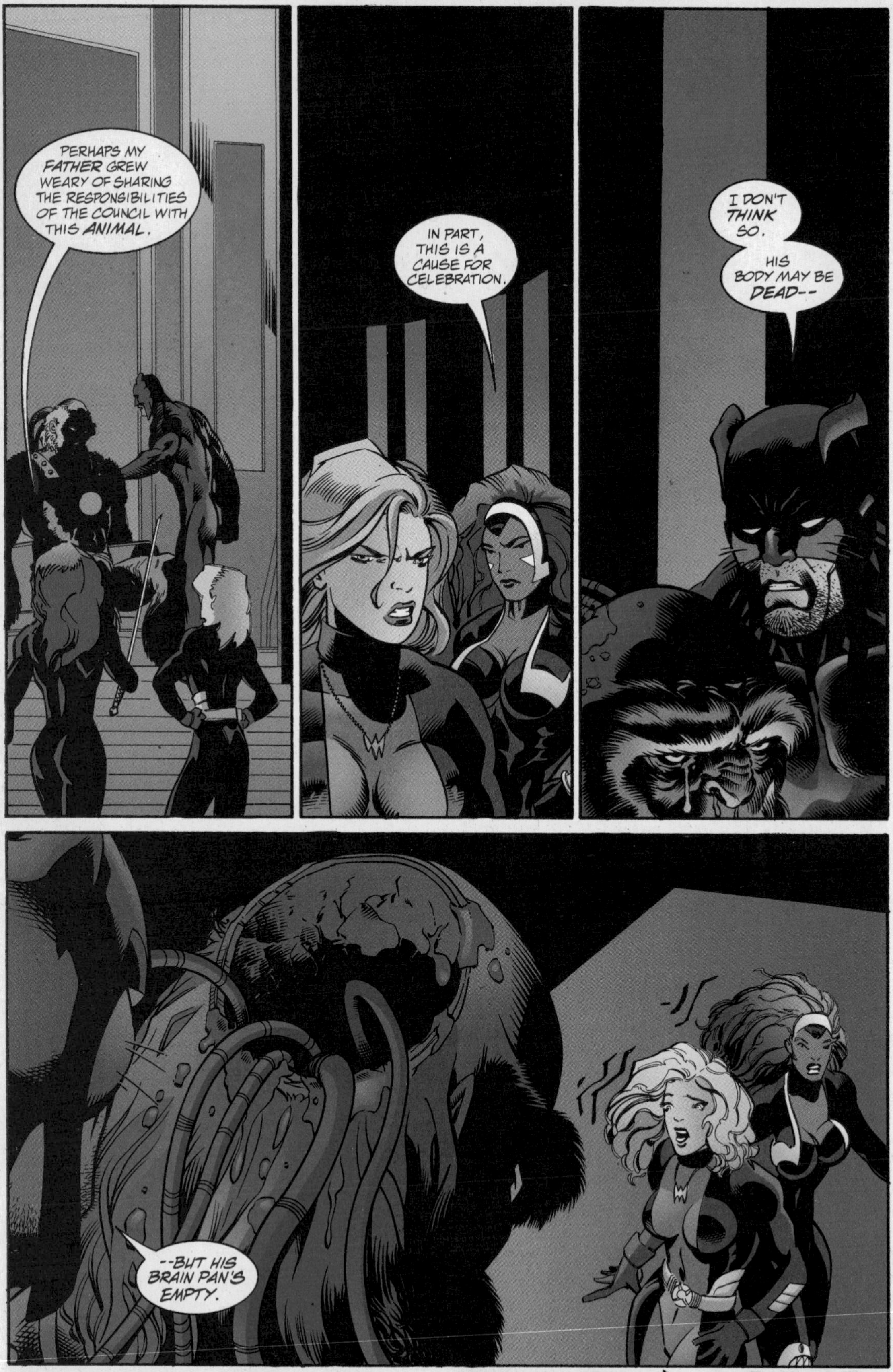
PERHAPS MY FATHER GREW WEARY OF SHARING THE RESPONSIBILITIES OF THE COUNCIL WITH THIS ANIMAL.
IN PART, THIS IS A CAUSE FOR CELEBRATION.
I DON'T THINK SO.
HIS BODY MAY BE DEAD--
--BUT HIS BRAIN PAN'S EMPTY.

THE END: FOR NOW...

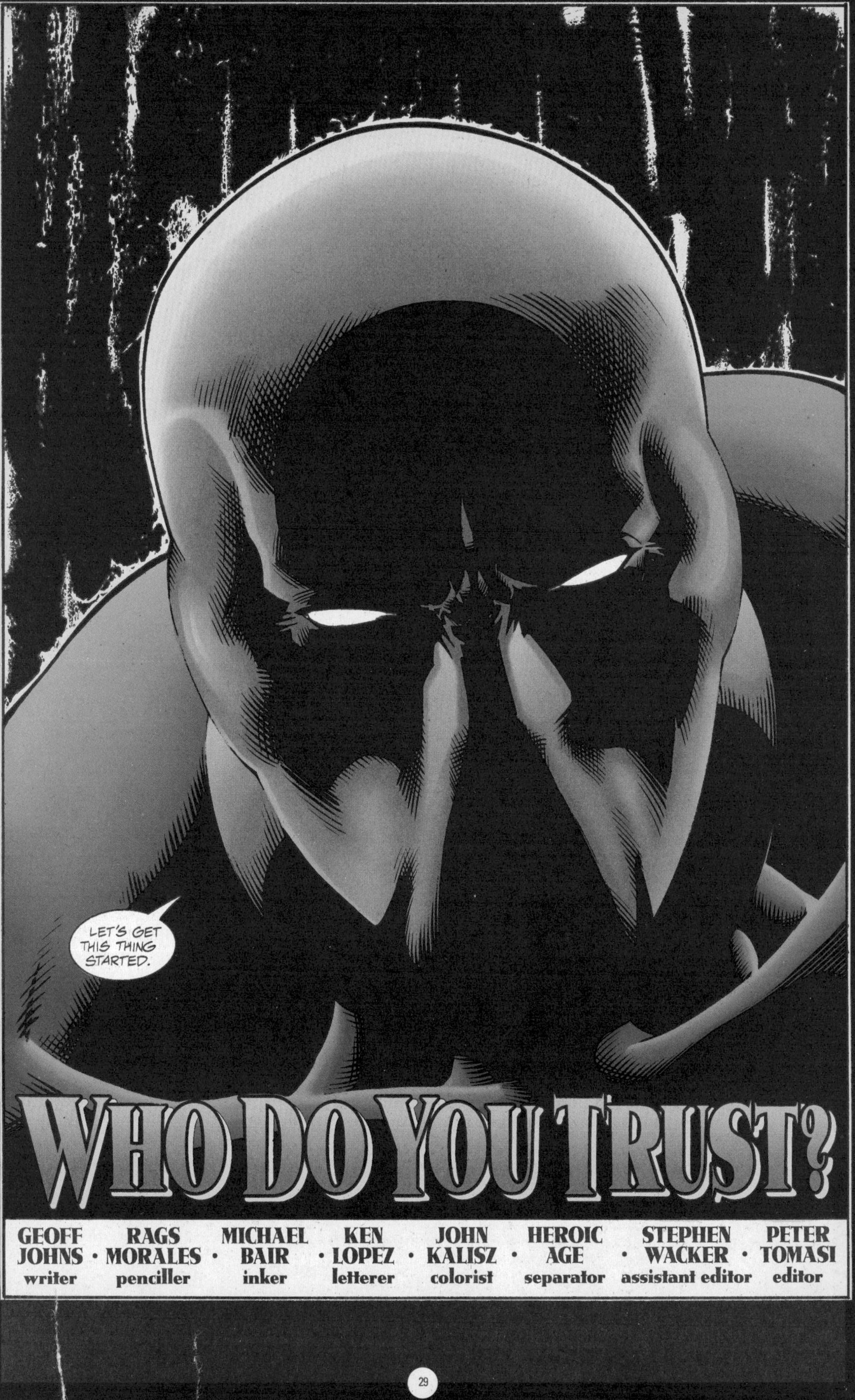
LET'S GET THIS THING STARTED.
WHO DO YOU TRUST?
GEOFF JOHNS writer · RAGS MORALES penciller · MICHAEL BAIR inker · KEN LOPEZ letterer · JOHN KALISZ colorist · HEROIC AGE separator · STEPHEN WACKER assistant editor · PETER TOMASI editor

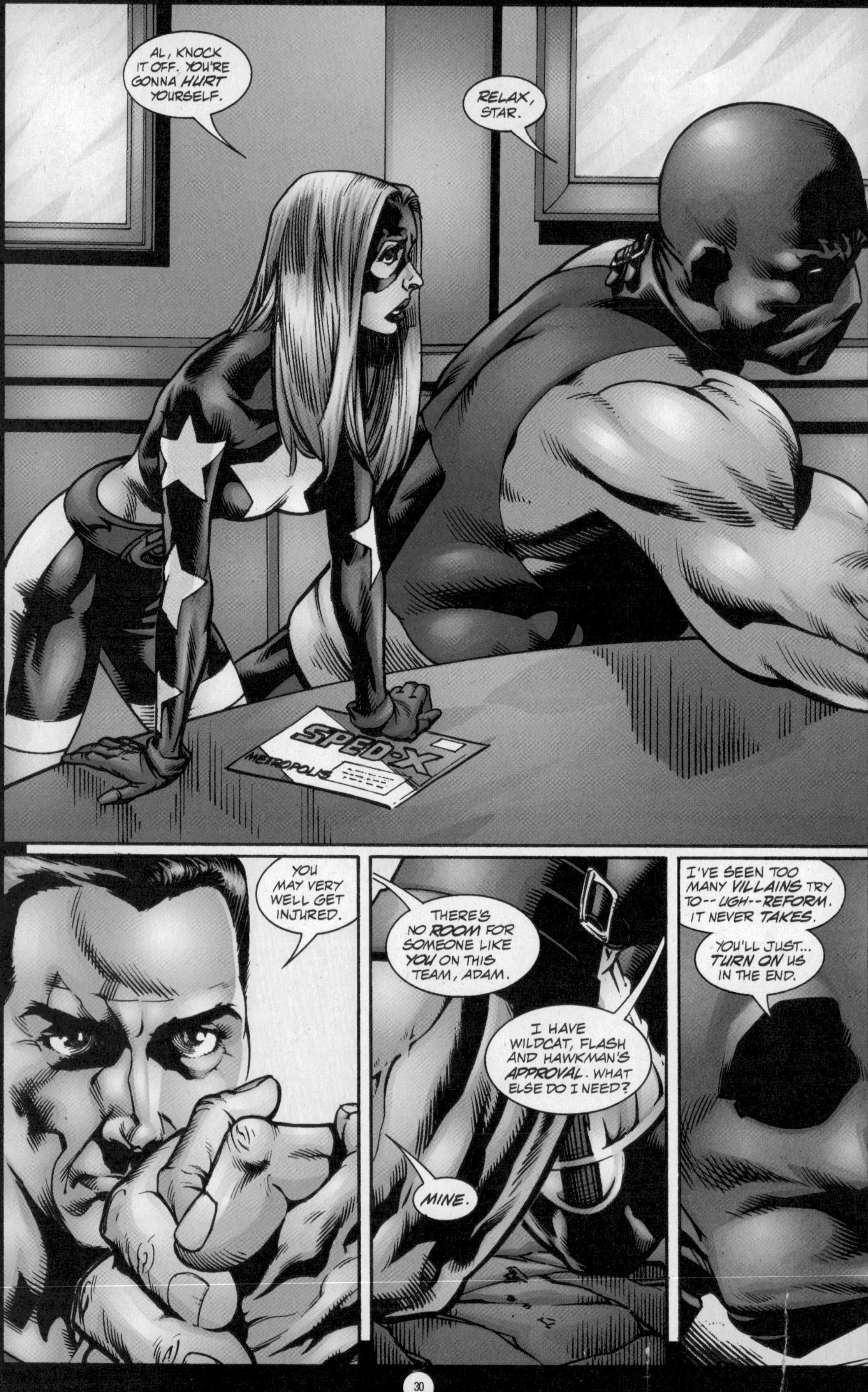
AL, KNOCK IT OFF. YOU'RE GONNA HURT YOURSELF.
RELAX, STAR.
SPED-X
METROPOLIS
YOU MAY VERY WELL GET INJURED.
THERE'S NO ROOM FOR SOMEONE LIKE YOU ON THIS TEAM, ADAM.
I HAVE WILDCAT, FLASH AND HAWKMAN'S APPROVAL. WHAT ELSE DO I NEED?
MINE.
I'VE SEEN TOO MANY VILLAINS TRY TO-- UGH-- REFORM. IT NEVER TAKES.
YOU'LL JUST... TURN ON US IN THE END.

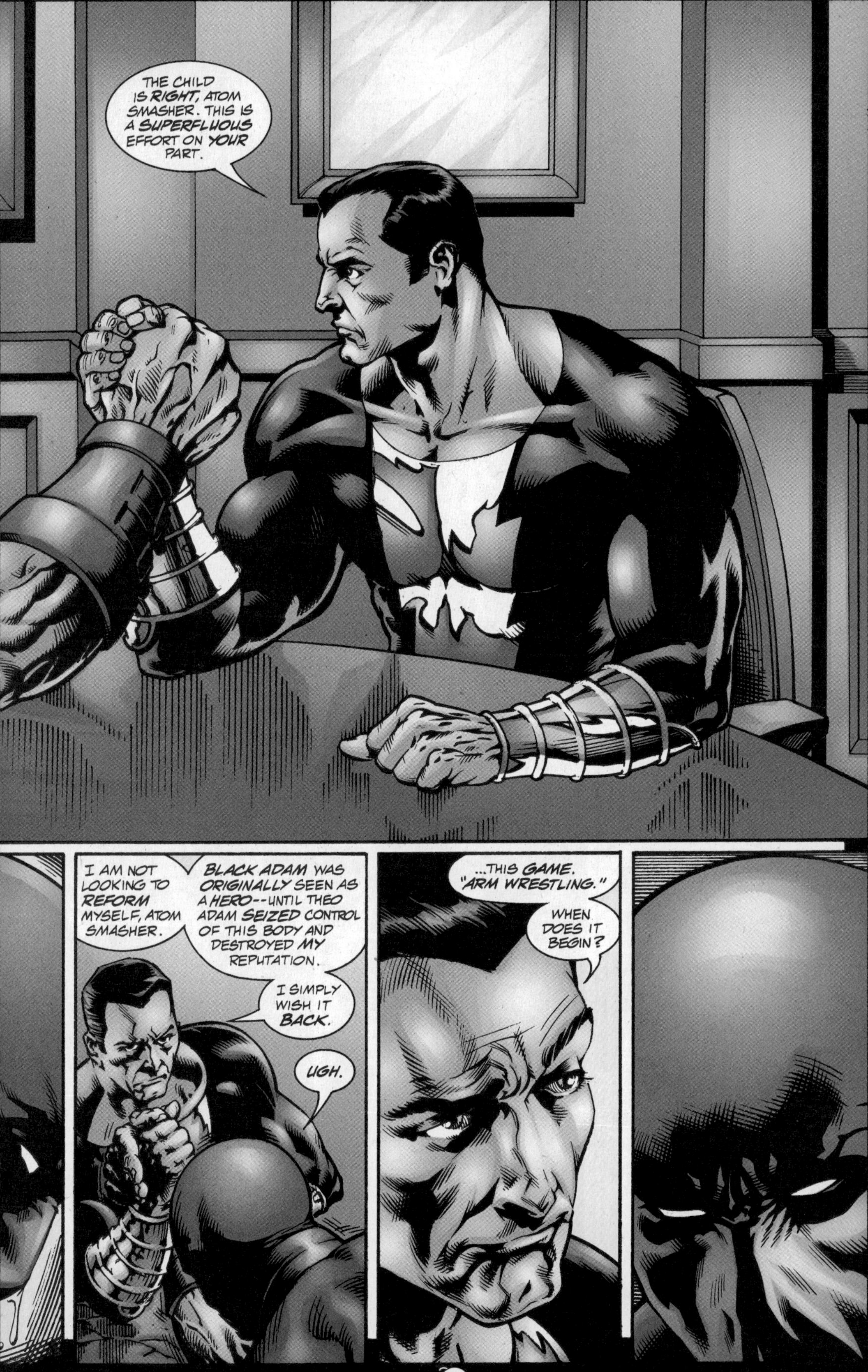
THE CHILD IS RIGHT, ATOM SMASHER. THIS IS A SUPERFLUOUS EFFORT ON YOUR PART.
I AM NOT LOOKING TO REFORM MYSELF, ATOM SMASHER.
BLACK ADAM WAS ORIGINALLY SEEN AS A HERO--UNTIL THEO ADAM SEIZED CONTROL OF THIS BODY AND DESTROYED MY REPUTATION.
I SIMPLY WISH IT BACK.
UGH.
...THIS GAME. "ARM WRESTLING."
WHEN DOES IT BEGIN?

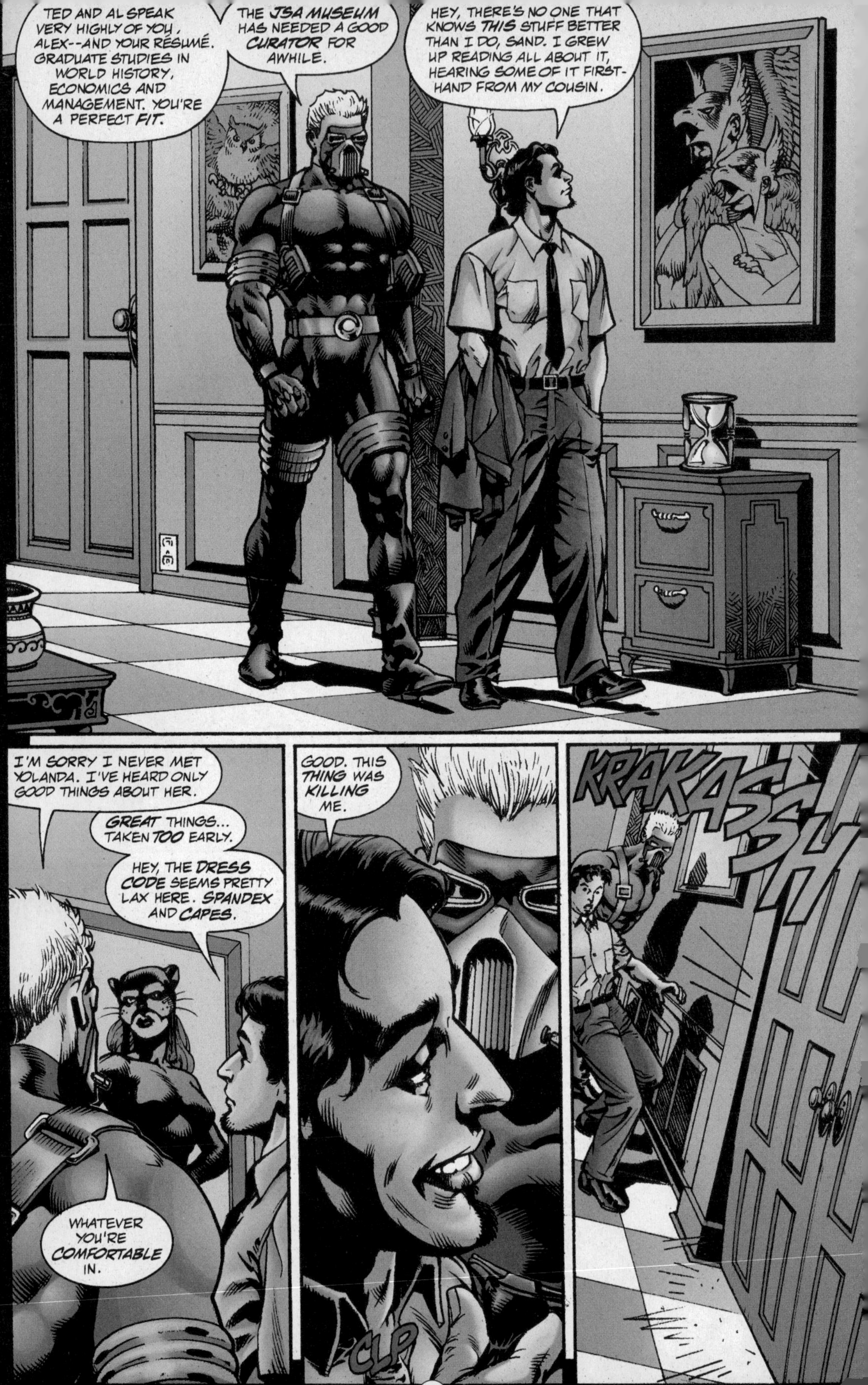
TED AND AL SPEAK VERY HIGHLY OF YOU, ALEX--AND YOUR RÉSUMÉ. GRADUATE STUDIES IN WORLD HISTORY, ECONOMICS AND MANAGEMENT. YOU'RE A PERFECT FIT.
THE JSA MUSEUM HAS NEEDED A GOOD CURATOR FOR AWHILE.
HEY, THERE'S NO ONE THAT KNOWS THIS STUFF BETTER THAN I DO, SAND. I GREW UP READING ALL ABOUT IT, HEARING SOME OF IT FIRST-HAND FROM MY COUSIN.
I'M SORRY I NEVER MET YOLANDA. I'VE HEARD ONLY GOOD THINGS ABOUT HER.
GREAT THINGS... TAKEN TOO EARLY.
HEY, THE DRESS CODE SEEMS PRETTY LAX HERE. SPANDEX AND CAPES.
WHATEVER YOU'RE COMFORTABLE IN.
GOOD. THIS THING WAS KILLING ME.
CLP
KRAKASSH

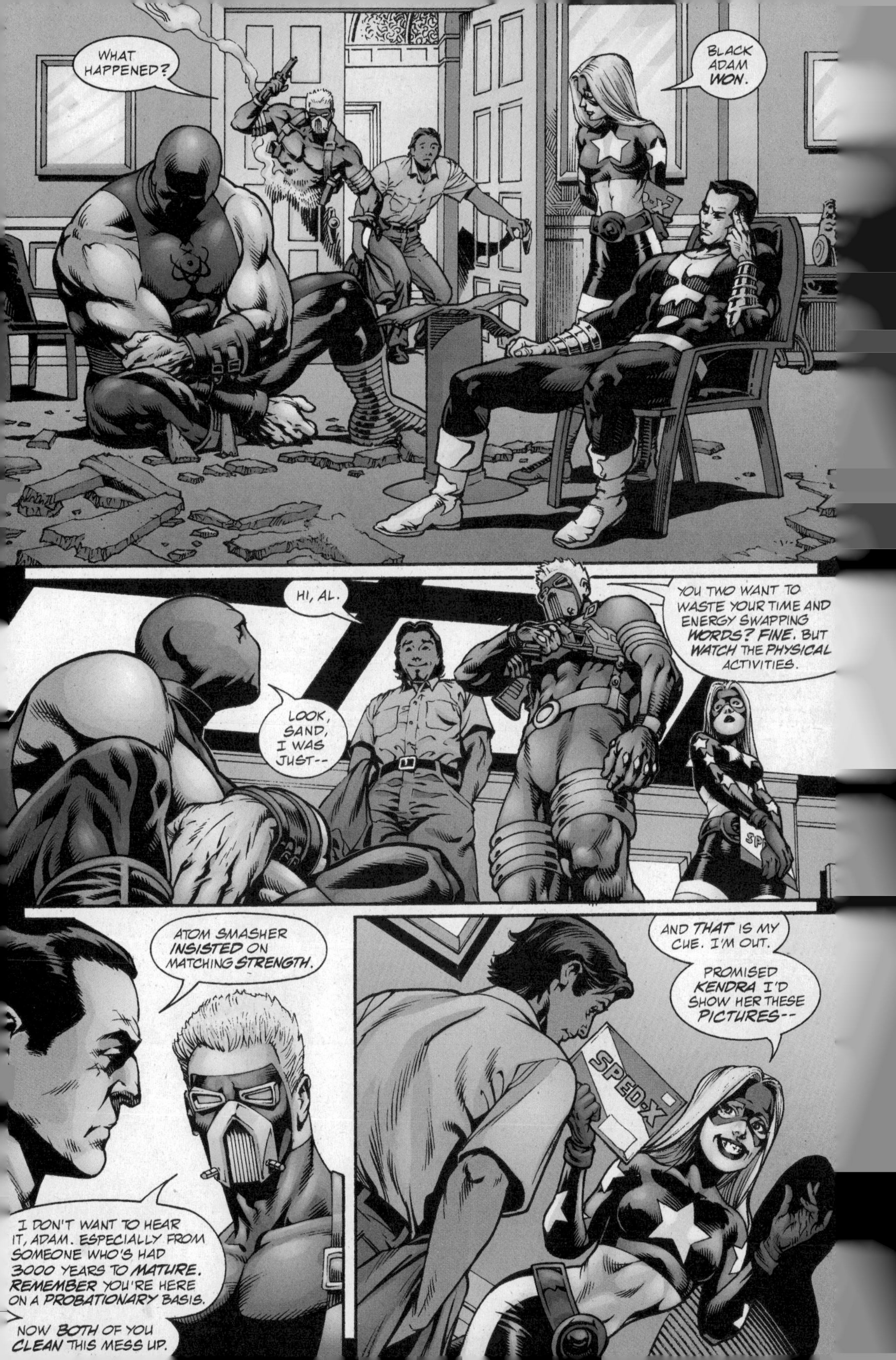
WHAT HAPPENED?
BLACK ADAM WON.
HI, AL.
LOOK, SAND, I WAS JUST--
YOU TWO WANT TO WASTE YOUR TIME AND ENERGY SWAPPING WORDS? FINE. BUT WATCH THE PHYSICAL ACTIVITIES.
ATOM SMASHER INSISTED ON MATCHING STRENGTH.
I DON'T WANT TO HEAR IT, ADAM. ESPECIALLY FROM SOMEONE WHO'S HAD 3000 YEARS TO MATURE. REMEMBER YOU'RE HERE ON A PROBATIONARY BASIS.
NOW BOTH OF YOU CLEAN THIS MESS UP.
AND THAT IS MY CUE. I'M OUT.
PROMISED KENDRA I'D SHOW HER THESE PICTURES--
SPED-X

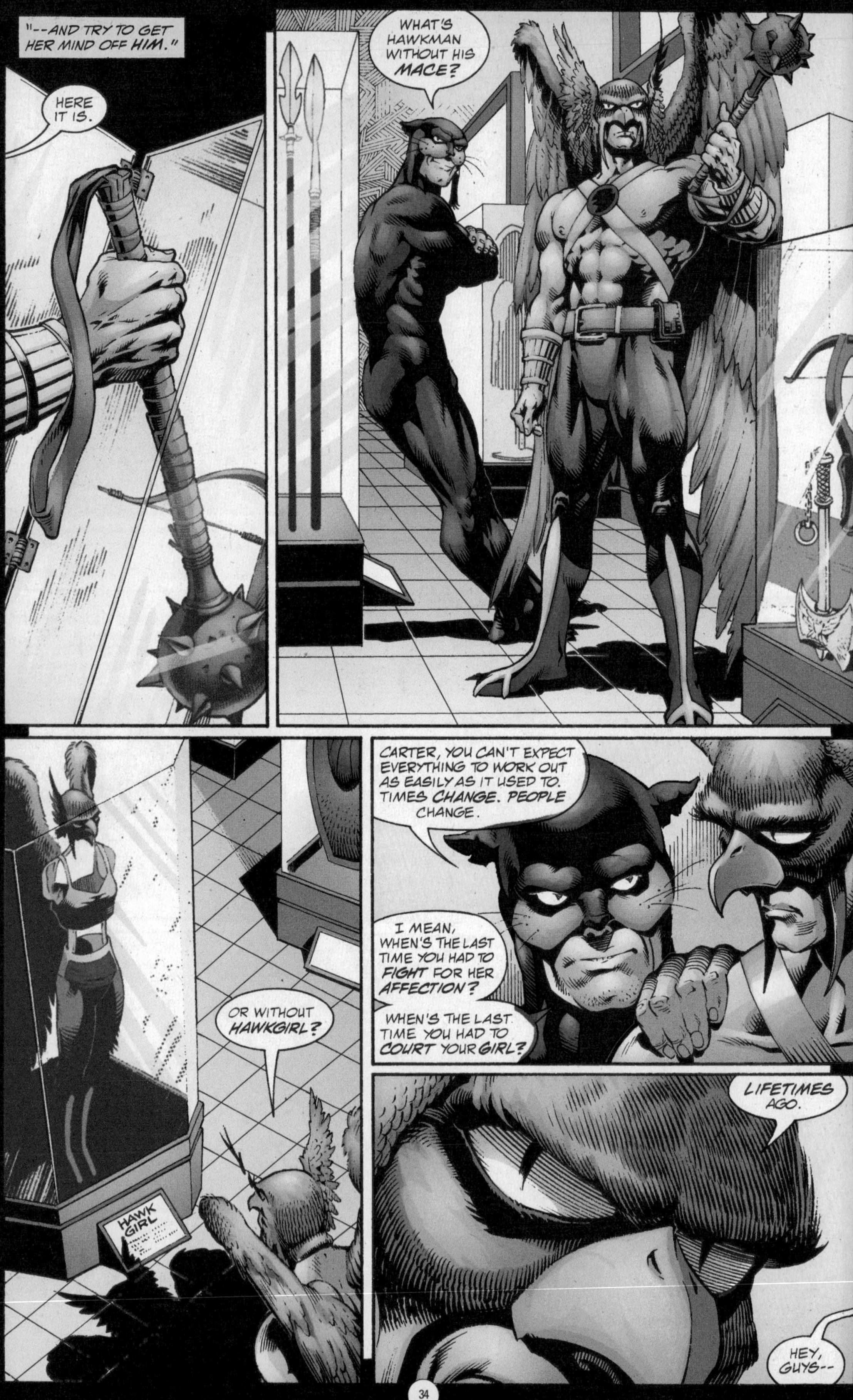
"--AND TRY TO GET HER MIND OFF HIM."
HERE IT IS.
WHAT'S HAWKMAN WITHOUT HIS MACE?
OR WITHOUT HAWKGIRL?
HAWK GIRL
CARTER, YOU CAN'T EXPECT EVERYTHING TO WORK OUT AS EASILY AS IT USED TO. TIMES CHANGE. PEOPLE CHANGE.
I MEAN, WHEN'S THE LAST TIME YOU HAD TO FIGHT FOR HER AFFECTION?
WHEN'S THE LAST TIME YOU HAD TO COURT YOUR GIRL?
LIFETIMES AGO.
HEY, GUYS--

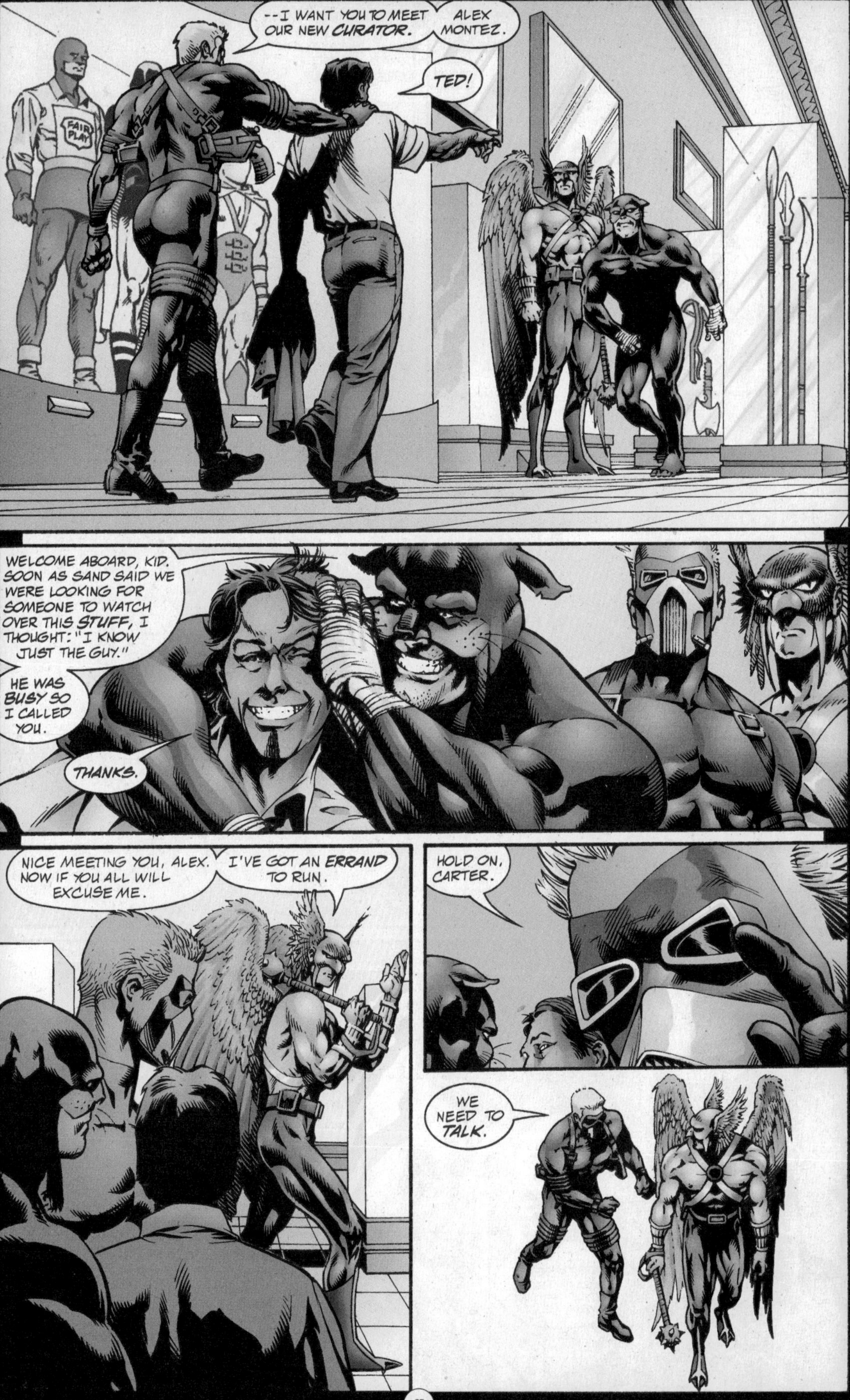
--I WANT YOU TO MEET OUR NEW CURATOR.
ALEX MONTEZ.
TED!
WELCOME ABOARD, KID. SOON AS SAND SAID WE WERE LOOKING FOR SOMEONE TO WATCH OVER THIS STUFF, I THOUGHT: "I KNOW JUST THE GUY."
HE WAS BUSY SO I CALLED YOU.
THANKS.
NICE MEETING YOU, ALEX. NOW IF YOU ALL WILL EXCUSE ME.
I'VE GOT AN ERRAND TO RUN.
HOLD ON, CARTER.
WE NEED TO TALK.

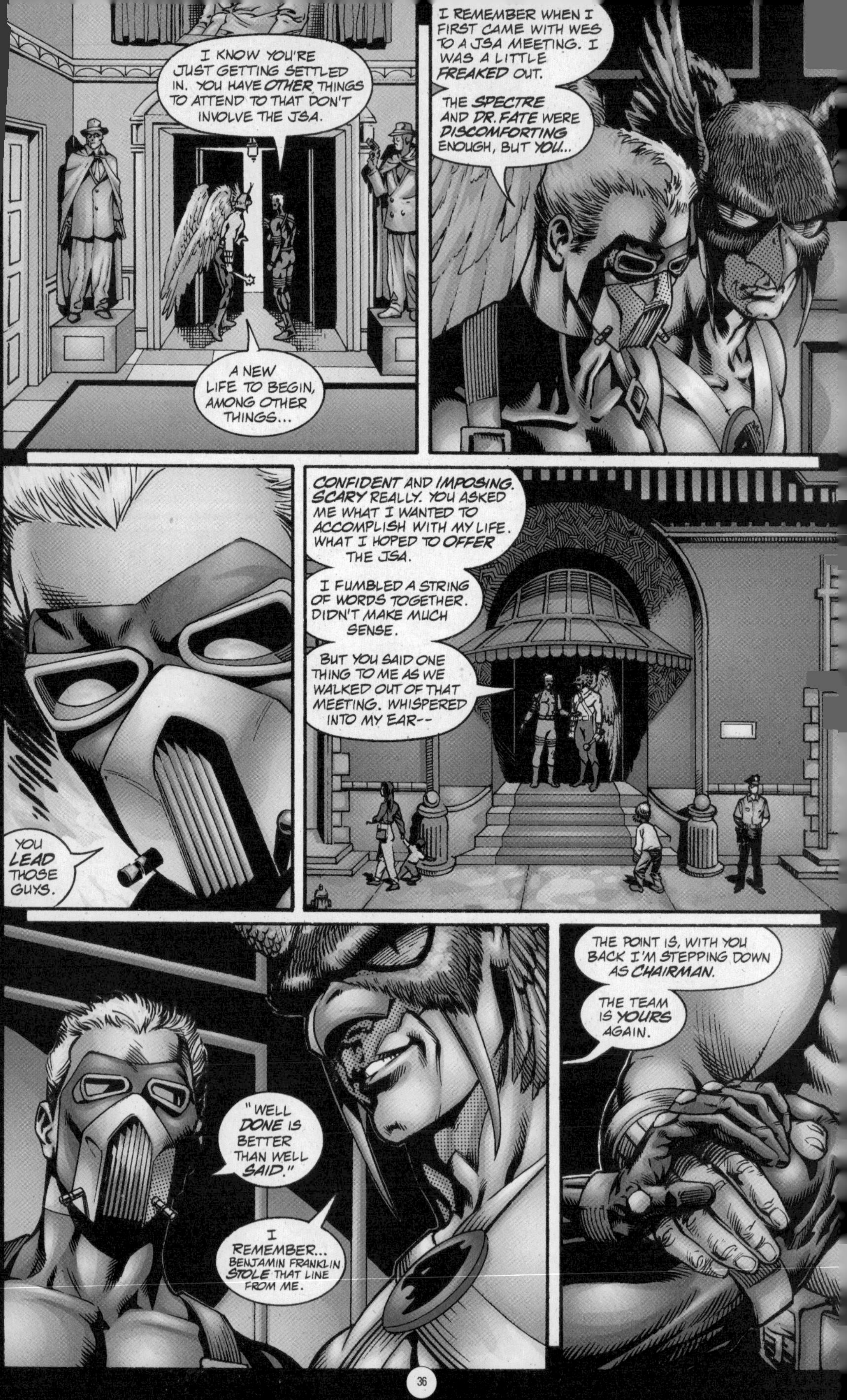
I KNOW YOU'RE JUST GETTING SETTLED IN. YOU HAVE OTHER THINGS TO ATTEND TO THAT DON'T INVOLVE THE JSA.
A NEW LIFE TO BEGIN, AMONG OTHER THINGS...
I REMEMBER WHEN I FIRST CAME WITH WES TO A JSA MEETING. I WAS A LITTLE FREAKED OUT.
THE SPECTRE AND DR. FATE WERE DISCOMFORTING ENOUGH, BUT YOU...
YOU LEAD THOSE GUYS.
CONFIDENT AND IMPOSING. SCARY REALLY. YOU ASKED ME WHAT I WANTED TO ACCOMPLISH WITH MY LIFE. WHAT I HOPED TO OFFER THE JSA.
I FUMBLED A STRING OF WORDS TOGETHER. DIDN'T MAKE MUCH SENSE.
BUT YOU SAID ONE THING TO ME AS WE WALKED OUT OF THAT MEETING. WHISPERED INTO MY EAR--
"WELL DONE IS BETTER THAN WELL SAID."
I REMEMBER... BENJAMIN FRANKLIN STOLE THAT LINE FROM ME.
THE POINT IS, WITH YOU BACK I'M STEPPING DOWN AS CHAIRMAN.
THE TEAM IS YOURS AGAIN.

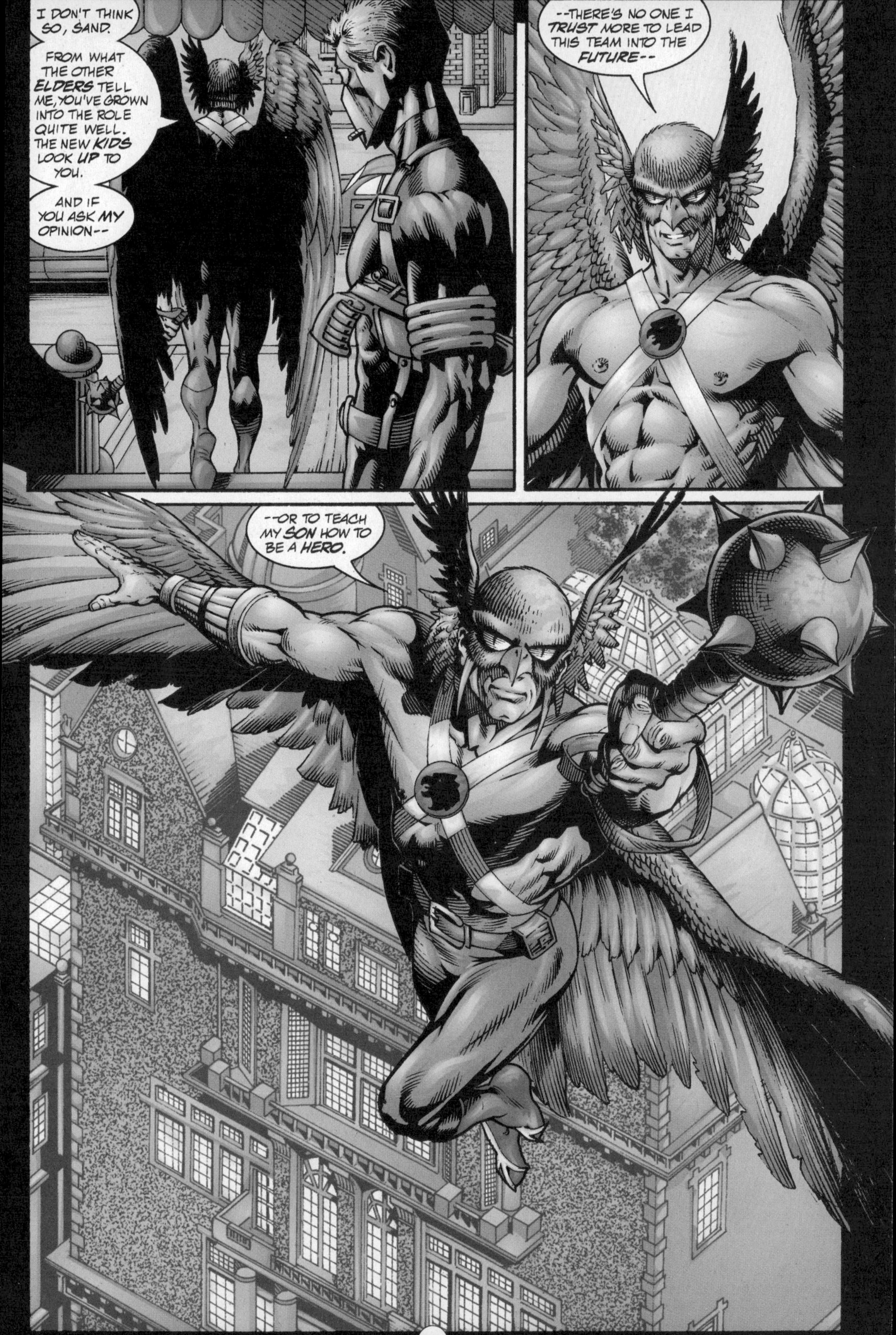
I DON'T THINK SO, SAND.
FROM WHAT THE OTHER ELDERS TELL ME, YOU'VE GROWN INTO THE ROLE QUITE WELL. THE NEW KIDS LOOK UP TO YOU.
AND IF YOU ASK MY OPINION--
--THERE'S NO ONE I TRUST MORE TO LEAD THIS TEAM INTO THE FUTURE--
--OR TO TEACH MY SON HOW TO BE A HERO.

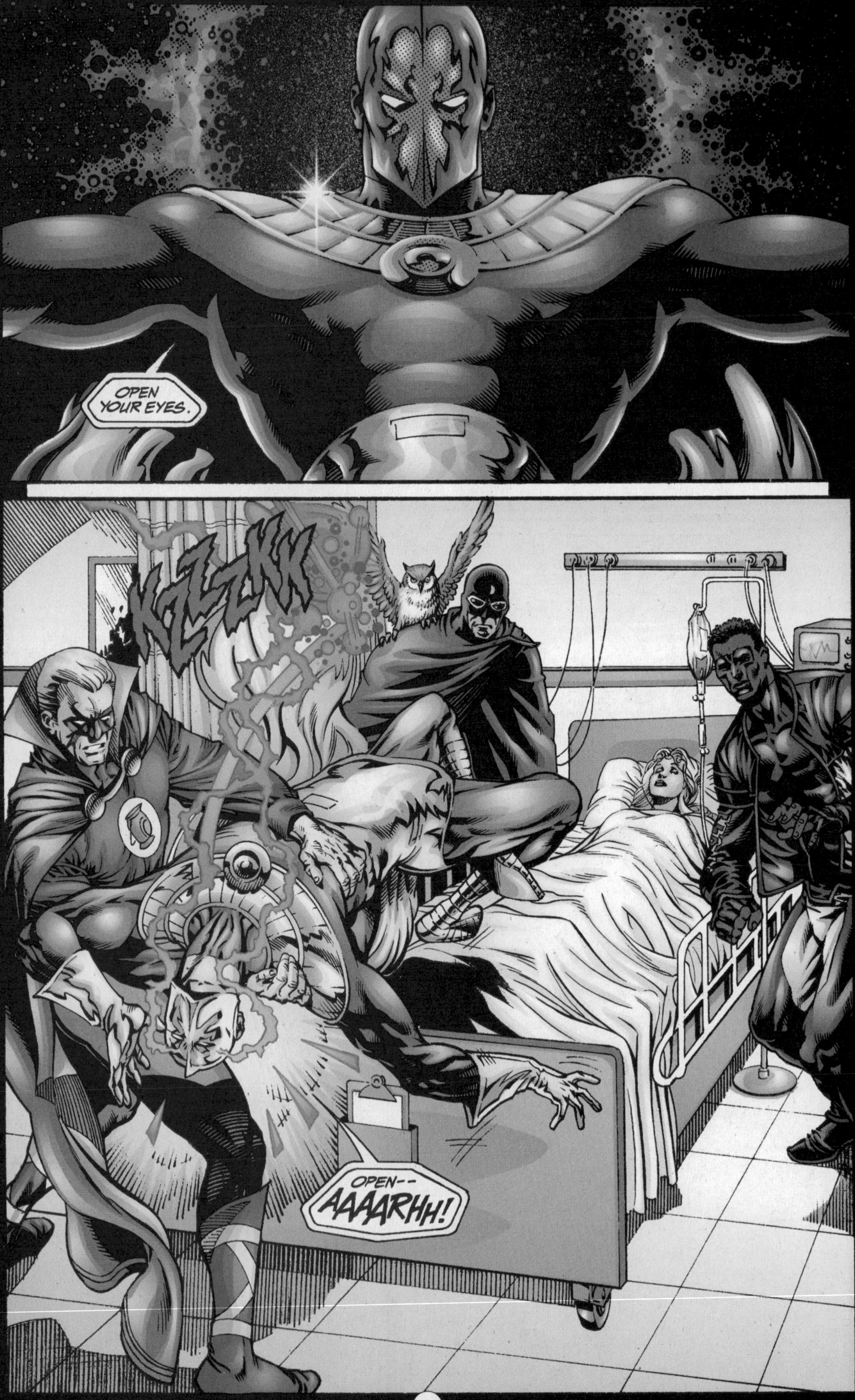
OPEN YOUR EYES.
KZZZKK
OPEN--
AAAARHH!

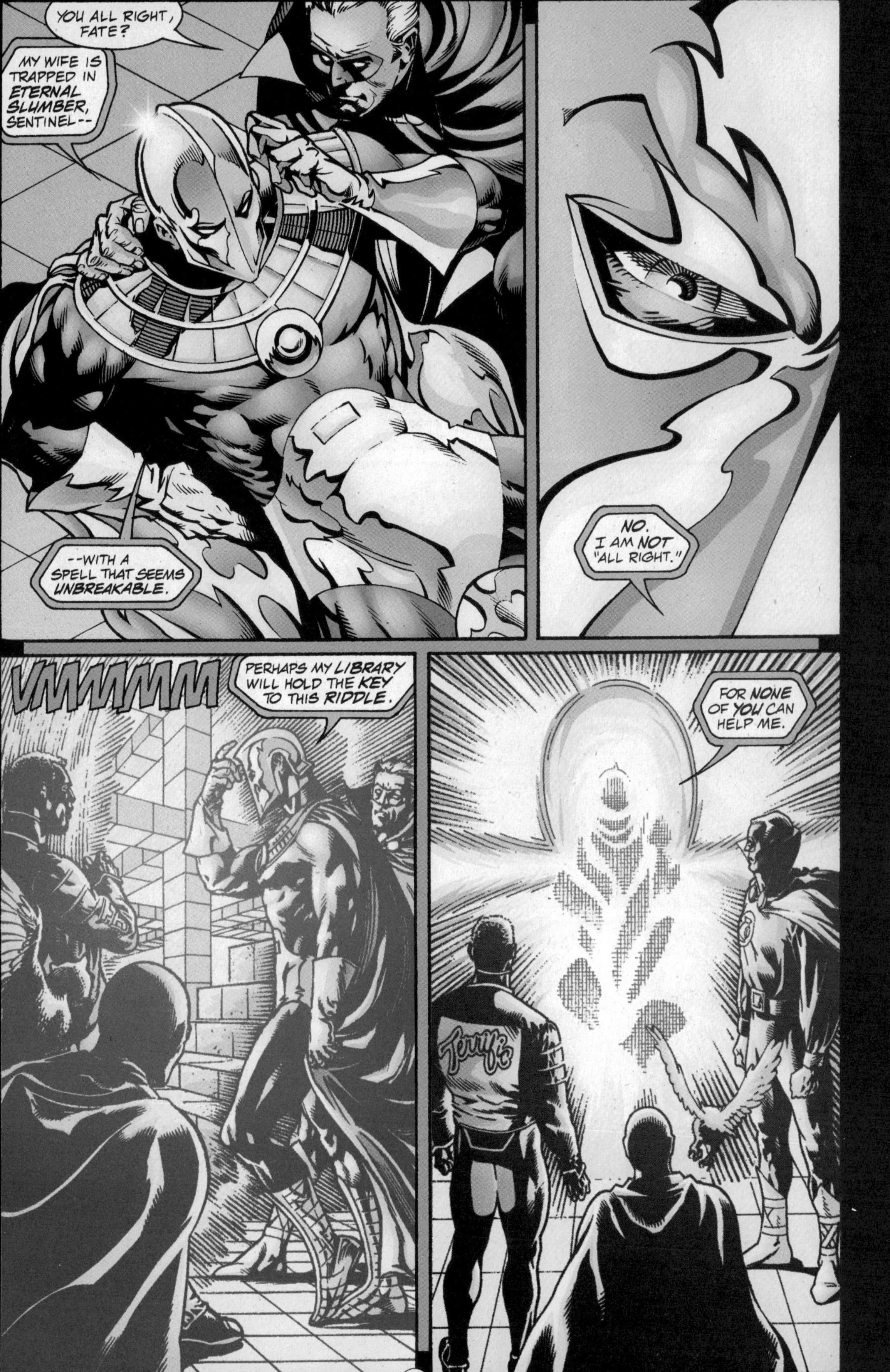
YOU ALL RIGHT, FATE?
MY WIFE IS TRAPPED IN ETERNAL SLUMBER, SENTINEL--
--WITH A SPELL THAT SEEMS UNBREAKABLE.
NO. I AM NOT "ALL RIGHT."
VMMMMM
PERHAPS MY LIBRARY WILL HOLD THE KEY TO THIS RIDDLE.
FOR NONE OF YOU CAN HELP ME.

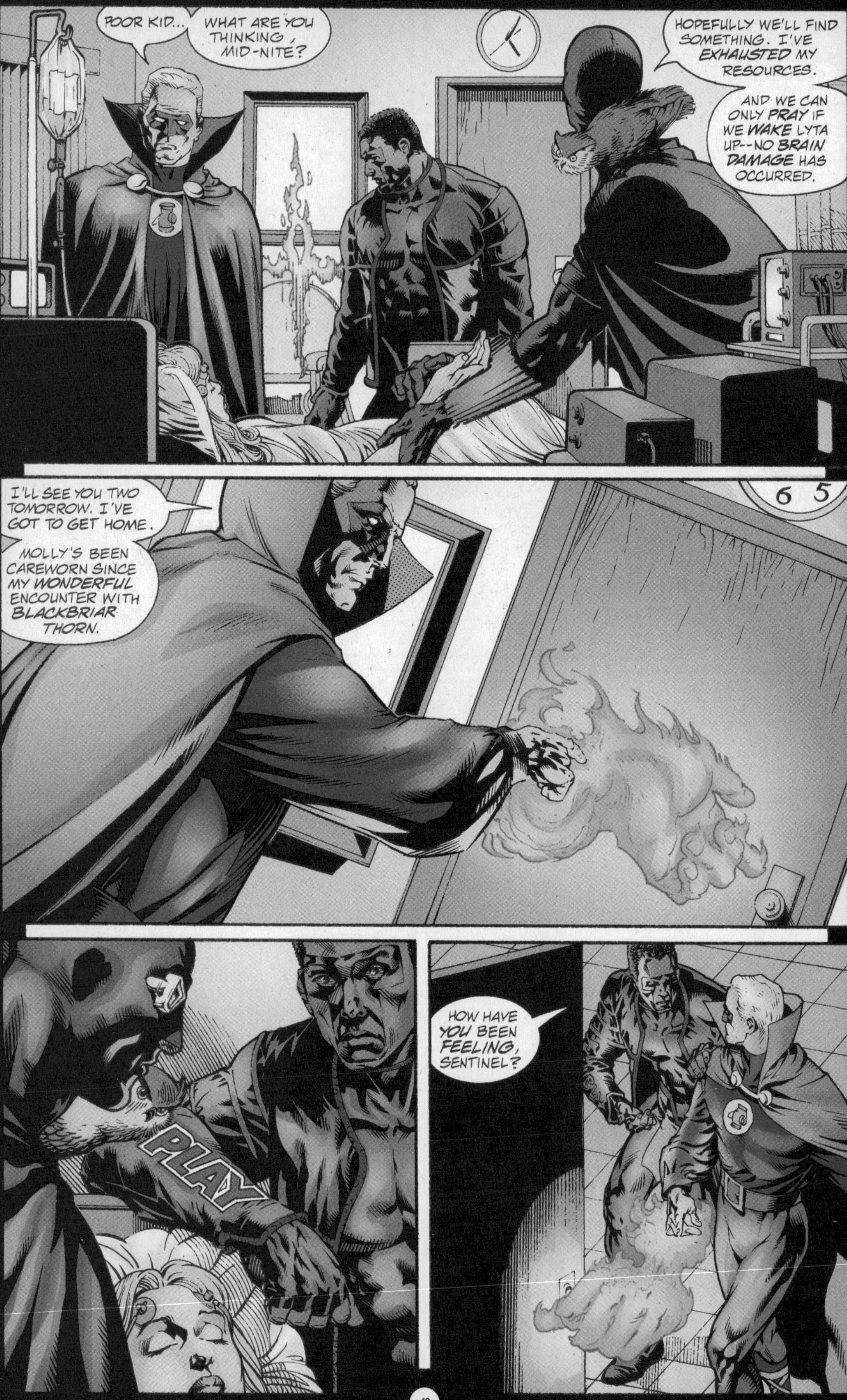
POOR KID...
WHAT ARE YOU THINKING, MID-NITE?
HOPEFULLY WE'LL FIND SOMETHING. I'VE EXHAUSTED MY RESOURCES.
AND WE CAN ONLY PRAY IF WE WAKE LYTA UP--NO BRAIN DAMAGE HAS OCCURRED.
I'LL SEE YOU TWO TOMORROW. I'VE GOT TO GET HOME.
MOLLY'S BEEN CAREWORN SINCE MY WONDERFUL ENCOUNTER WITH BLACKBRIAR THORN.
PLAY
HOW HAVE YOU BEEN FEELING, SENTINEL?

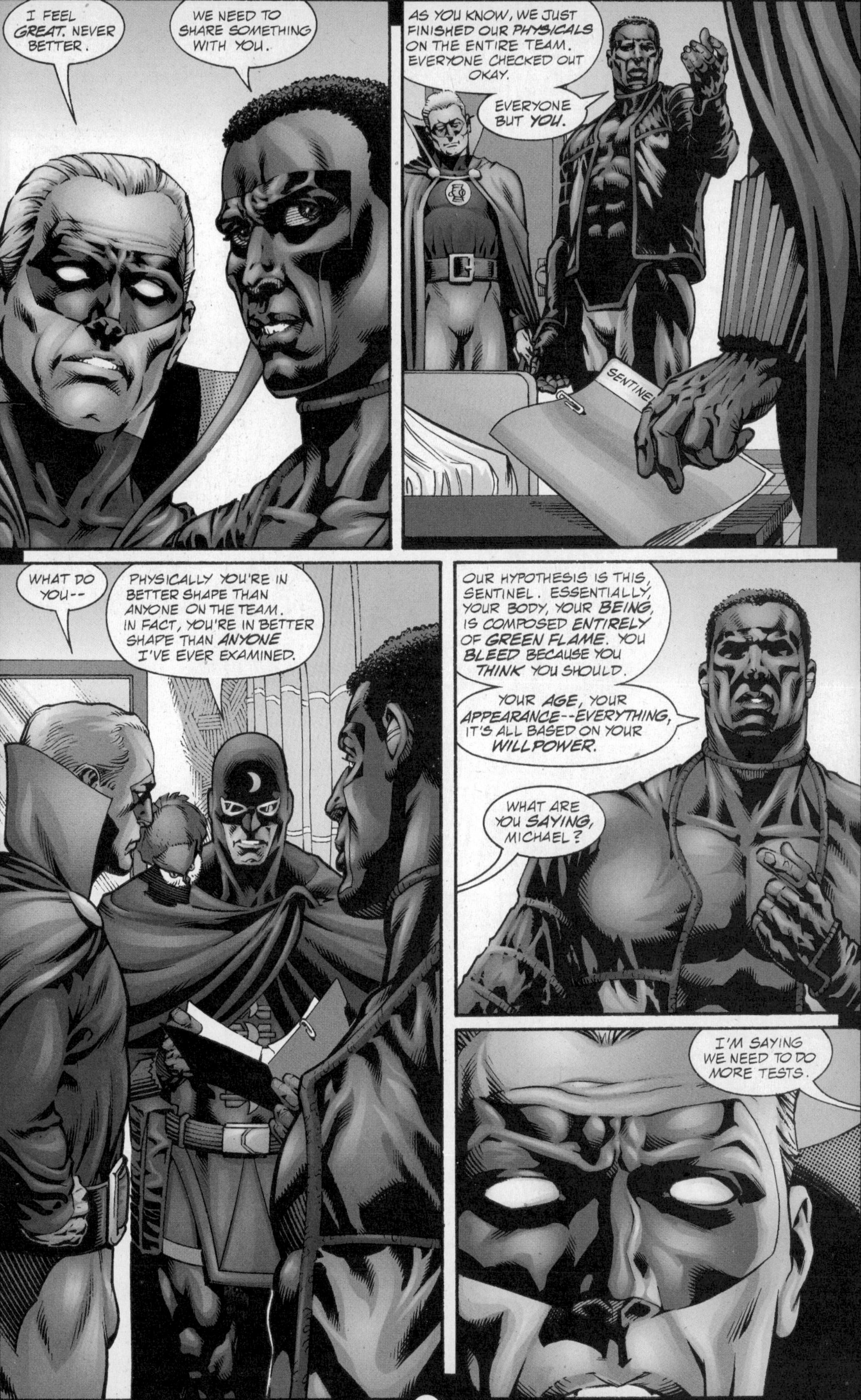
I FEEL GREAT. NEVER BETTER.
WE NEED TO SHARE SOMETHING WITH YOU.
AS YOU KNOW, WE JUST FINISHED OUR PHYSICALS ON THE ENTIRE TEAM. EVERYONE CHECKED OUT OKAY.
EVERYONE BUT YOU.
SENTINE
WHAT DO YOU--
PHYSICALLY YOU'RE IN BETTER SHAPE THAN ANYONE ON THE TEAM. IN FACT, YOU'RE IN BETTER SHAPE THAN ANYONE I'VE EVER EXAMINED.
OUR HYPOTHESIS IS THIS, SENTINEL. ESSENTIALLY, YOUR BODY, YOUR BEING, IS COMPOSED ENTIRELY OF GREEN FLAME. YOU BLEED BECAUSE YOU THINK YOU SHOULD.
YOUR AGE, YOUR APPEARANCE--EVERYTHING, IT'S ALL BASED ON YOUR WILLPOWER.
WHAT ARE YOU SAYING, MICHAEL?
I'M SAYING WE NEED TO DO MORE TESTS.

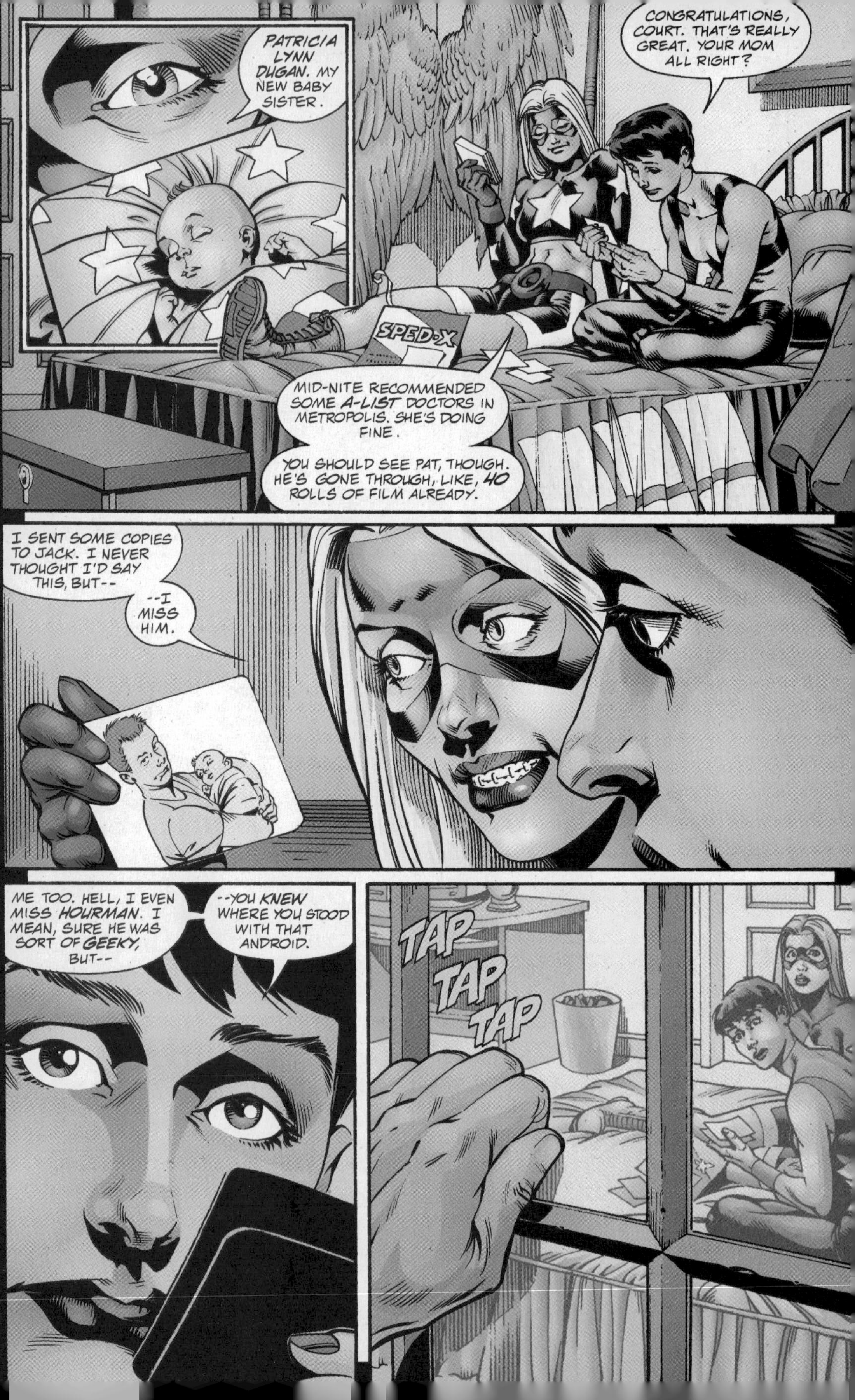
PATRICIA LYNN DUGAN. MY NEW BABY SISTER.
CONGRATULATIONS, COURT. THAT'S REALLY GREAT. YOUR MOM ALL RIGHT?
SPED-X
MID-NITE RECOMMENDED SOME A-LIST DOCTORS IN METROPOLIS. SHE'S DOING FINE.
YOU SHOULD SEE PAT, THOUGH. HE'S GONE THROUGH, LIKE, 40 ROLLS OF FILM ALREADY.
I SENT SOME COPIES TO JACK. I NEVER THOUGHT I'D SAY THIS, BUT--
--I MISS HIM.
ME TOO. HELL, I EVEN MISS HOURMAN. I MEAN, SURE HE WAS SORT OF GEEKY, BUT--
--YOU KNEW WHERE YOU STOOD WITH THAT ANDROID.
TAP TAP TAP

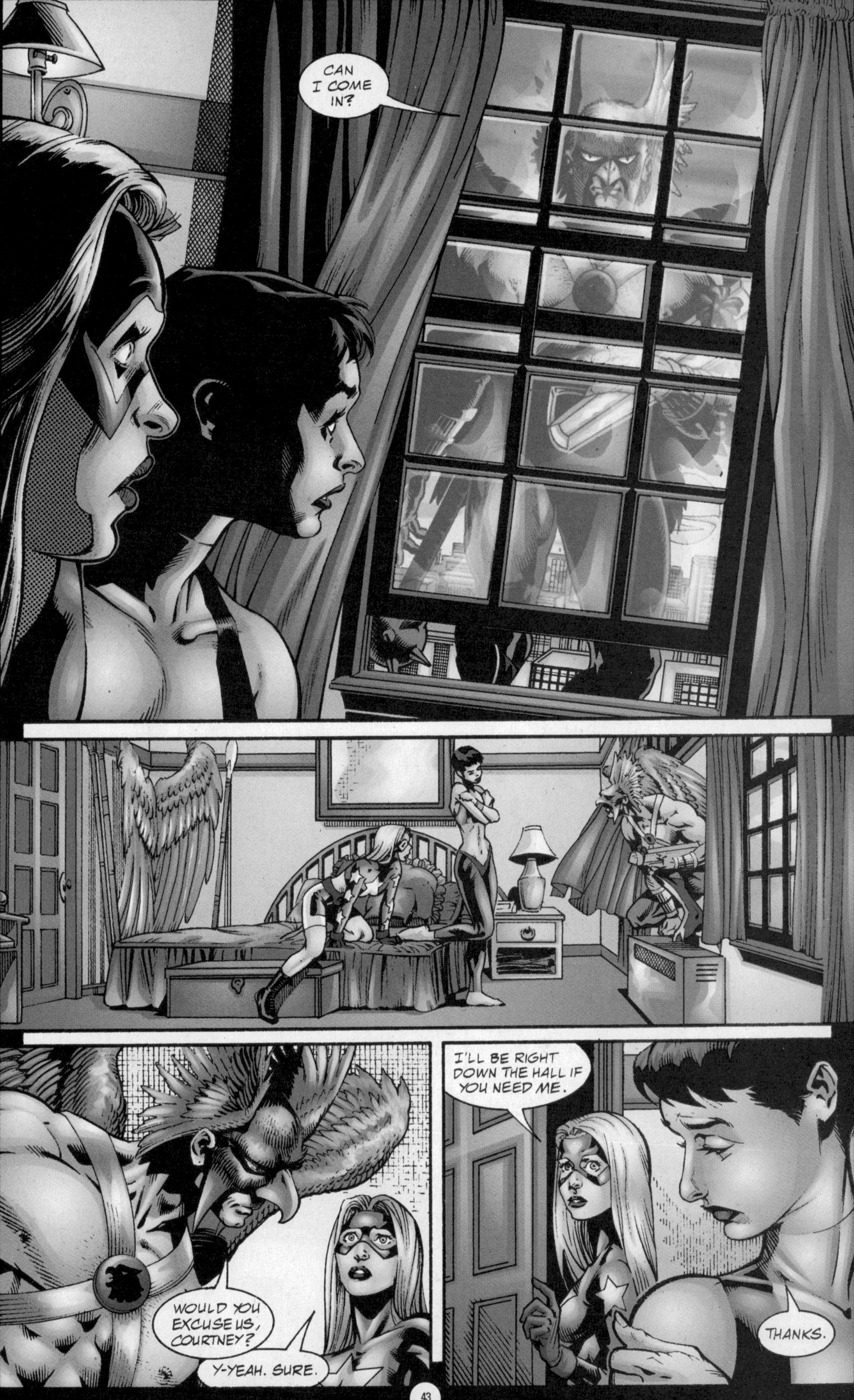
CAN I COME IN?
WOULD YOU EXCUSE US, COURTNEY?
Y-YEAH. SURE.
I'LL BE RIGHT DOWN THE HALL IF YOU NEED ME.
THANKS.

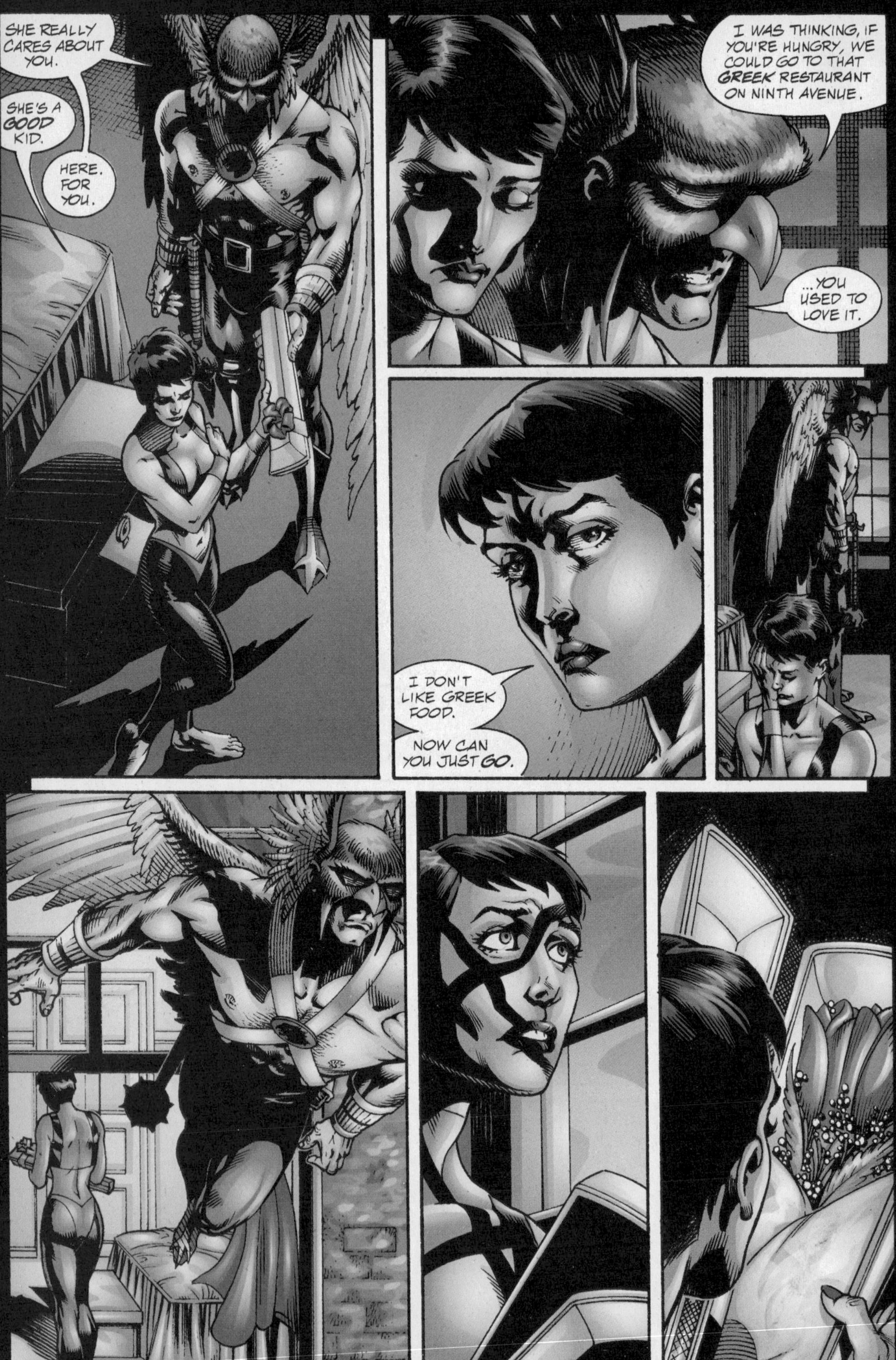
SHE REALLY CARES ABOUT YOU.
SHE'S A GOOD KID.
HERE. FOR YOU.
I WAS THINKING, IF YOU'RE HUNGRY, WE COULD GO TO THAT GREEK RESTAURANT ON NINTH AVENUE.
...YOU USED TO LOVE IT.
I DON'T LIKE GREEK FOOD.
NOW CAN YOU JUST GO.

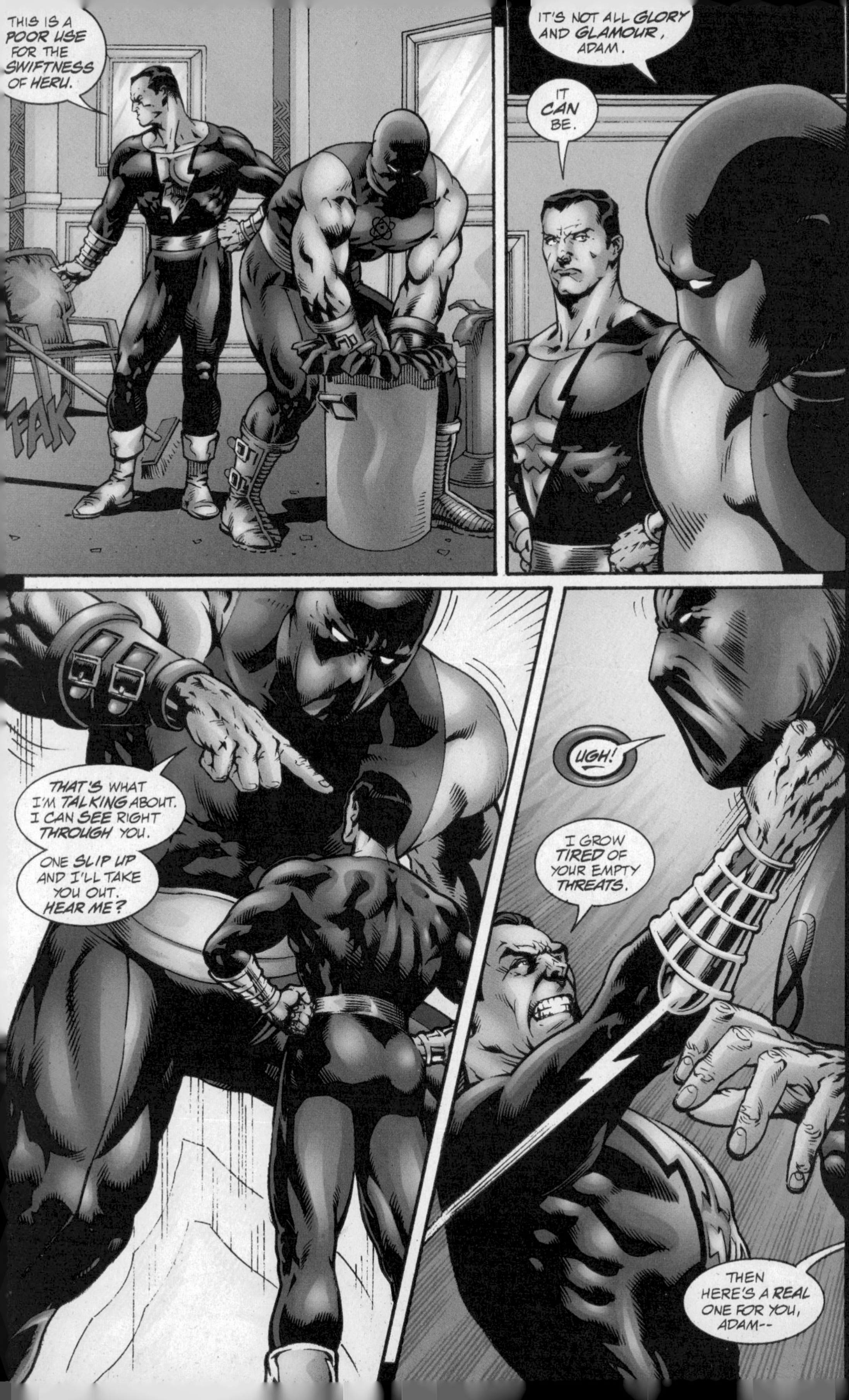

THIS IS A POOR USE FOR THE SWIFTNESS OF HERU.
FAK
IT'S NOT ALL GLORY AND GLAMOUR, ADAM.
IT CAN BE.
THAT'S WHAT I'M TALKING ABOUT. I CAN SEE RIGHT THROUGH YOU.
ONE SLIP UP AND I'LL TAKE YOU OUT. HEAR ME?
UGH!
I GROW TIRED OF YOUR EMPTY THREATS.
THEN HERE'S A REAL ONE FOR YOU, ADAM--

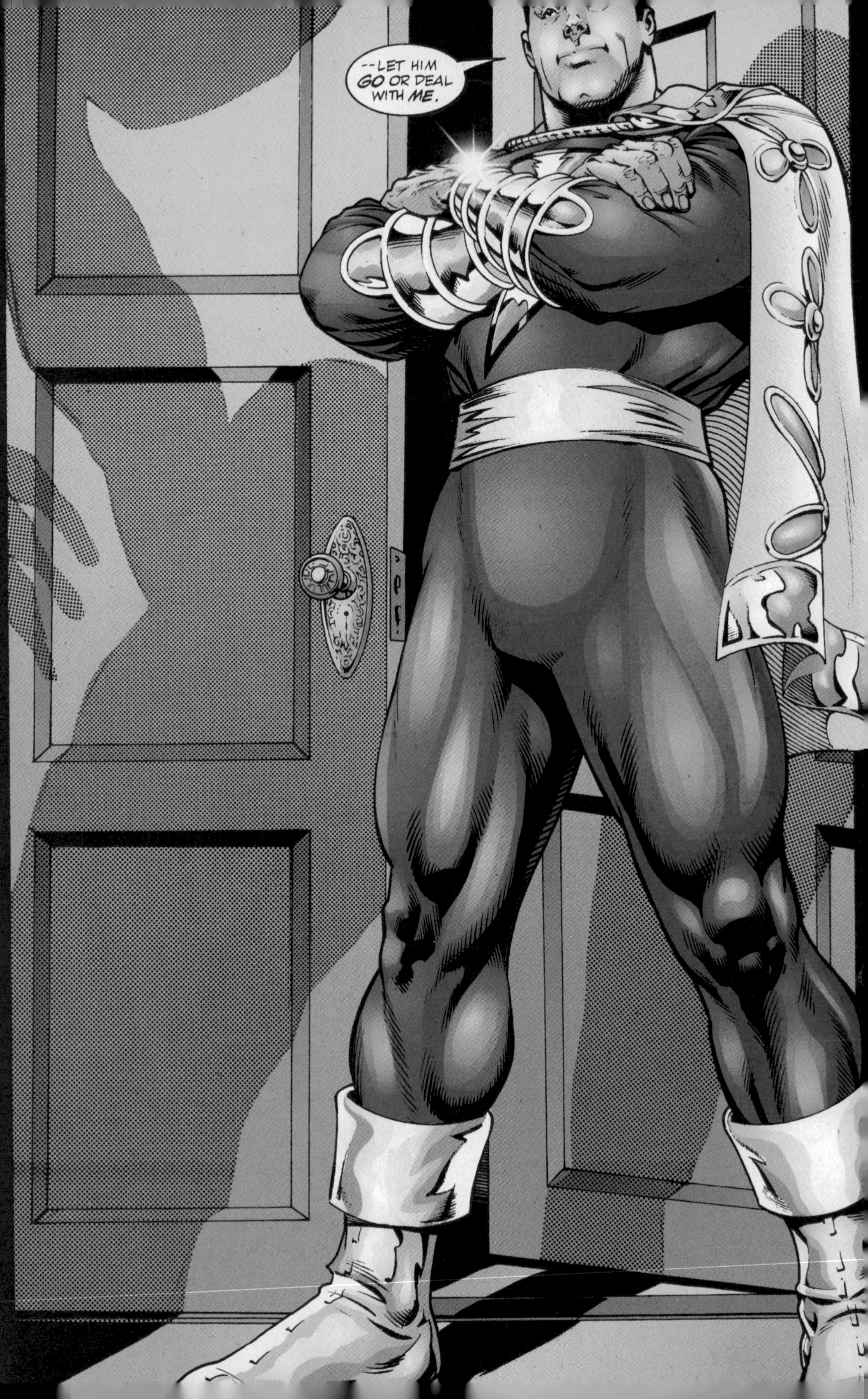
--LET HIM GO OR DEAL WITH ME.

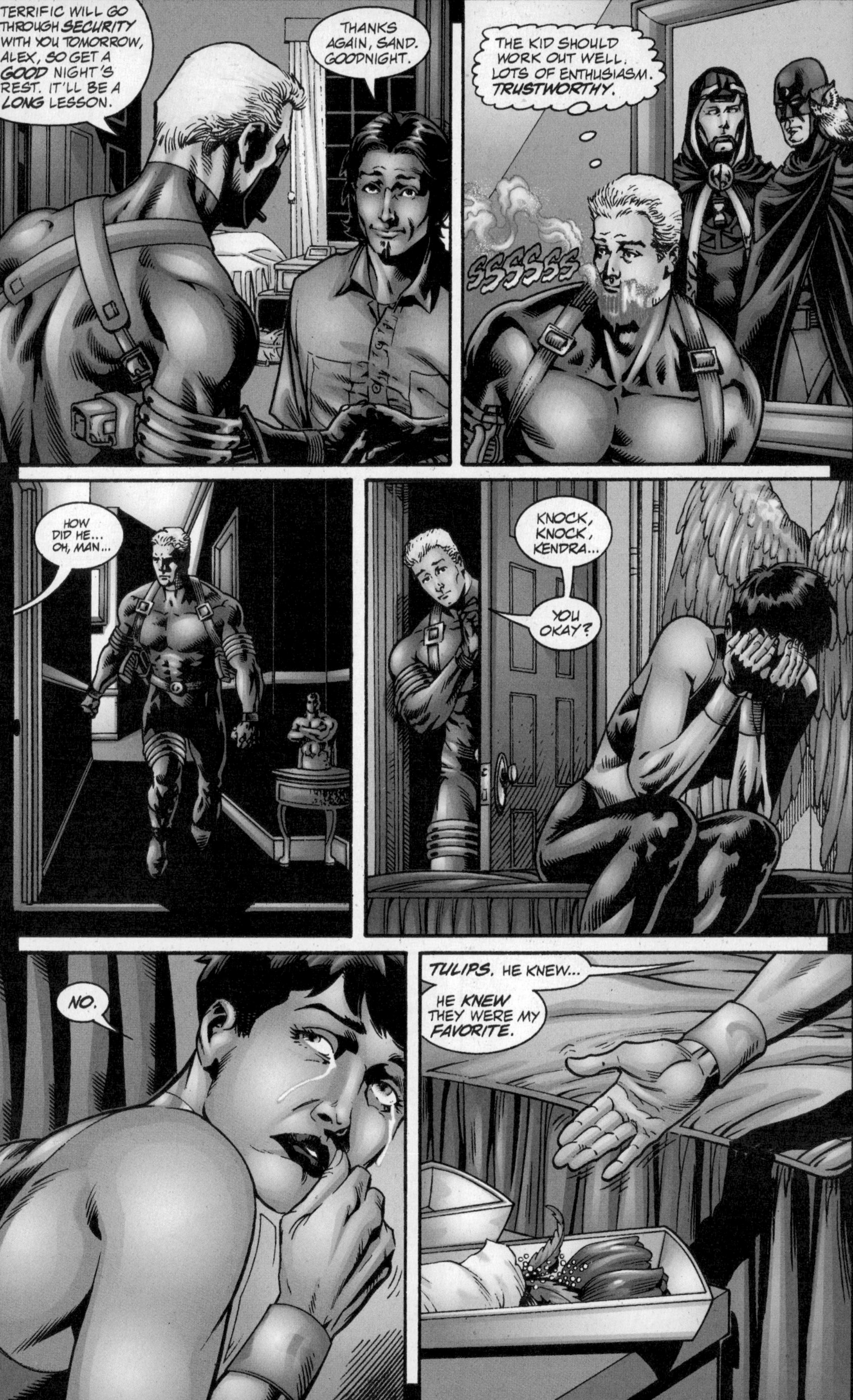
TERRIFIC WILL GO THROUGH SECURITY WITH YOU TOMORROW, ALEX, SO GET A GOOD NIGHT'S REST. IT'LL BE A LONG LESSON.
THANKS AGAIN, SAND. GOODNIGHT.
THE KID SHOULD WORK OUT WELL. LOTS OF ENTHUSIASM. TRUSTWORTHY.
SSSSSS
HOW DID HE... OH, MAN...
KNOCK, KNOCK, KENDRA...
YOU OKAY?
NO.
TULIPS. HE KNEW...
HE KNEW THEY WERE MY FAVORITE.

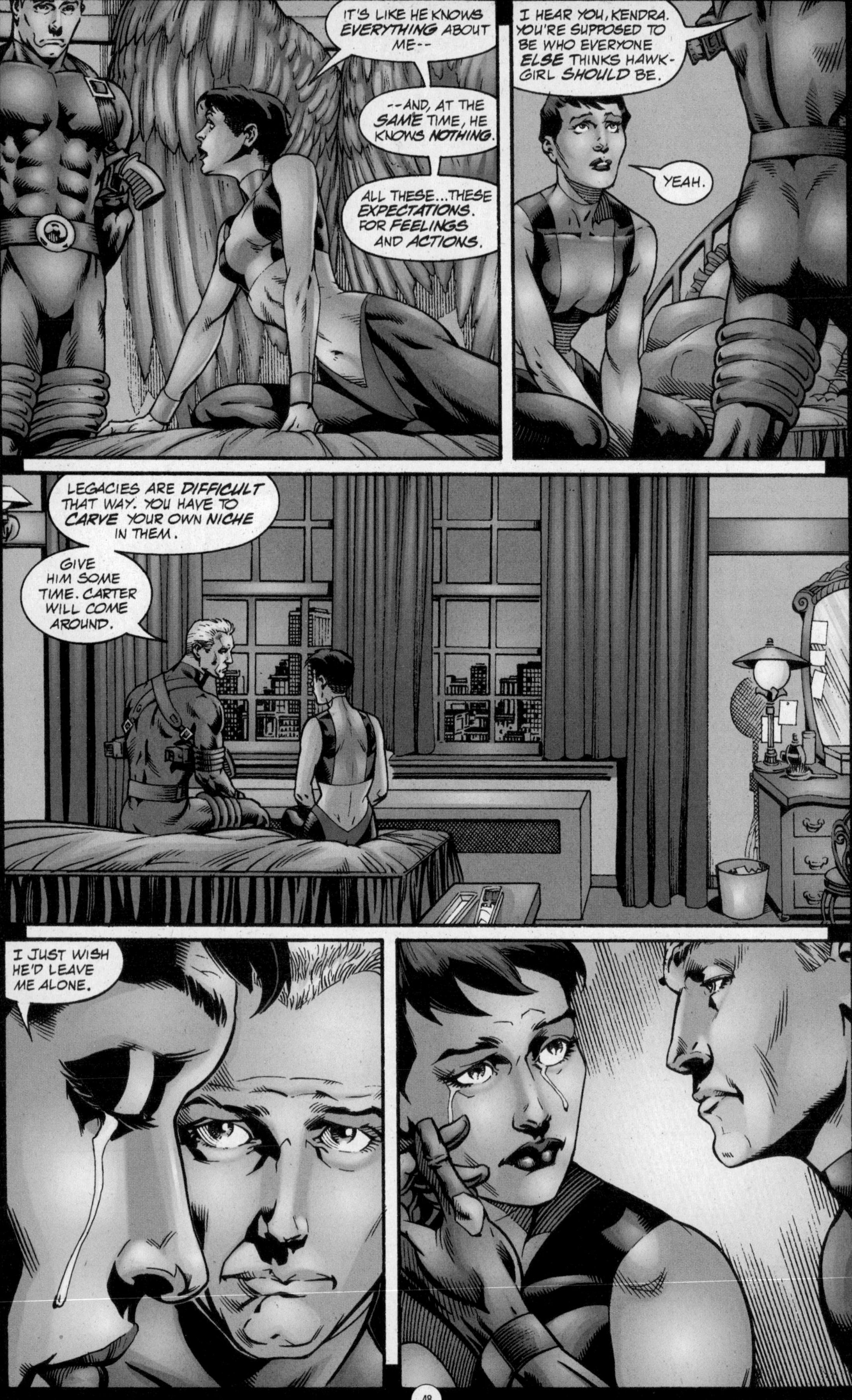
IT'S LIKE HE KNOWS EVERYTHING ABOUT ME--
--AND, AT THE SAME TIME, HE KNOWS NOTHING.
ALL THESE...THESE EXPECTATIONS. FOR FEELINGS AND ACTIONS.
I HEAR YOU, KENDRA. YOU'RE SUPPOSED TO BE WHO EVERYONE ELSE THINKS HAWK-GIRL SHOULD BE.
YEAH.
LEGACIES ARE DIFFICULT THAT WAY. YOU HAVE TO CARVE YOUR OWN NICHE IN THEM.
GIVE HIM SOME TIME. CARTER WILL COME AROUND.
I JUST WISH HE'D LEAVE ME ALONE.

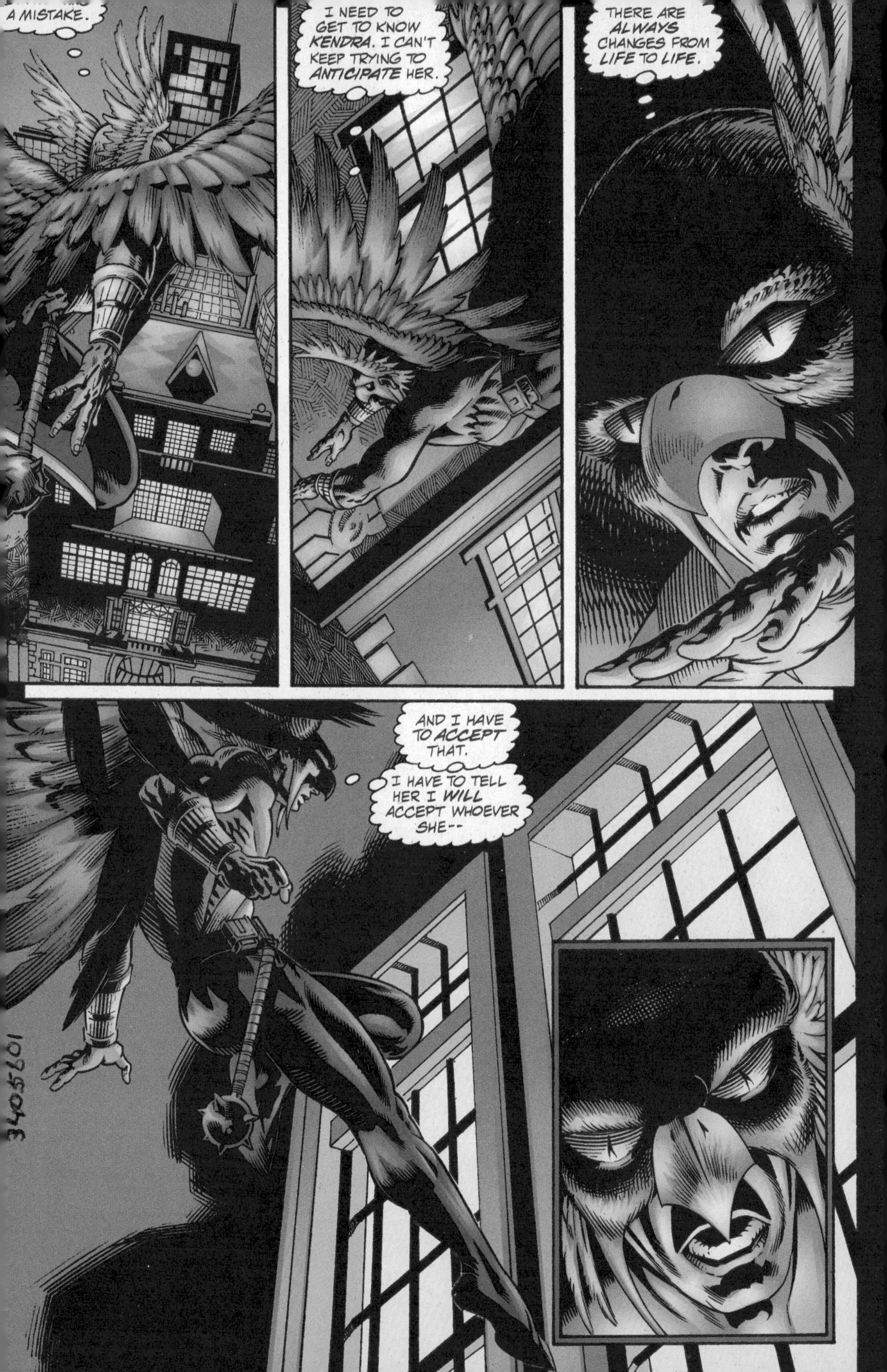

A MISTAKE.
I NEED TO GET TO KNOW KENDRA. I CAN'T KEEP TRYING TO ANTICIPATE HER.
THERE ARE ALWAYS CHANGES FROM LIFE TO LIFE.
AND I HAVE TO ACCEPT THAT.
I HAVE TO TELL HER I WILL ACCEPT WHOEVER SHE--

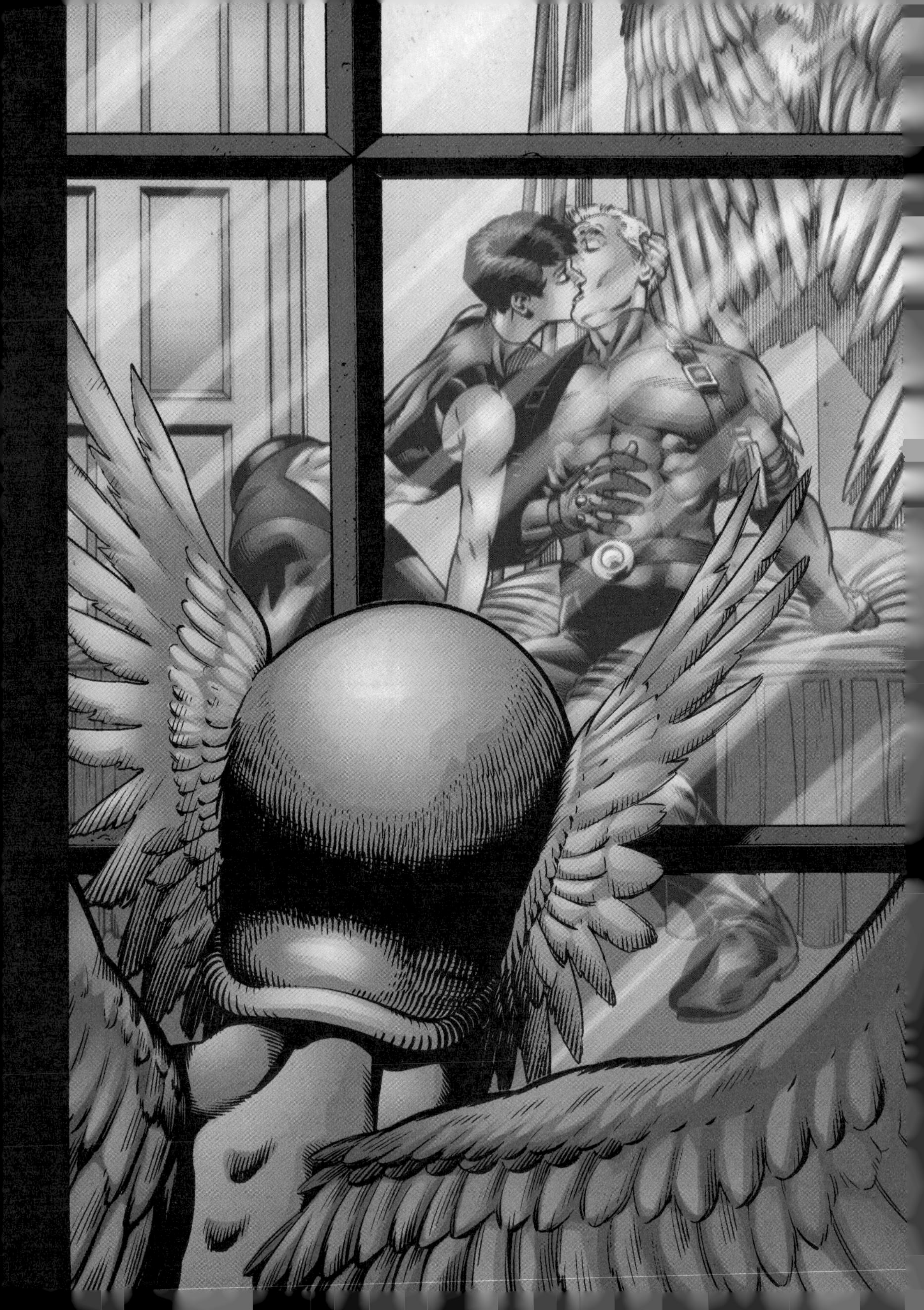

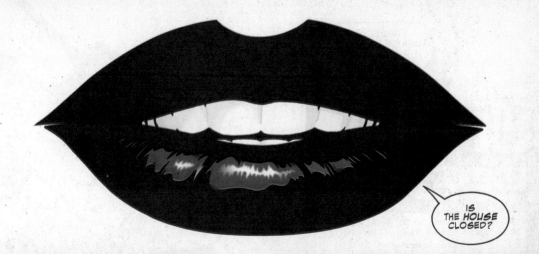

IS THE *HOUSE* CLOSED?

ALL THE BETS ARE IN, *ROULETTE*.

WHAT *BETS* THERE ARE. THIS TURNOUT'S *PATHETIC*.

I NEED *BIGGER* VENUES, DO YOU *UNDERSTAND?* MY *GRANDFATHER* DIDN'T FINANCE THE *HOUSE* TO SEE IT TURN INTO A *NON-PROFIT* ORGANIZATION.

OUR MAIN EVENT ISN'T *MAIN* ENOUGH. I MEAN, LOOK AT THEM--

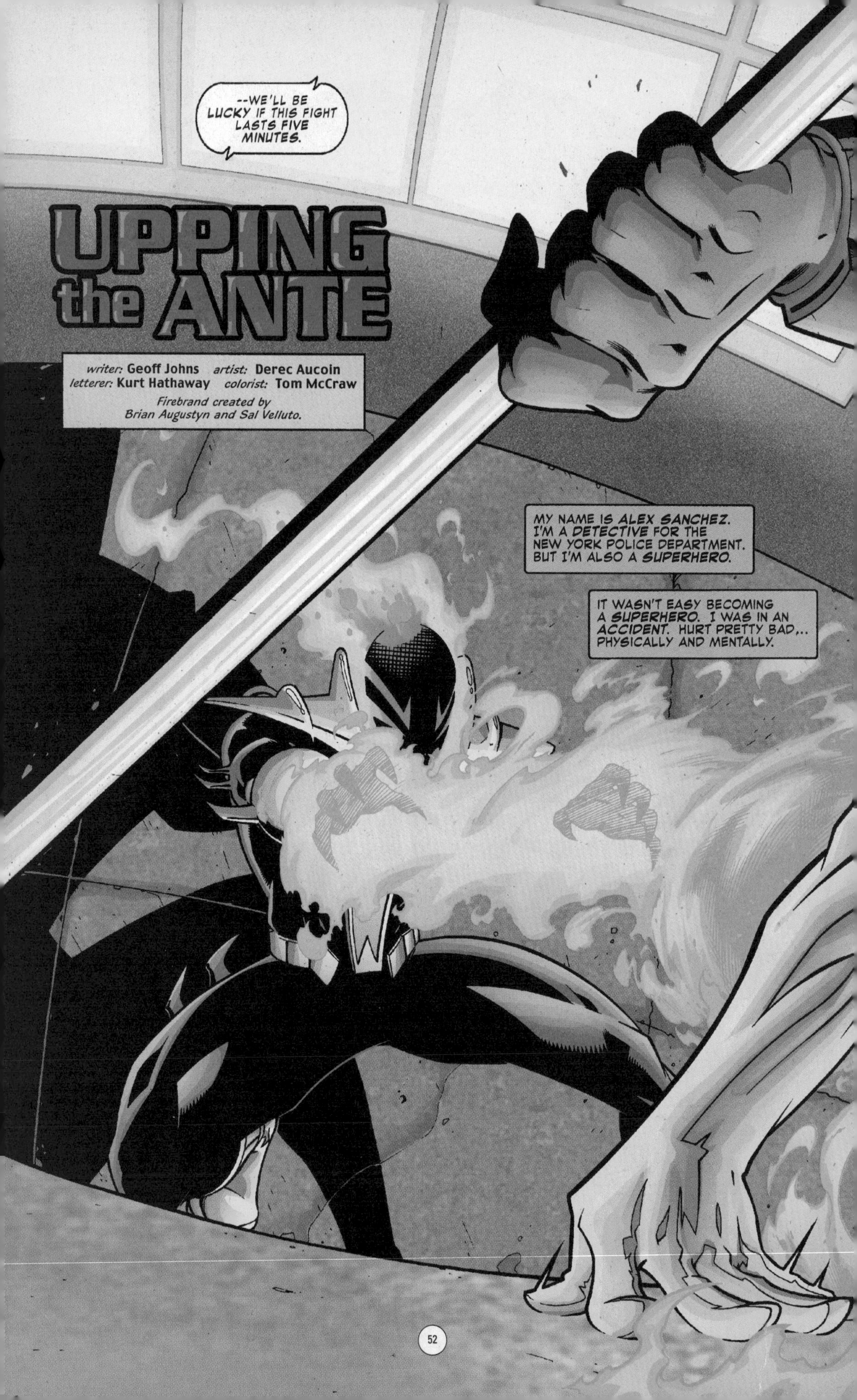

--WE'LL BE LUCKY IF THIS FIGHT LASTS FIVE MINUTES.
UPPING the ANTE
writer: Geoff Johns artist: Derec Aucoin
letterer: Kurt Hathaway colorist: Tom McCraw
Firebrand created by Brian Augustyn and Sal Velluto.
MY NAME IS ALEX SANCHEZ. I'M A DETECTIVE FOR THE NEW YORK POLICE DEPARTMENT. BUT I'M ALSO A SUPERHERO.
IT WASN'T EASY BECOMING A SUPERHERO. I WAS IN AN ACCIDENT. HURT PRETTY BAD... PHYSICALLY AND MENTALLY.

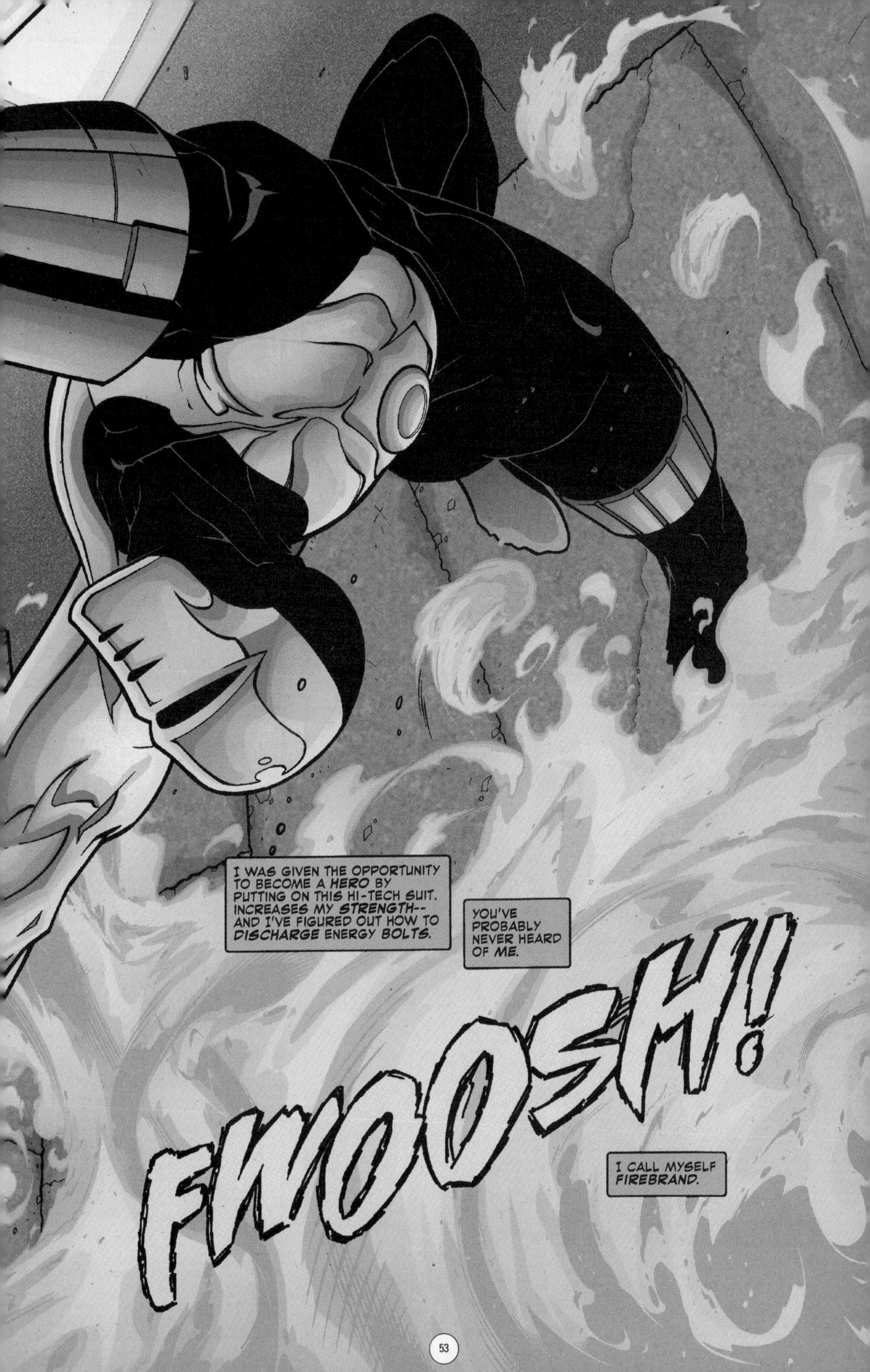
I WAS GIVEN THE OPPORTUNITY TO BECOME A *HERO* BY PUTTING ON THIS HI-TECH SUIT. INCREASES MY *STRENGTH*-- AND I'VE FIGURED OUT HOW TO *DISCHARGE* ENERGY *BOLTS*.
YOU'VE PROBABLY NEVER HEARD OF *ME*.
FWOOSH!
I CALL MYSELF *FIREBRAND*.

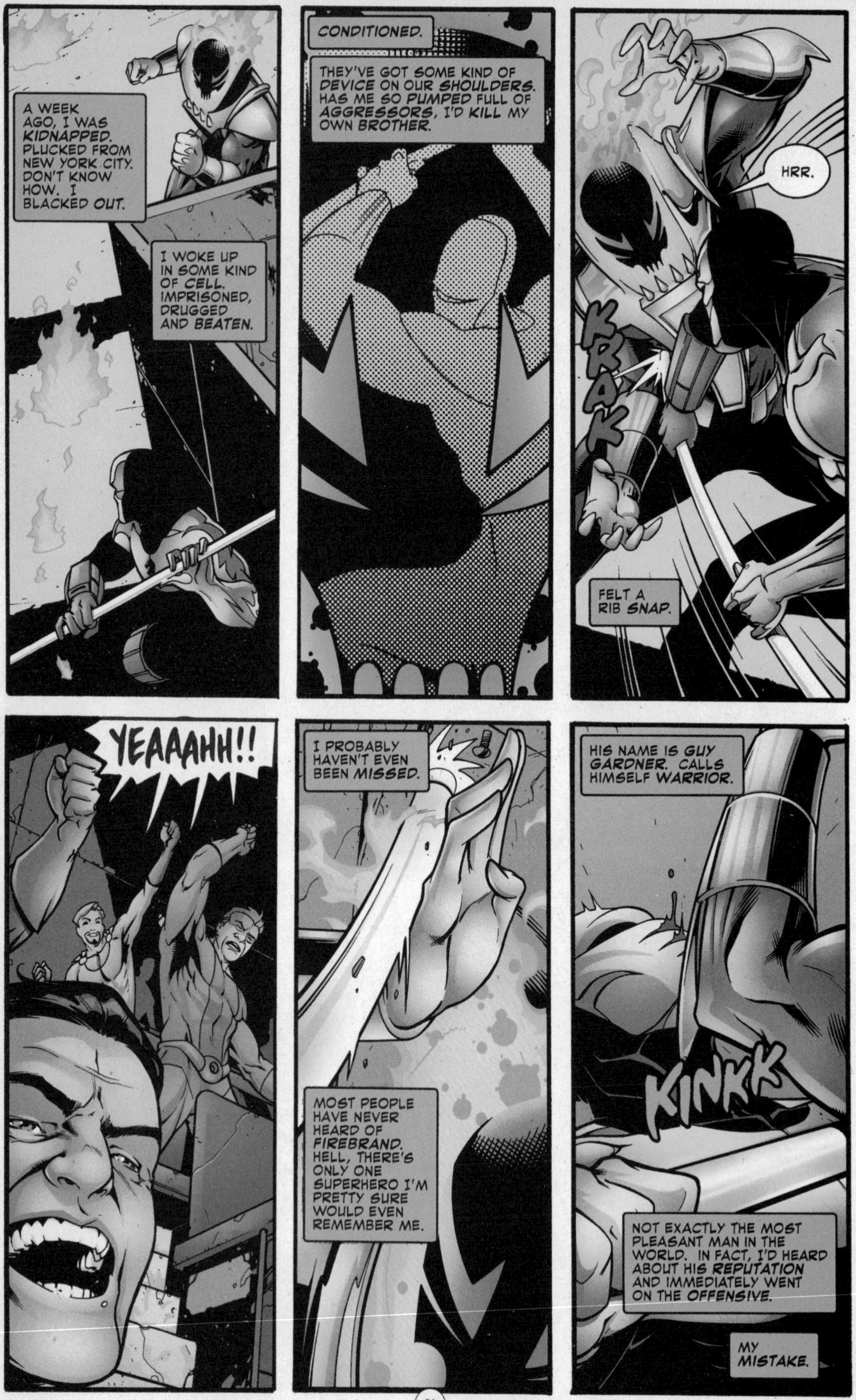
A WEEK AGO, I WAS KIDNAPPED. PLUCKED FROM NEW YORK CITY. DON'T KNOW HOW. I BLACKED OUT.
I WOKE UP IN SOME KIND OF CELL. IMPRISONED, DRUGGED AND BEATEN.
CONDITIONED.
THEY'VE GOT SOME KIND OF DEVICE ON OUR SHOULDERS. HAS ME SO PUMPED FULL OF AGGRESSORS, I'D KILL MY OWN BROTHER.
HRR.
KRAK
FELT A RIB SNAP.
YEAAAHH!!
I PROBABLY HAVEN'T EVEN BEEN MISSED.
MOST PEOPLE HAVE NEVER HEARD OF FIREBRAND. HELL, THERE'S ONLY ONE SUPERHERO I'M PRETTY SURE WOULD EVEN REMEMBER ME.
HIS NAME IS GUY GARDNER. CALLS HIMSELF WARRIOR.
KINKK
NOT EXACTLY THE MOST PLEASANT MAN IN THE WORLD. IN FACT, I'D HEARD ABOUT HIS REPUTATION AND IMMEDIATELY WENT ON THE OFFENSIVE.
MY MISTAKE.

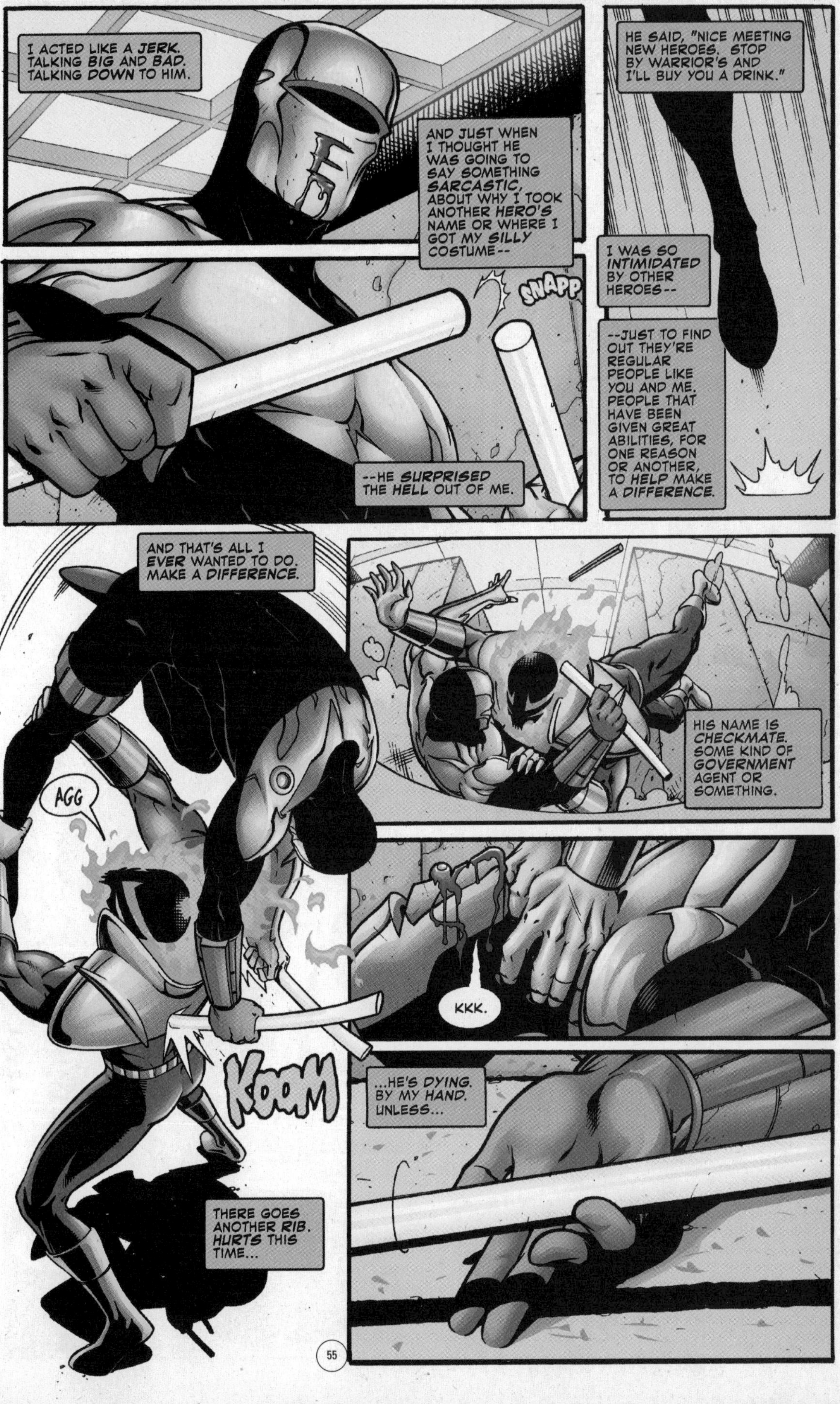
I ACTED LIKE A JERK. TALKING BIG AND BAD. TALKING DOWN TO HIM.
AND JUST WHEN I THOUGHT HE WAS GOING TO SAY SOMETHING SARCASTIC, ABOUT WHY I TOOK ANOTHER HERO'S NAME OR WHERE I GOT MY SILLY COSTUME--
SNAPP
--HE SURPRISED THE HELL OUT OF ME.
HE SAID, "NICE MEETING NEW HEROES. STOP BY WARRIOR'S AND I'LL BUY YOU A DRINK."
I WAS SO INTIMIDATED BY OTHER HEROES--
--JUST TO FIND OUT THEY'RE REGULAR PEOPLE LIKE YOU AND ME. PEOPLE THAT HAVE BEEN GIVEN GREAT ABILITIES, FOR ONE REASON OR ANOTHER, TO HELP MAKE A DIFFERENCE.
AND THAT'S ALL I EVER WANTED TO DO. MAKE A DIFFERENCE.
AGG
KOOM
THERE GOES ANOTHER RIB. HURTS THIS TIME...
HIS NAME IS CHECKMATE. SOME KIND OF GOVERNMENT AGENT OR SOMETHING.
KKK.
...HE'S DYING. BY MY HAND. UNLESS...

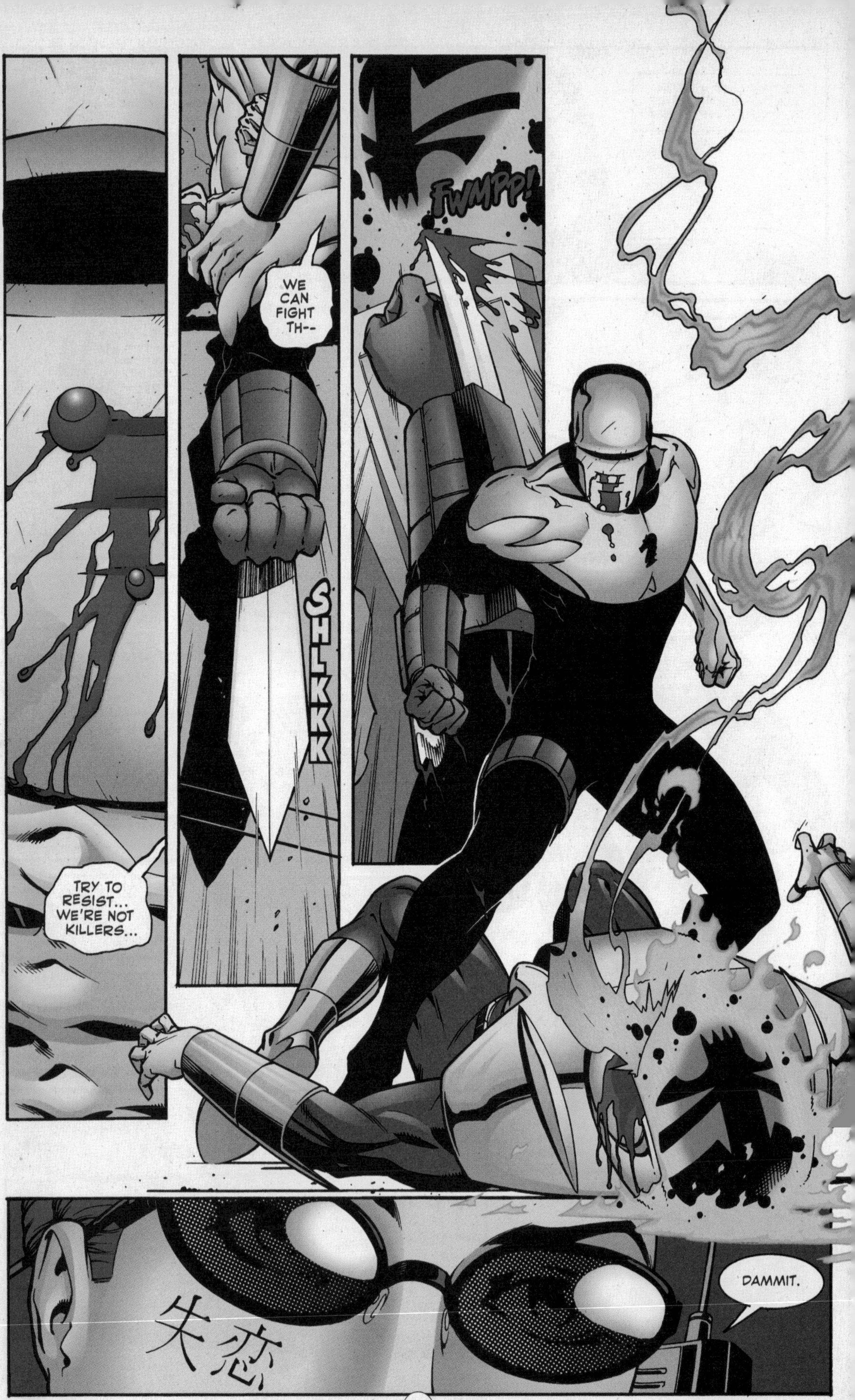
TRY TO RESIST... WE'RE NOT KILLERS...
WE CAN FIGHT TH--
SHLKKK
FWMPP!
DAMMIT.
失恋

I TOLD YOU IT'D LAST FIVE MINUTES.

AND THE CHECKMATE IDIOT WON.

DO YOU REALIZE HOW MUCH WE JUST LOST?

YES, SEND THE G-MAN HOME. LET HIM LIVE WITH THE GUILT OF MURDER.

SOMETHING I'M SURE HE WON'T DO FOR LONG.

SOLD OUT

FUTURE BUSINESS. WE NEED BIG NAMES. NOW.

WE NEED--

ODDS & EVENTS

HAWKMAN RETURNS TO THE JSA!

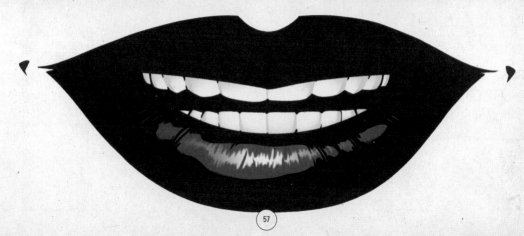

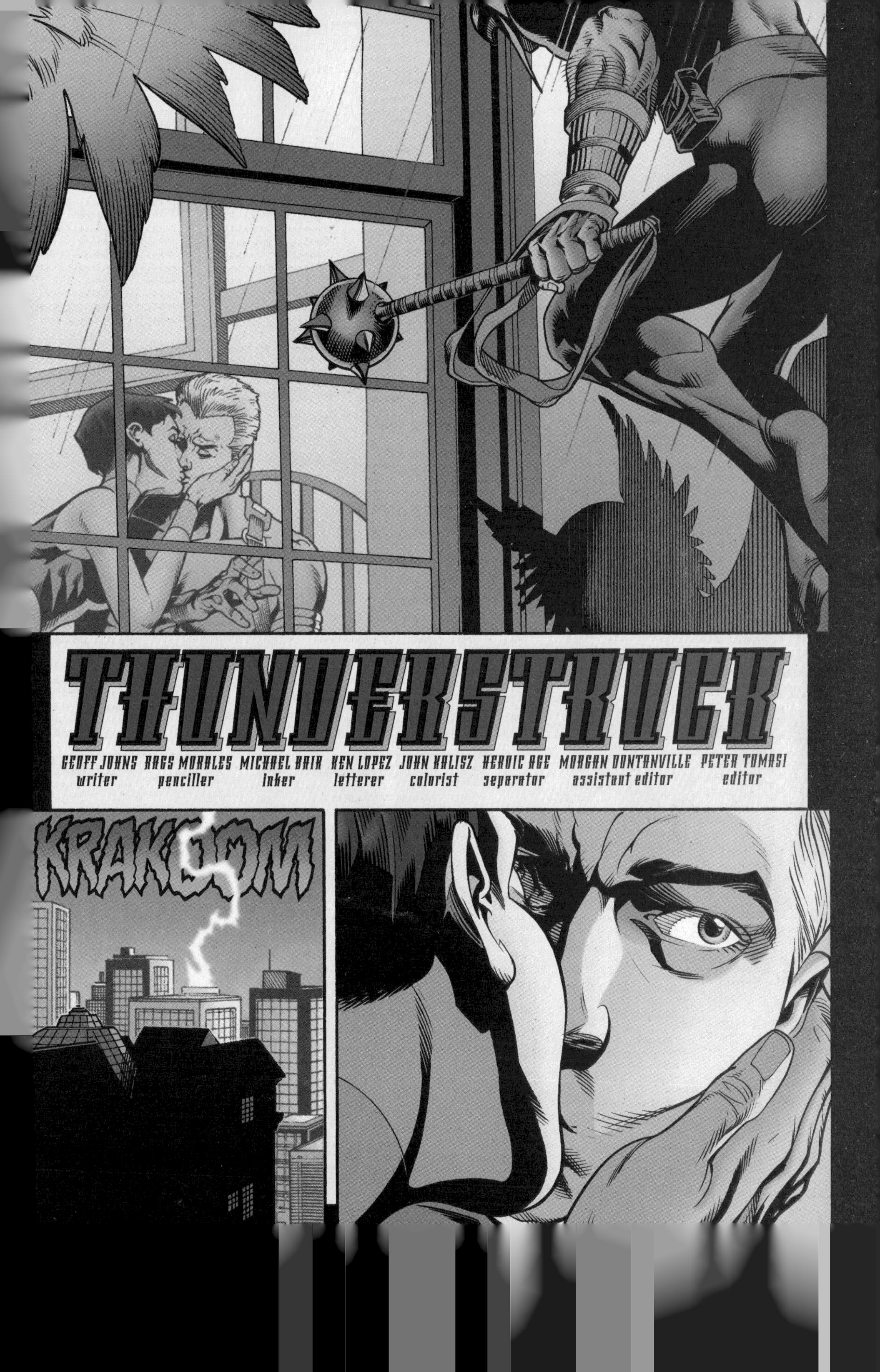
THUNDERSTRUCK
GEOFF JOHNS writer
RAGS MORALES penciller
MICHAEL BAIR inker
KEN LOPEZ letterer
JOHN KALISZ colorist
HEROIC AGE separator
MORGAN DONTANVILLE assistant editor
PETER TOMASI editor
KRAKOOM

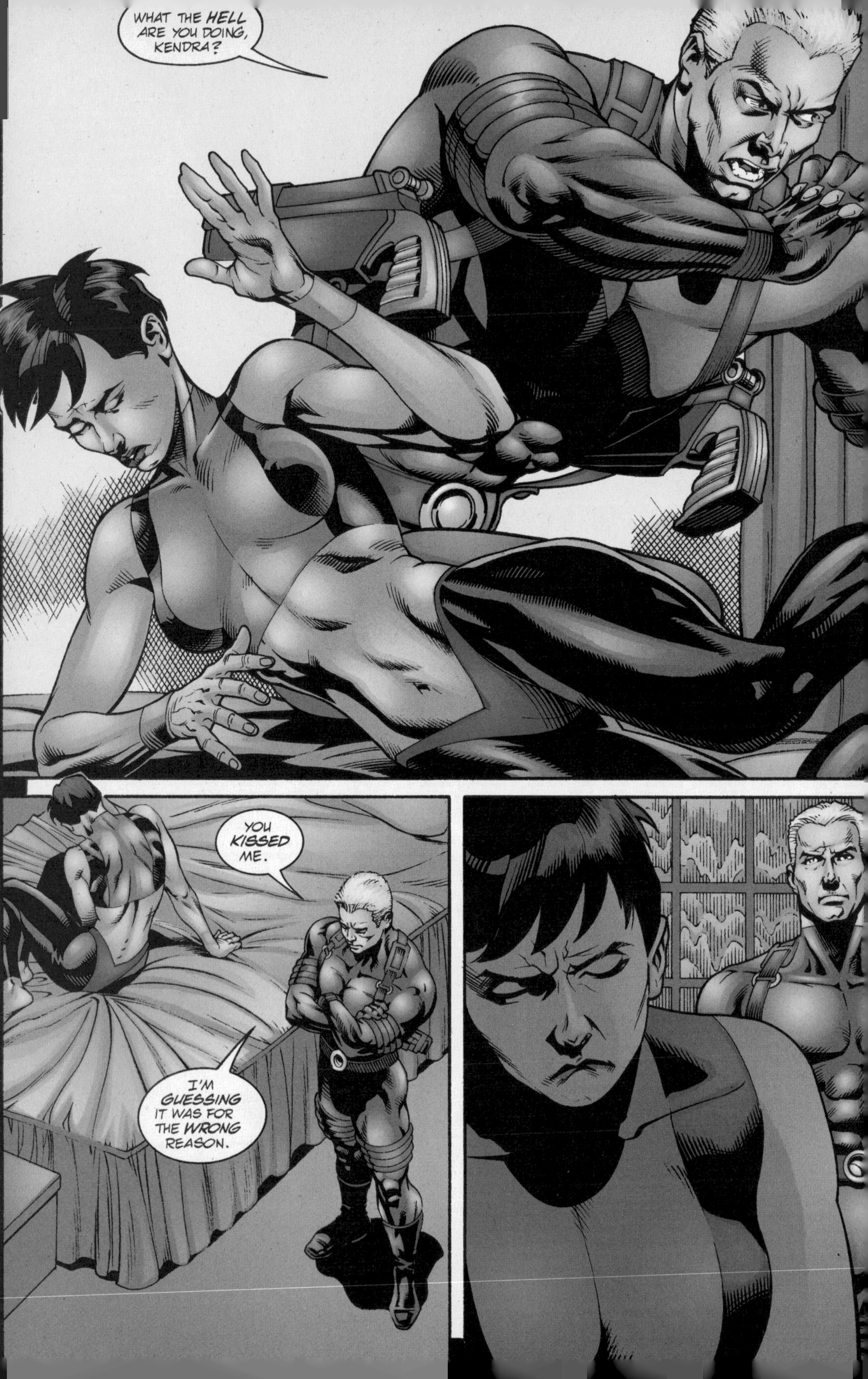

WHAT THE HELL ARE YOU DOING, KENDRA?
YOU KISSED ME.
I'M GUESSING IT WAS FOR THE WRONG REASON.

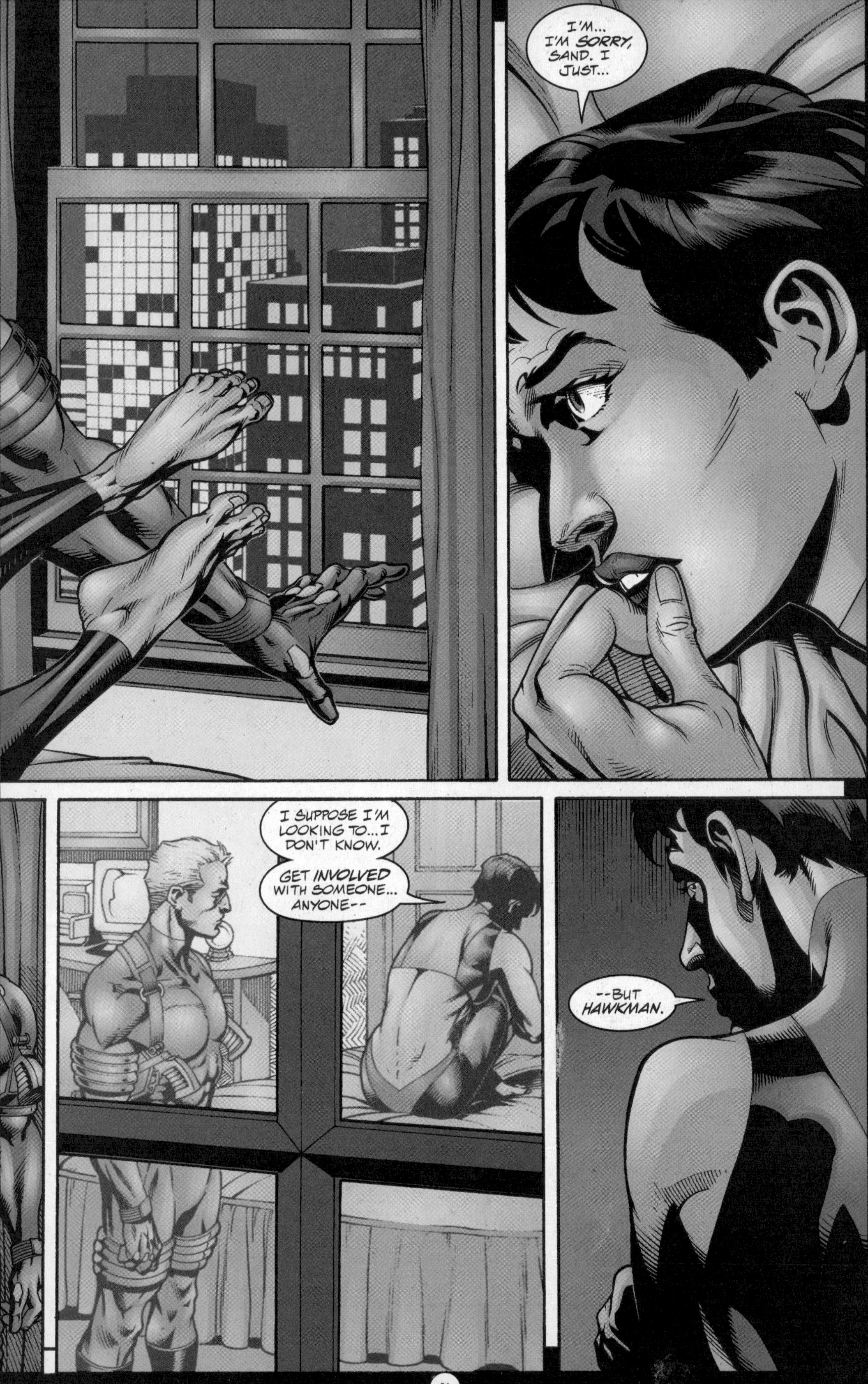
I'M... I'M SORRY, SAND. I JUST...
I SUPPOSE I'M LOOKING TO... I DON'T KNOW.
GET INVOLVED WITH SOMEONE... ANYONE--
--BUT HAWKMAN.

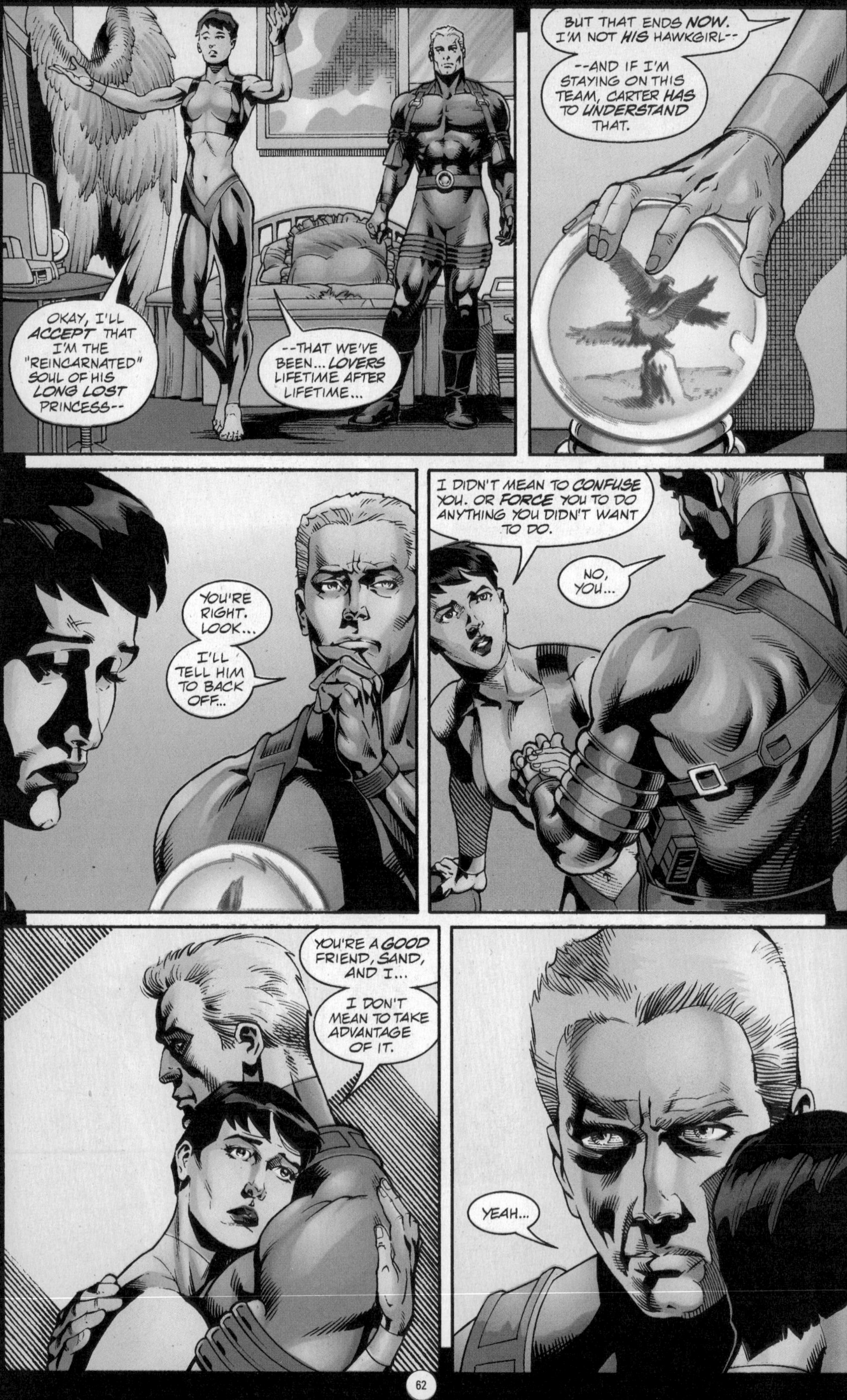
OKAY, I'LL ACCEPT THAT I'M THE "REINCARNATED" SOUL OF HIS LONG LOST PRINCESS--
--THAT WE'VE BEEN... LOVERS LIFETIME AFTER LIFETIME...
BUT THAT ENDS NOW. I'M NOT HIS HAWKGIRL--
--AND IF I'M STAYING ON THIS TEAM, CARTER HAS TO UNDERSTAND THAT.
YOU'RE RIGHT. LOOK...
I'LL TELL HIM TO BACK OFF...
I DIDN'T MEAN TO CONFUSE YOU. OR FORCE YOU TO DO ANYTHING YOU DIDN'T WANT TO DO.
NO, YOU...
YOU'RE A GOOD FRIEND, SAND, AND I...
I DON'T MEAN TO TAKE ADVANTAGE OF IT.
YEAH...

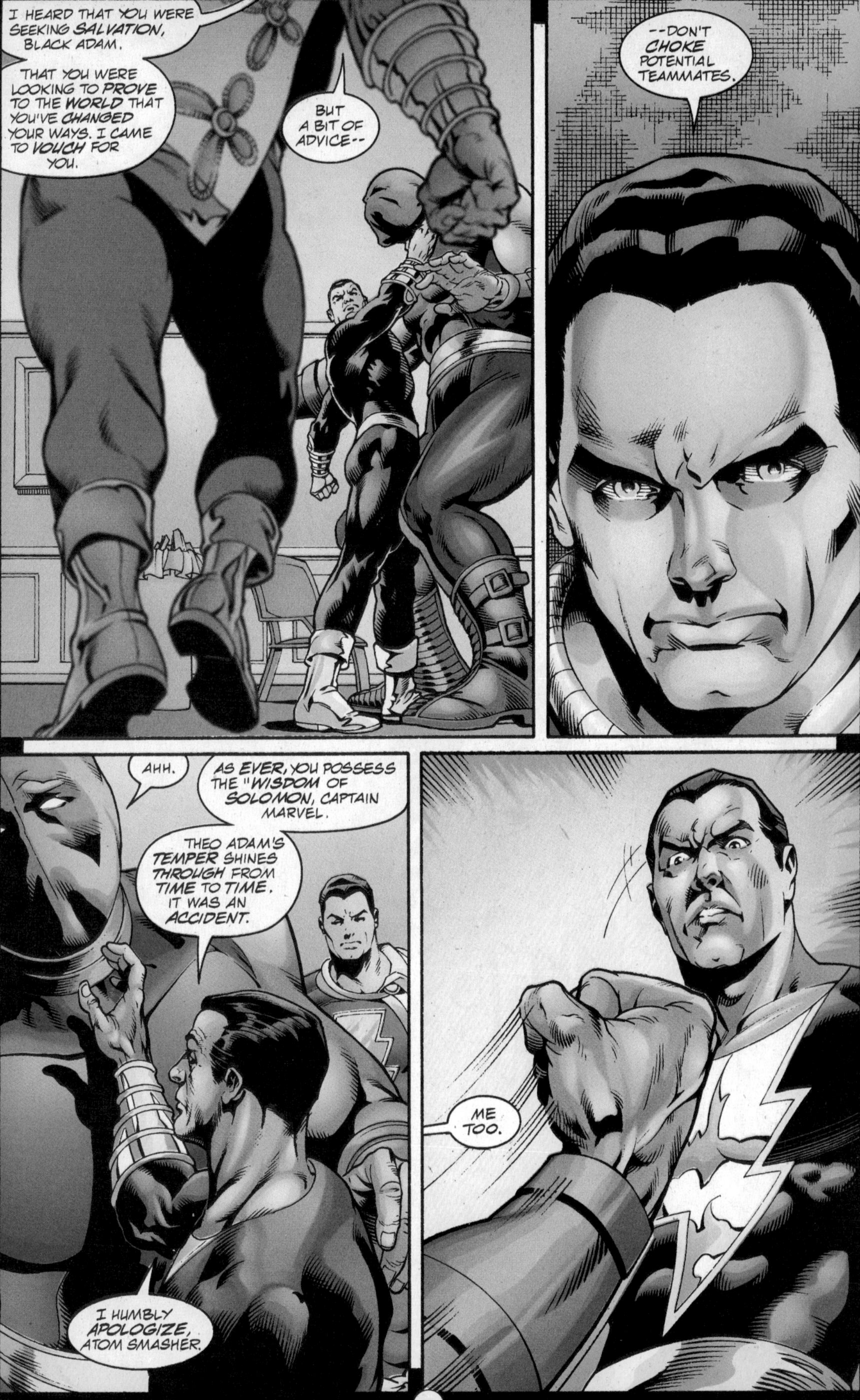
I HEARD THAT YOU WERE SEEKING SALVATION, BLACK ADAM.
THAT YOU WERE LOOKING TO PROVE TO THE WORLD THAT YOU'VE CHANGED YOUR WAYS. I CAME TO VOUCH FOR YOU.
BUT A BIT OF ADVICE--
--DON'T CHOKE POTENTIAL TEAMMATES.
AHH.
AS EVER, YOU POSSESS THE "WISDOM OF SOLOMON, CAPTAIN MARVEL.
THEO ADAM'S TEMPER SHINES THROUGH FROM TIME TO TIME. IT WAS AN ACCIDENT.
I HUMBLY APOLOGIZE, ATOM SMASHER.
ME TOO.

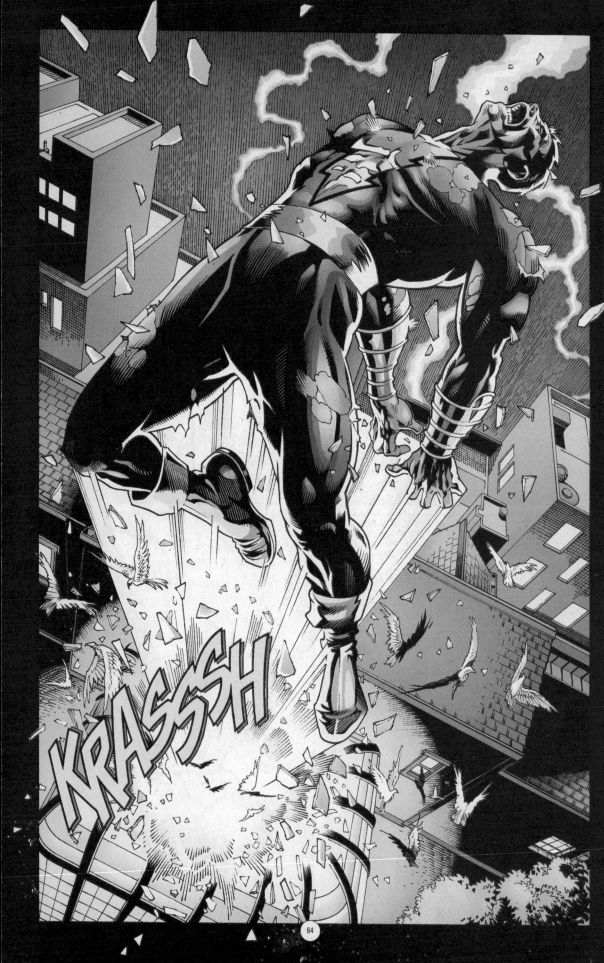

KRASSSH

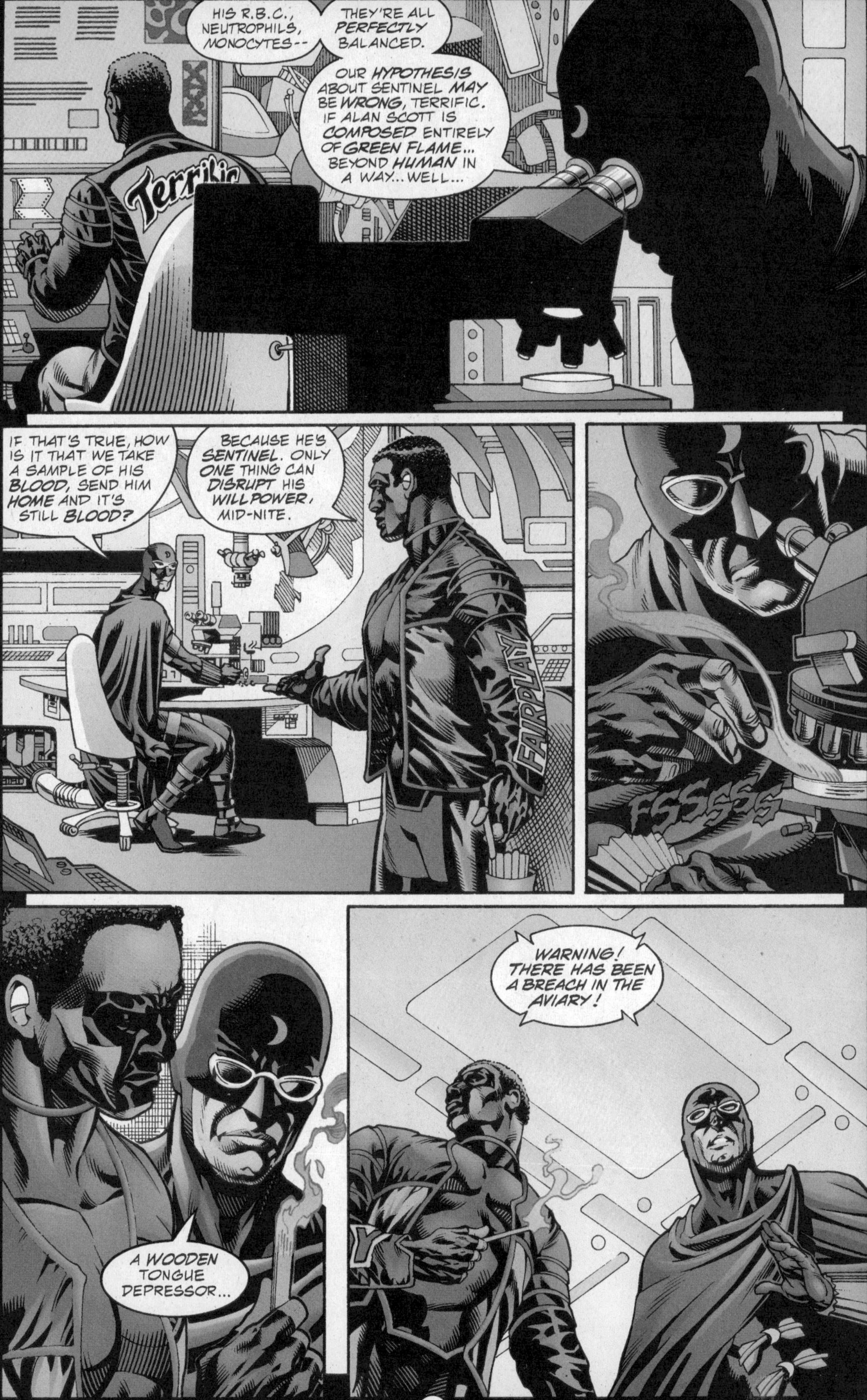
HIS R.B.C., NEUTROPHILS, MONOCYTES--
THEY'RE ALL PERFECTLY BALANCED.
OUR HYPOTHESIS ABOUT SENTINEL MAY BE WRONG, TERRIFIC. IF ALAN SCOTT IS COMPOSED ENTIRELY OF GREEN FLAME... BEYOND HUMAN IN A WAY... WELL...
Terrific
IF THAT'S TRUE, HOW IS IT THAT WE TAKE A SAMPLE OF HIS BLOOD, SEND HIM HOME AND IT'S STILL BLOOD?
BECAUSE HE'S SENTINEL. ONLY ONE THING CAN DISRUPT HIS WILLPOWER, MID-NITE.
FAIRPLAY
FSSSSS
A WOODEN TONGUE DEPRESSOR...
WARNING! THERE HAS BEEN A BREACH IN THE AVIARY!

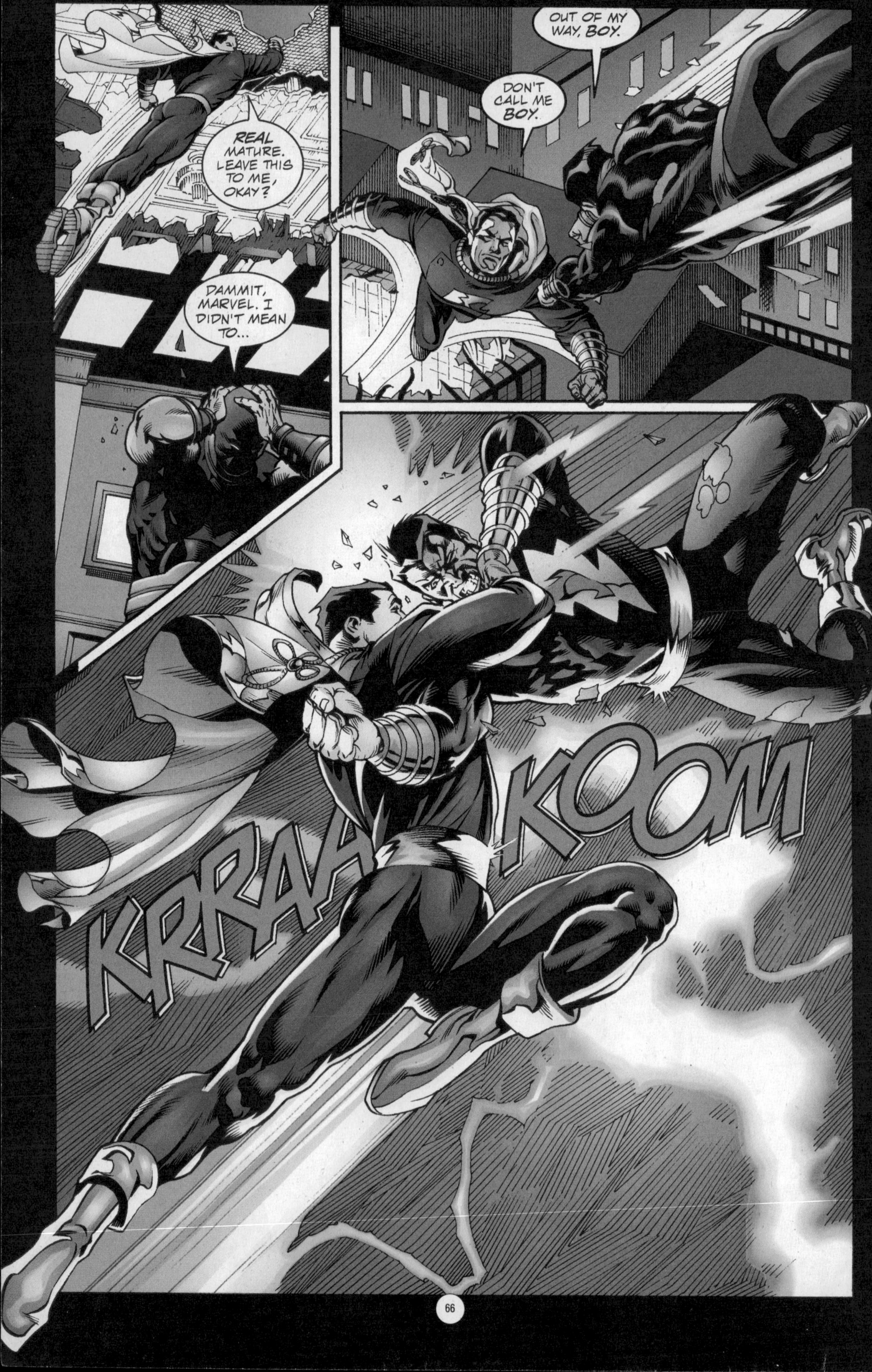
REAL MATURE. LEAVE THIS TO ME, OKAY?
DAMMIT, MARVEL. I DIDN'T MEAN TO...
OUT OF MY WAY, BOY.
DON'T CALL ME BOY.
KRRAA KOOM

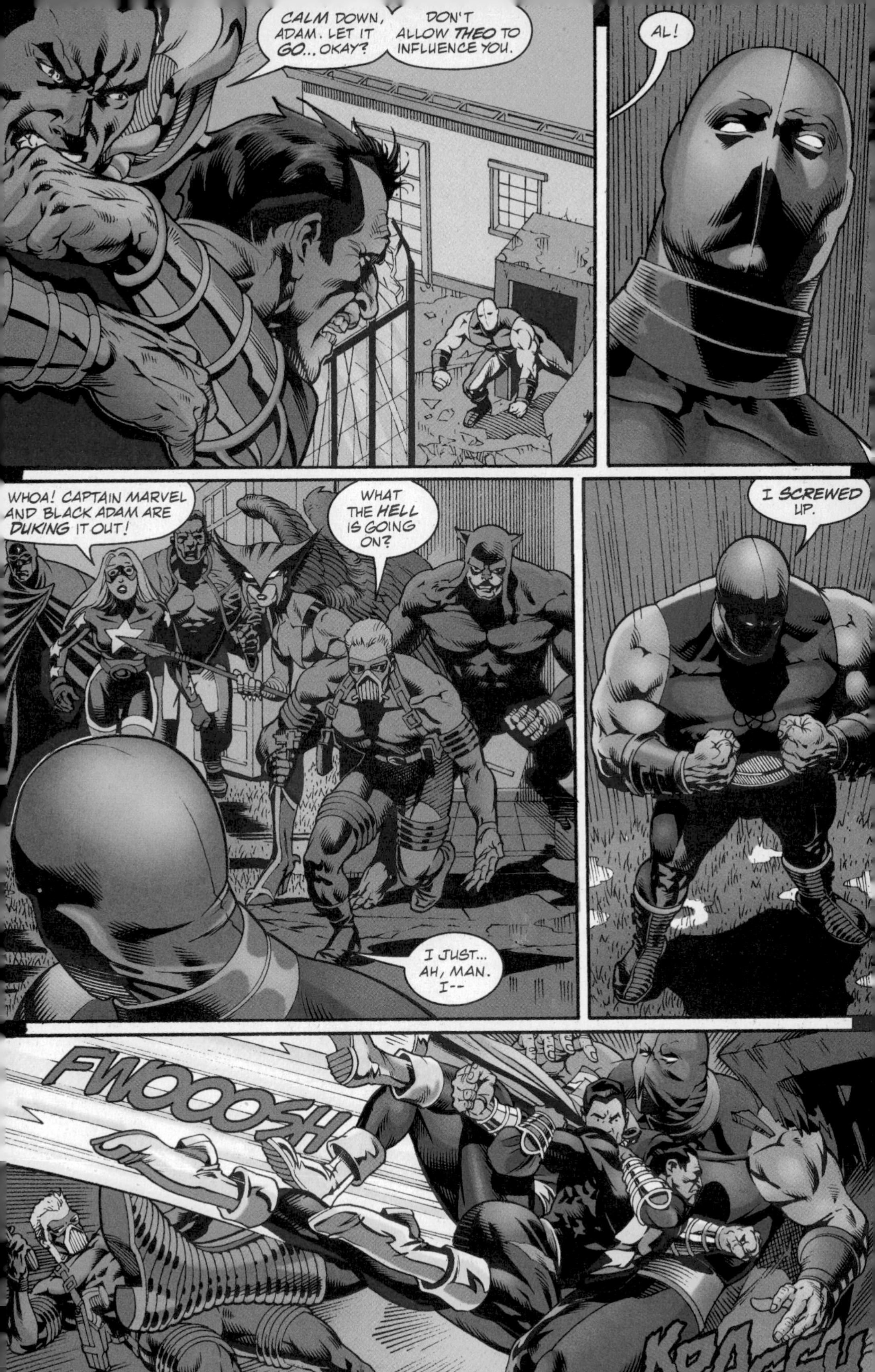
CALM DOWN, ADAM. LET IT GO... OKAY?
DON'T ALLOW THEO TO INFLUENCE YOU.
AL!
WHOA! CAPTAIN MARVEL AND BLACK ADAM ARE DUKING IT OUT!
WHAT THE HELL IS GOING ON?
I JUST... AH, MAN. I--
I SCREWED UP.
FWOOOSH
KRASSH

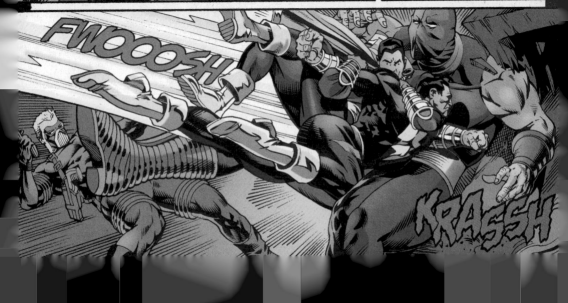

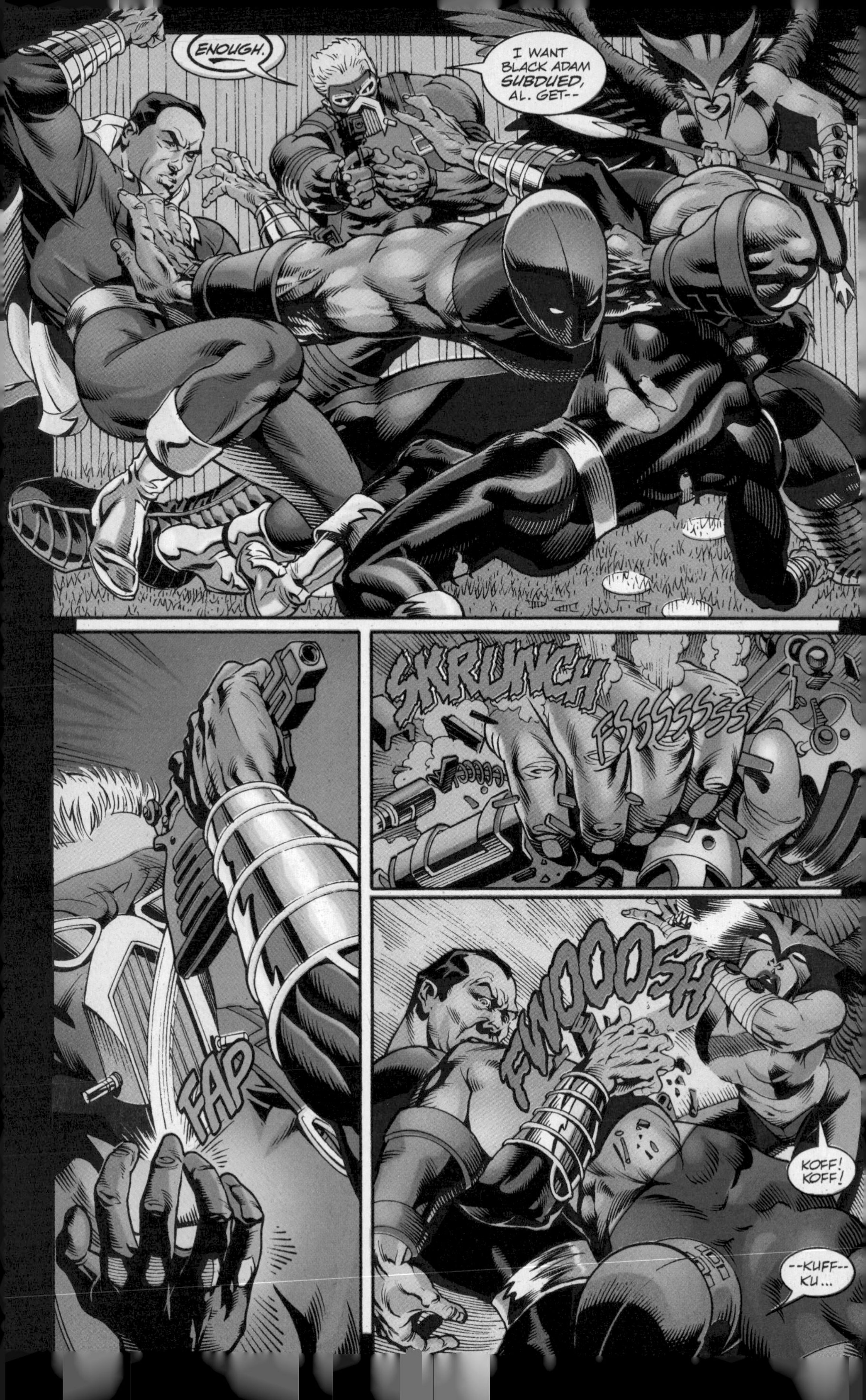
ENOUGH.
I WANT BLACK ADAM SUBDUED, AL. GET--
FAP
SKRUNCH
FSSSSSSS
FWOOOSH
KOFF! KOFF!
--KUFF-- KU...

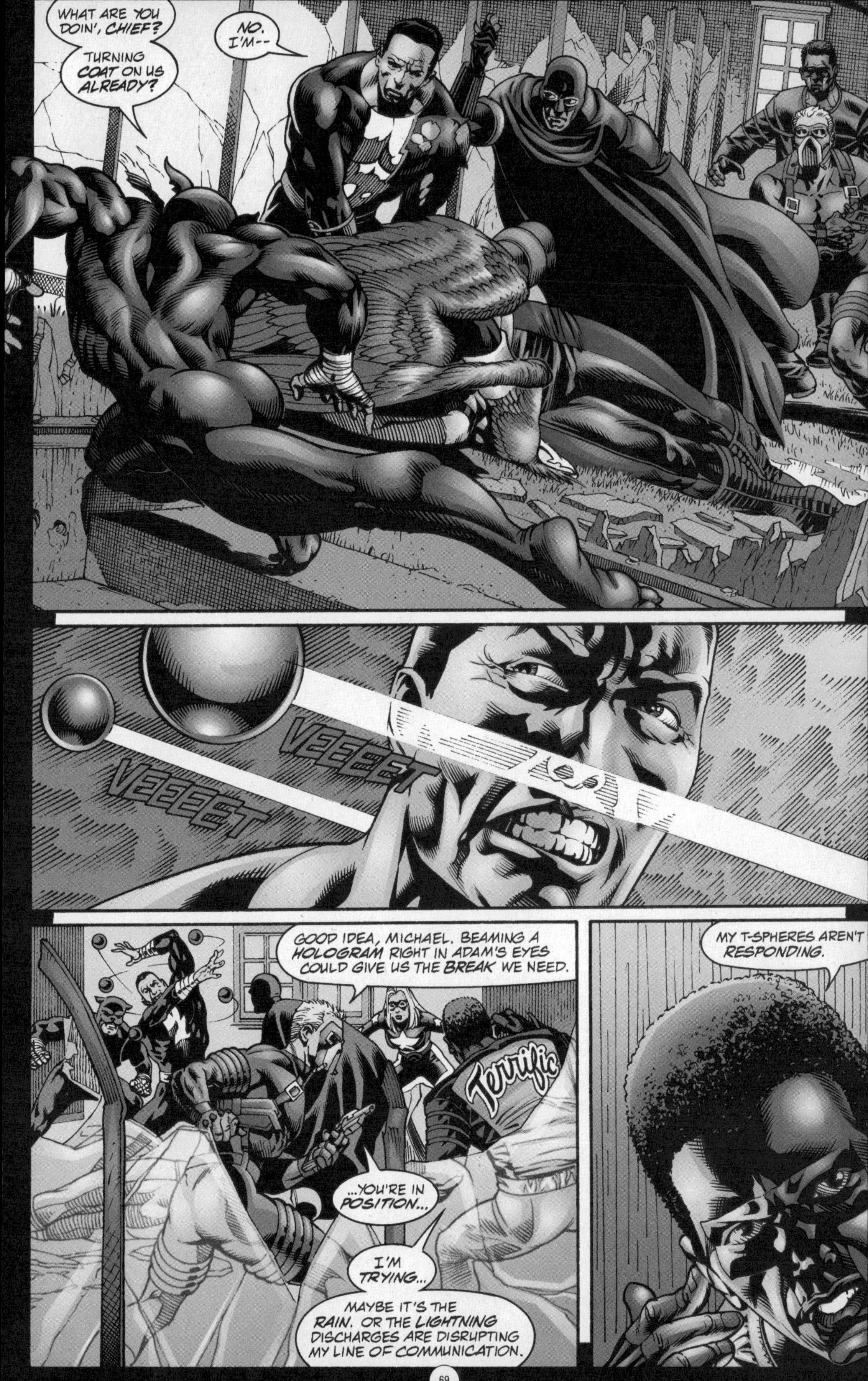
WHAT ARE YOU DOIN', CHIEF?
TURNING COAT ON US ALREADY?
NO. I'M--
VEEEET
VEEEET
GOOD IDEA, MICHAEL. BEAMING A HOLOGRAM RIGHT IN ADAM'S EYES COULD GIVE US THE BREAK WE NEED.
...YOU'RE IN POSITION...
I'M TRYING...
MAYBE IT'S THE RAIN. OR THE LIGHTNING DISCHARGES ARE DISRUPTING MY LINE OF COMMUNICATION.
MY T-SPHERES AREN'T RESPONDING.

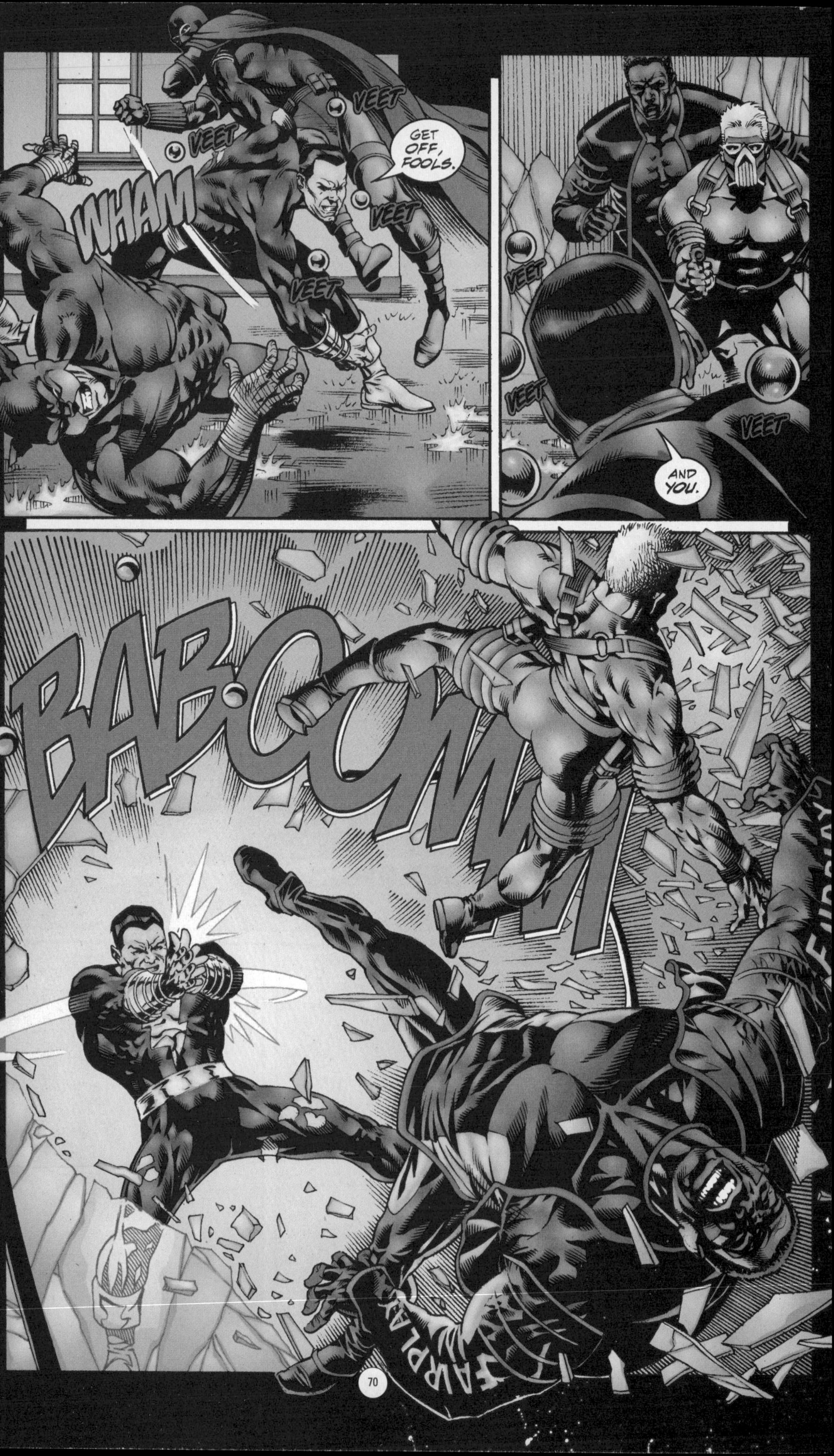
VEET
VEET
WHAM
GET OFF, FOOLS.
VEET
VEET
VEET
VEET
VEET
AND YOU.
BABOOM

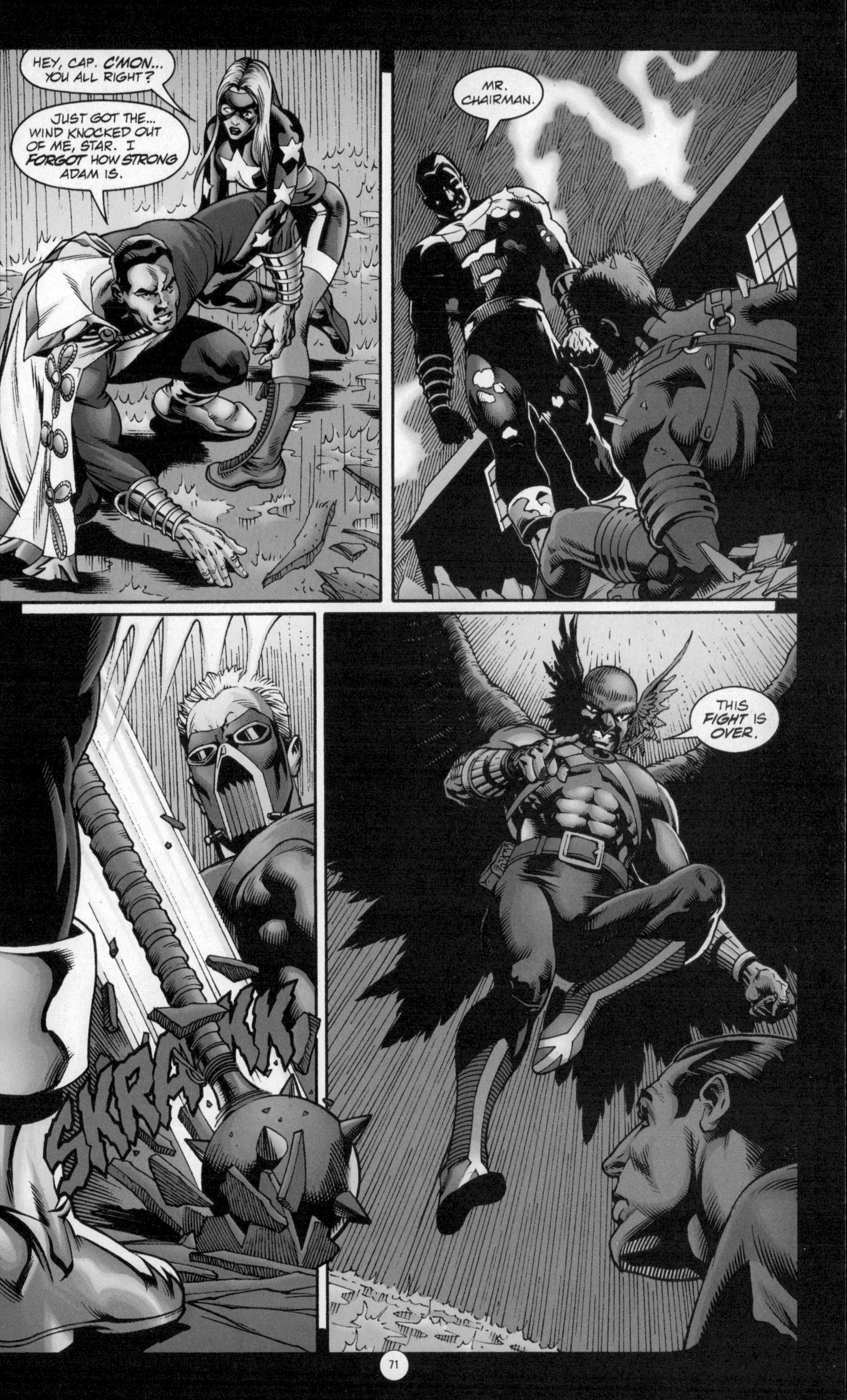
HEY, CAP. C'MON... YOU ALL RIGHT?
JUST GOT THE... WIND KNOCKED OUT OF ME, STAR. I FORGOT HOW STRONG ADAM IS.
MR. CHAIRMAN.
SKRAKK!
THIS FIGHT IS OVER.

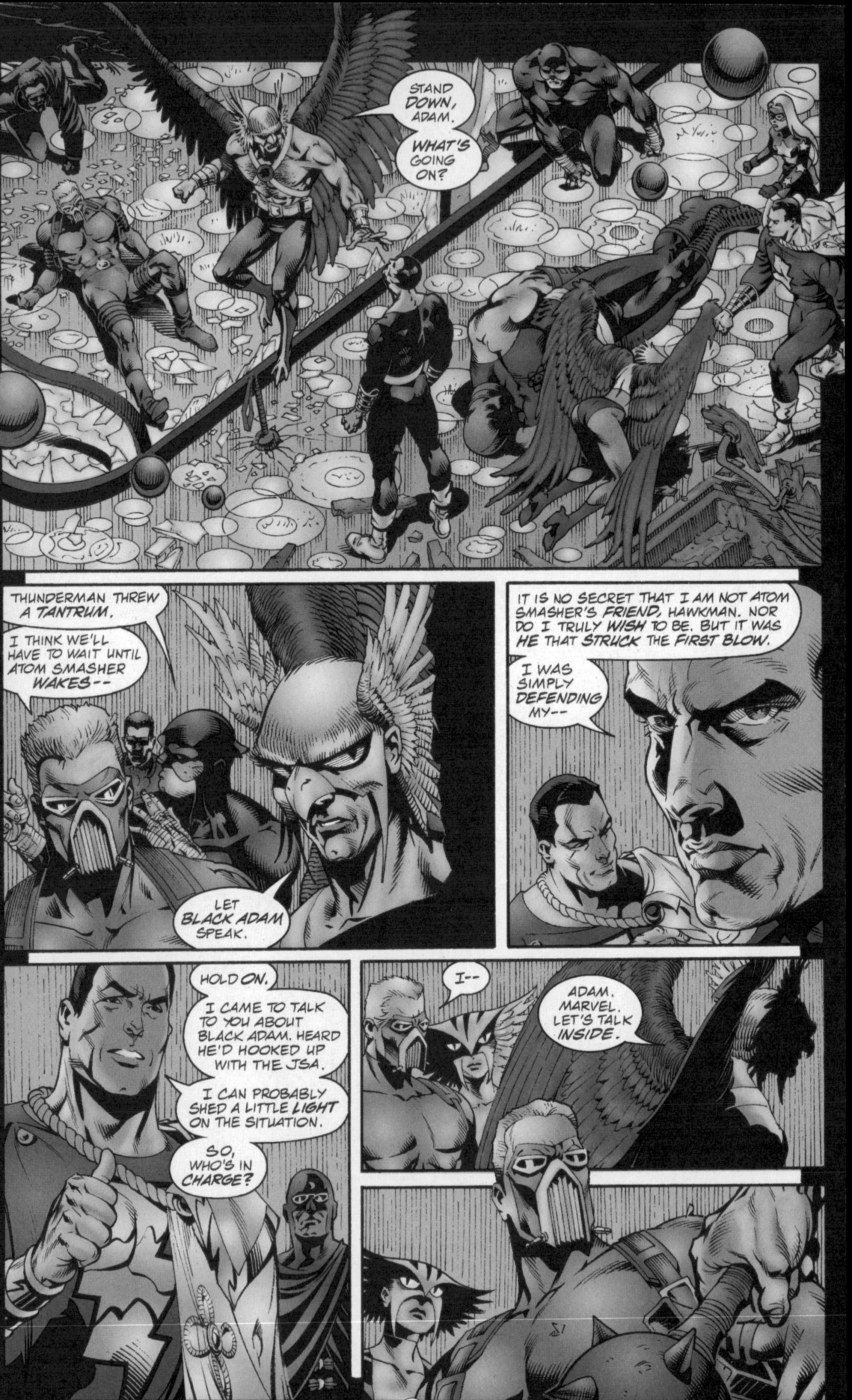

STAND DOWN, ADAM.
WHAT'S GOING ON?
THUNDERMAN THREW A TANTRUM.
I THINK WE'LL HAVE TO WAIT UNTIL ATOM SMASHER WAKES--
LET BLACK ADAM SPEAK.
IT IS NO SECRET THAT I AM NOT ATOM SMASHER'S FRIEND, HAWKMAN. NOR DO I TRULY WISH TO BE. BUT IT WAS HE THAT STRUCK THE FIRST BLOW.
I WAS SIMPLY DEFENDING MY--
HOLD ON.
I CAME TO TALK TO YOU ABOUT BLACK ADAM. HEARD HE'D HOOKED UP WITH THE JSA.
I CAN PROBABLY SHED A LITTLE LIGHT ON THE SITUATION.
SO, WHO'S IN CHARGE?
I--
ADAM. MARVEL. LET'S TALK INSIDE.

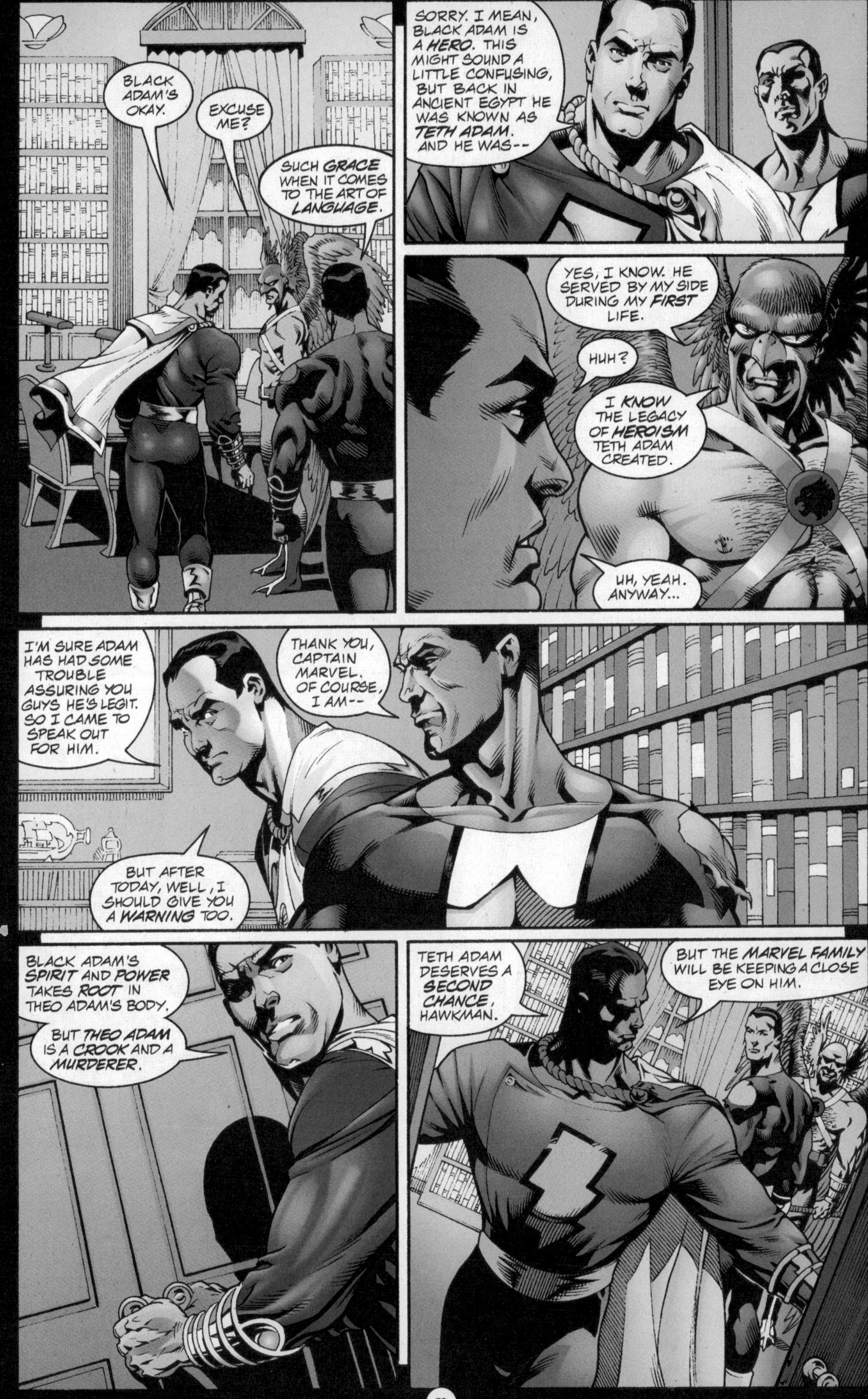
BLACK ADAM'S OKAY.
EXCUSE ME?
SUCH GRACE WHEN IT COMES TO THE ART OF LANGUAGE.
SORRY. I MEAN, BLACK ADAM IS A HERO. THIS MIGHT SOUND A LITTLE CONFUSING, BUT BACK IN ANCIENT EGYPT HE WAS KNOWN AS TETH ADAM. AND HE WAS--
YES, I KNOW. HE SERVED BY MY SIDE DURING MY FIRST LIFE.
HUH?
I KNOW THE LEGACY OF HEROISM TETH ADAM CREATED.
UH, YEAH. ANYWAY...
I'M SURE ADAM HAS HAD SOME TROUBLE ASSURING YOU GUYS HE'S LEGIT. SO I CAME TO SPEAK OUT FOR HIM.
THANK YOU, CAPTAIN MARVEL. OF COURSE, I AM--
BUT AFTER TODAY, WELL, I SHOULD GIVE YOU A WARNING TOO.
BLACK ADAM'S SPIRIT AND POWER TAKES ROOT IN THEO ADAM'S BODY.
BUT THEO ADAM IS A CROOK AND A MURDERER.
TETH ADAM DESERVES A SECOND CHANCE, HAWKMAN.
BUT THE MARVEL FAMILY WILL BE KEEPING A CLOSE EYE ON HIM.

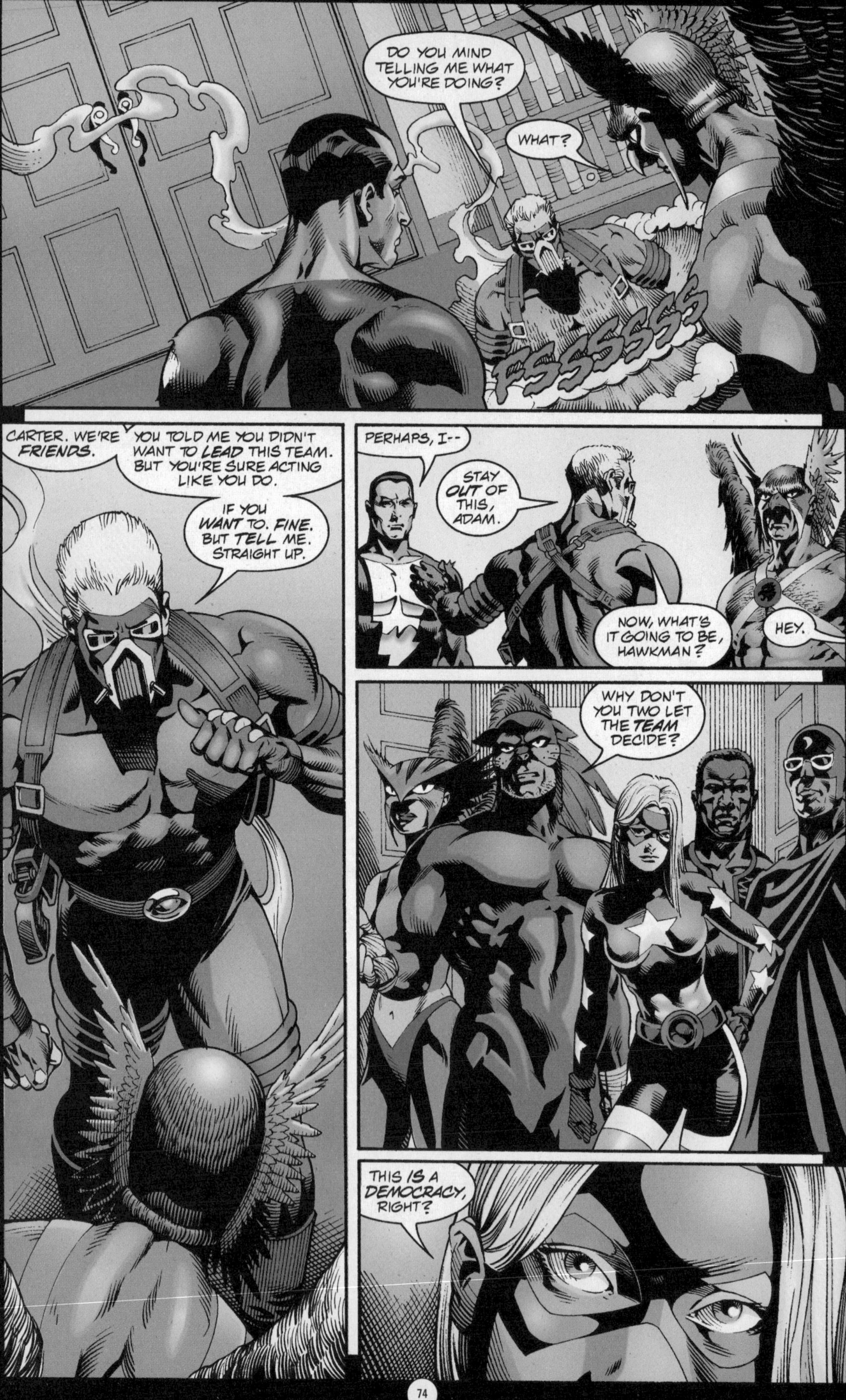
DO YOU MIND TELLING ME WHAT YOU'RE DOING?
WHAT?
FSSSSSSS
CARTER. WE'RE FRIENDS.
YOU TOLD ME YOU DIDN'T WANT TO LEAD THIS TEAM. BUT YOU'RE SURE ACTING LIKE YOU DO.
IF YOU WANT TO. FINE. BUT TELL ME. STRAIGHT UP.
PERHAPS, I--
STAY OUT OF THIS, ADAM.
NOW, WHAT'S IT GOING TO BE, HAWKMAN?
HEY.
WHY DON'T YOU TWO LET THE TEAM DECIDE?
THIS IS A DEMOCRACY, RIGHT?

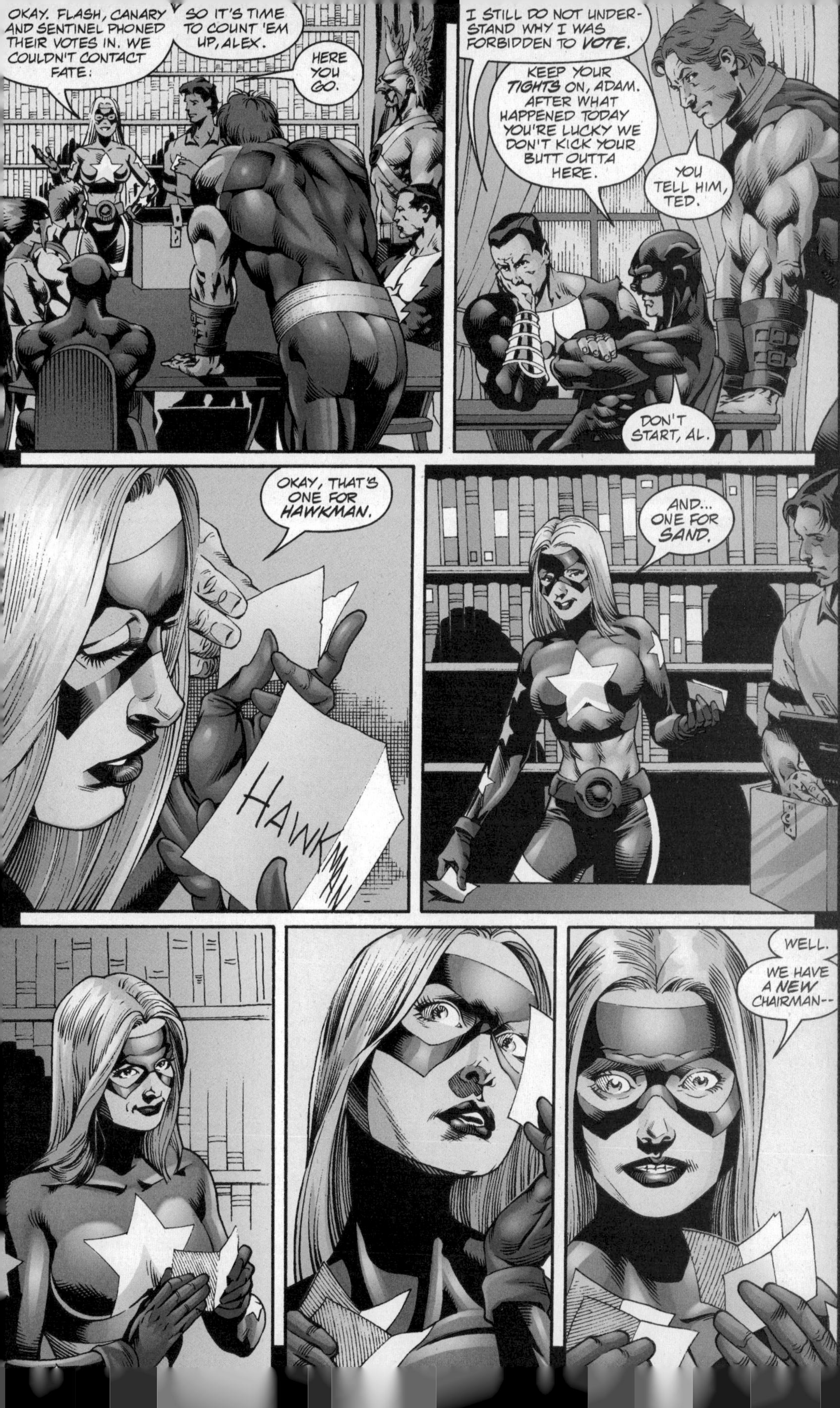
OKAY. FLASH, CANARY AND SENTINEL PHONED THEIR VOTES IN. WE COULDN'T CONTACT FATE:
SO IT'S TIME TO COUNT 'EM UP, ALEX.
HERE YOU GO.
I STILL DO NOT UNDERSTAND WHY I WAS FORBIDDEN TO VOTE.
KEEP YOUR TIGHTS ON, ADAM. AFTER WHAT HAPPENED TODAY YOU'RE LUCKY WE DON'T KICK YOUR BUTT OUTTA HERE.
YOU TELL HIM, TED.
DON'T START, AL.
OKAY, THAT'S ONE FOR HAWKMAN.
HAWKMAN
AND... ONE FOR SAND.
WELL.
WE HAVE A NEW CHAIRMAN--

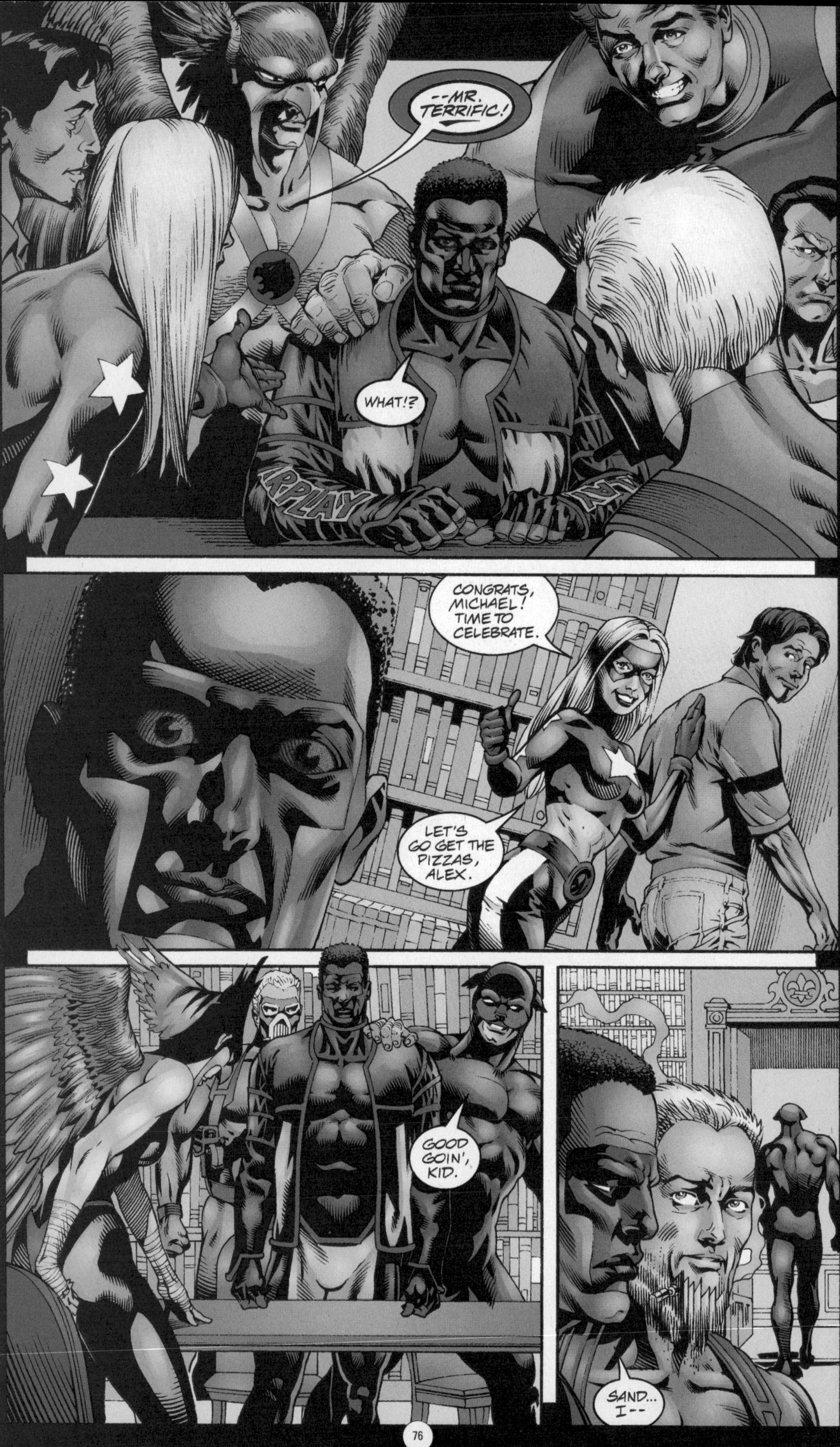
--MR. TERRIFIC!
WHAT!?
RPLAY
CONGRATS, MICHAEL! TIME TO CELEBRATE.
LET'S GO GET THE PIZZAS, ALEX.
GOOD GOIN', KID.
SAND... I--

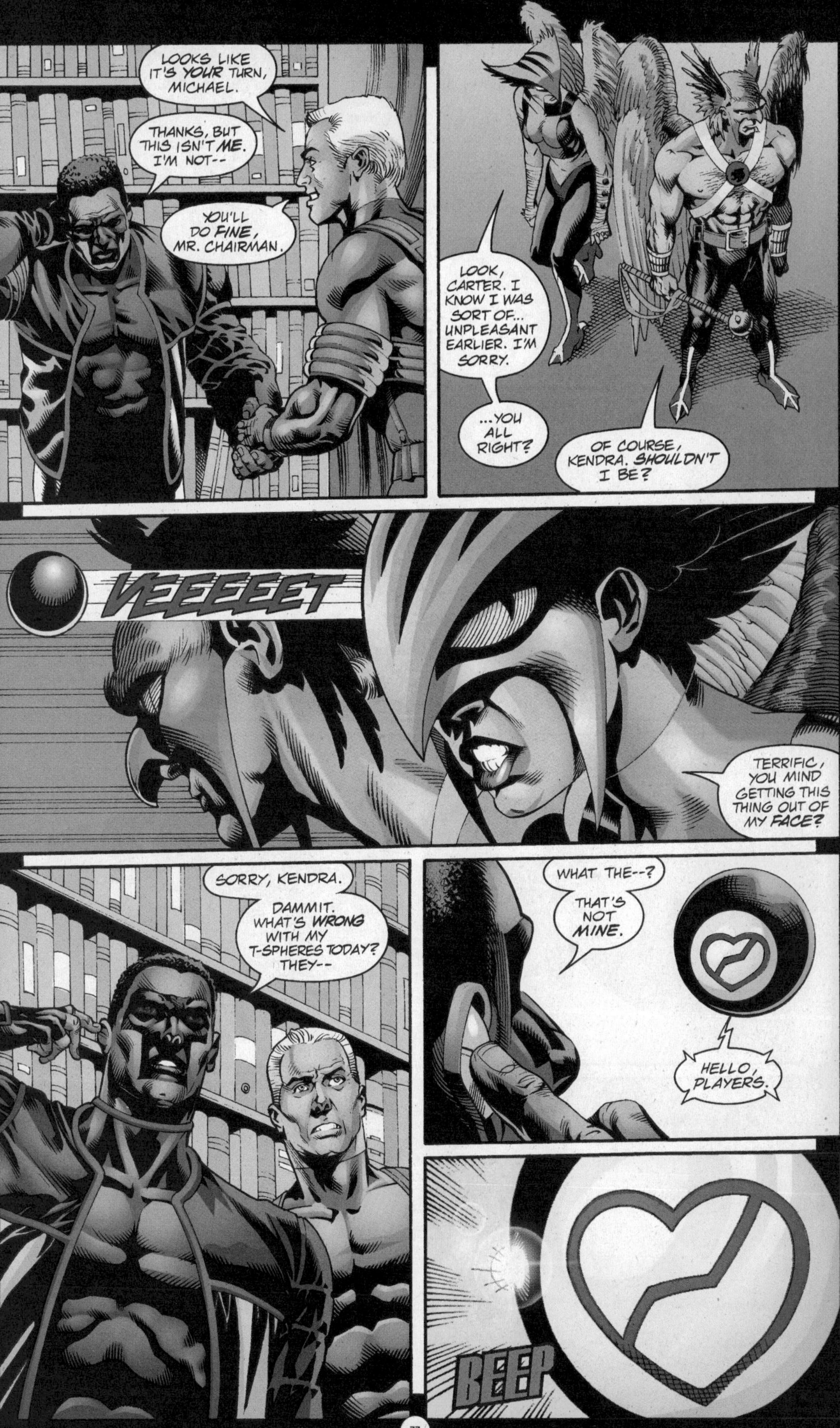
LOOKS LIKE IT'S YOUR TURN, MICHAEL.
THANKS, BUT THIS ISN'T ME. I'M NOT--
YOU'LL DO FINE, MR. CHAIRMAN.
LOOK, CARTER. I KNOW I WAS SORT OF... UNPLEASANT EARLIER. I'M SORRY.
...YOU ALL RIGHT?
OF COURSE, KENDRA. SHOULDN'T I BE?
VEEEEEET
TERRIFIC, YOU MIND GETTING THIS THING OUT OF MY FACE?
SORRY, KENDRA.
DAMMIT. WHAT'S WRONG WITH MY T-SPHERES TODAY? THEY--
WHAT THE--?
THAT'S NOT MINE.
HELLO, PLAYERS.
BEEP

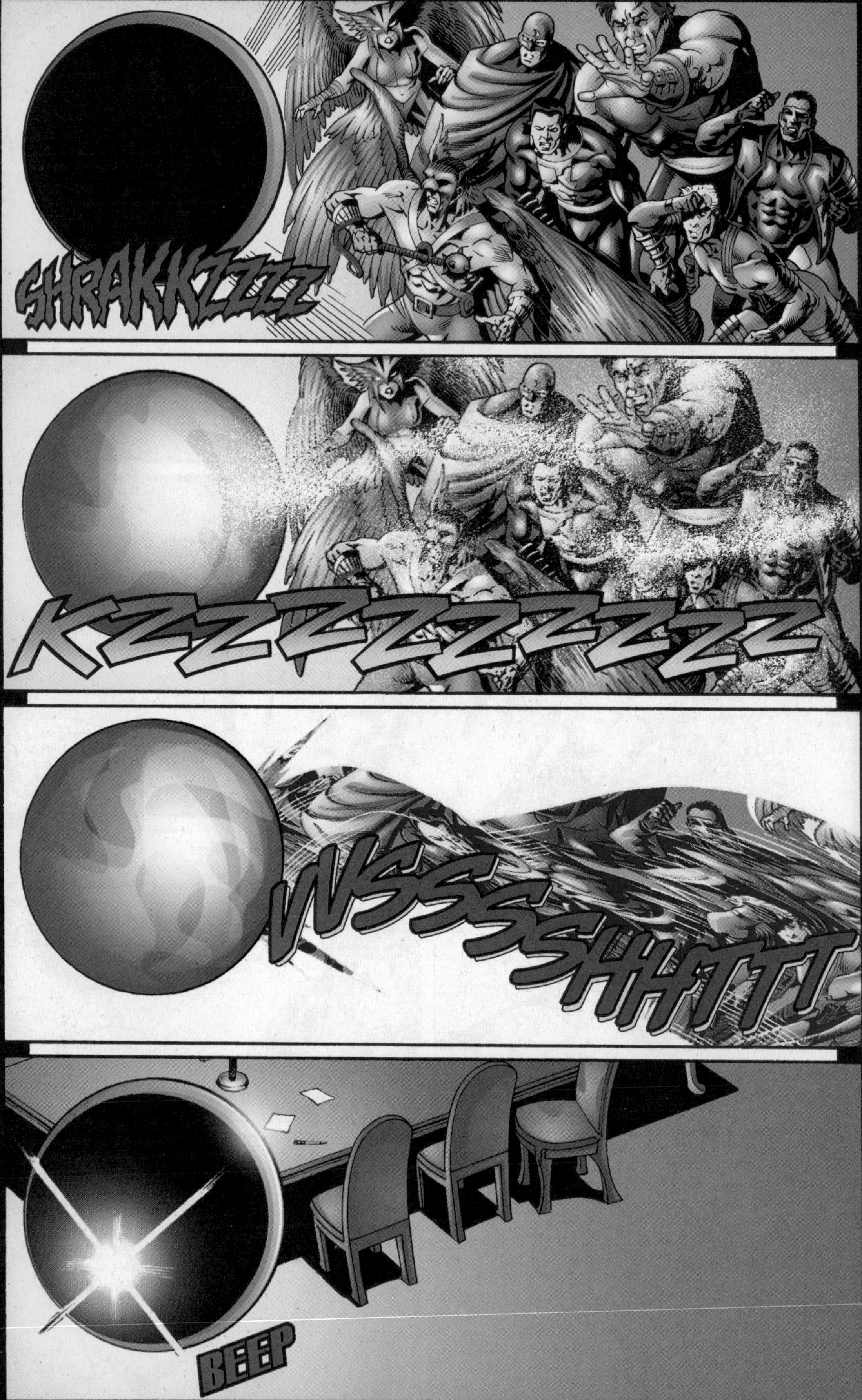
SHRAKKZZZZ
KZZZZZZZZZZ
VVSSSSHHTTT
BEEEP

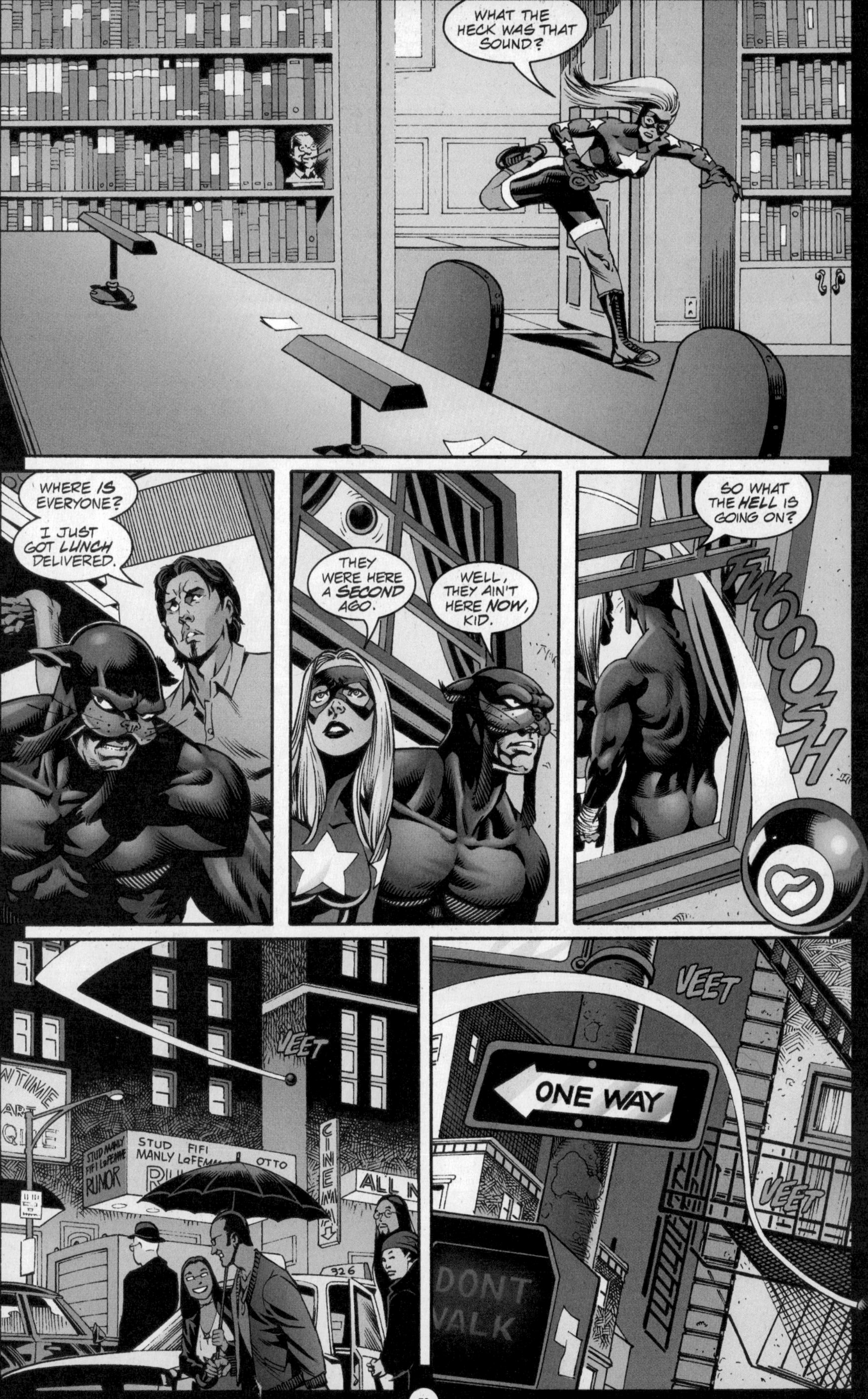
WHAT THE HECK WAS THAT SOUND?
WHERE IS EVERYONE?
I JUST GOT LUNCH DELIVERED.
THEY WERE HERE A SECOND AGO.
WELL, THEY AIN'T HERE NOW, KID.
SO WHAT THE HELL IS GOING ON?
FWOOOOOSH
VEET
STUD FIFI MANLY LaFEMM
OTTO
STUD MANLY FIFI LaFEMME RUMOR
CINEMA
ALL N
326
VEET
ONE WAY
VEET
DONT WALK

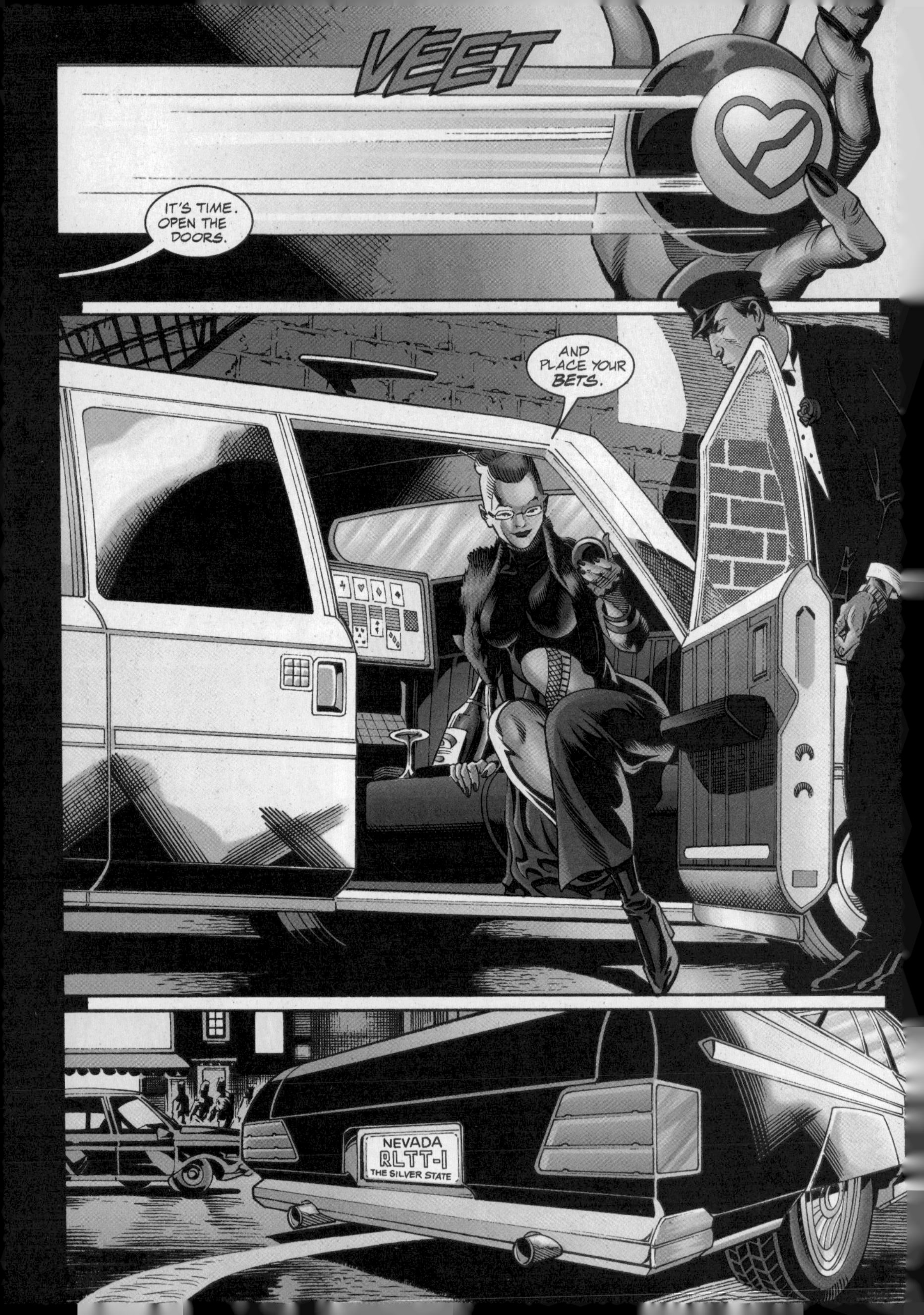
VEET
IT'S TIME. OPEN THE DOORS.
AND PLACE YOUR BETS.
NEVADA
RLTT-1
THE SILVER STATE

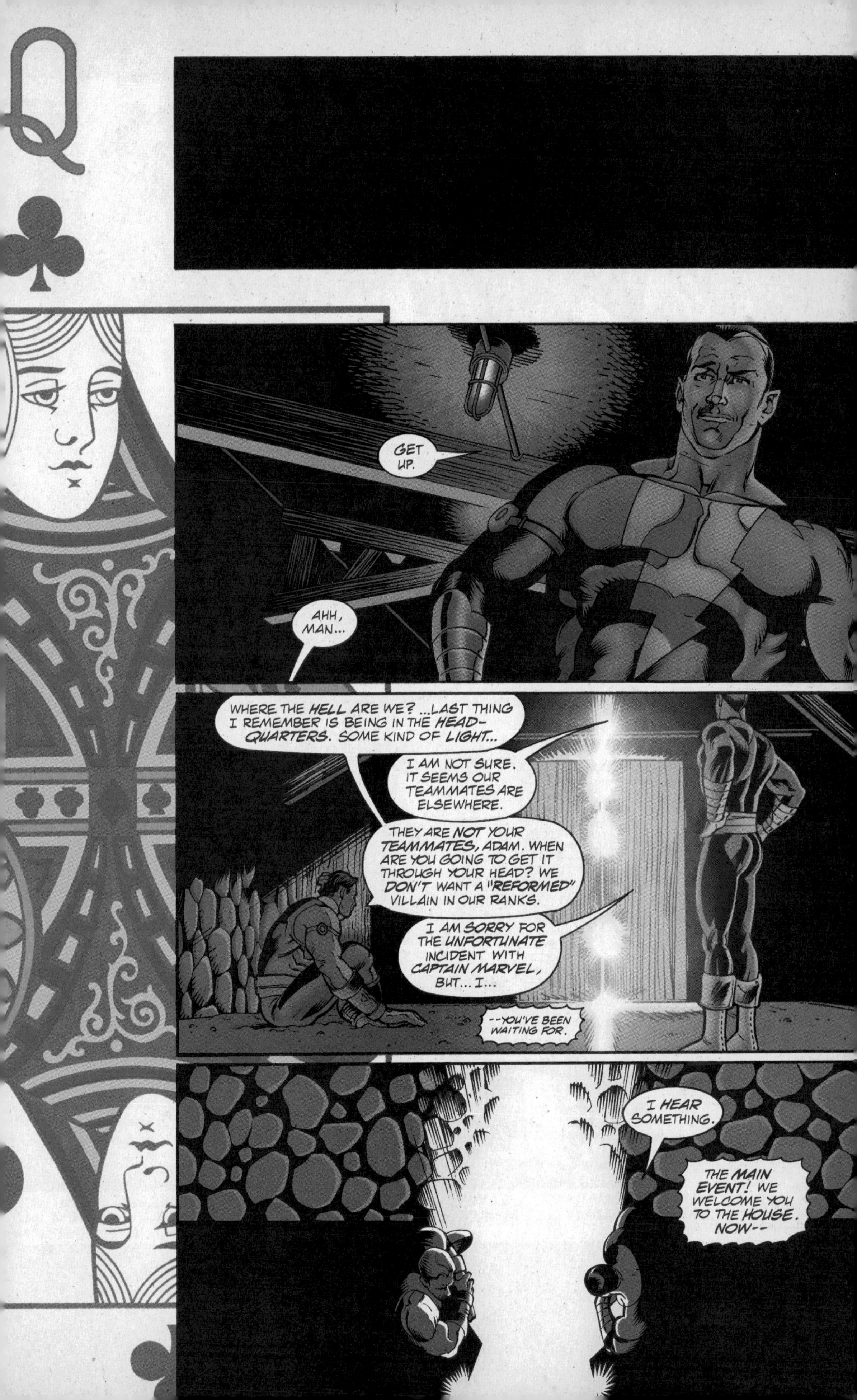
GET UP.
AHH, MAN...
WHERE THE HELL ARE WE? ...LAST THING I REMEMBER IS BEING IN THE HEAD-QUARTERS. SOME KIND OF LIGHT...
I AM NOT SURE. IT SEEMS OUR TEAMMATES ARE ELSEWHERE.
THEY ARE NOT YOUR TEAMMATES, ADAM. WHEN ARE YOU GOING TO GET IT THROUGH YOUR HEAD? WE DON'T WANT A "REFORMED" VILLAIN IN OUR RANKS.
I AM SORRY FOR THE UNFORTUNATE INCIDENT WITH CAPTAIN MARVEL, BUT... I...
--YOU'VE BEEN WAITING FOR.
I HEAR SOMETHING.
THE MAIN EVENT! WE WELCOME YOU TO THE HOUSE. NOW--

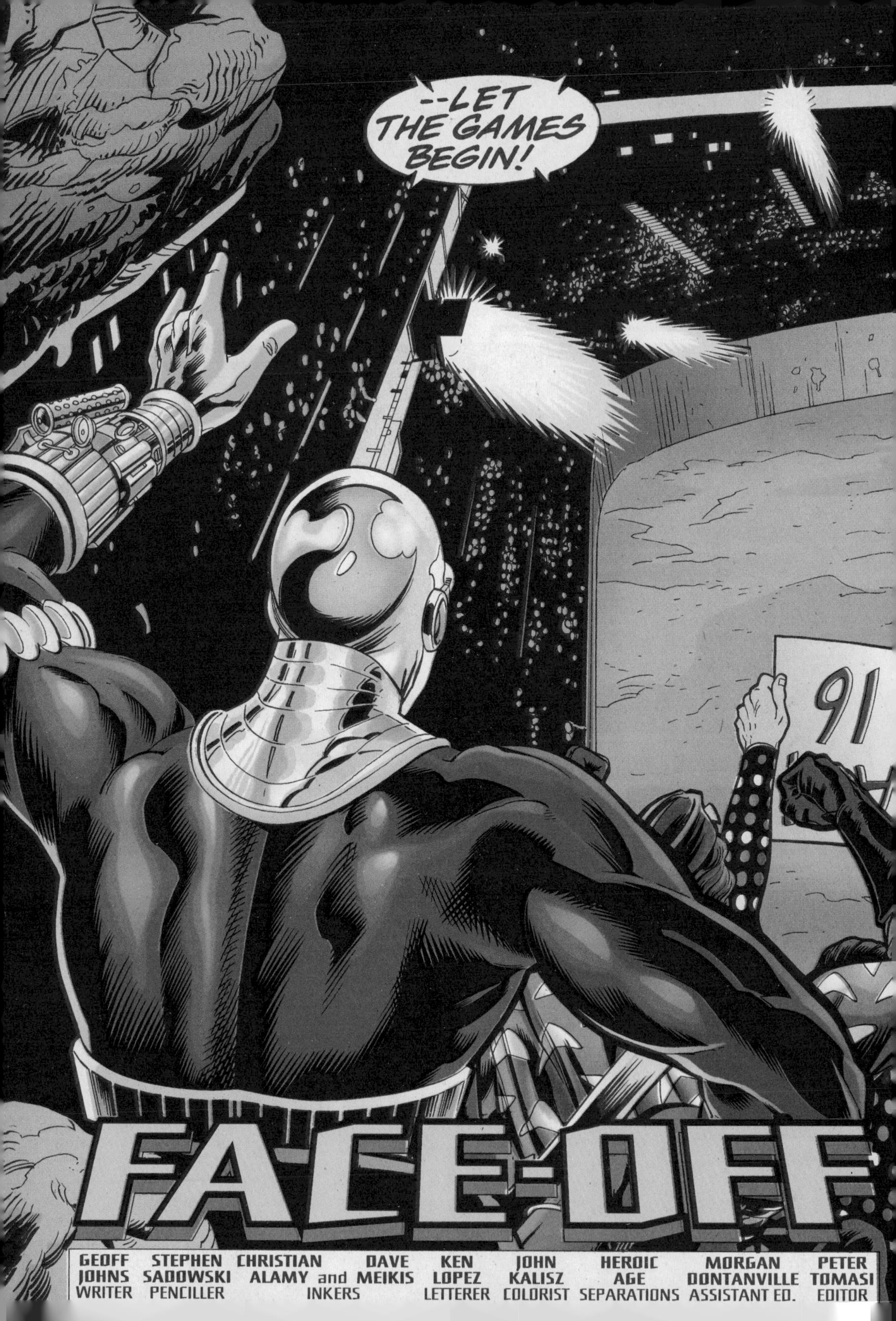
--LET THE GAMES BEGIN!
91
FACE-OFF
GEOFF JOHNS WRITER
STEPHEN SADOWSKI PENCILLER
CHRISTIAN ALAMY and DAVE MEIKIS INKERS
KEN LOPEZ LETTERER
JOHN KALISZ COLORIST
HEROIC AGE SEPARATIONS
MORGAN DONTANVILLE ASSISTANT ED.
PETER TOMASI EDITOR

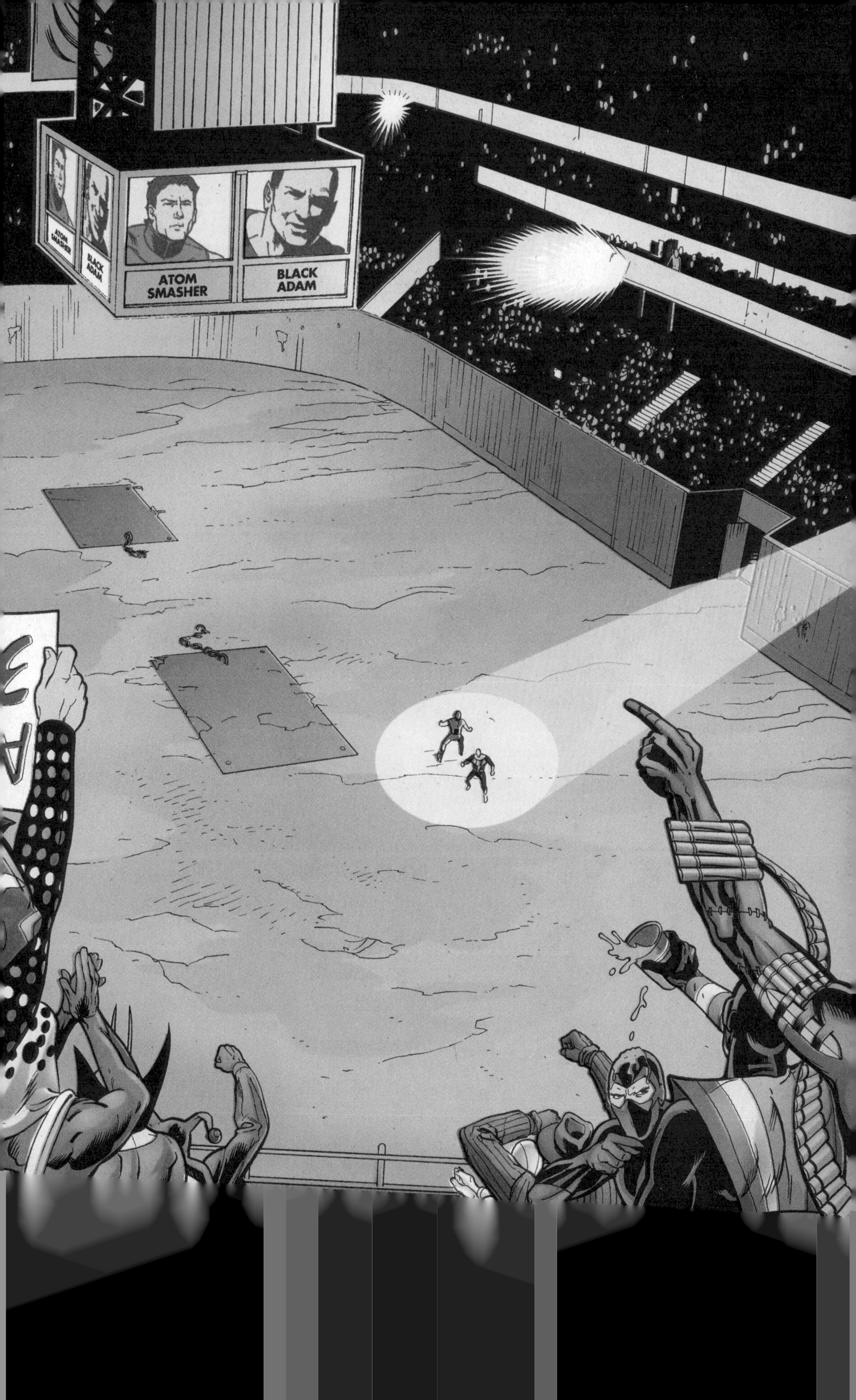
ATOM SMASHER
BLACK ADAM
ATOM SMASHER
BLACK ADAM

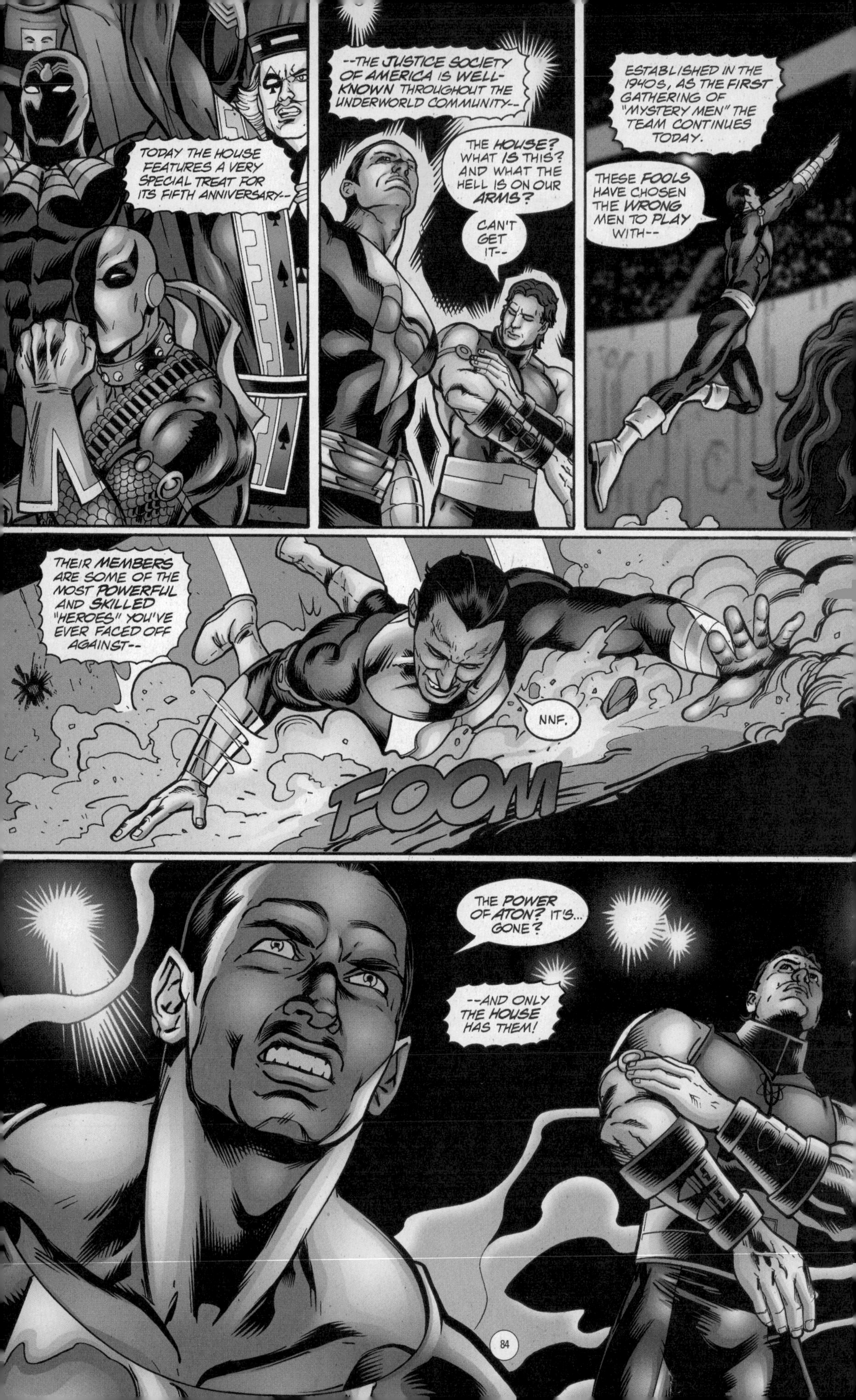
TODAY THE HOUSE FEATURES A VERY SPECIAL TREAT FOR ITS FIFTH ANNIVERSARY--
--THE JUSTICE SOCIETY OF AMERICA IS WELL-KNOWN THROUGHOUT THE UNDERWORLD COMMUNITY--
THE HOUSE? WHAT IS THIS? AND WHAT THE HELL IS ON OUR ARMS?
CAN'T GET IT--
ESTABLISHED IN THE 1940S, AS THE FIRST GATHERING OF "MYSTERY MEN" THE TEAM CONTINUES TODAY.
THESE FOOLS HAVE CHOSEN THE WRONG MEN TO PLAY WITH--
THEIR MEMBERS ARE SOME OF THE MOST POWERFUL AND SKILLED "HEROES" YOU'VE EVER FACED OFF AGAINST--
NNF.
FOOM
THE POWER OF ATON? IT'S... GONE?
--AND ONLY THE HOUSE HAS THEM!

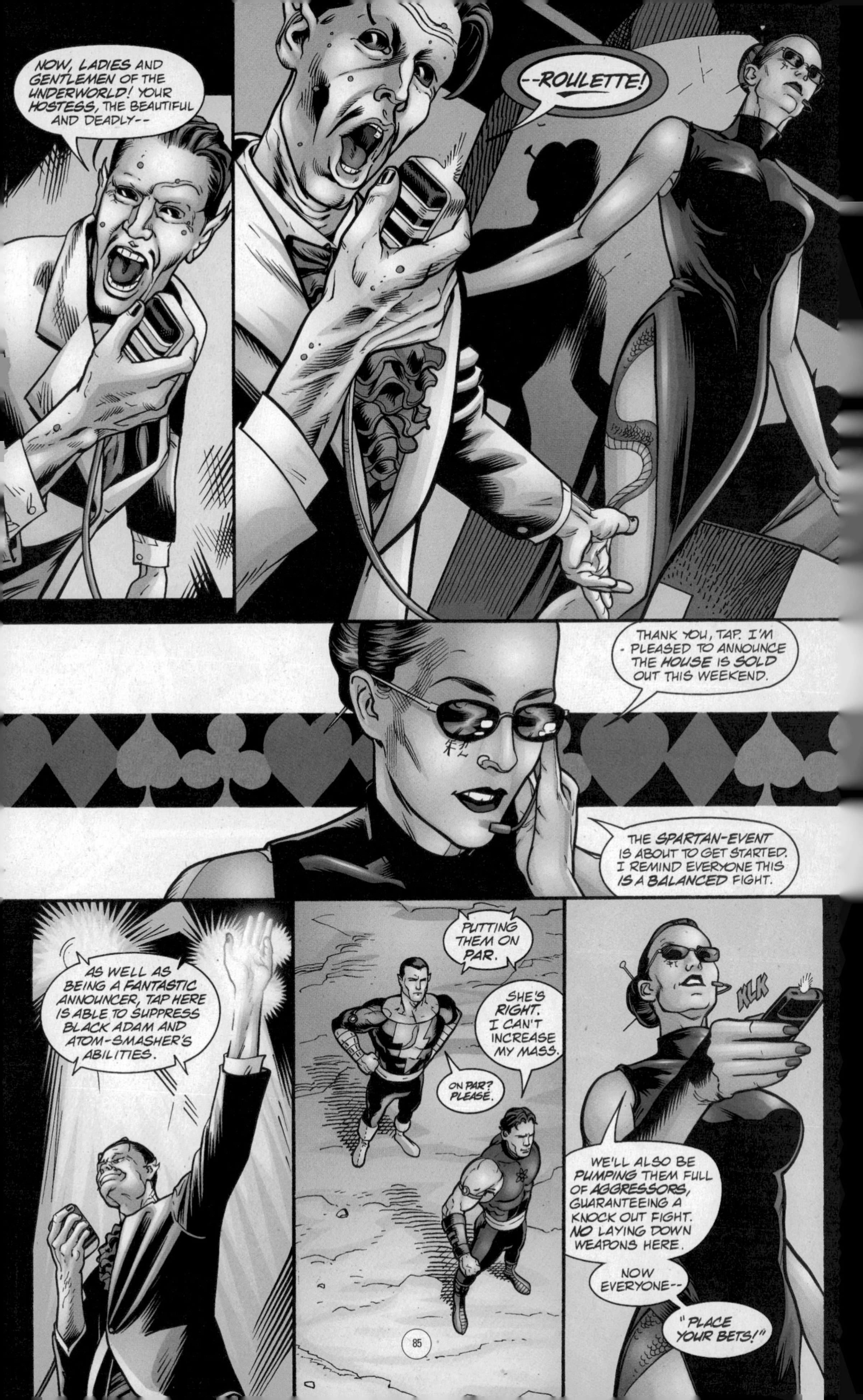
NOW, LADIES AND GENTLEMEN OF THE UNDERWORLD! YOUR HOSTESS, THE BEAUTIFUL AND DEADLY--
--ROULETTE!
THANK YOU, TAP. I'M PLEASED TO ANNOUNCE THE HOUSE IS SOLD OUT THIS WEEKEND.
THE SPARTAN-EVENT IS ABOUT TO GET STARTED. I REMIND EVERYONE THIS IS A BALANCED FIGHT.
AS WELL AS BEING A FANTASTIC ANNOUNCER, TAP HERE IS ABLE TO SUPPRESS BLACK ADAM AND ATOM-SMASHER'S ABILITIES.
PUTTING THEM ON PAR.
SHE'S RIGHT. I CAN'T INCREASE MY MASS.
ON PAR? PLEASE.
KLK
WE'LL ALSO BE PUMPING THEM FULL OF AGGRESSORS, GUARANTEEING A KNOCK OUT FIGHT. NO LAYING DOWN WEAPONS HERE.
NOW EVERYONE--
"PLACE YOUR BETS!"

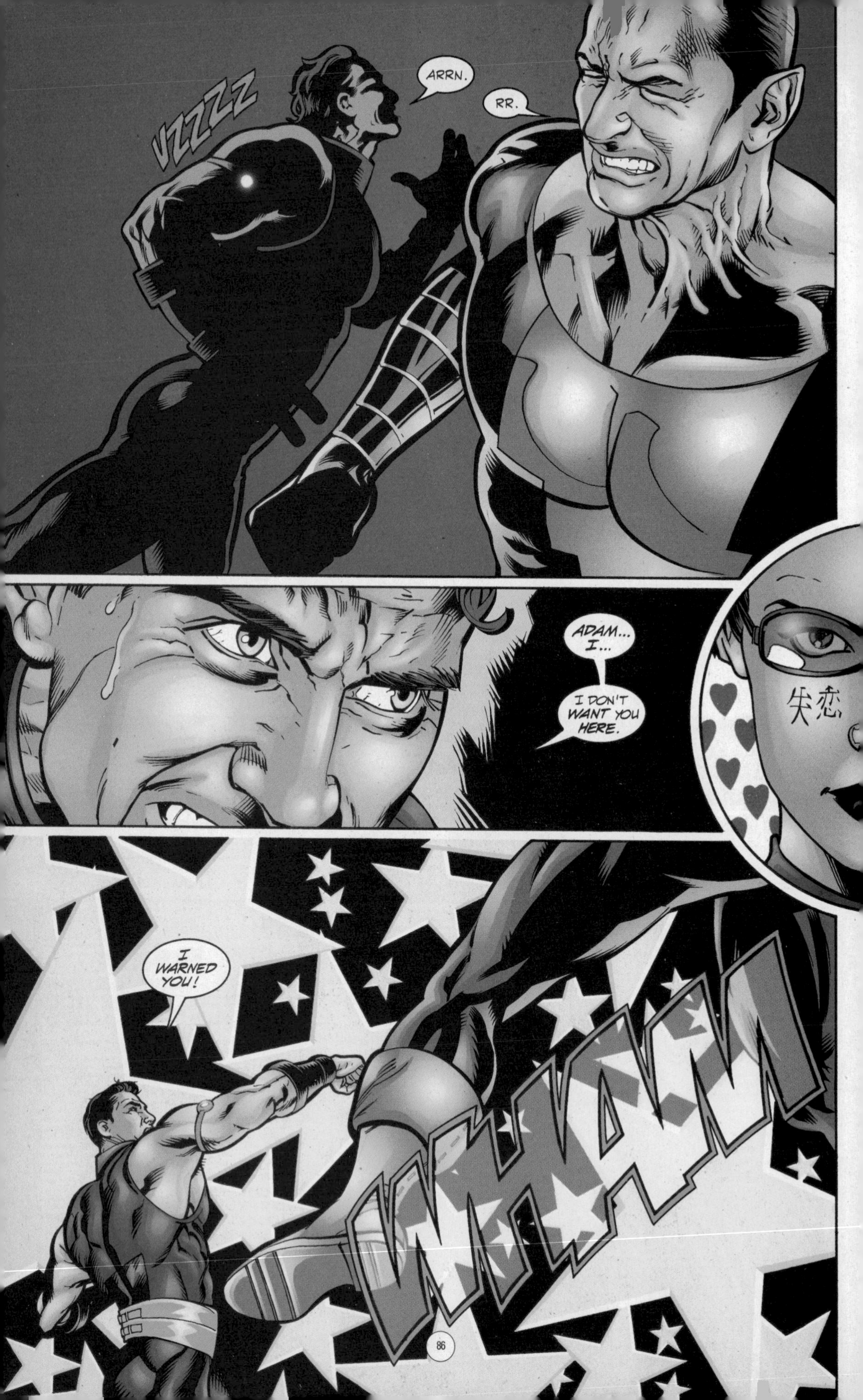
VZZZZ
ARRN.
RR.
ADAM... I...
I DON'T WANT YOU HERE.
失恋
I WARNED YOU!
WHAM

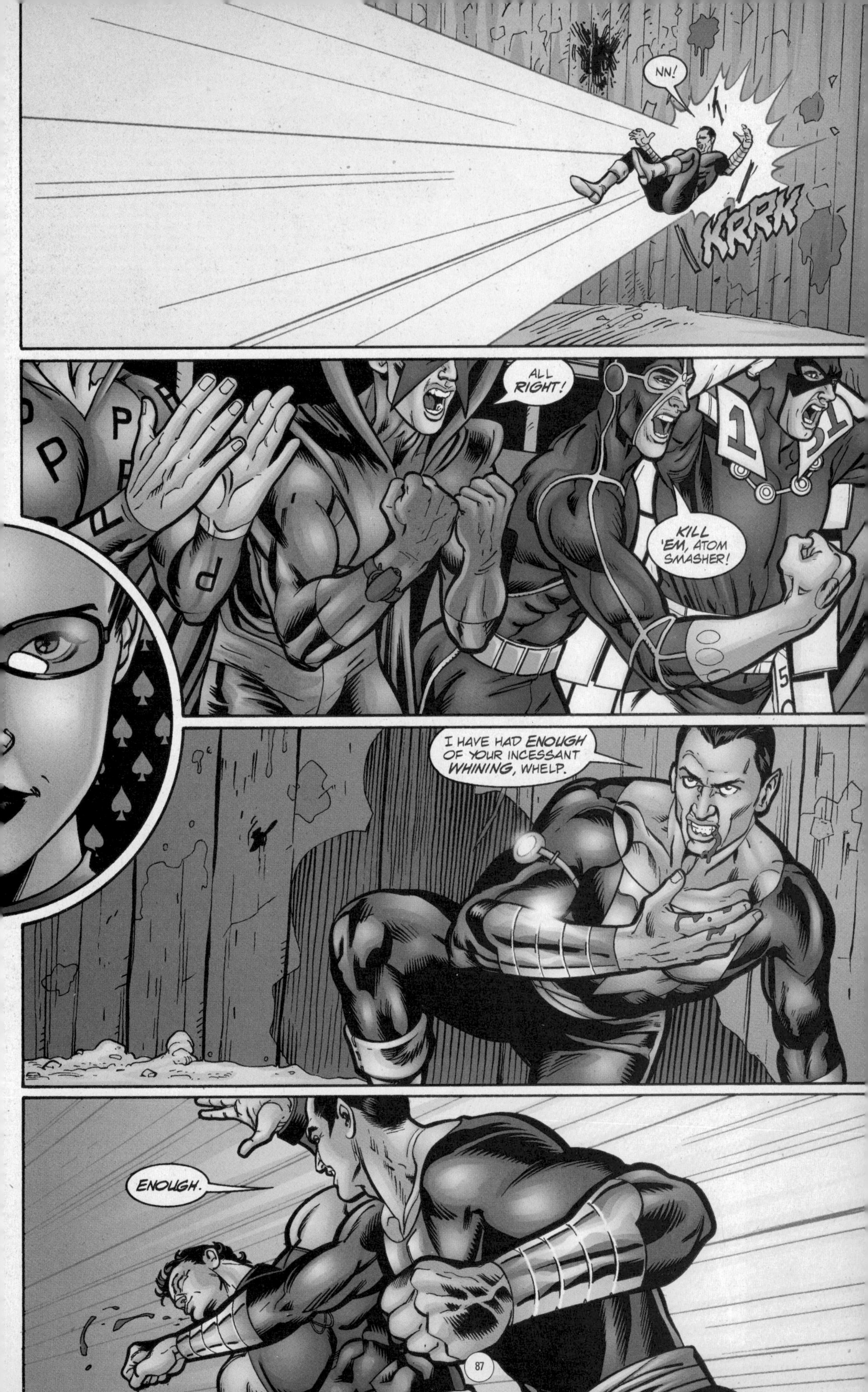
NN!
KRRK
ALL RIGHT!
KILL 'EM, ATOM SMASHER!
I HAVE HAD ENOUGH OF YOUR INCESSANT WHINING, WHELP.
ENOUGH.

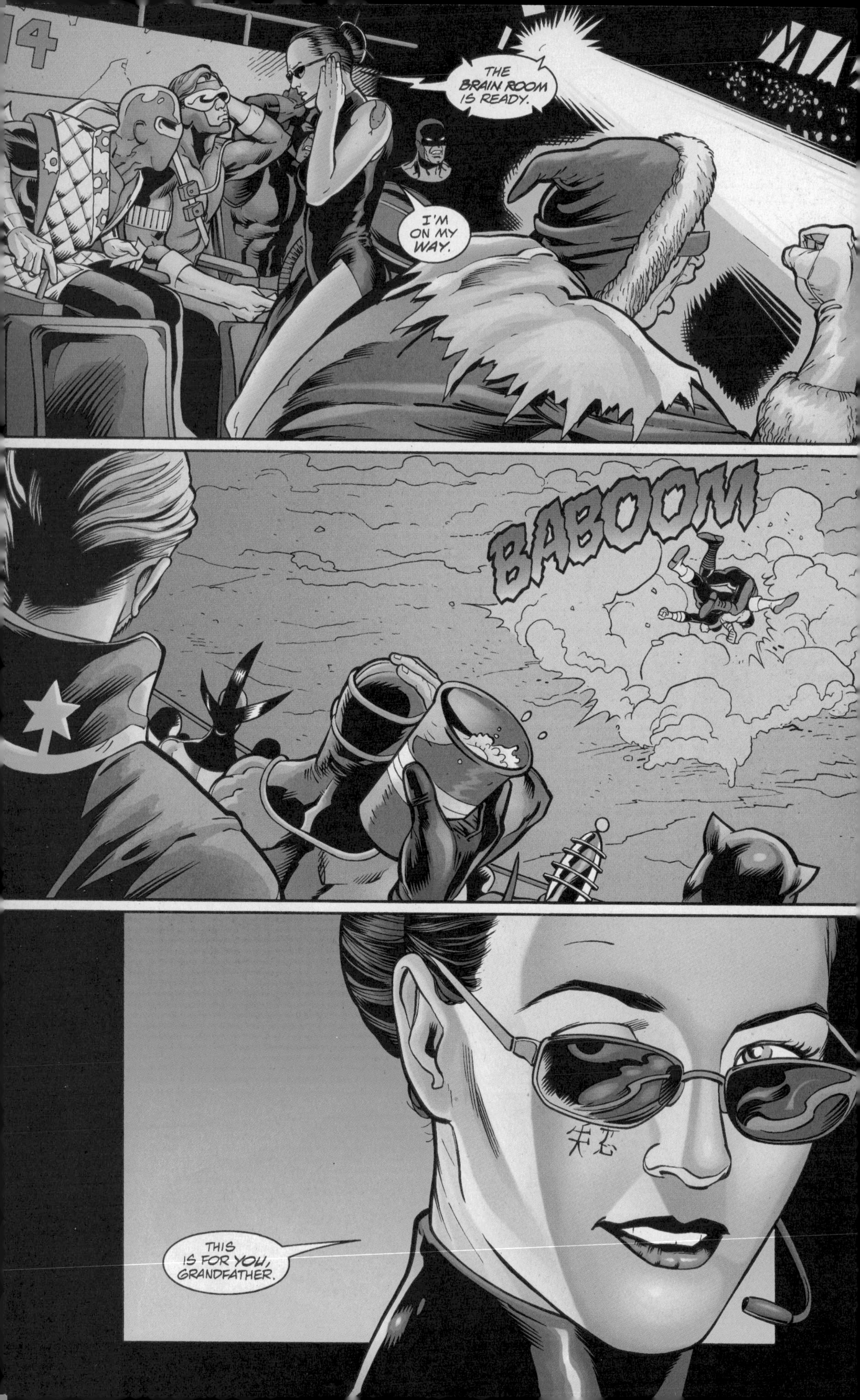
THE BRAIN ROOM IS READY.
I'M ON MY WAY.
BABOOM
THIS IS FOR YOU, GRANDFATHER.

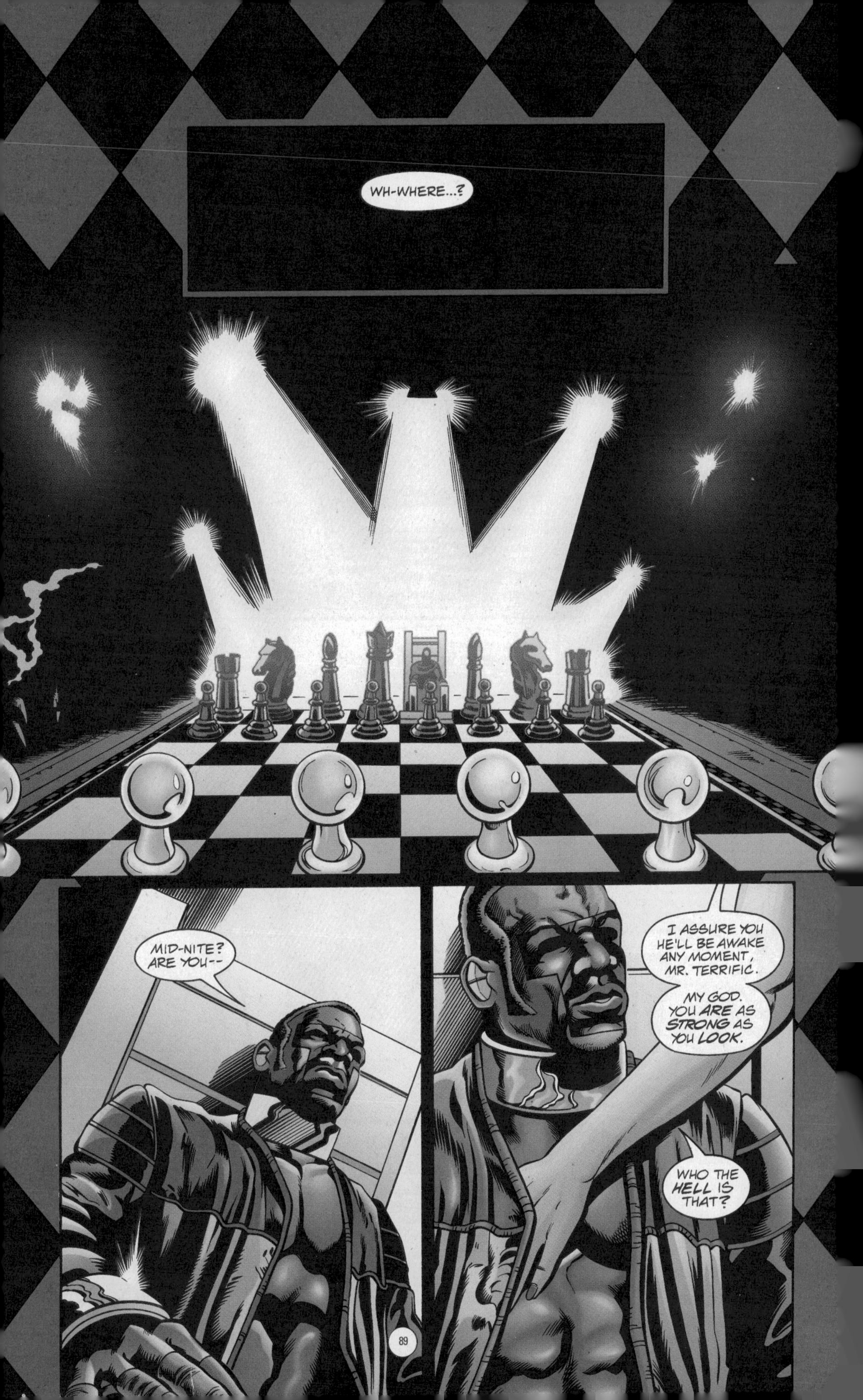
WH-WHERE...?
MID-NITE? ARE YOU--
I ASSURE YOU HE'LL BE AWAKE ANY MOMENT, MR. TERRIFIC.
MY GOD. YOU ARE AS STRONG AS YOU LOOK.
WHO THE HELL IS THAT?

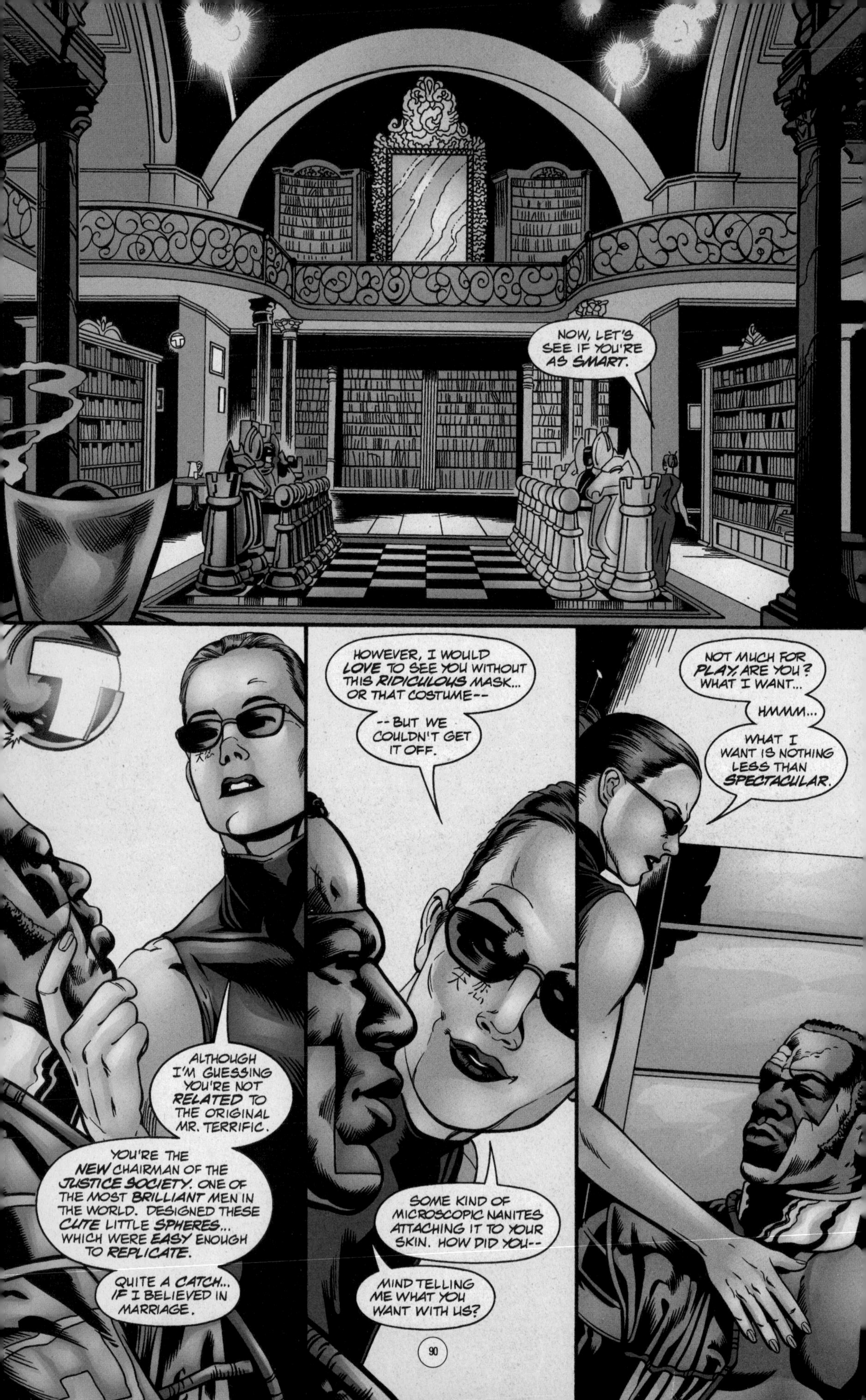
NOW, LET'S SEE IF YOU'RE AS SMART.
ALTHOUGH I'M GUESSING YOU'RE NOT RELATED TO THE ORIGINAL MR. TERRIFIC.
YOU'RE THE NEW CHAIRMAN OF THE JUSTICE SOCIETY. ONE OF THE MOST BRILLIANT MEN IN THE WORLD. DESIGNED THESE CUTE LITTLE SPHERES... WHICH WERE EASY ENOUGH TO REPLICATE.
QUITE A CATCH... IF I BELIEVED IN MARRIAGE.
HOWEVER, I WOULD LOVE TO SEE YOU WITHOUT THIS RIDICULOUS MASK... OR THAT COSTUME--
--BUT WE COULDN'T GET IT OFF.
SOME KIND OF MICROSCOPIC NANITES ATTACHING IT TO YOUR SKIN. HOW DID YOU--
MIND TELLING ME WHAT YOU WANT WITH US?
NOT MUCH FOR PLAY, ARE YOU? WHAT I WANT...
HMMM...
WHAT I WANT IS NOTHING LESS THAN SPECTACULAR.

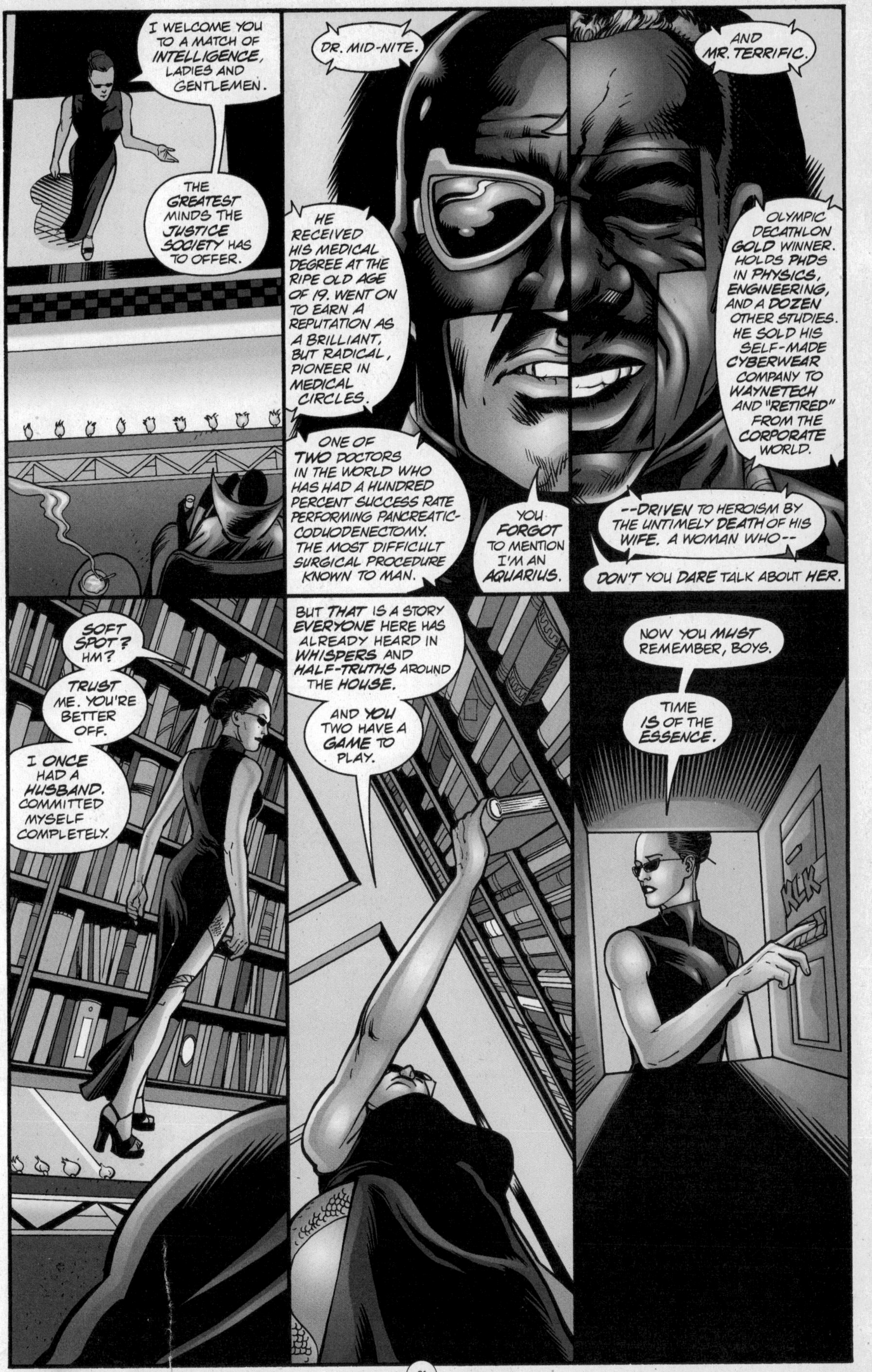
I WELCOME YOU TO A MATCH OF INTELLIGENCE, LADIES AND GENTLEMEN.
THE GREATEST MINDS THE JUSTICE SOCIETY HAS TO OFFER.
DR. MID-NITE.
AND MR. TERRIFIC.
HE RECEIVED HIS MEDICAL DEGREE AT THE RIPE OLD AGE OF 19. WENT ON TO EARN A REPUTATION AS A BRILLIANT, BUT RADICAL, PIONEER IN MEDICAL CIRCLES.
ONE OF TWO DOCTORS IN THE WORLD WHO HAS HAD A HUNDRED PERCENT SUCCESS RATE PERFORMING PANCREATIC-CODUODENECTOMY. THE MOST DIFFICULT SURGICAL PROCEDURE KNOWN TO MAN.
YOU FORGOT TO MENTION I'M AN AQUARIUS.
OLYMPIC DECATHLON GOLD WINNER. HOLDS PHDS IN PHYSICS, ENGINEERING, AND A DOZEN OTHER STUDIES. HE SOLD HIS SELF-MADE CYBERWEAR COMPANY TO WAYNETECH AND "RETIRED" FROM THE CORPORATE WORLD.
--DRIVEN TO HEROISM BY THE UNTIMELY DEATH OF HIS WIFE. A WOMAN WHO--
DON'T YOU DARE TALK ABOUT HER.
SOFT SPOT? HM?
TRUST ME. YOU'RE BETTER OFF.
I ONCE HAD A HUSBAND. COMMITTED MYSELF COMPLETELY.
BUT THAT IS A STORY EVERYONE HERE HAS ALREADY HEARD IN WHISPERS AND HALF-TRUTHS AROUND THE HOUSE.
AND YOU TWO HAVE A GAME TO PLAY.
NOW YOU MUST REMEMBER, BOYS.
TIME IS OF THE ESSENCE.
KLIK

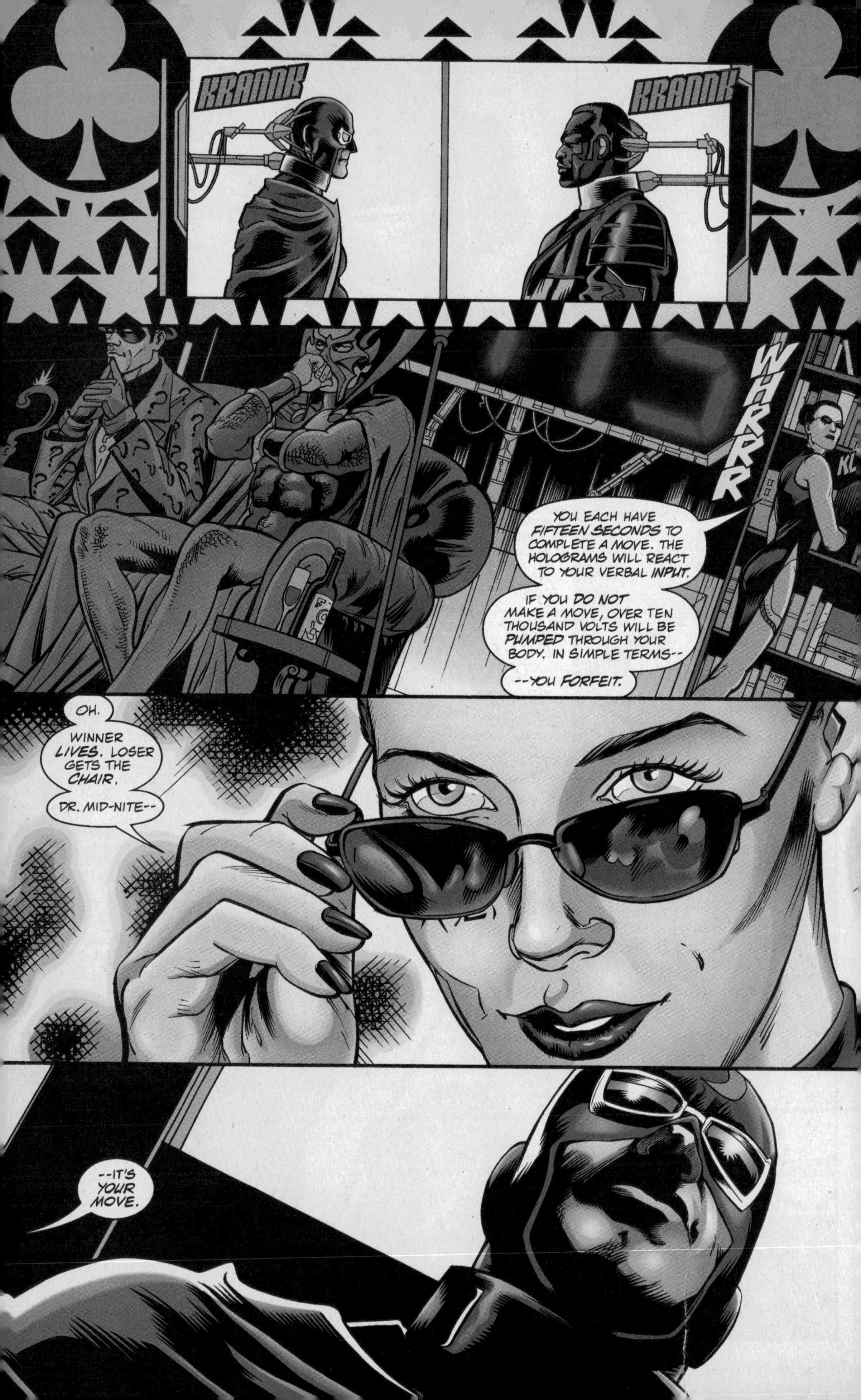
KRANNK
KRANNK
WHRRRR
YOU EACH HAVE FIFTEEN SECONDS TO COMPLETE A MOVE. THE HOLOGRAMS WILL REACT TO YOUR VERBAL INPUT.
IF YOU DO NOT MAKE A MOVE, OVER TEN THOUSAND VOLTS WILL BE PUMPED THROUGH YOUR BODY. IN SIMPLE TERMS--
--YOU FORFEIT.
OH.
WINNER LIVES. LOSER GETS THE CHAIR.
DR. MID-NITE--
--IT'S YOUR MOVE.

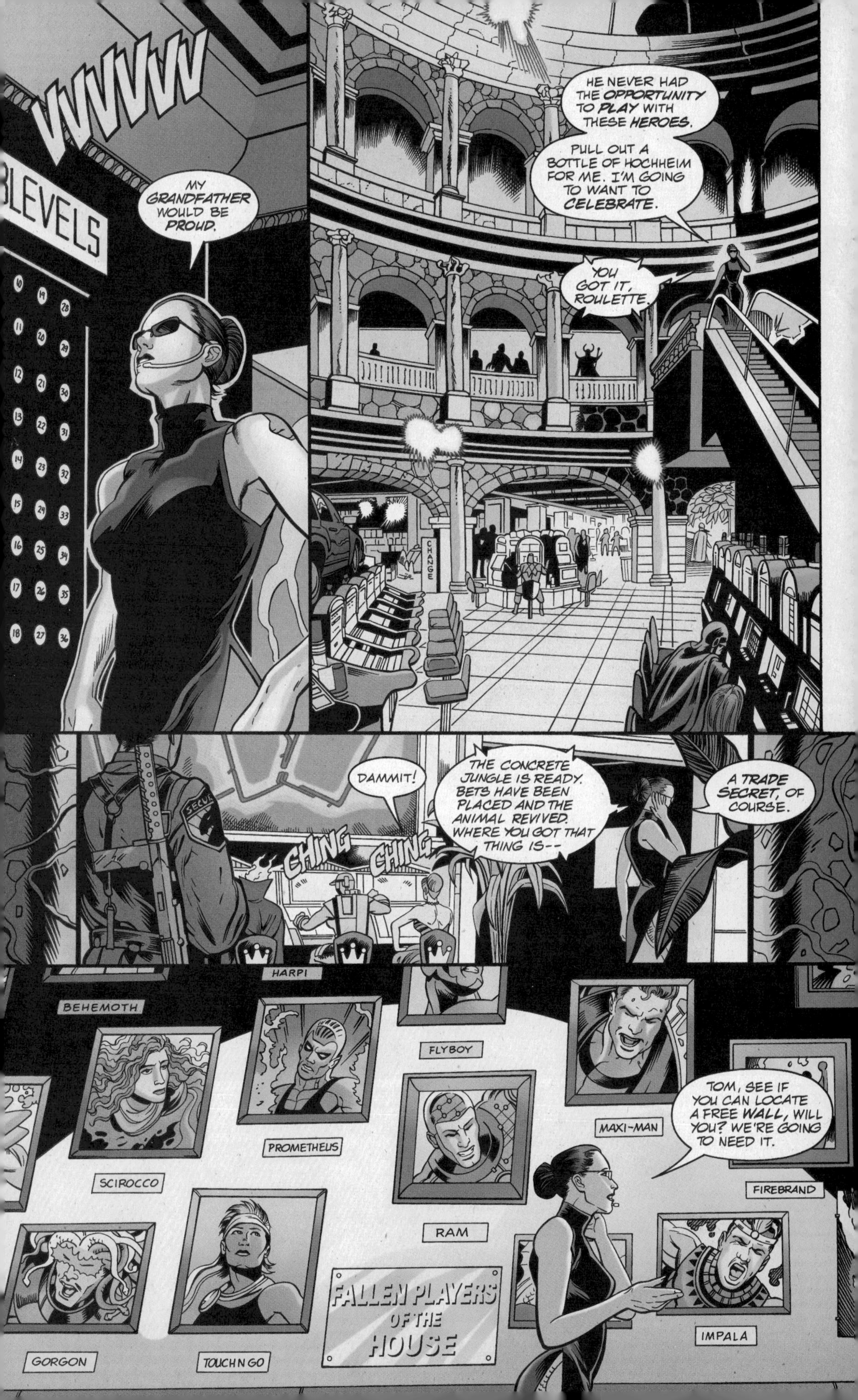
VVVVVV
LEVELS
MY GRANDFATHER WOULD BE PROUD.
HE NEVER HAD THE OPPORTUNITY TO PLAY WITH THESE HEROES.
PULL OUT A BOTTLE OF HOCHHEIM FOR ME. I'M GOING TO WANT TO CELEBRATE.
YOU GOT IT, ROULETTE.
CHANGE
DAMMIT!
CHING
CHING
THE CONCRETE JUNGLE IS READY. BETS HAVE BEEN PLACED AND THE ANIMAL REVIVED. WHERE YOU GOT THAT THING IS--
A TRADE SECRET, OF COURSE.
HARPI
BEHEMOTH
FLYBOY
MAXI-MAN
PROMETHEUS
SCIROCCO
TOM, SEE IF YOU CAN LOCATE A FREE WALL, WILL YOU? WE'RE GOING TO NEED IT.
FIREBRAND
RAM
FALLEN PLAYERS OF THE HOUSE
IMPALA
GORGON
TOUCH N GO

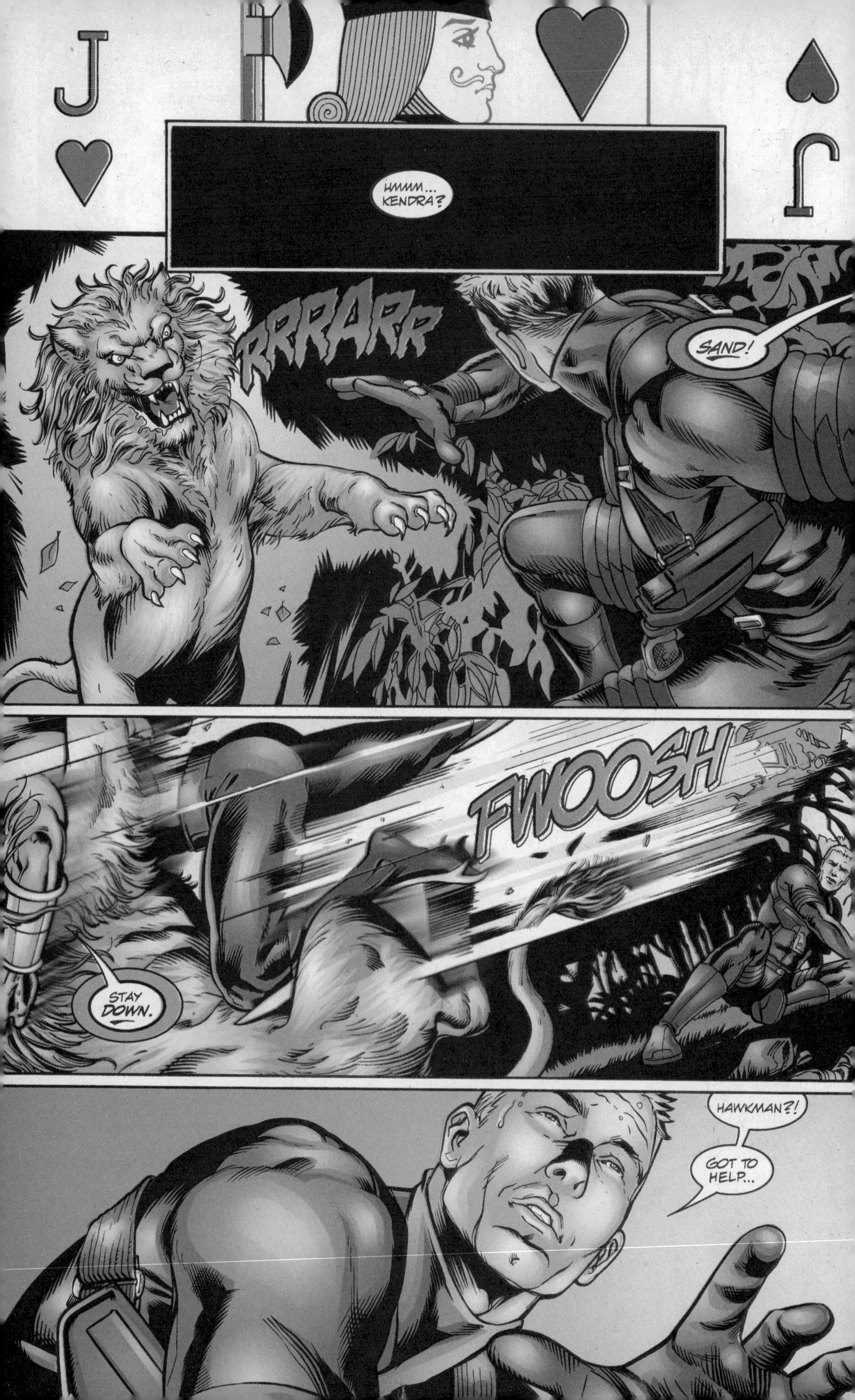
HMMM... KENDRA?
RRRARR
SAND!
FWOOSH
STAY DOWN.
HAWKMAN?!
GOT TO HELP...

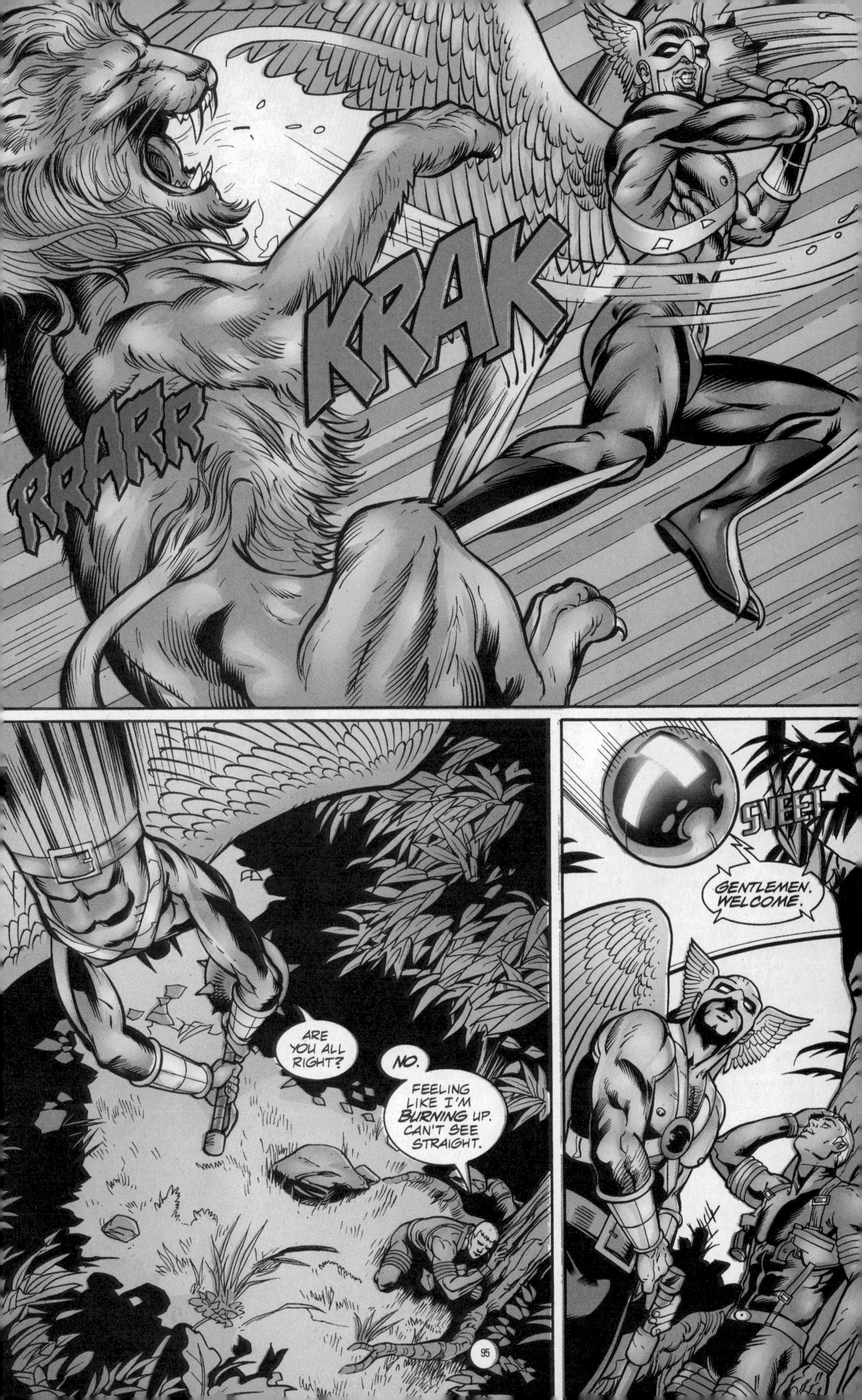
KRAK
RRARR
ARE YOU ALL RIGHT?
NO.
FEELING LIKE I'M BURNING UP. CAN'T SEE STRAIGHT.
SVEET
GENTLEMEN. WELCOME.

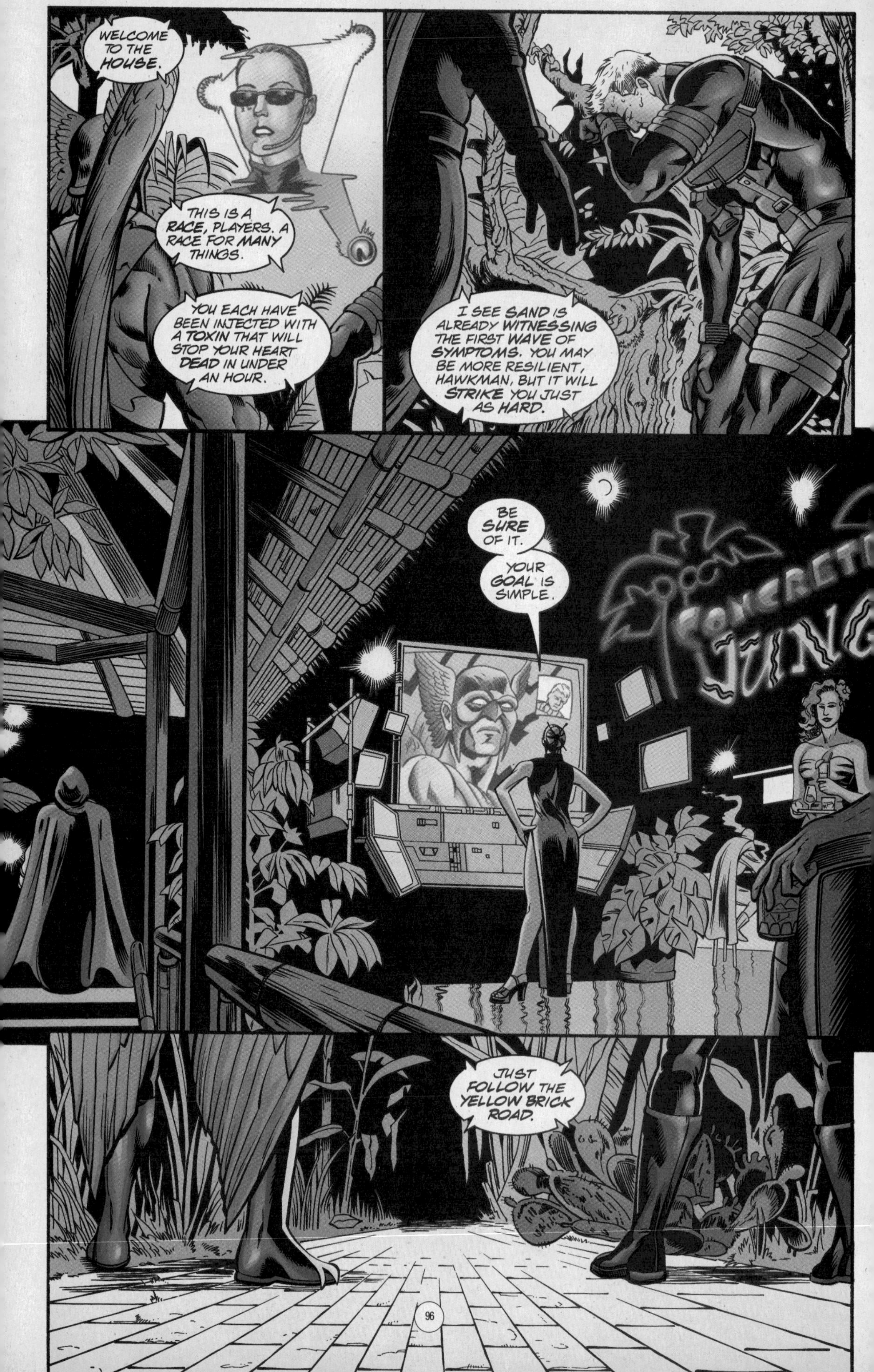
WELCOME TO THE HOUSE.
THIS IS A RACE, PLAYERS. A RACE FOR MANY THINGS.
YOU EACH HAVE BEEN INJECTED WITH A TOXIN THAT WILL STOP YOUR HEART DEAD IN UNDER AN HOUR.
I SEE SAND IS ALREADY WITNESSING THE FIRST WAVE OF SYMPTOMS. YOU MAY BE MORE RESILIENT, HAWKMAN, BUT IT WILL STRIKE YOU JUST AS HARD.
BE SURE OF IT.
YOUR GOAL IS SIMPLE.
JUST FOLLOW THE YELLOW BRICK ROAD.

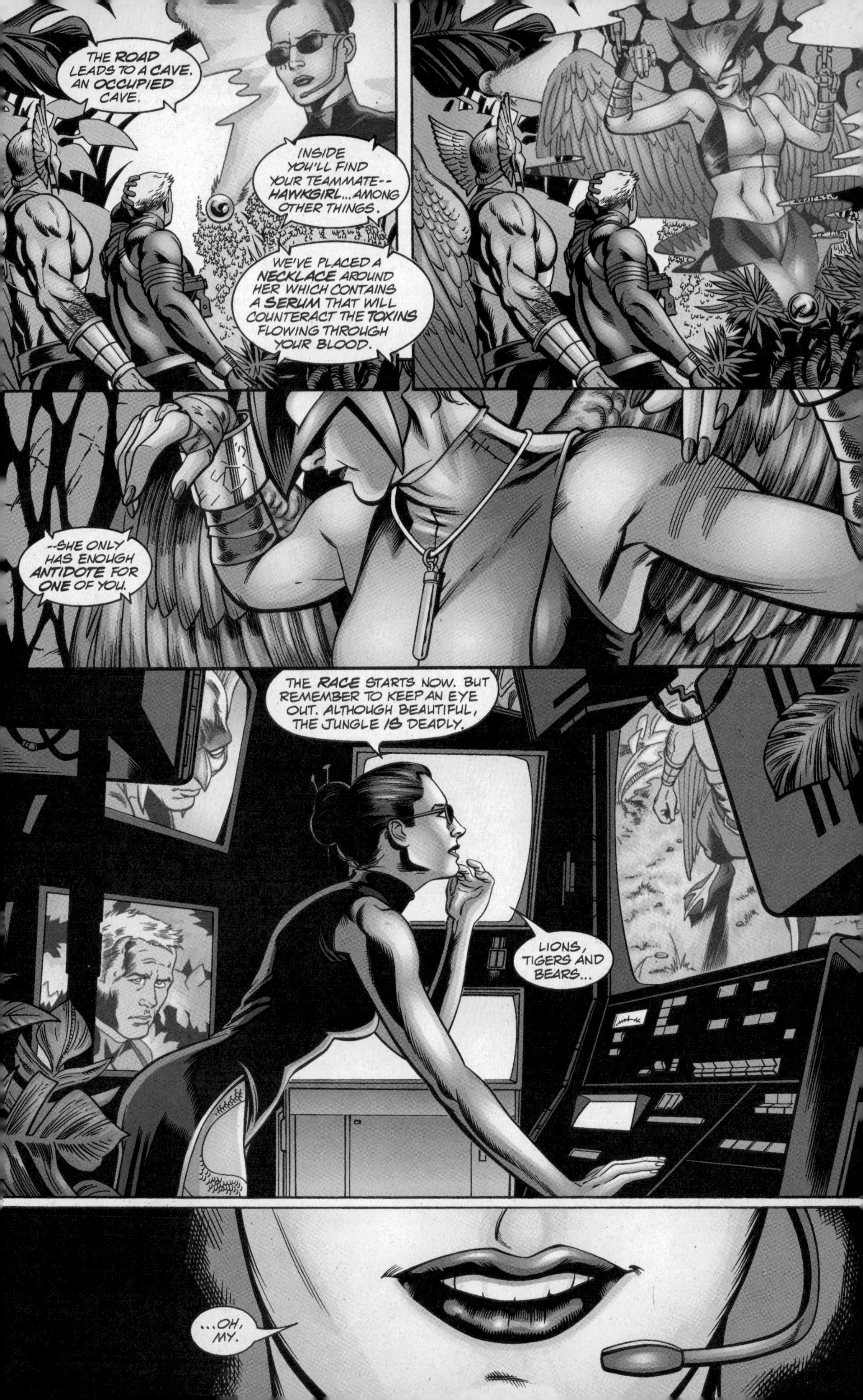
THE ROAD LEADS TO A CAVE. AN OCCUPIED CAVE.
INSIDE YOU'LL FIND YOUR TEAMMATE-- HAWKGIRL... AMONG OTHER THINGS.
WE'VE PLACED A NECKLACE AROUND HER WHICH CONTAINS A SERUM THAT WILL COUNTERACT THE TOXINS FLOWING THROUGH YOUR BLOOD.
--SHE ONLY HAS ENOUGH ANTIDOTE FOR ONE OF YOU.
THE RACE STARTS NOW. BUT REMEMBER TO KEEP AN EYE OUT. ALTHOUGH BEAUTIFUL, THE JUNGLE IS DEADLY.
LIONS, TIGERS AND BEARS...
...OH, MY.

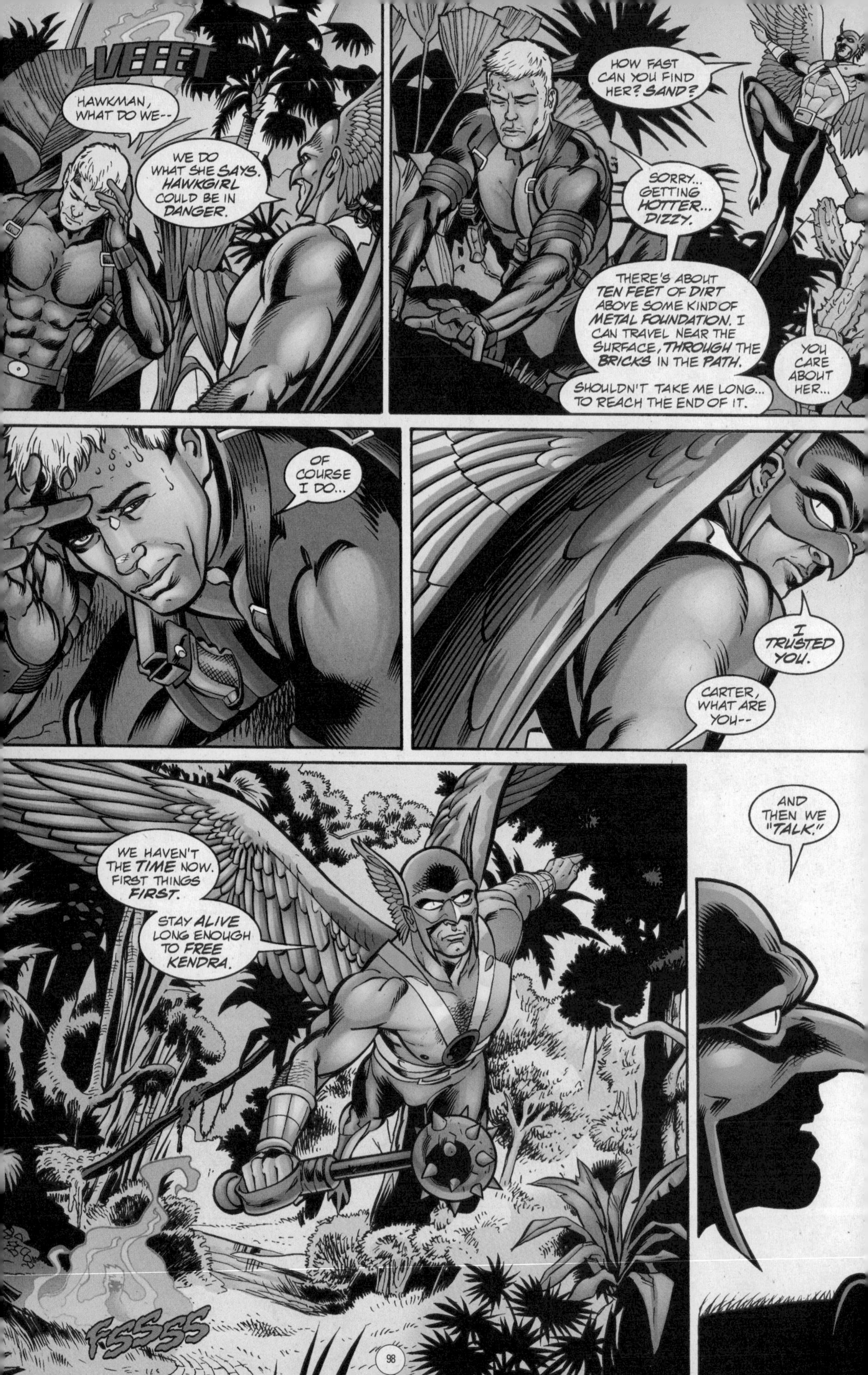
VEEEET
HAWKMAN, WHAT DO WE--
WE DO WHAT SHE SAYS. HAWKGIRL COULD BE IN DANGER.
HOW FAST CAN YOU FIND HER? SAND?
SORRY... GETTING HOTTER... DIZZY.
THERE'S ABOUT TEN FEET OF DIRT ABOVE SOME KIND OF METAL FOUNDATION. I CAN TRAVEL NEAR THE SURFACE, THROUGH THE BRICKS IN THE PATH.
SHOULDN'T TAKE ME LONG... TO REACH THE END OF IT.
YOU CARE ABOUT HER...
OF COURSE I DO...
I TRUSTED YOU.
CARTER, WHAT ARE YOU--
WE HAVEN'T THE TIME NOW. FIRST THINGS FIRST.
STAY ALIVE LONG ENOUGH TO FREE KENDRA.
AND THEN WE "TALK."
FSSSSS

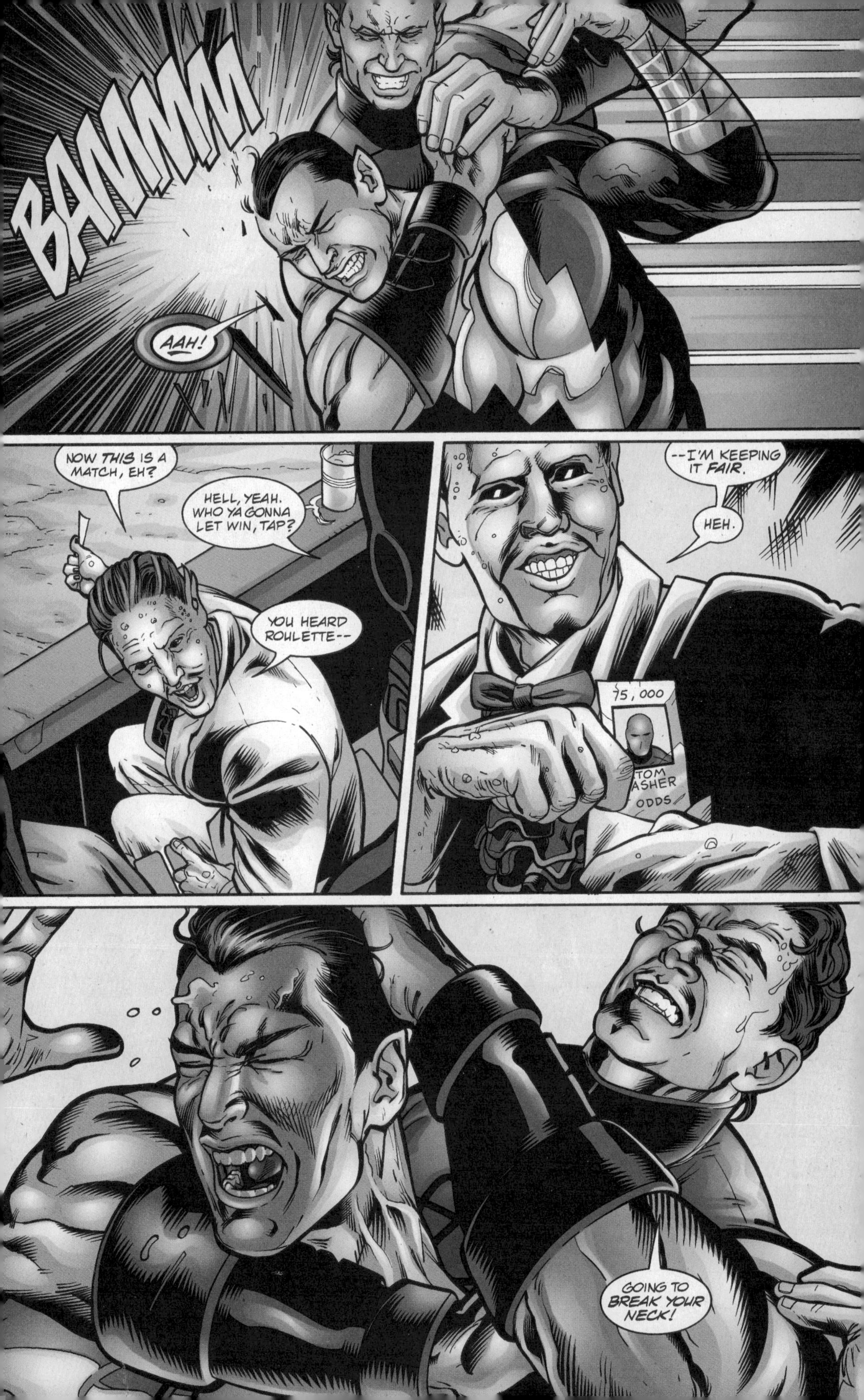
BAMMMM
AAH!
NOW THIS IS A MATCH, EH?
HELL, YEAH. WHO YA GONNA LET WIN, TAP?
YOU HEARD ROULETTE--
--I'M KEEPING IT FAIR.
HEH.
75,000
TOM ASHER
ODDS
GOING TO BREAK YOUR NECK!

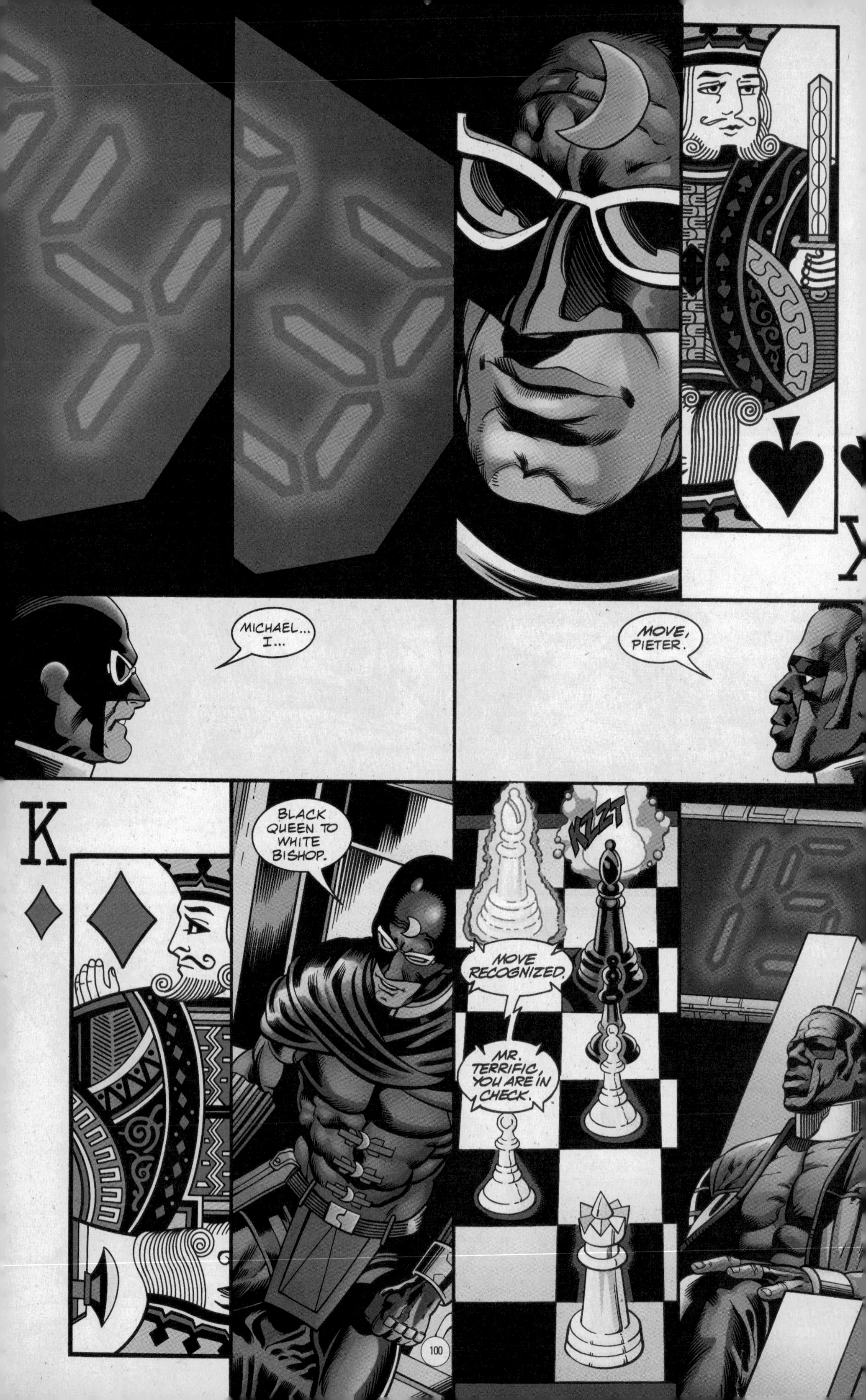

MICHAEL... I...
MOVE, PIETER.
BLACK QUEEN TO WHITE BISHOP.
KZZT
MOVE RECOGNIZED.
MR. TERRIFIC, YOU ARE IN CHECK.

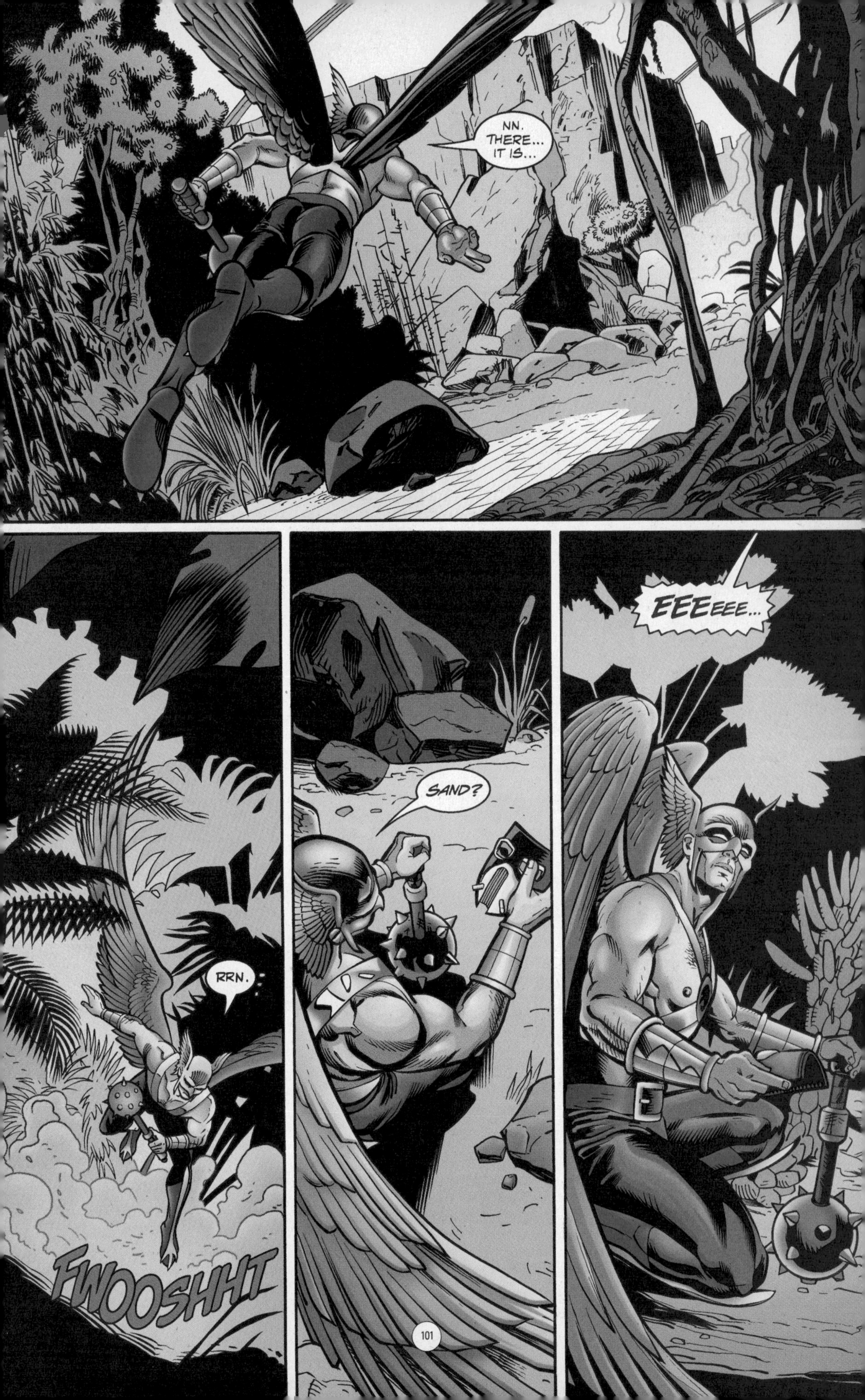
NN. THERE... IT IS...
RRN.
FWOOSHHT
SAND?
EEEeee...

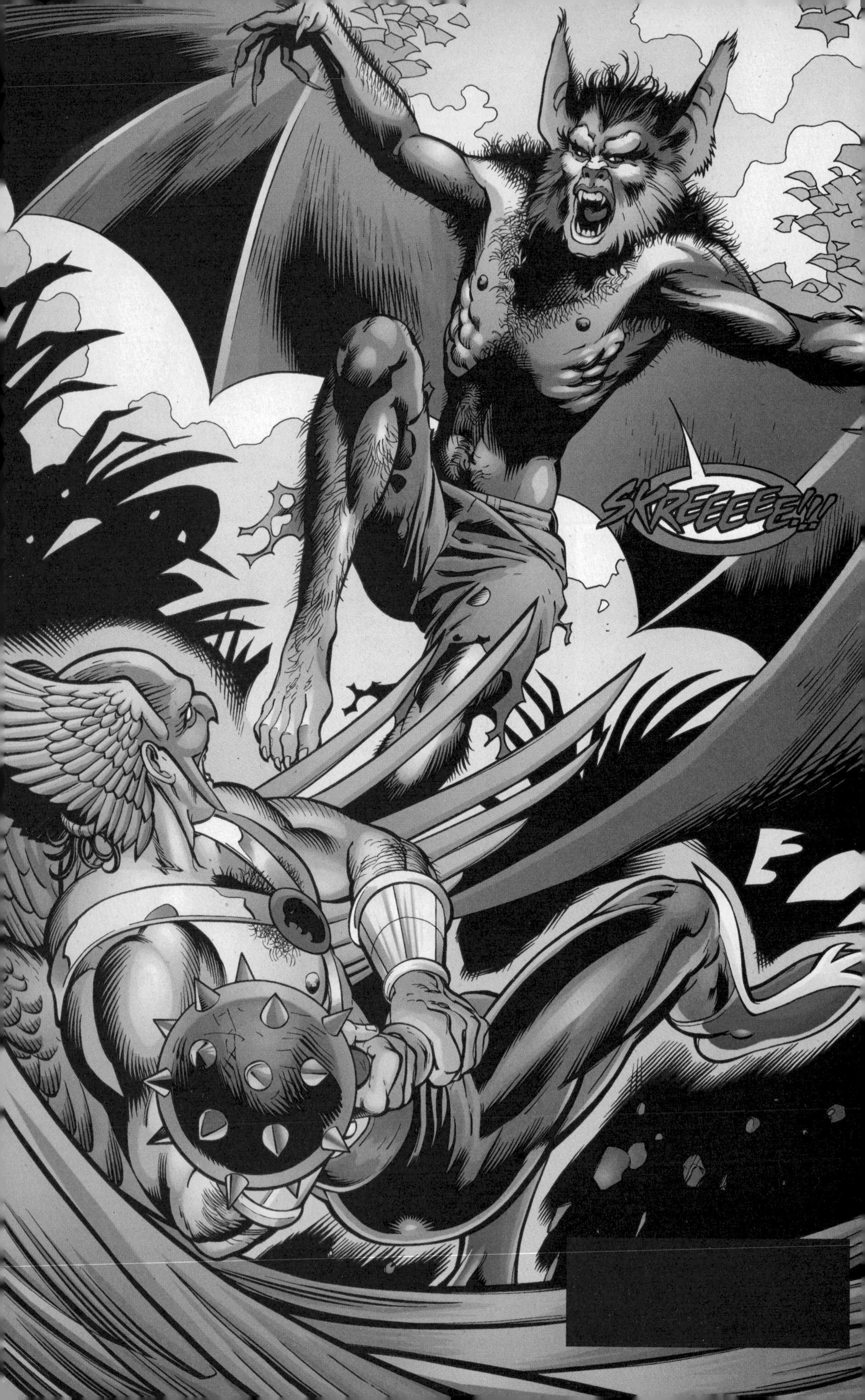
SKREEEEE!!!
[redacted]

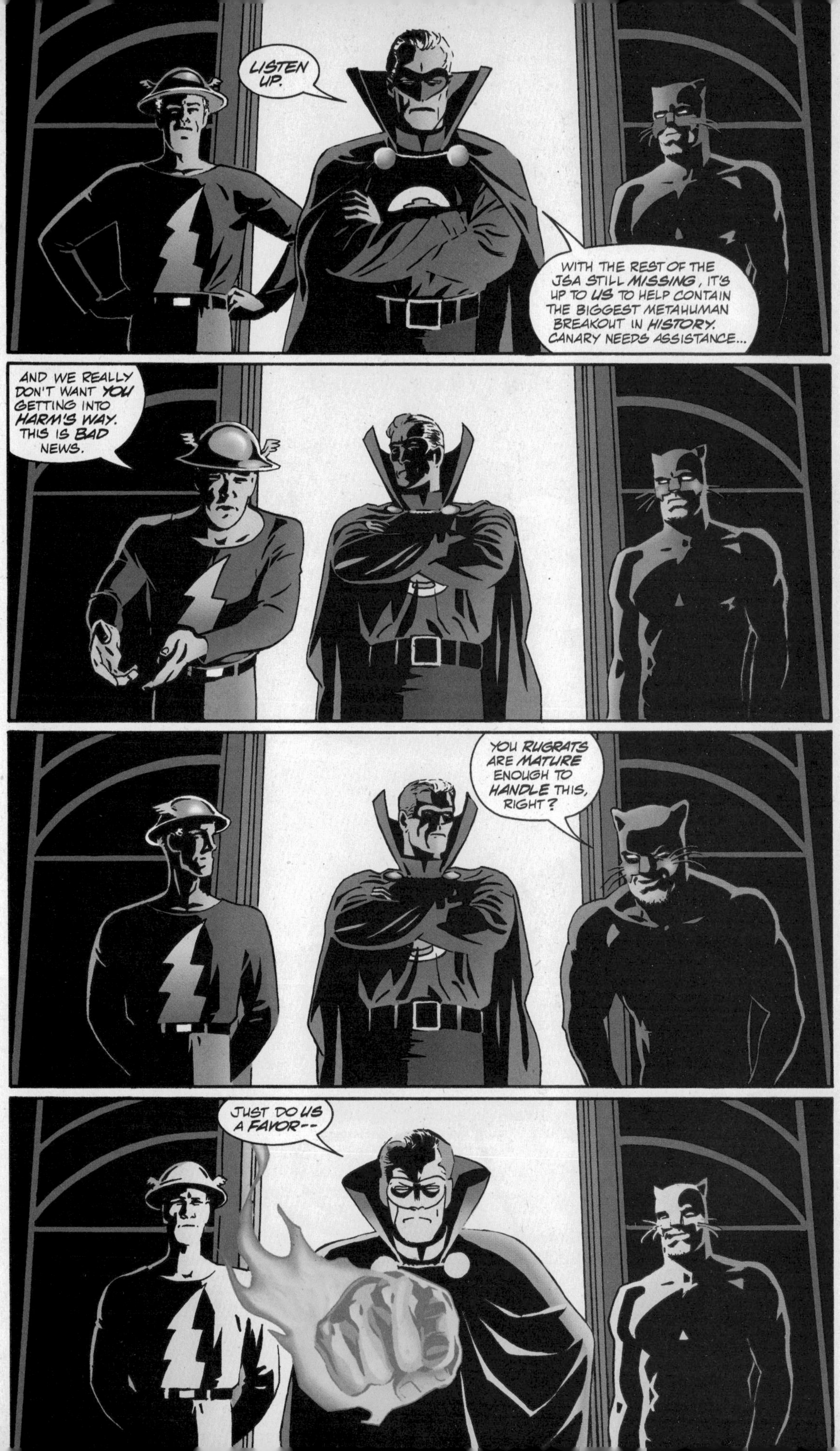
LISTEN UP.
WITH THE REST OF THE JSA STILL MISSING, IT'S UP TO US TO HELP CONTAIN THE BIGGEST METAHUMAN BREAKOUT IN HISTORY. CANARY NEEDS ASSISTANCE...
AND WE REALLY DON'T WANT YOU GETTING INTO HARM'S WAY. THIS IS BAD NEWS.
YOU RUGRATS ARE MATURE ENOUGH TO HANDLE THIS, RIGHT?
JUST DO US A FAVOR--

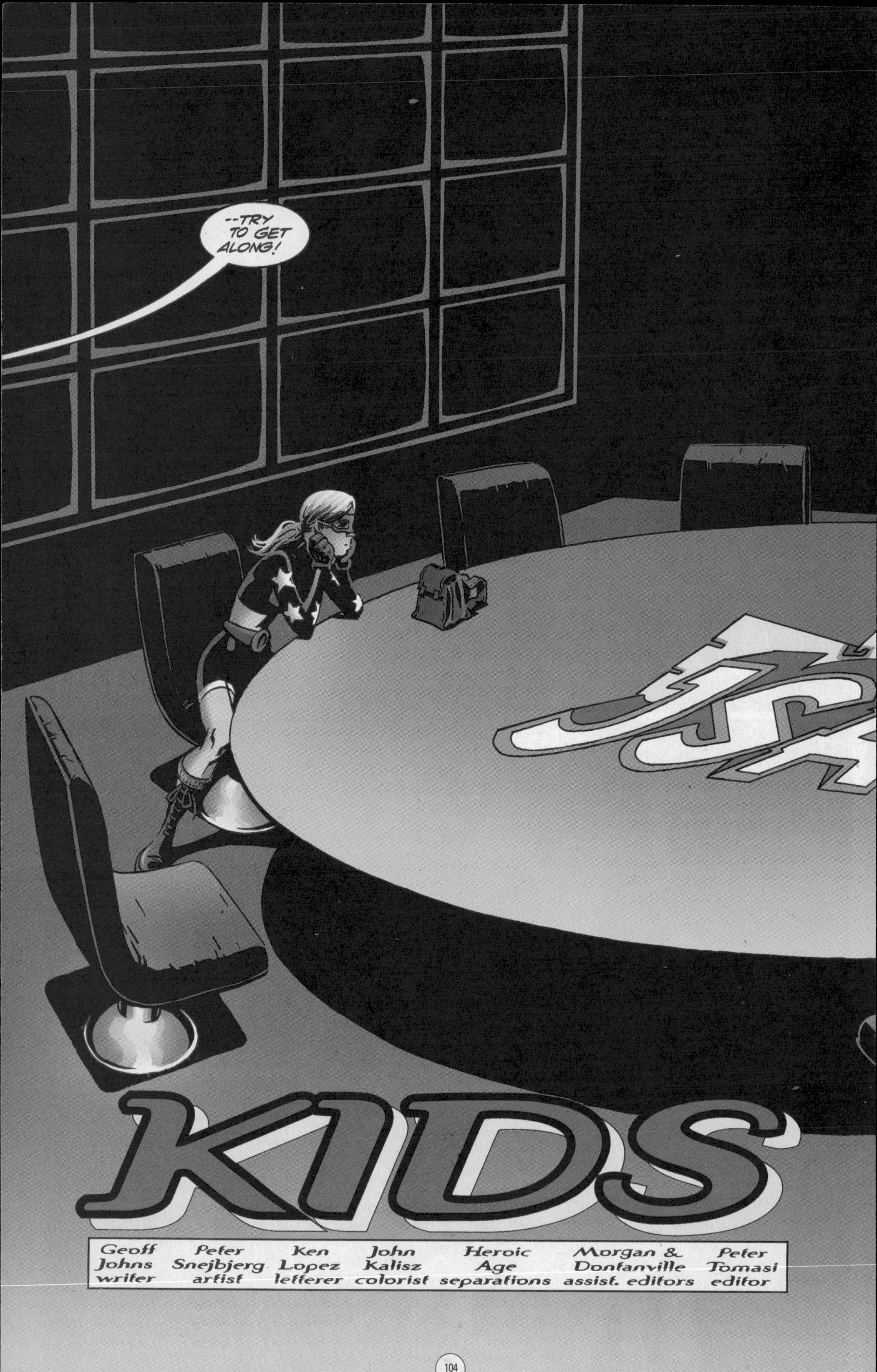
--TRY TO GET ALONG!
KIDS
Geoff Johns writer
Peter Snejbjerg artist
Ken Lopez letterer
John Kalisz colorist
Heroic Age separations
Morgan & Dontanville assist. editors
Peter Tomasi editor

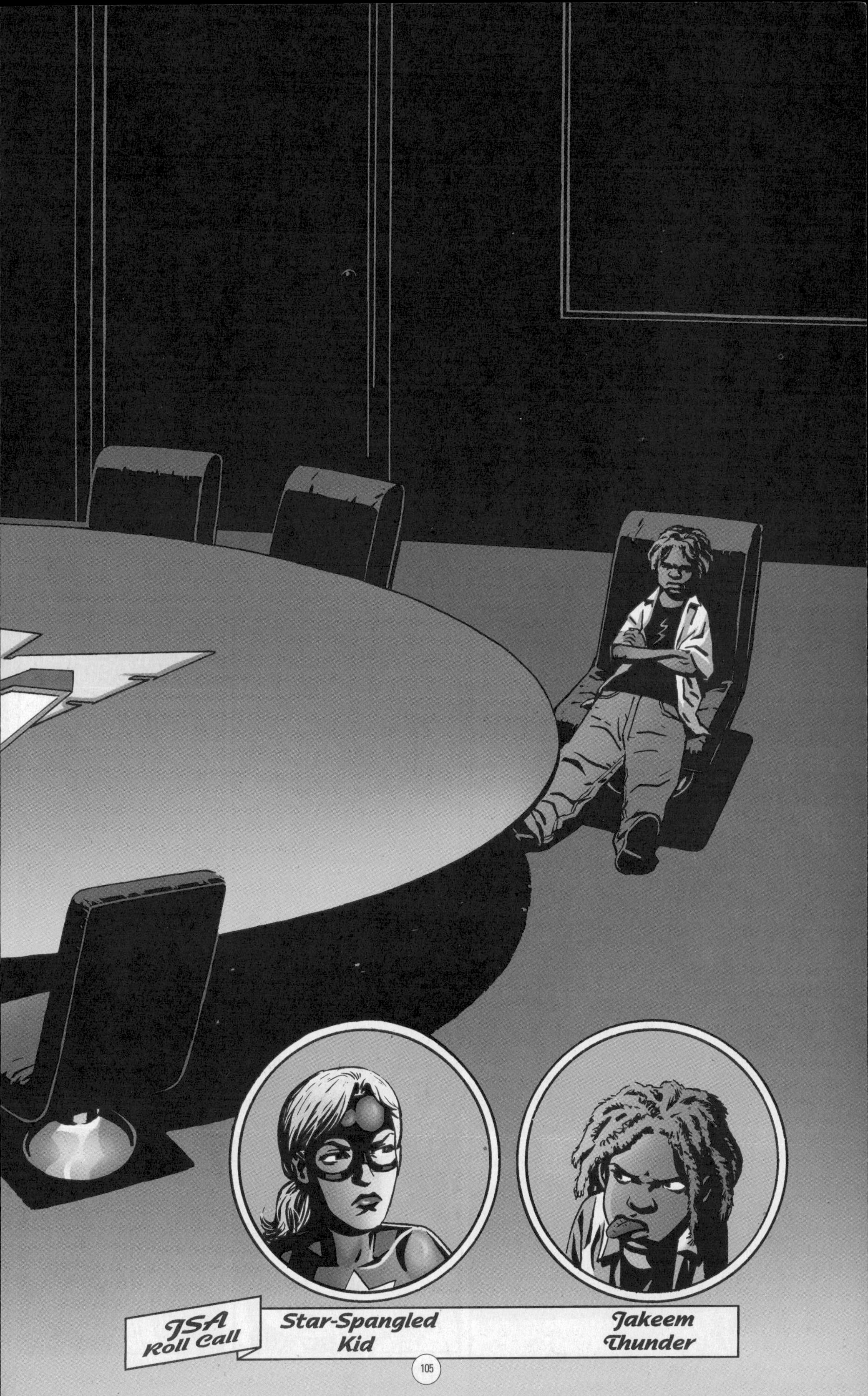
JSA Roll Call
Star-Spangled Kid
Jakeem Thunder

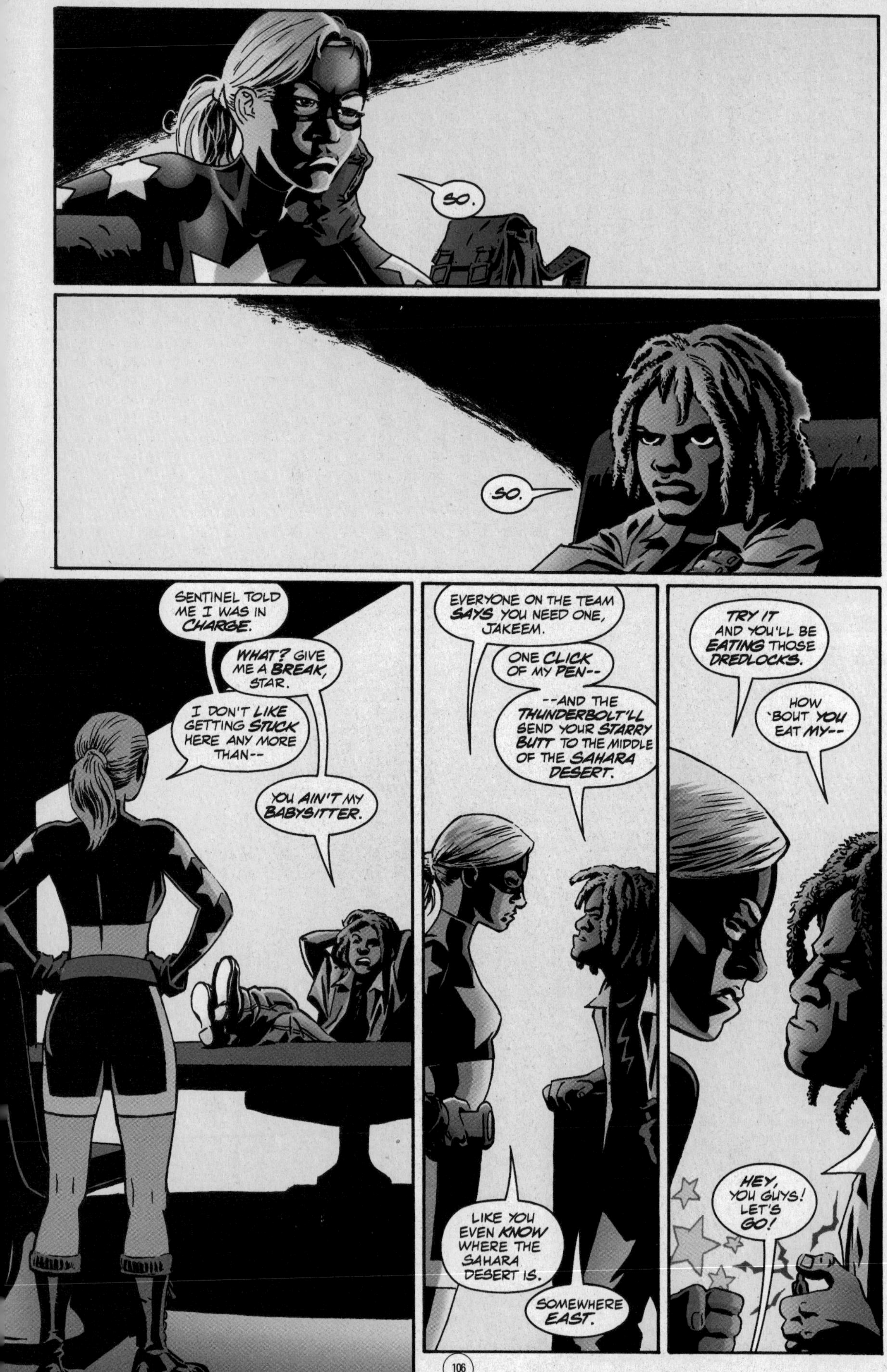

SO.
SO.
SENTINEL TOLD ME I WAS IN CHARGE.
WHAT? GIVE ME A BREAK, STAR.
I DON'T LIKE GETTING STUCK HERE ANY MORE THAN--
YOU AIN'T MY BABYSITTER.
EVERYONE ON THE TEAM SAYS YOU NEED ONE, JAKEEM.
ONE CLICK OF MY PEN--
--AND THE THUNDERBOLT'LL SEND YOUR STARRY BUTT TO THE MIDDLE OF THE SAHARA DESERT.
LIKE YOU EVEN KNOW WHERE THE SAHARA DESERT IS.
SOMEWHERE EAST.
TRY IT AND YOU'LL BE EATING THOSE DREDLOCKS.
HOW 'BOUT YOU EAT MY--
HEY, YOU GUYS! LET'S GO!

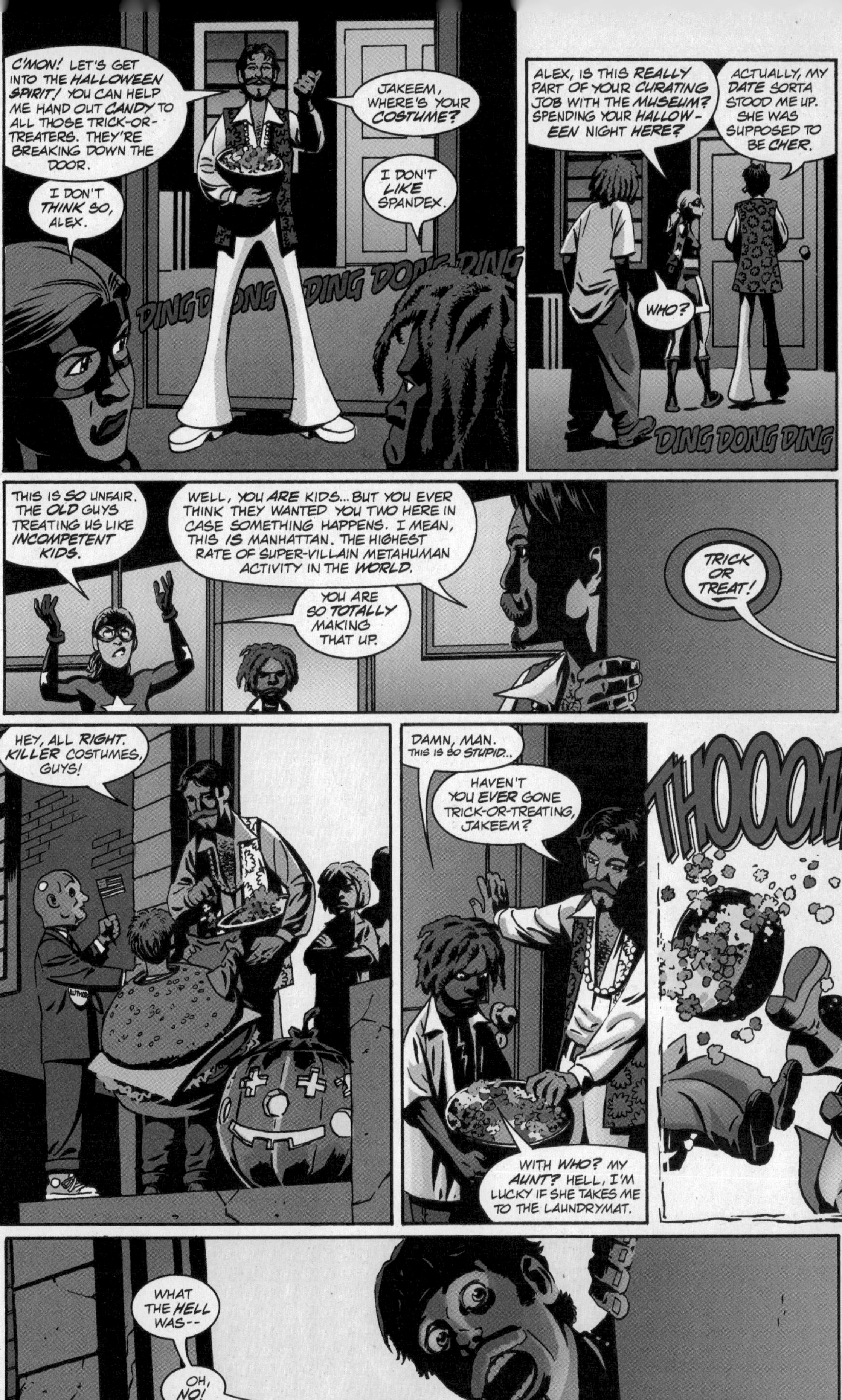
C'MON! LET'S GET INTO THE HALLOWEEN SPIRIT! YOU CAN HELP ME HAND OUT CANDY TO ALL THOSE TRICK-OR-TREATERS. THEY'RE BREAKING DOWN THE DOOR.
I DON'T THINK SO, ALEX.
JAKEEM, WHERE'S YOUR COSTUME?
I DON'T LIKE SPANDEX.
DING DONG DING DONG DING
ALEX, IS THIS REALLY PART OF YOUR CURATING JOB WITH THE MUSEUM? SPENDING YOUR HALLOW-EEN NIGHT HERE?
ACTUALLY, MY DATE SORTA STOOD ME UP. SHE WAS SUPPOSED TO BE CHER.
WHO?
DING DONG DING
THIS IS SO UNFAIR. THE OLD GUYS TREATING US LIKE INCOMPETENT KIDS.
WELL, YOU ARE KIDS... BUT YOU EVER THINK THEY WANTED YOU TWO HERE IN CASE SOMETHING HAPPENS. I MEAN, THIS IS MANHATTAN. THE HIGHEST RATE OF SUPER-VILLAIN METAHUMAN ACTIVITY IN THE WORLD.
YOU ARE SO TOTALLY MAKING THAT UP.
TRICK OR TREAT!
HEY, ALL RIGHT. KILLER COSTUMES, GUYS!
LUTHOR
DAMN, MAN. THIS IS SO STUPID...
HAVEN'T YOU EVER GONE TRICK-OR-TREATING, JAKEEM?
WITH WHO? MY AUNT? HELL, I'M LUCKY IF SHE TAKES ME TO THE LAUNDRYMAT.
THOOOM
WHAT THE HELL WAS--
OH, NO!

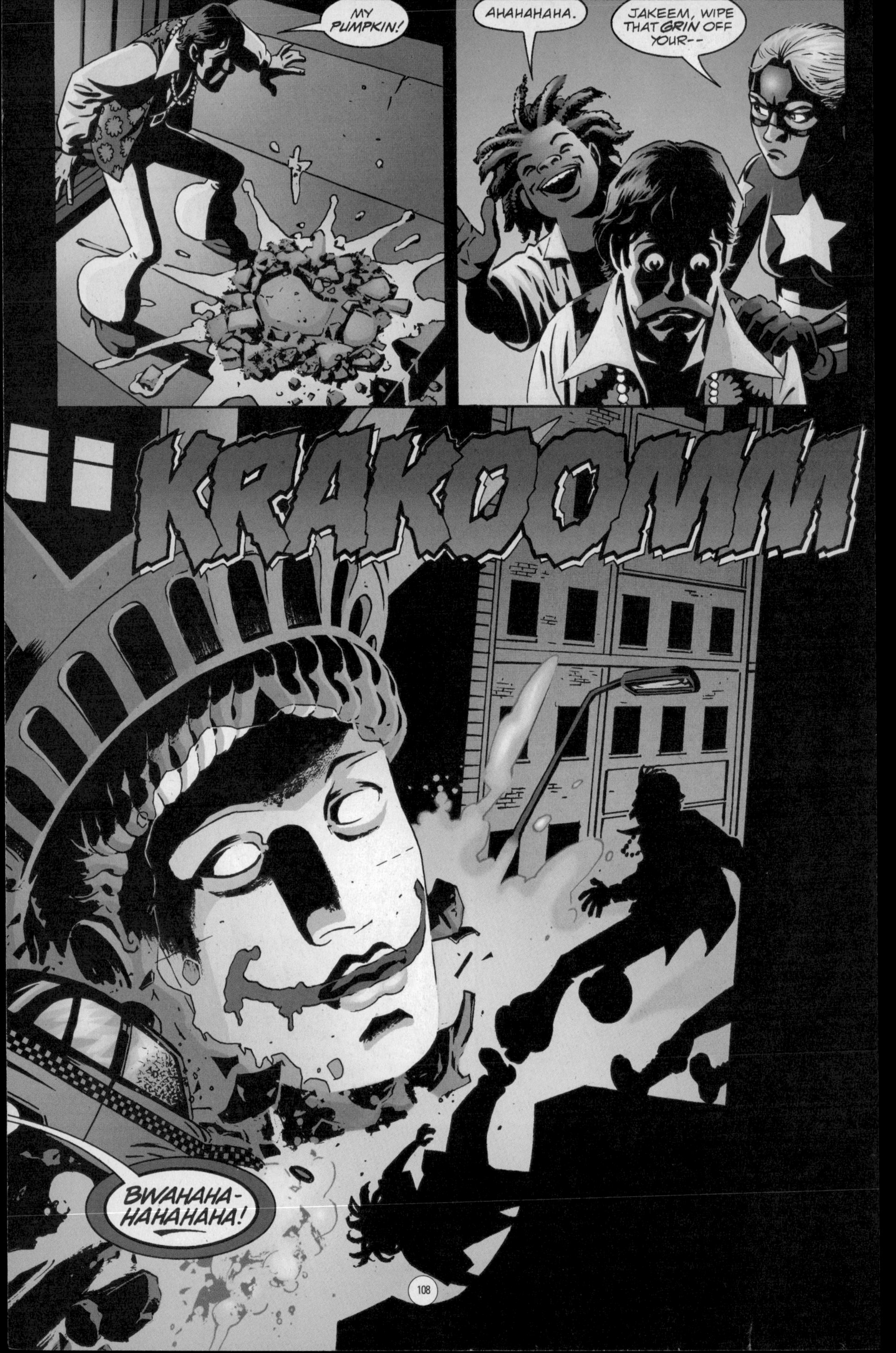
MY PUMPKIN!
AHAHAHAHA.
JAKEEM, WIPE THAT GRIN OFF YOUR--
KRAKOOMM
BWAHAHA-HAHAHAHA!

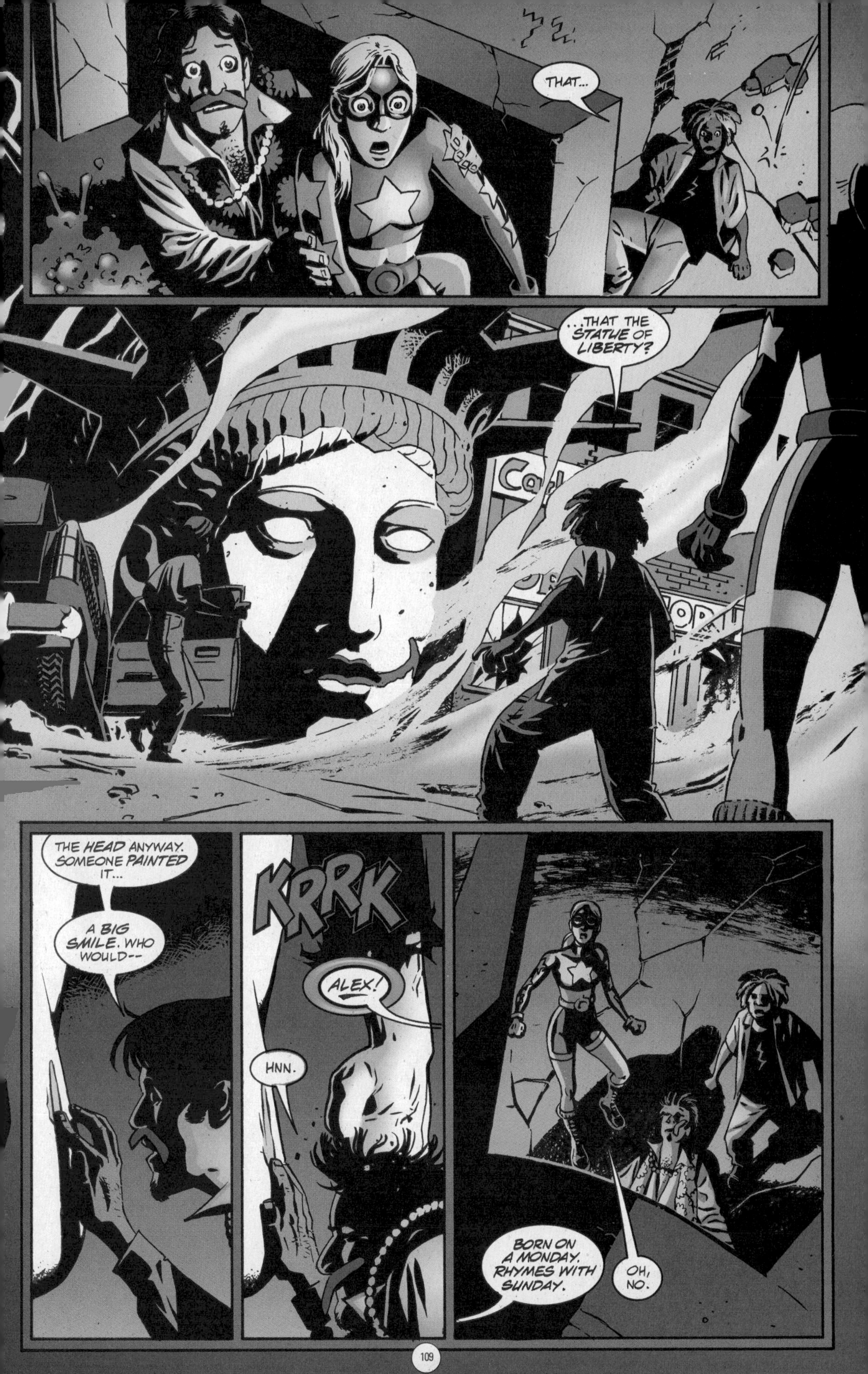
THAT...
...THAT THE STATUE OF LIBERTY?
THE HEAD ANYWAY. SOMEONE PAINTED IT...
A BIG SMILE. WHO WOULD--
KRRK
ALEX!
HNN.
BORN ON A MONDAY. RHYMES WITH SUNDAY.
OH, NO.

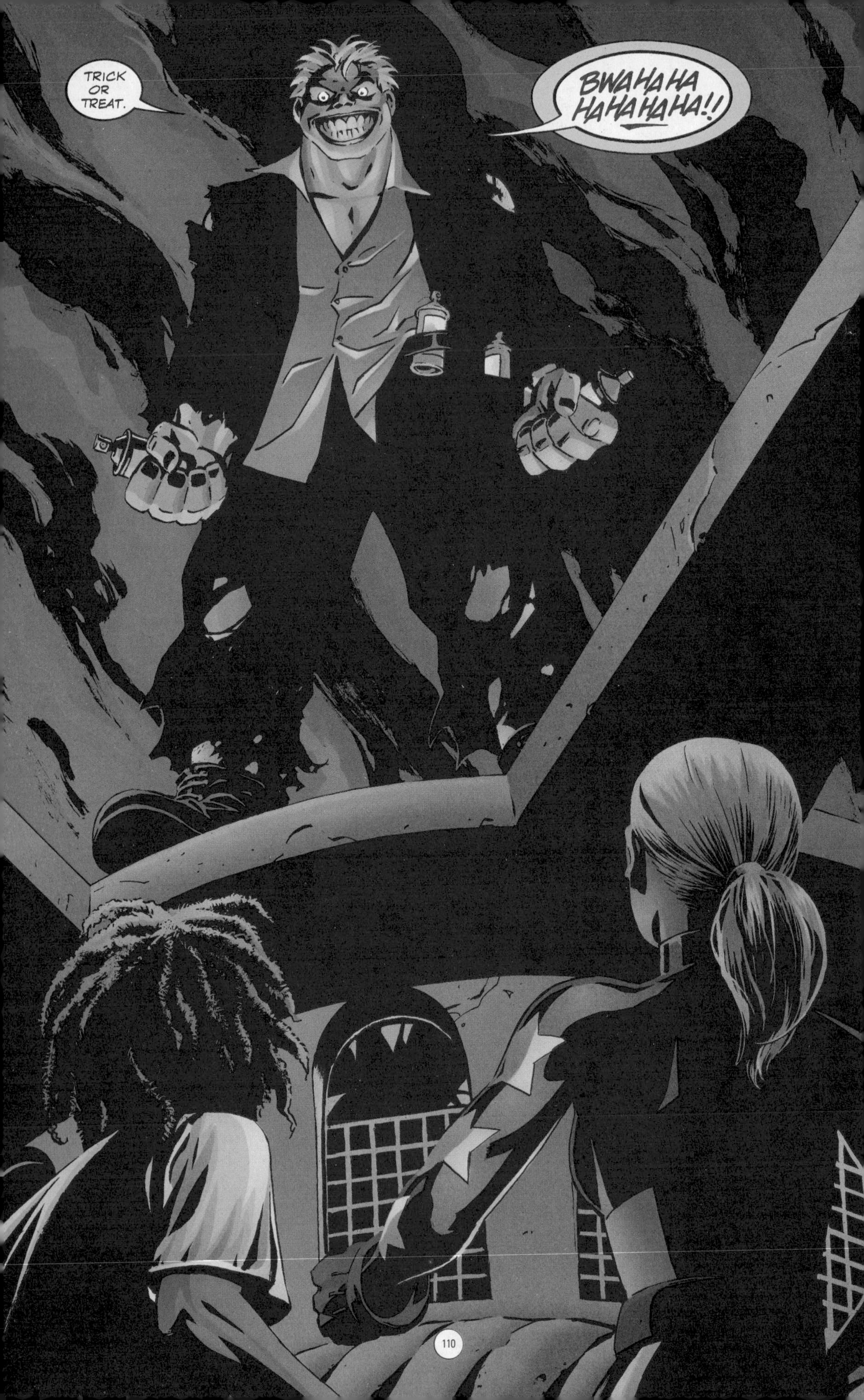
TRICK OR TREAT.
BWAHAHA HAHAHAHA!!

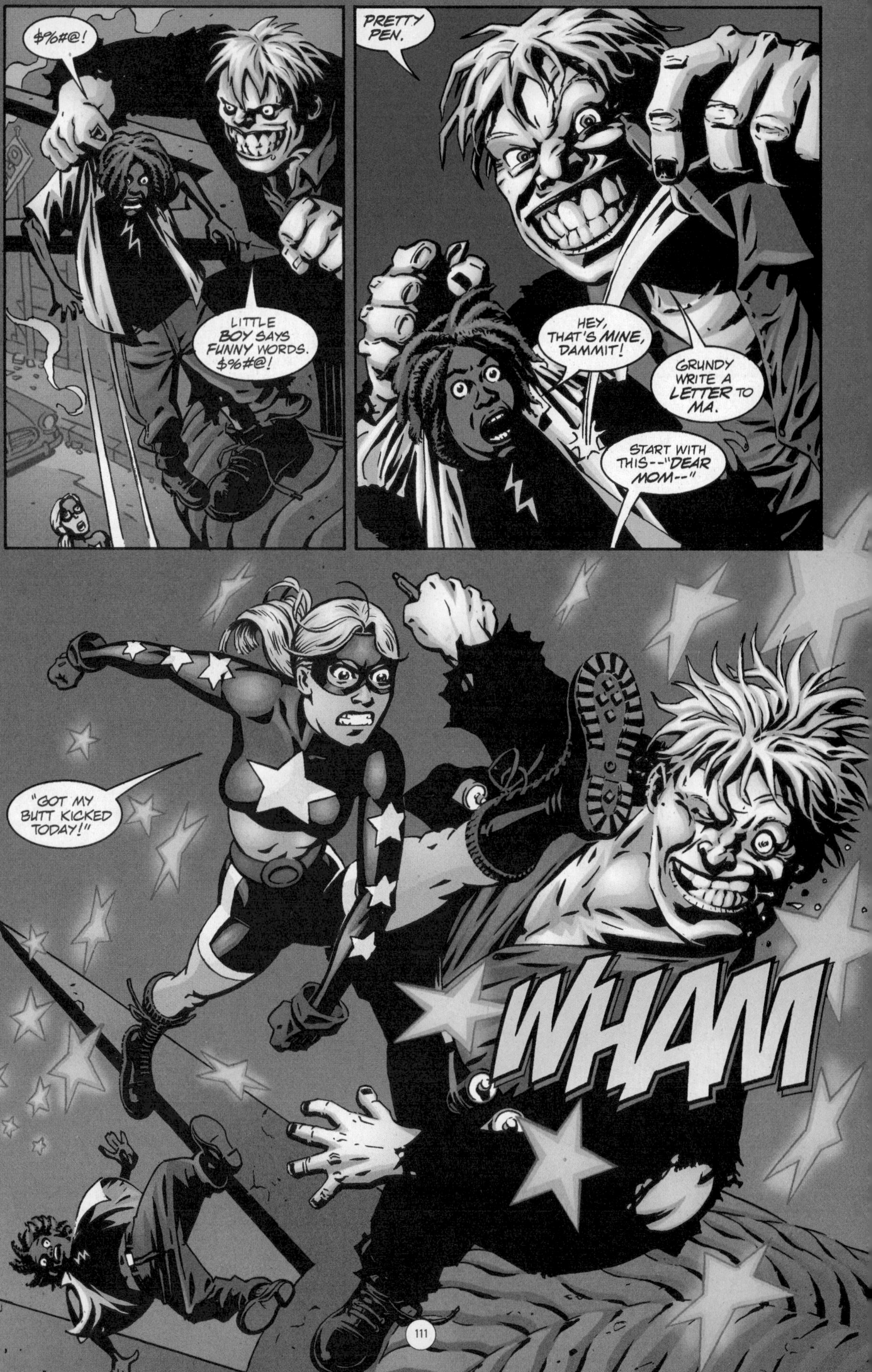
$%#@!
LITTLE BOY SAYS FUNNY WORDS. $%#@!
PRETTY PEN.
HEY, THAT'S MINE, DAMMIT!
GRUNDY WRITE A LETTER TO MA.
START WITH THIS--"DEAR MOM--"
"GOT MY BUTT KICKED TODAY!"
WHAM

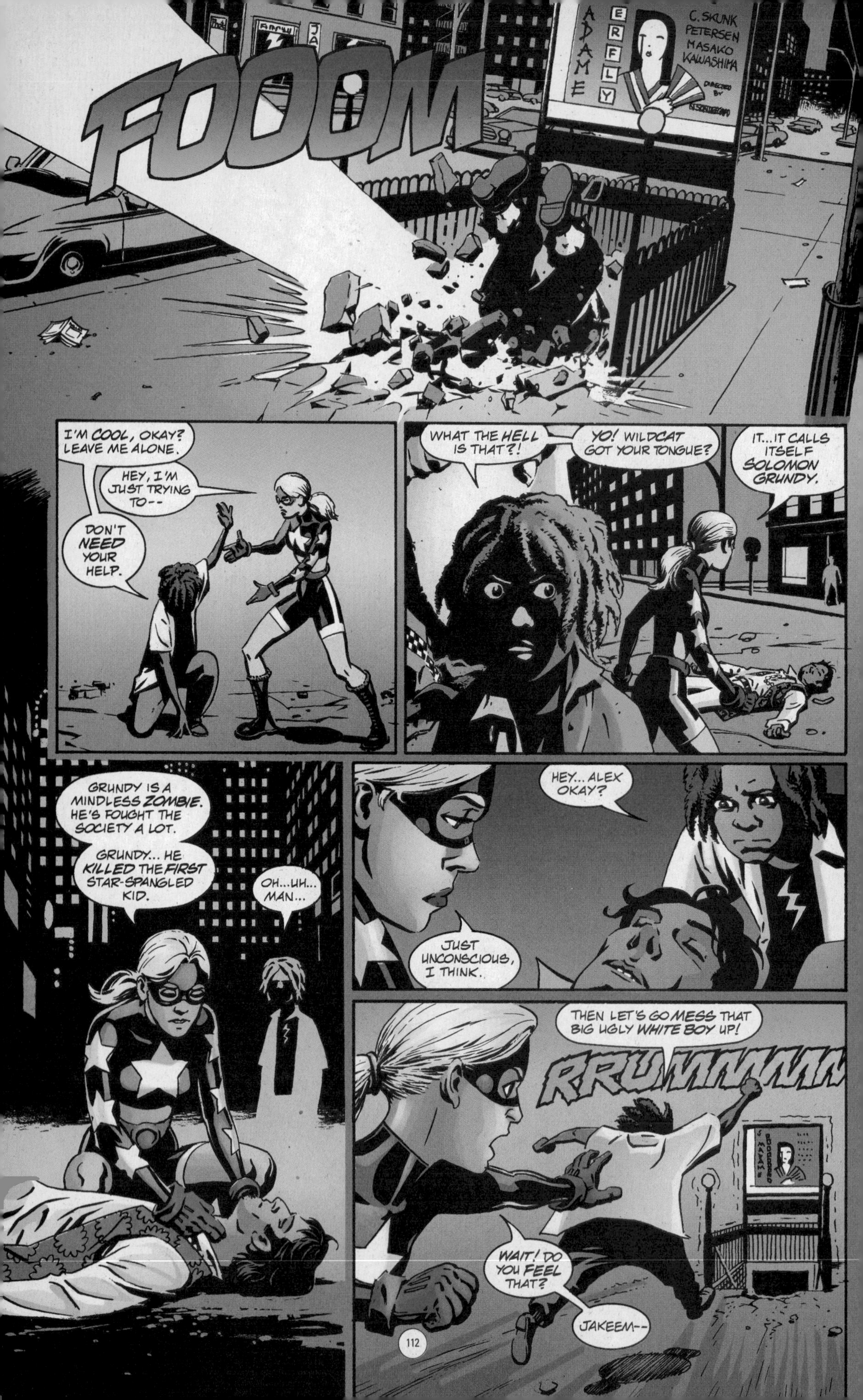

FOOOM
C. SKUNK
PETERSEN
MASAKO
KAWASHIMA
DIRECTED BY
I'M COOL, OKAY? LEAVE ME ALONE.
HEY, I'M JUST TRYING TO--
DON'T NEED YOUR HELP.
WHAT THE HELL IS THAT?!
YO! WILDCAT GOT YOUR TONGUE?
IT...IT CALLS ITSELF SOLOMON GRUNDY.
GRUNDY IS A MINDLESS ZOMBIE. HE'S FOUGHT THE SOCIETY A LOT.
GRUNDY... HE KILLED THE FIRST STAR-SPANGLED KID.
OH...UH... MAN...
HEY... ALEX OKAY?
JUST UNCONSCIOUS, I THINK.
THEN LET'S GO MESS THAT BIG UGLY WHITE BOY UP!
RRUMMMMM
WAIT! DO YOU FEEL THAT?
JAKEEM--

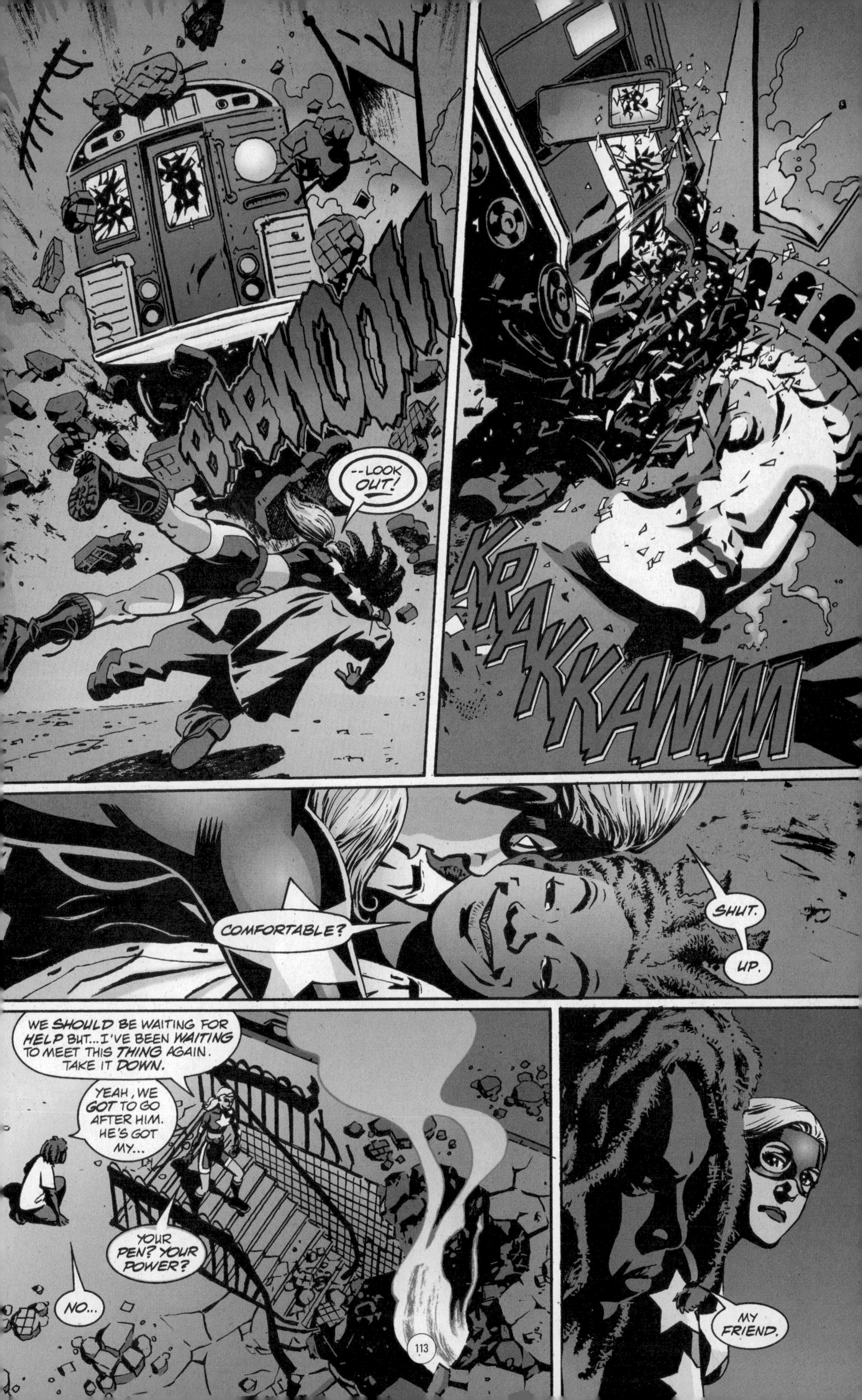
BABWOOM
--LOOK OUT!
KRAKKAMM
COMFORTABLE?
SHUT.
UP.
WE SHOULD BE WAITING FOR HELP BUT... I'VE BEEN WAITING TO MEET THIS THING AGAIN. TAKE IT DOWN.
YEAH, WE GOT TO GO AFTER HIM. HE'S GOT MY...
YOUR PEN? YOUR POWER?
NO...
MY FRIEND.

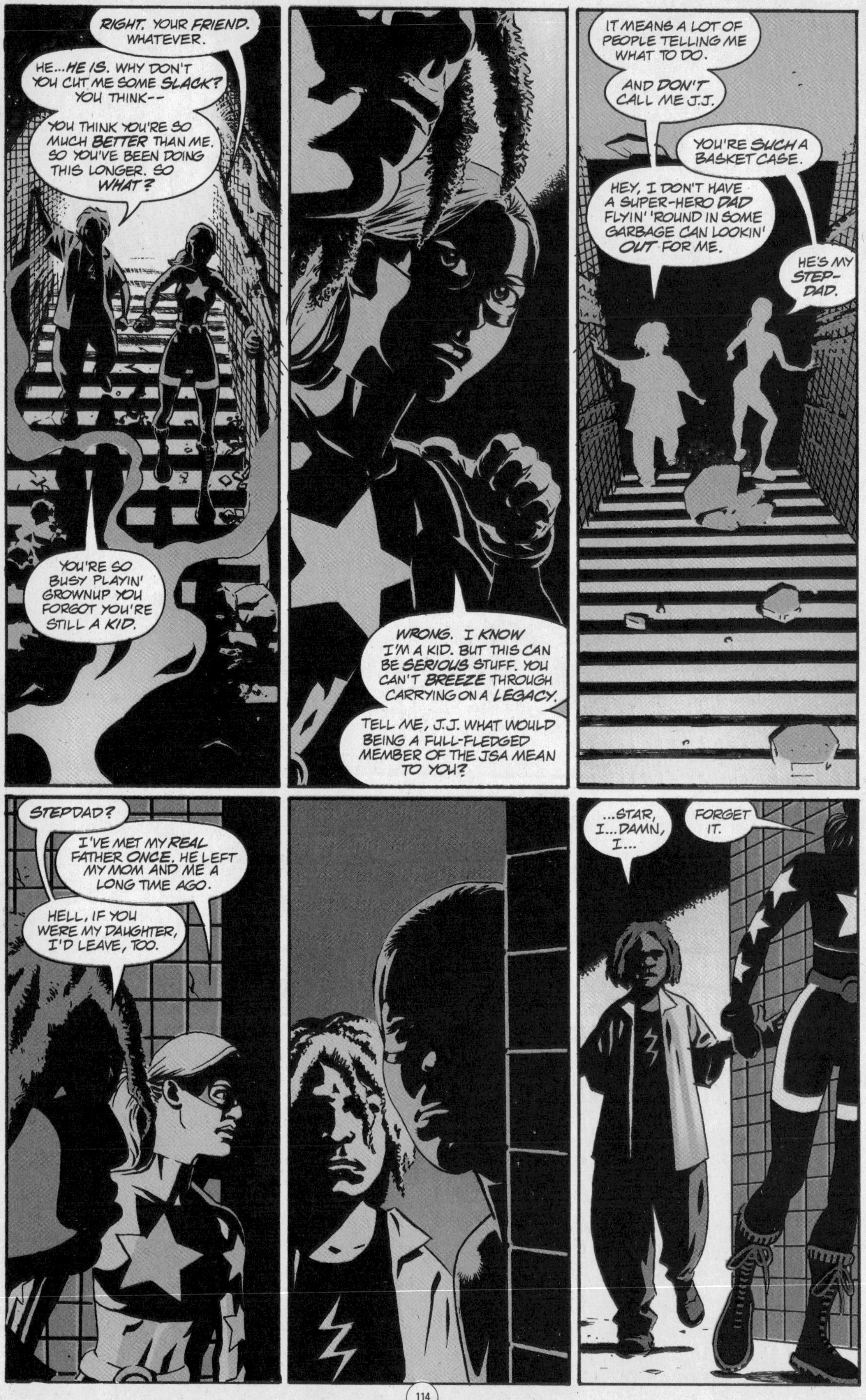
RIGHT. YOUR FRIEND. WHATEVER.
HE...HE IS. WHY DON'T YOU CUT ME SOME SLACK? YOU THINK--
YOU THINK YOU'RE SO MUCH BETTER THAN ME. SO YOU'VE BEEN DOING THIS LONGER. SO WHAT?
YOU'RE SO BUSY PLAYIN' GROWNUP YOU FORGOT YOU'RE STILL A KID.
WRONG. I KNOW I'M A KID. BUT THIS CAN BE SERIOUS STUFF. YOU CAN'T BREEZE THROUGH CARRYING ON A LEGACY.
TELL ME, J.J. WHAT WOULD BEING A FULL-FLEDGED MEMBER OF THE JSA MEAN TO YOU?
IT MEANS A LOT OF PEOPLE TELLING ME WHAT TO DO.
AND DON'T CALL ME J.J.
YOU'RE SUCH A BASKET CASE.
HEY, I DON'T HAVE A SUPER-HERO DAD FLYIN' 'ROUND IN SOME GARBAGE CAN LOOKIN' OUT FOR ME.
HE'S MY STEP-DAD.
STEPDAD?
I'VE MET MY REAL FATHER ONCE. HE LEFT MY MOM AND ME A LONG TIME AGO.
HELL, IF YOU WERE MY DAUGHTER, I'D LEAVE, TOO.
...STAR, I...DAMN, I...
FORGET IT.

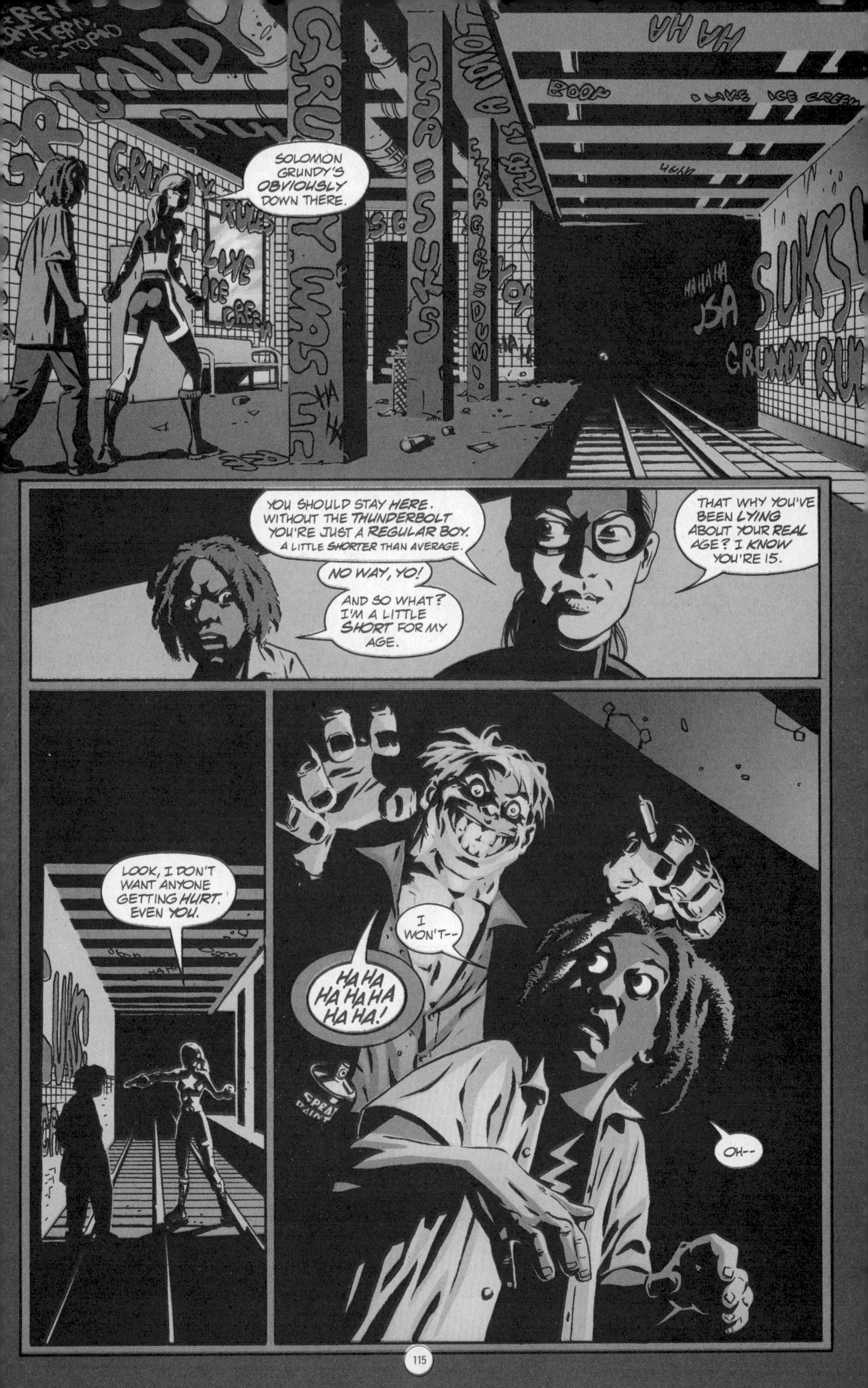
SOLOMON GRUNDY'S OBVIOUSLY DOWN THERE.
YOU SHOULD STAY HERE. WITHOUT THE THUNDERBOLT YOU'RE JUST A REGULAR BOY. A LITTLE SHORTER THAN AVERAGE.
NO WAY, YO!
AND SO WHAT? I'M A LITTLE SHORT FOR MY AGE.
THAT WHY YOU'VE BEEN LYING ABOUT YOUR REAL AGE? I KNOW YOU'RE 15.
LOOK, I DON'T WANT ANYONE GETTING HURT. EVEN YOU.
I WON'T--
HA HA HA HA HA HA HA!
OH--

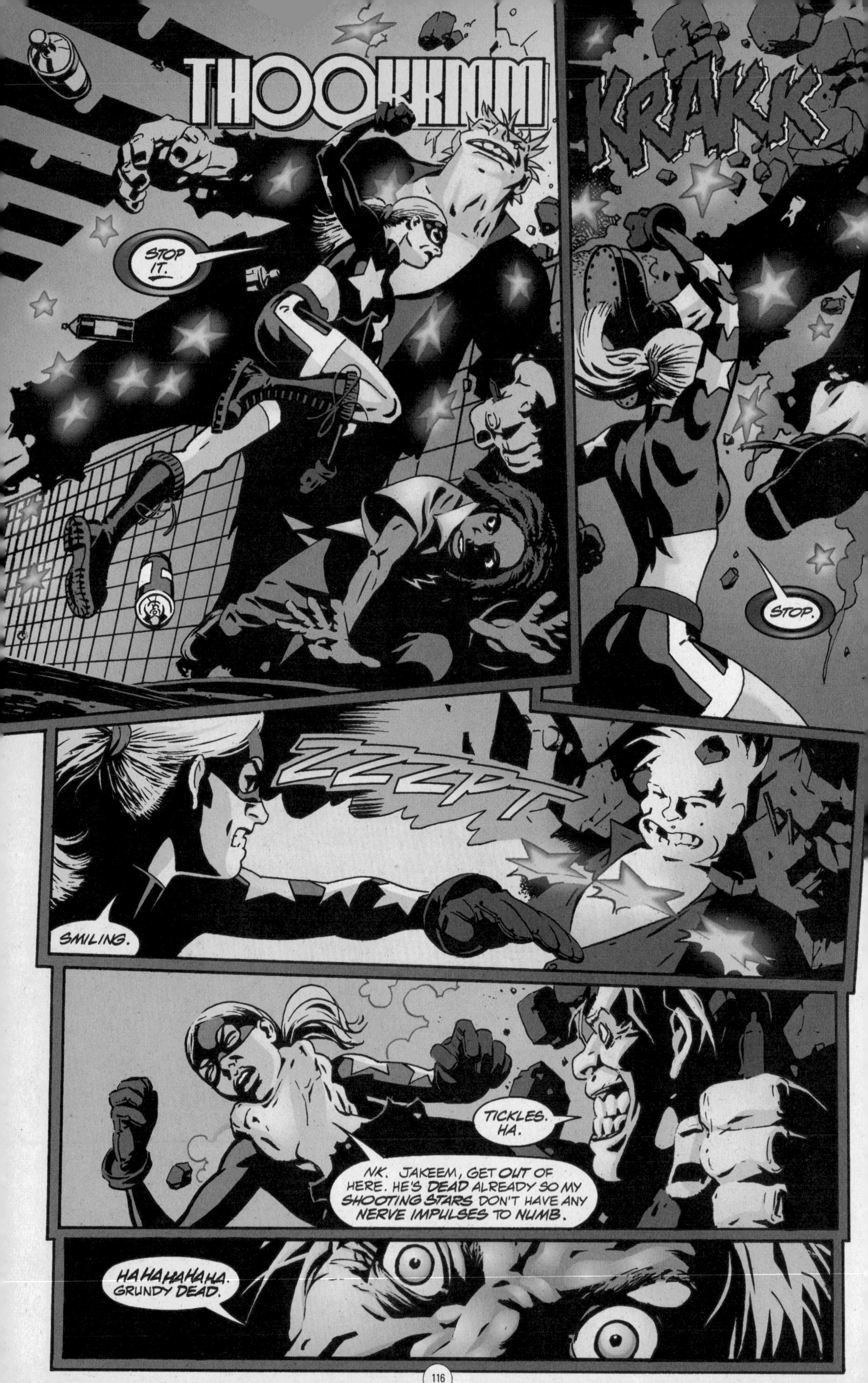
THOOKKMM
STOP IT.
KRAKKS
STOP.
ZZZPT
SMILING.
TICKLES. HA.
NK. JAKEEM, GET OUT OF HERE. HE'S DEAD ALREADY SO MY SHOOTING STARS DON'T HAVE ANY NERVE IMPULSES TO NUMB.
HA HA HA HA HA HA. GRUNDY DEAD.

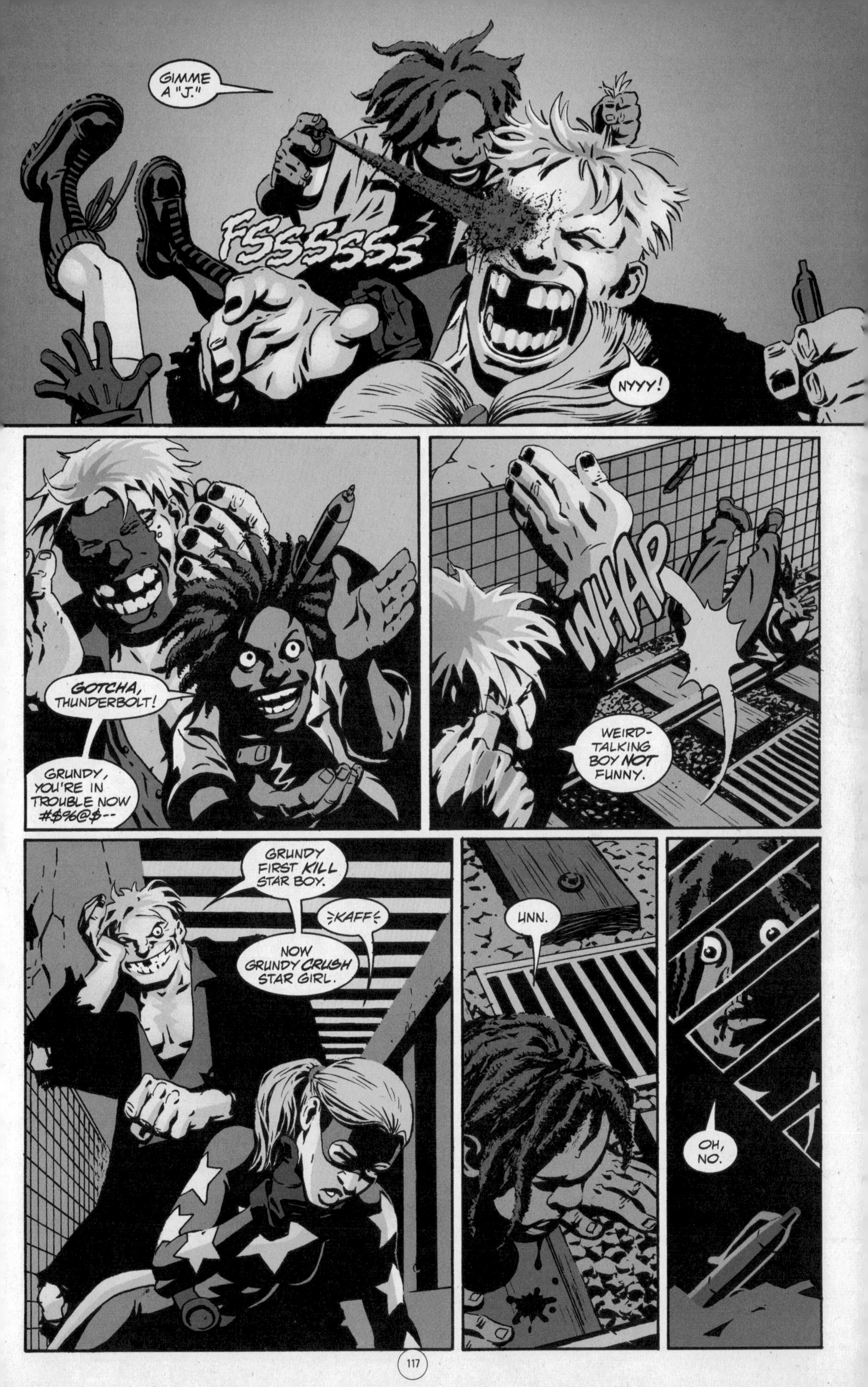

GIMME A "J."
FSSSSSSS
NYYY!
GOTCHA, THUNDERBOLT!
GRUNDY, YOU'RE IN TROUBLE NOW #$%@$--
WHAP
WEIRD-TALKING BOY NOT FUNNY.
GRUNDY FIRST KILL STAR BOY.
NOW GRUNDY CRUSH STAR GIRL.
KAFF
UNN.
OH, NO.

NNN. LET. GO.

ME TELL YOU *SECRET,* STAR GIRL. EVERYONE THINK GRUNDY NOT MEAN TO KILL STAR BOY. THAT GRUNDY *TRICKED* INTO BEING BAD BY GREEN GIRL.

BIG *LIE.*

GRUNDY KNOW *EXACTLY* WHAT ME DO.

GRUNDY *BAD.*

K-KILL YOU...

OKAY. BE LIKE GRUNDY.

STAR GIRL BE *DEAD!* HAHAHAHA!

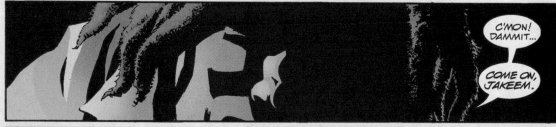

C'MON! DAMMIT...

COME ON, JAKEEM.

YOU CAN REACH IT.

WHOA!

KZZZTT

HOW'D I DO THAT?

KLIK

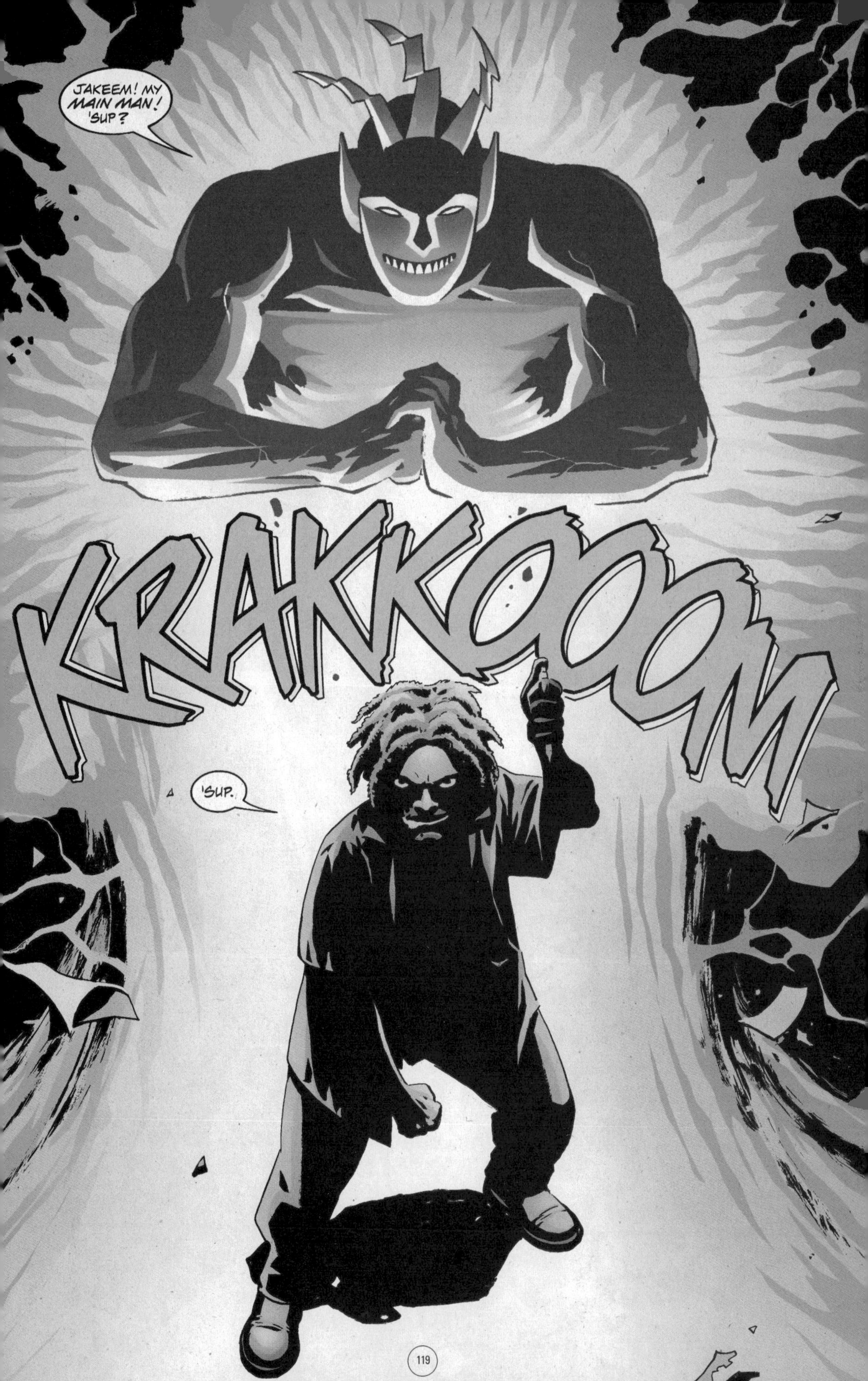
JAKEEM! MY MAIN MAN! 'SUP?
KRAKKOOOM
'SUP.

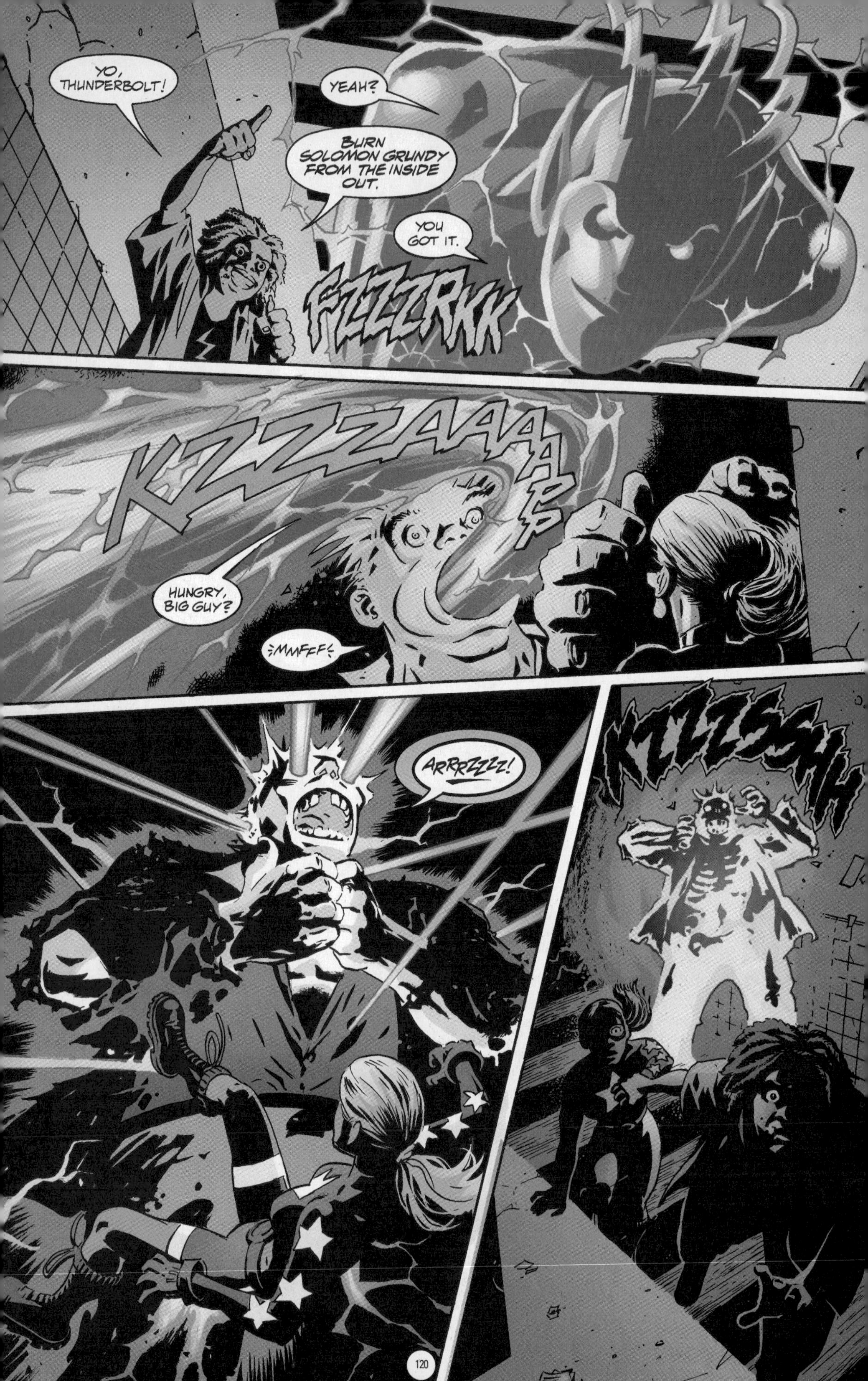
YO, THUNDERBOLT!
YEAH?
BURN SOLOMON GRUNDY FROM THE INSIDE OUT.
YOU GOT IT.
FZZZRKK
KZZZAAAARB
HUNGRY, BIG GUY?
MMFFF
ARRRZZZZ!
KZZZSSHH

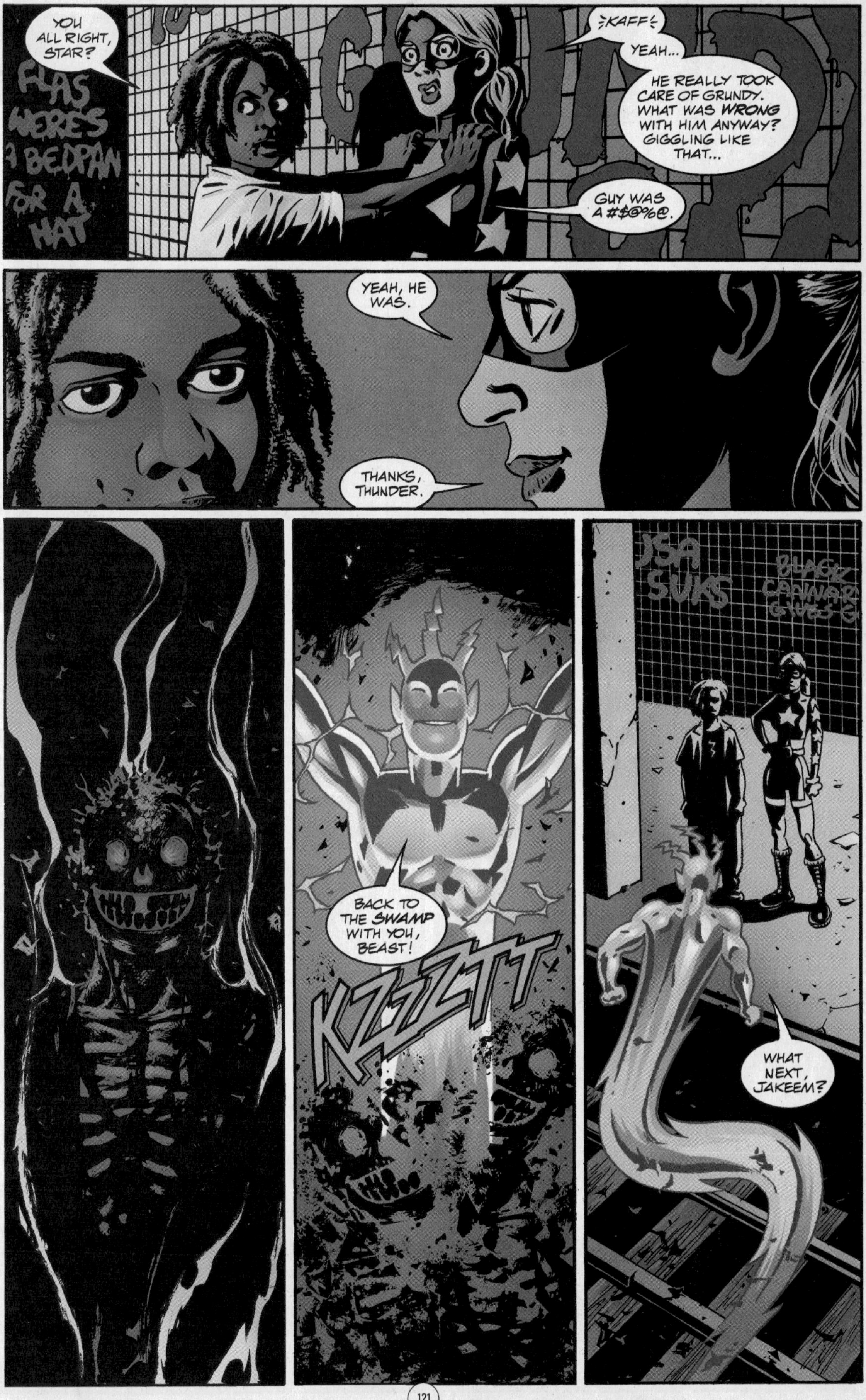
YOU ALL RIGHT, STAR?
FLAS WERE'S A BEDPAN FOR A HAT
KAFF
YEAH...
HE REALLY TOOK CARE OF GRUNDY. WHAT WAS WRONG WITH HIM ANYWAY? GIGGLING LIKE THAT...
GUY WAS A #$@%@.
YEAH, HE WAS.
THANKS, THUNDER.
BACK TO THE SWAMP WITH YOU, BEAST!
KZZZTT
JSA SUKS
WHAT NEXT, JAKEEM?

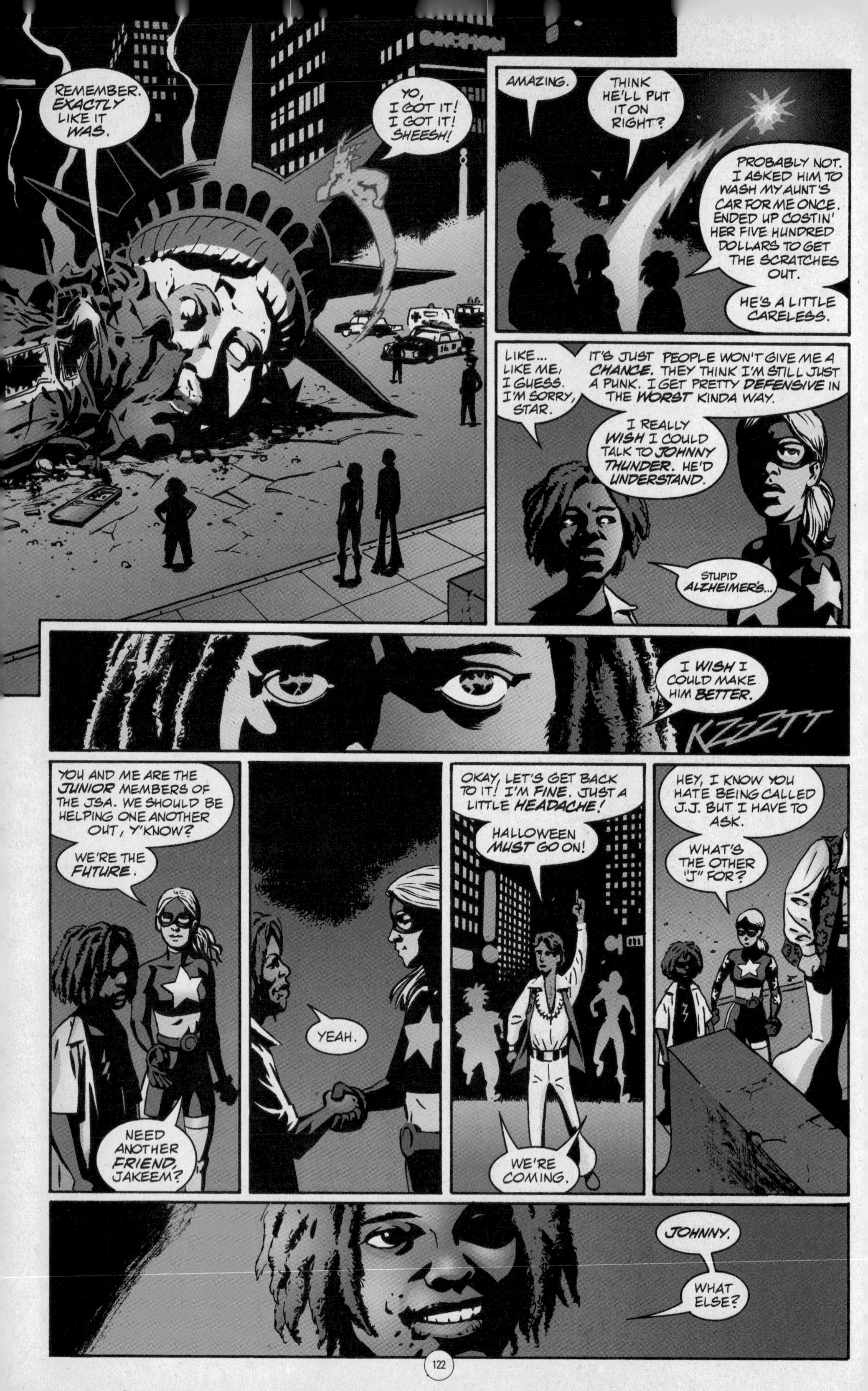

REMEMBER. EXACTLY LIKE IT WAS.
YO, I GOT IT! I GOT IT! SHEESH!
AMAZING.
THINK HE'LL PUT IT ON RIGHT?
PROBABLY NOT. I ASKED HIM TO WASH MY AUNT'S CAR FOR ME ONCE. ENDED UP COSTIN' HER FIVE HUNDRED DOLLARS TO GET THE SCRATCHES OUT.
HE'S A LITTLE CARELESS.
LIKE... LIKE ME, I GUESS. I'M SORRY, STAR.
IT'S JUST PEOPLE WON'T GIVE ME A CHANCE. THEY THINK I'M STILL JUST A PUNK. I GET PRETTY DEFENSIVE IN THE WORST KINDA WAY.
I REALLY WISH I COULD TALK TO JOHNNY THUNDER. HE'D UNDERSTAND.
STUPID ALZHEIMER'S...
I WISH I COULD MAKE HIM BETTER.
KZZZTT
YOU AND ME ARE THE JUNIOR MEMBERS OF THE JSA. WE SHOULD BE HELPING ONE ANOTHER OUT, Y'KNOW?
WE'RE THE FUTURE.
NEED ANOTHER FRIEND, JAKEEM?
YEAH.
OKAY, LET'S GET BACK TO IT! I'M FINE. JUST A LITTLE HEADACHE!
HALLOWEEN MUST GO ON!
WE'RE COMING.
HEY, I KNOW YOU HATE BEING CALLED J.J. BUT I HAVE TO ASK.
WHAT'S THE OTHER "J" FOR?
JOHNNY.
WHAT ELSE?

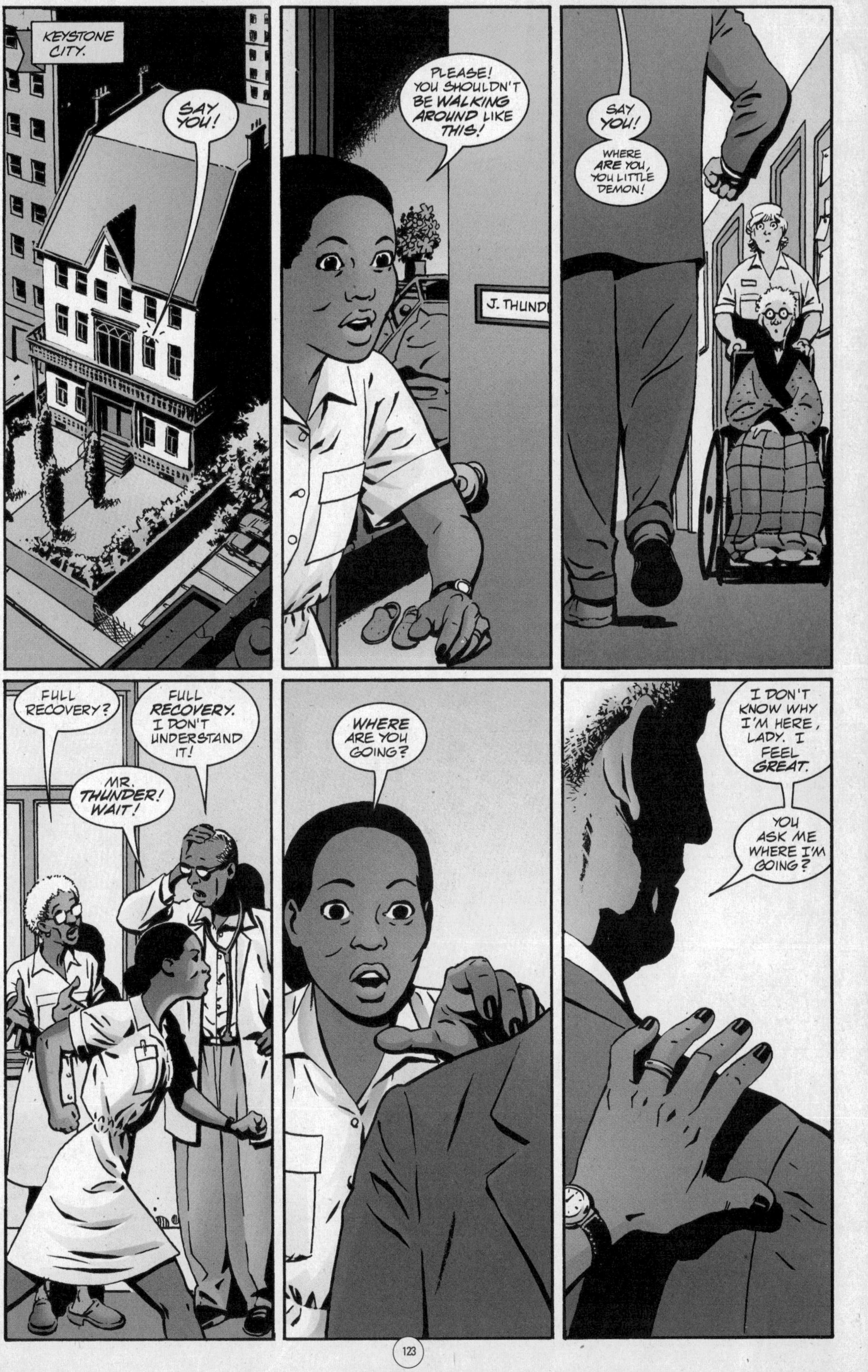
KEYSTONE CITY.
SAY YOU!
PLEASE! YOU SHOULDN'T BE WALKING AROUND LIKE THIS!
J. THUND
SAY YOU!
WHERE ARE YOU, YOU LITTLE DEMON!
FULL RECOVERY?
FULL RECOVERY. I DON'T UNDERSTAND IT!
MR. THUNDER! WAIT!
WHERE ARE YOU GOING?
I DON'T KNOW WHY I'M HERE, LADY. I FEEL GREAT.
YOU ASK ME WHERE I'M GOING?

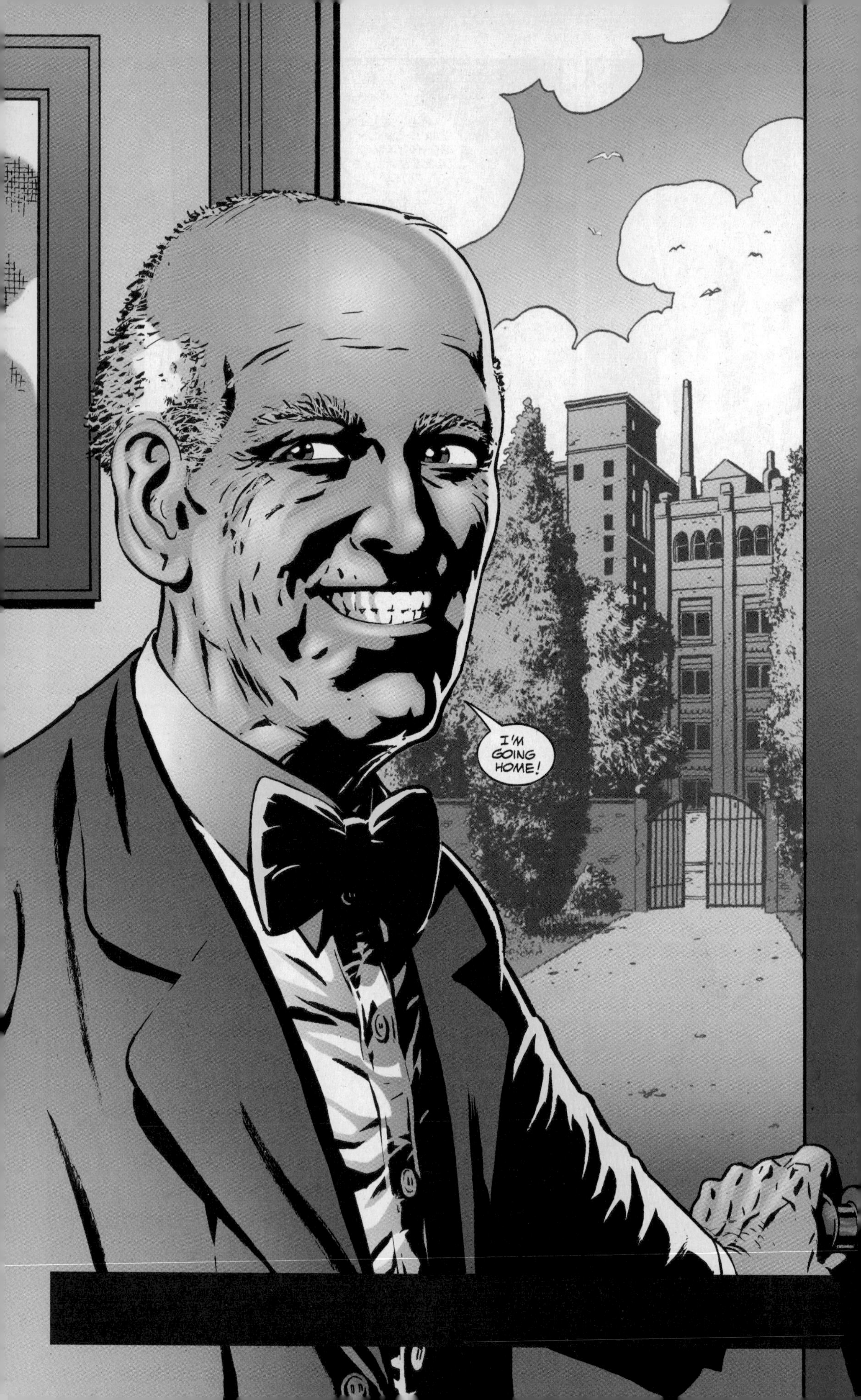
I'M GOING HOME!

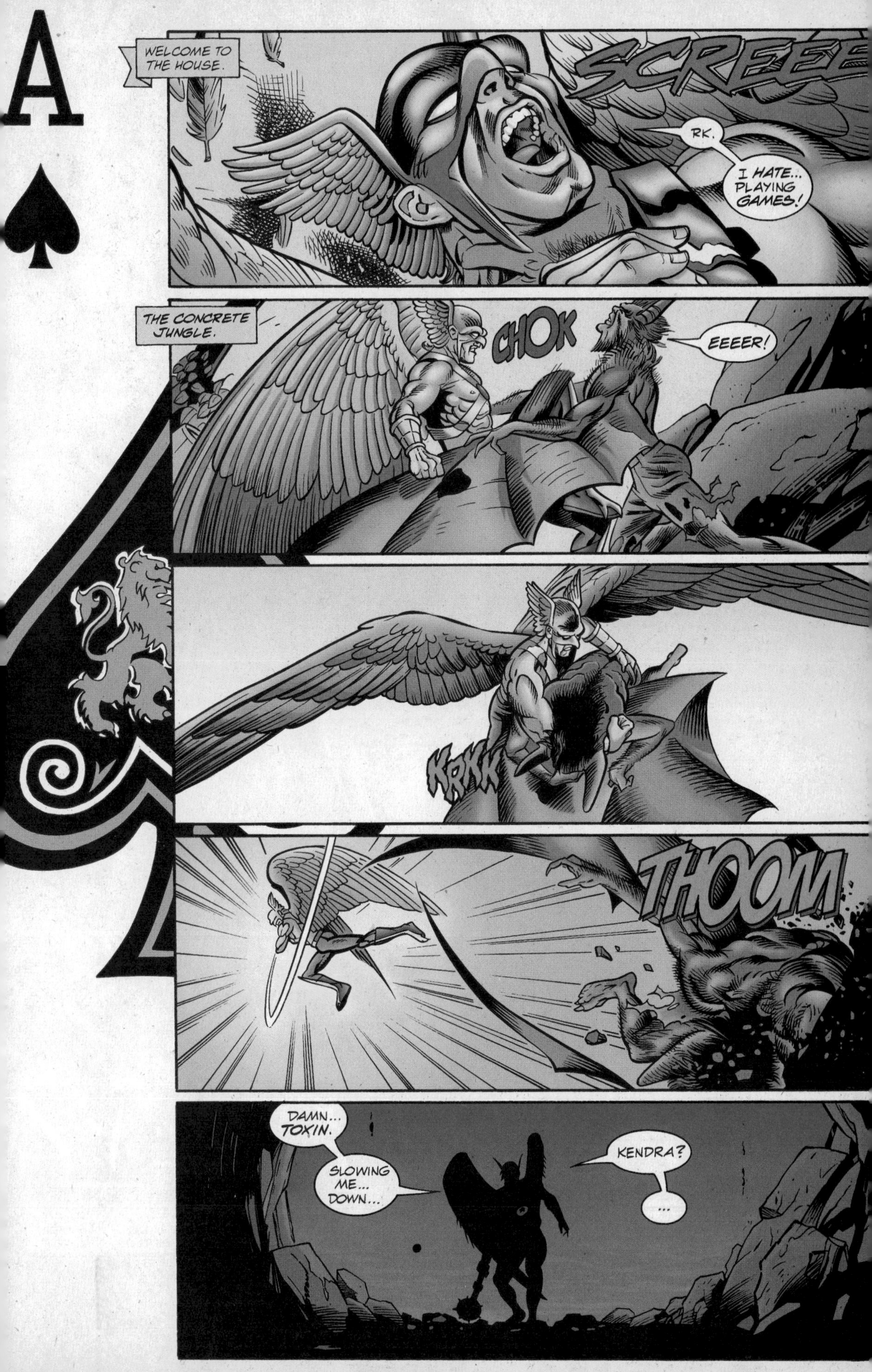
WELCOME TO THE HOUSE.
SCREEE
RK.
I HATE... PLAYING GAMES!
THE CONCRETE JUNGLE.
CHOK
EEEER!
KRKK
THOOM
DAMN... TOXIN.
SLOWING ME... DOWN...
KENDRA?
...

LET THE GAMES BEGIN Part 2: FAIR PLAY

GEOFF JOHNS	STEPHEN SADOWSKI	KEITH CHAMPAGNE	KEN LOPEZ	JOHN KALISZ	HEROIC AGE	MORGAN DONTANVILLE	PETER TOMASI
writer	penciller	inker	letterer	colorist	separator	assistant editor	editor

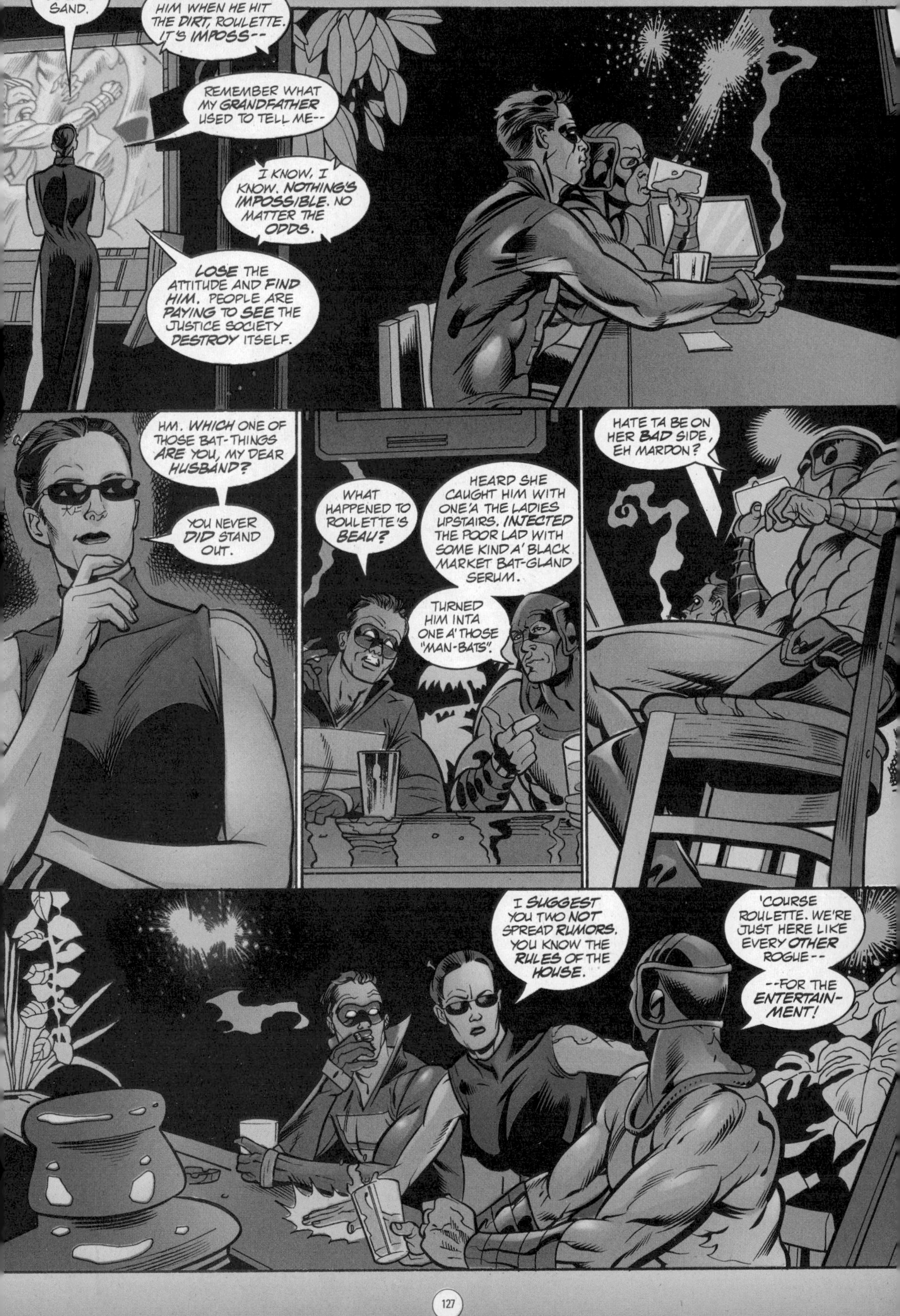
TOM, LOCATE SAND.
CAMERAS LOST HIM WHEN HE HIT THE DIRT, ROULETTE. IT'S IMPOSS--
REMEMBER WHAT MY GRANDFATHER USED TO TELL ME--
I KNOW. I KNOW. NOTHING'S IMPOSSIBLE. NO MATTER THE ODDS.
LOSE THE ATTITUDE AND FIND HIM. PEOPLE ARE PAYING TO SEE THE JUSTICE SOCIETY DESTROY ITSELF.
HM. WHICH ONE OF THOSE BAT-THINGS ARE YOU, MY DEAR HUSBAND?
YOU NEVER DID STAND OUT.
WHAT HAPPENED TO ROULETTE'S BEAU?
HEARD SHE CAUGHT HIM WITH ONE'A THE LADIES UPSTAIRS. INJECTED THE POOR LAD WITH SOME KIND A' BLACK MARKET BAT-GLAND SERUM.
TURNED HIM INTA ONE A' THOSE "MAN-BATS".
HATE TA BE ON HER BAD SIDE, EH MARDON?
I SUGGEST YOU TWO NOT SPREAD RUMORS. YOU KNOW THE RULES OF THE HOUSE.
'COURSE ROULETTE. WE'RE JUST HERE LIKE EVERY OTHER ROGUE--
--FOR THE ENTERTAINMENT!

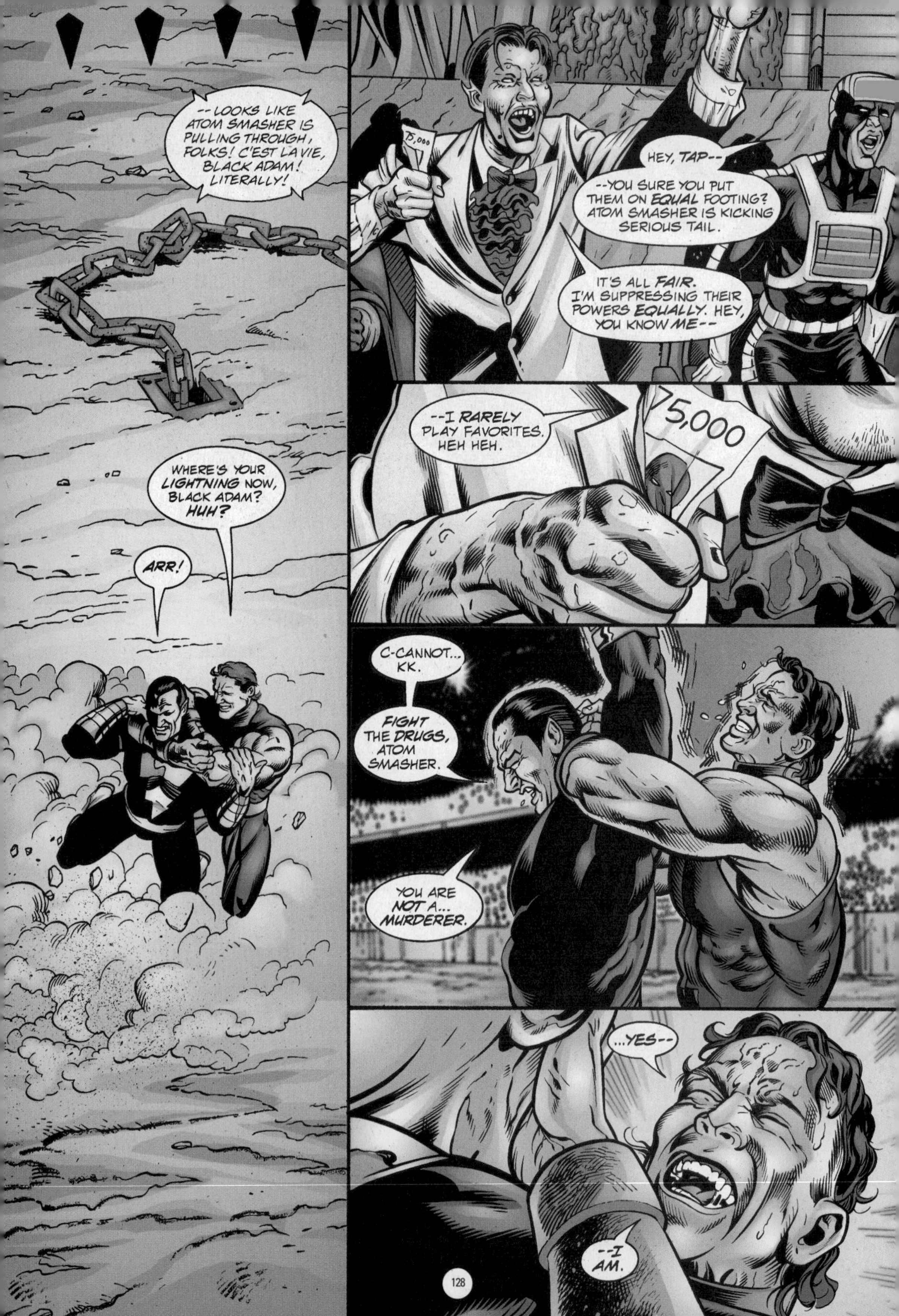
--LOOKS LIKE ATOM SMASHER IS PULLING THROUGH, FOLKS! C'EST LA VIE, BLACK ADAM! LITERALLY!
HEY, TAP--
--YOU SURE YOU PUT THEM ON EQUAL FOOTING? ATOM SMASHER IS KICKING SERIOUS TAIL.
IT'S ALL FAIR. I'M SUPPRESSING THEIR POWERS EQUALLY. HEY, YOU KNOW ME--
75,000
--I RARELY PLAY FAVORITES. HEH HEH.
75,000
WHERE'S YOUR LIGHTNING NOW, BLACK ADAM? HUH?
ARR!
C-CANNOT... KK.
FIGHT THE DRUGS, ATOM SMASHER.
YOU ARE NOT A... MURDERER.
...YES--
--I AM.

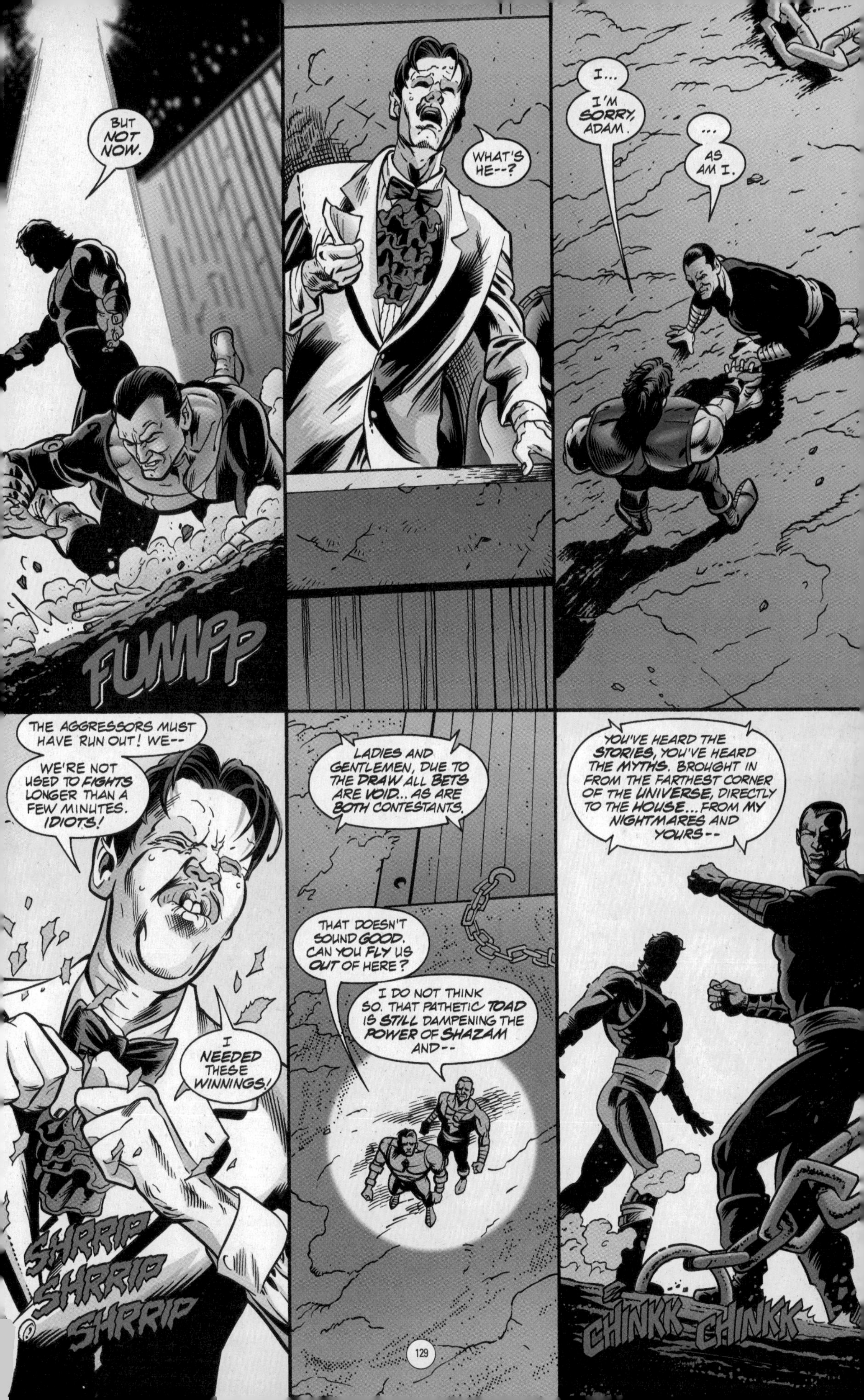

BUT NOT NOW.
FUMPP
WHAT'S HE--?
I... I'M SORRY, ADAM.
... AS AM I.
THE AGGRESSORS MUST HAVE RUN OUT! WE--
WE'RE NOT USED TO FIGHTS LONGER THAN A FEW MINUTES. IDIOTS!
I NEEDED THESE WINNINGS!
SHRRIP SHRRIP SHRRIP
LADIES AND GENTLEMEN, DUE TO THE DRAW ALL BETS ARE VOID... AS ARE BOTH CONTESTANTS.
THAT DOESN'T SOUND GOOD. CAN YOU FLY US OUT OF HERE?
I DO NOT THINK SO. THAT PATHETIC TOAD IS STILL DAMPENING THE POWER OF SHAZAM AND--
YOU'VE HEARD THE STORIES, YOU'VE HEARD THE MYTHS. BROUGHT IN FROM THE FARTHEST CORNER OF THE UNIVERSE, DIRECTLY TO THE HOUSE... FROM MY NIGHTMARES AND YOURS--
CHINKK CHINKK

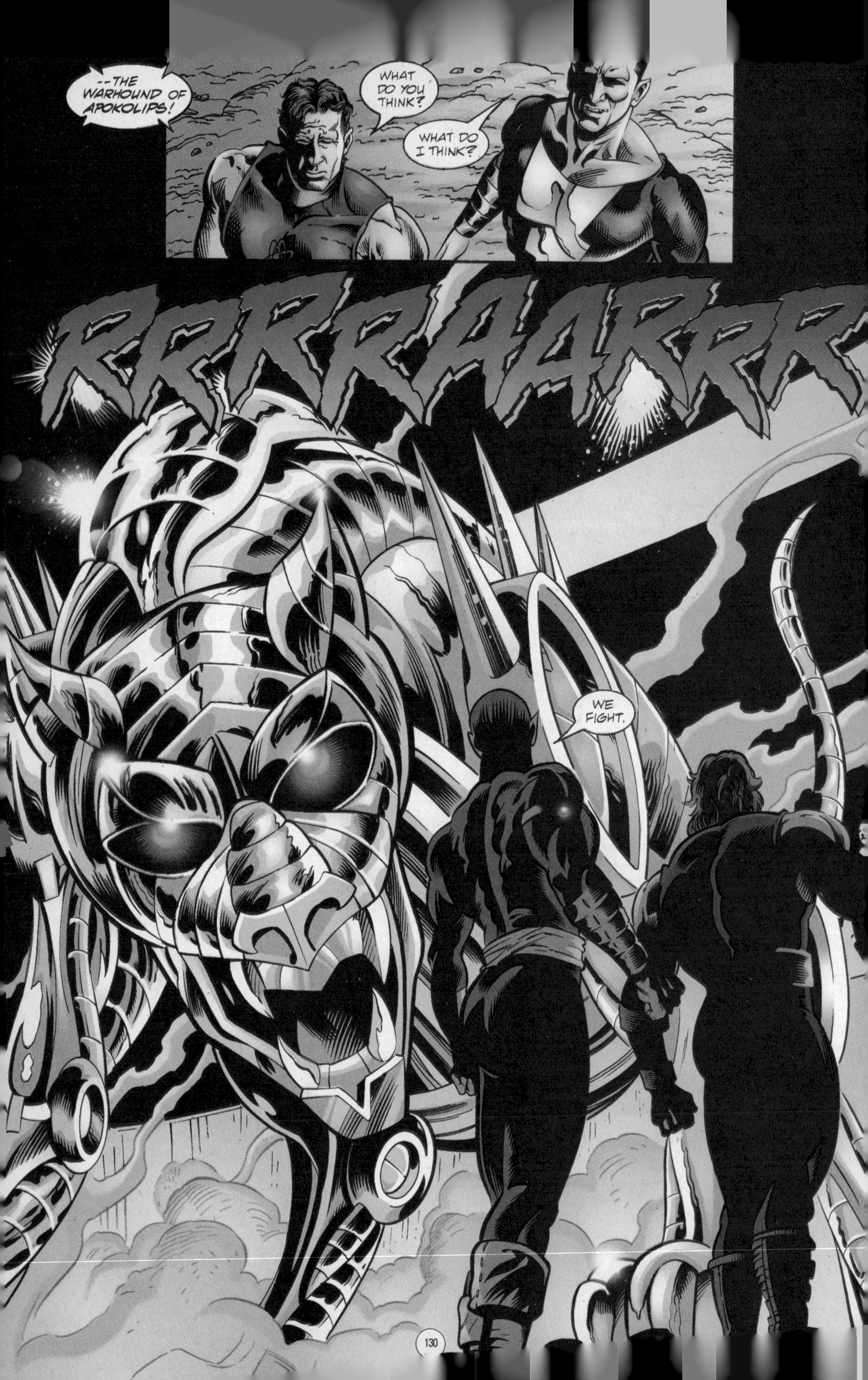
--THE WARHOUND OF APOKOLIPS!
WHAT DO YOU THINK?
WHAT DO I THINK?
RRRRAARRR
WE FIGHT.

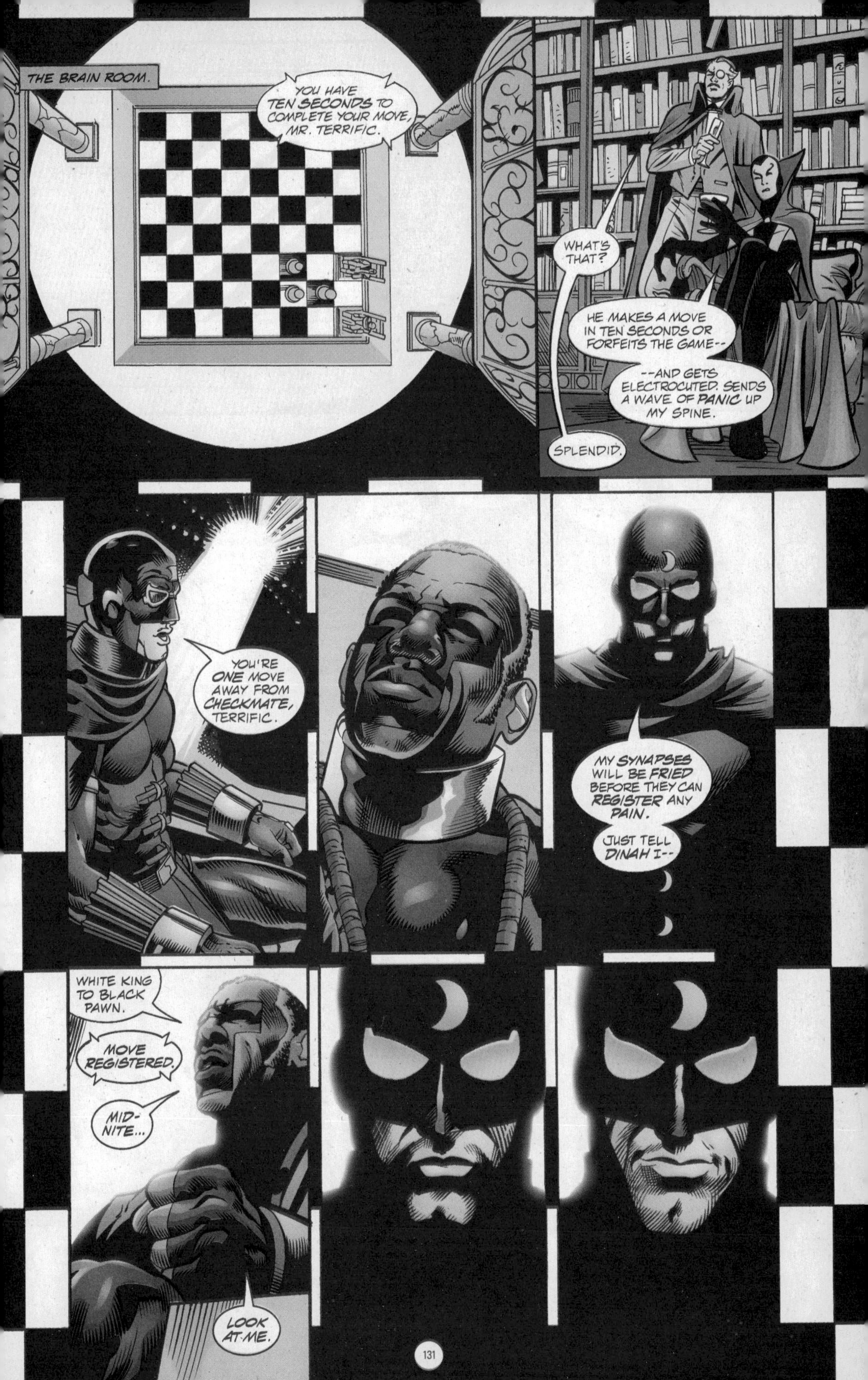
THE BRAIN ROOM.
YOU HAVE TEN SECONDS TO COMPLETE YOUR MOVE, MR. TERRIFIC.
WHAT'S THAT?
HE MAKES A MOVE IN TEN SECONDS OR FORFEITS THE GAME--
--AND GETS ELECTROCUTED. SENDS A WAVE OF PANIC UP MY SPINE.
SPLENDID.
YOU'RE ONE MOVE AWAY FROM CHECKMATE, TERRIFIC.
MY SYNAPSES WILL BE FRIED BEFORE THEY CAN REGISTER ANY PAIN.
JUST TELL DINAH I--
WHITE KING TO BLACK PAWN.
MOVE REGISTERED.
MID-NITE...
LOOK AT ME.

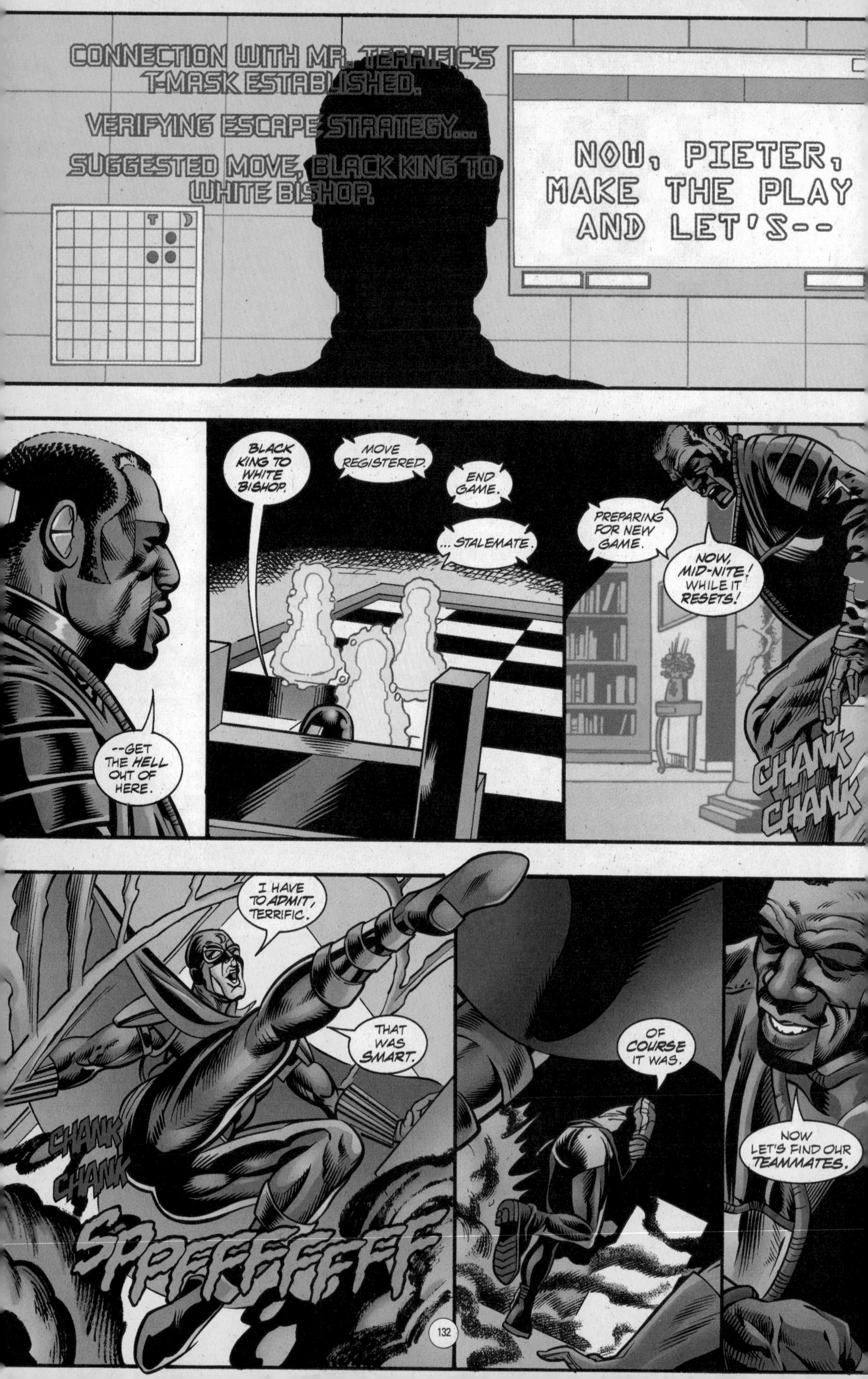

CONNECTION WITH MR. TERRIFIC'S T-MASK ESTABLISHED.
VERIFYING ESCAPE STRATEGY...
SUGGESTED MOVE, BLACK KING TO WHITE BISHOP.
NOW, PIETER, MAKE THE PLAY AND LET'S--
--GET THE HELL OUT OF HERE.
BLACK KING TO WHITE BISHOP.
MOVE REGISTERED.
END GAME.
...STALEMATE.
PREPARING FOR NEW GAME.
NOW, MID-NITE! WHILE IT RESETS!
CHANK CHANK
I HAVE TO ADMIT, TERRIFIC.
THAT WAS SMART.
CHANK CHANK
SPPFFFFFFFF
OF COURSE IT WAS.
NOW LET'S FIND OUR TEAMMATES.

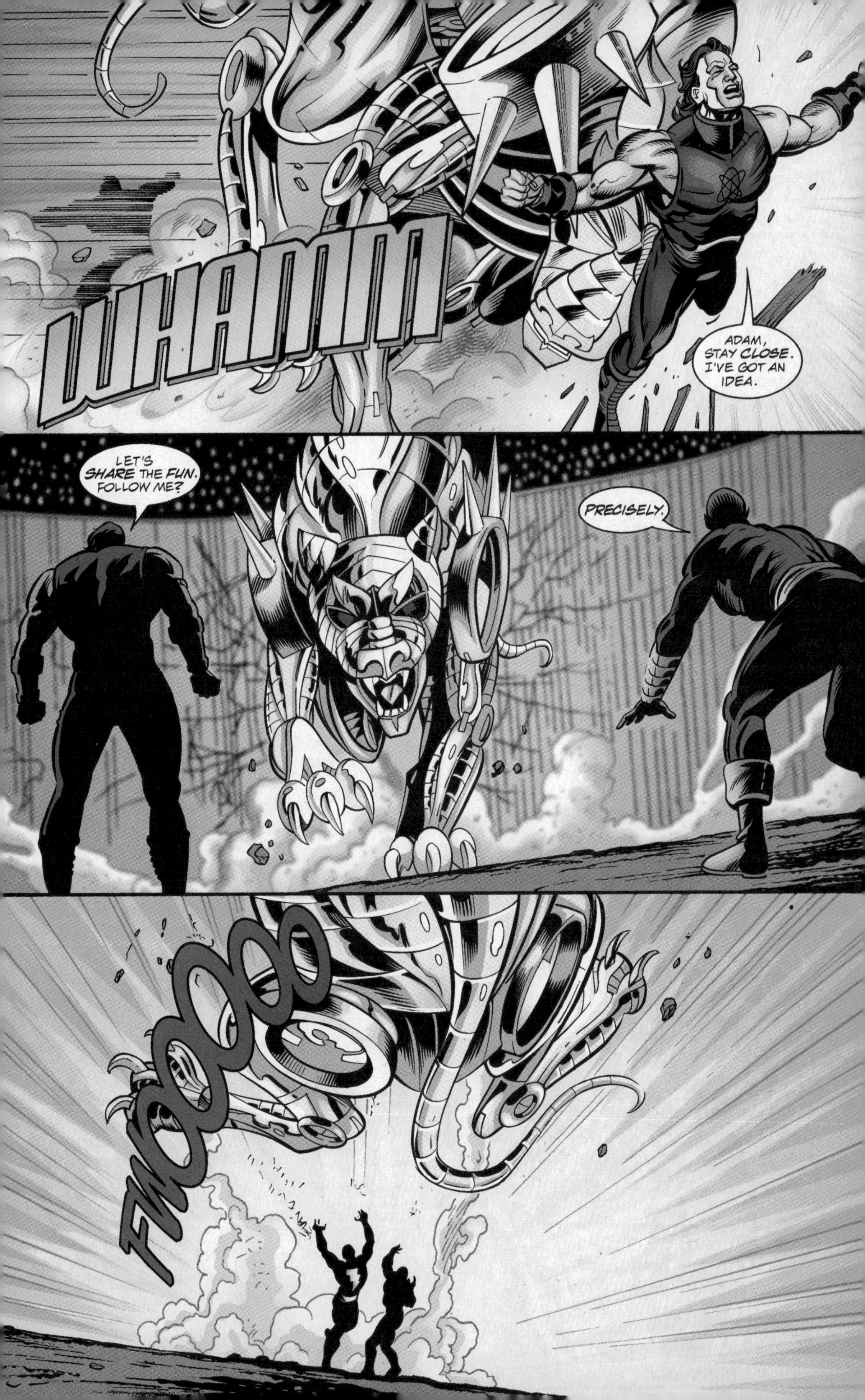
WHAMM
ADAM, STAY CLOSE. I'VE GOT AN IDEA.
LET'S SHARE THE FUN. FOLLOW ME?
PRECISELY.
FWOOOOO

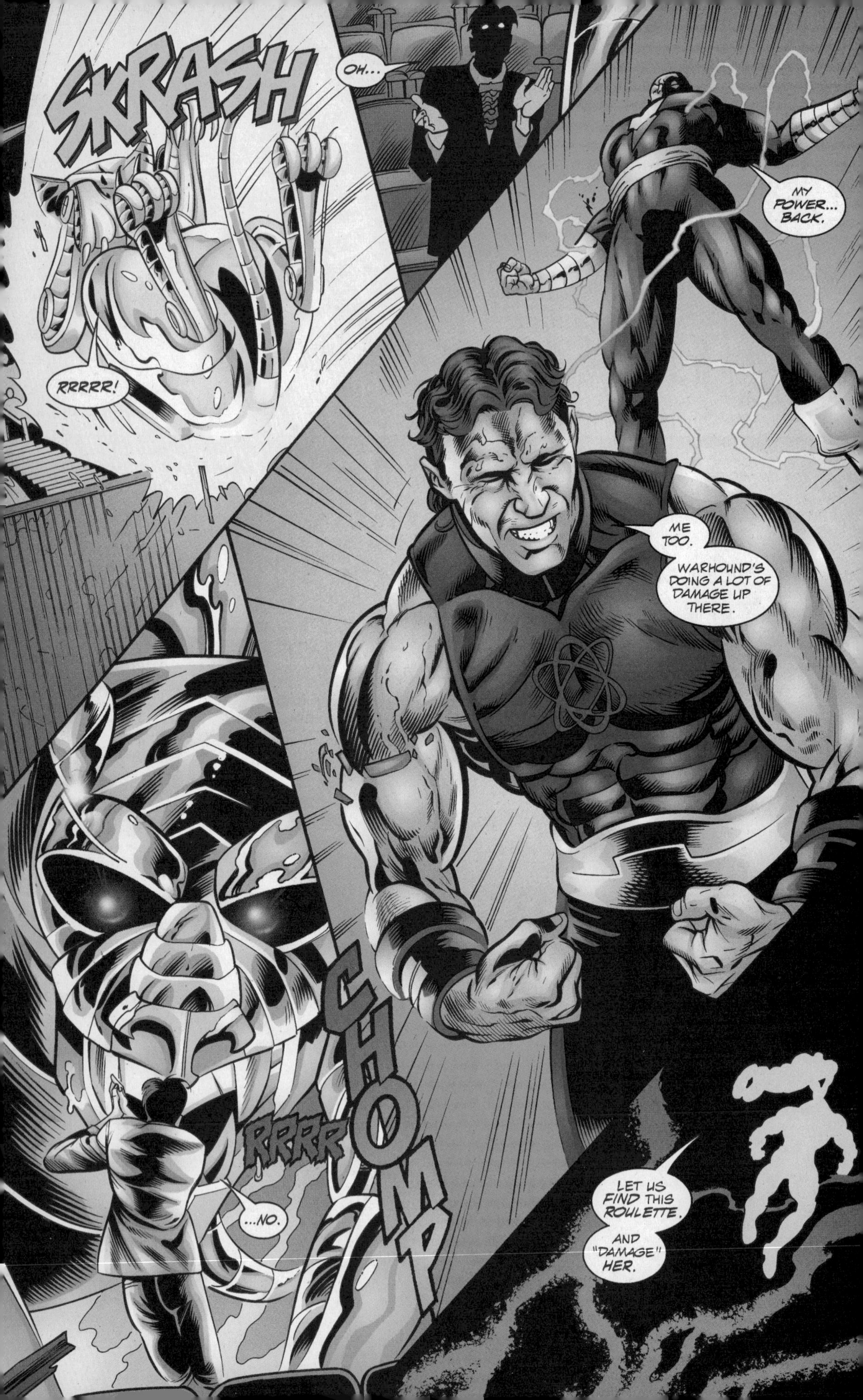
SKRASH
OH...
MY POWER... BACK.
RRRRR!
ME TOO.
WARHOUND'S DOING A LOT OF DAMAGE UP THERE.
RRRR
CHOMP
...NO.
LET US FIND THIS ROULETTE.
AND "DAMAGE" HER.

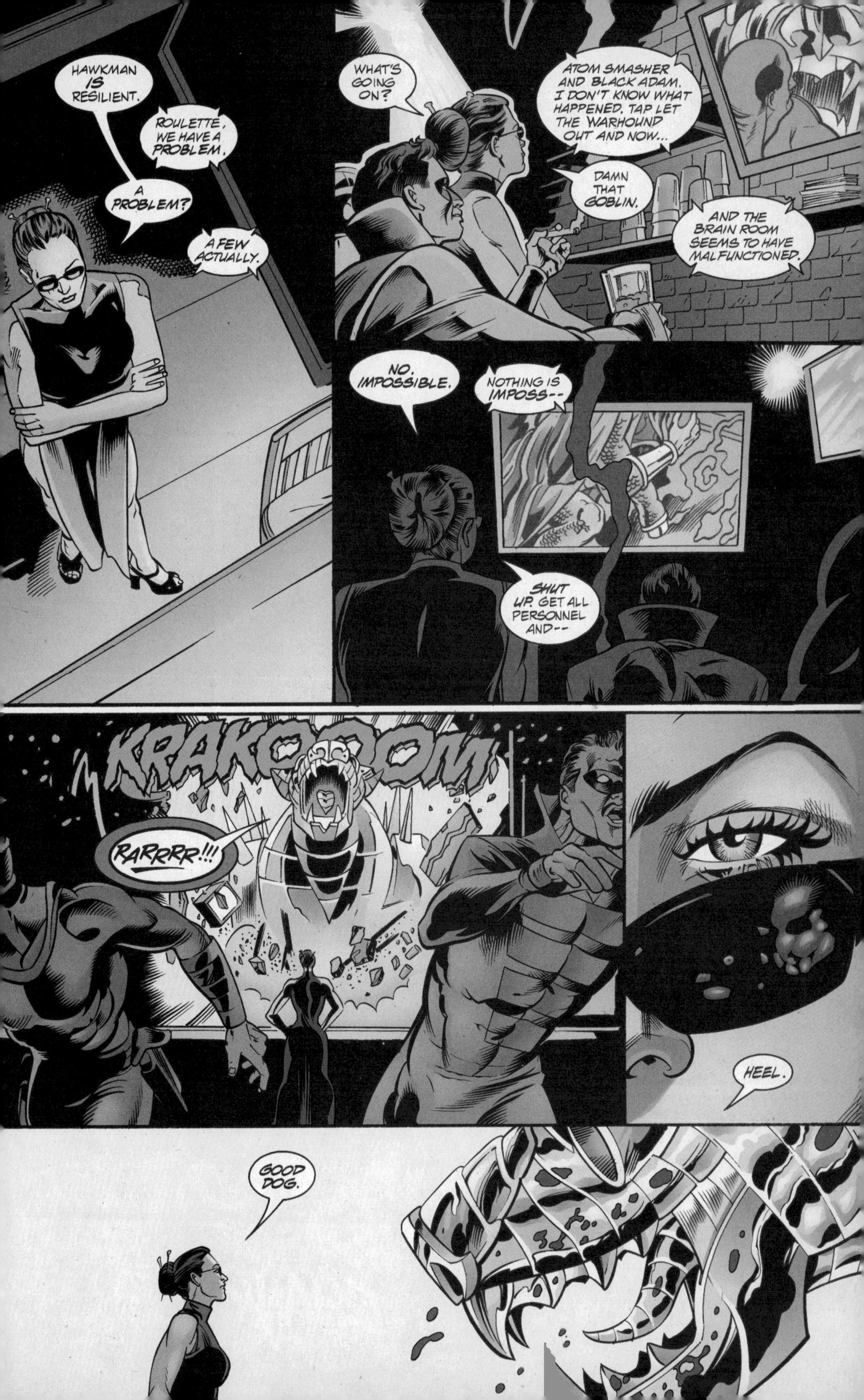
HAWKMAN IS RESILIENT.
ROULETTE, WE HAVE A PROBLEM.
A PROBLEM?
A FEW ACTUALLY.
WHAT'S GOING ON?
ATOM SMASHER AND BLACK ADAM. I DON'T KNOW WHAT HAPPENED. TAP LET THE WARHOUND OUT AND NOW...
DAMN THAT GOBLIN.
AND THE BRAIN ROOM SEEMS TO HAVE MALFUNCTIONED.
NO. IMPOSSIBLE.
NOTHING IS IMPOSS--
SHUT UP. GET ALL PERSONNEL AND--
KRAKOOOOM
RARRRR!!!
HEEL.
GOOD DOG.

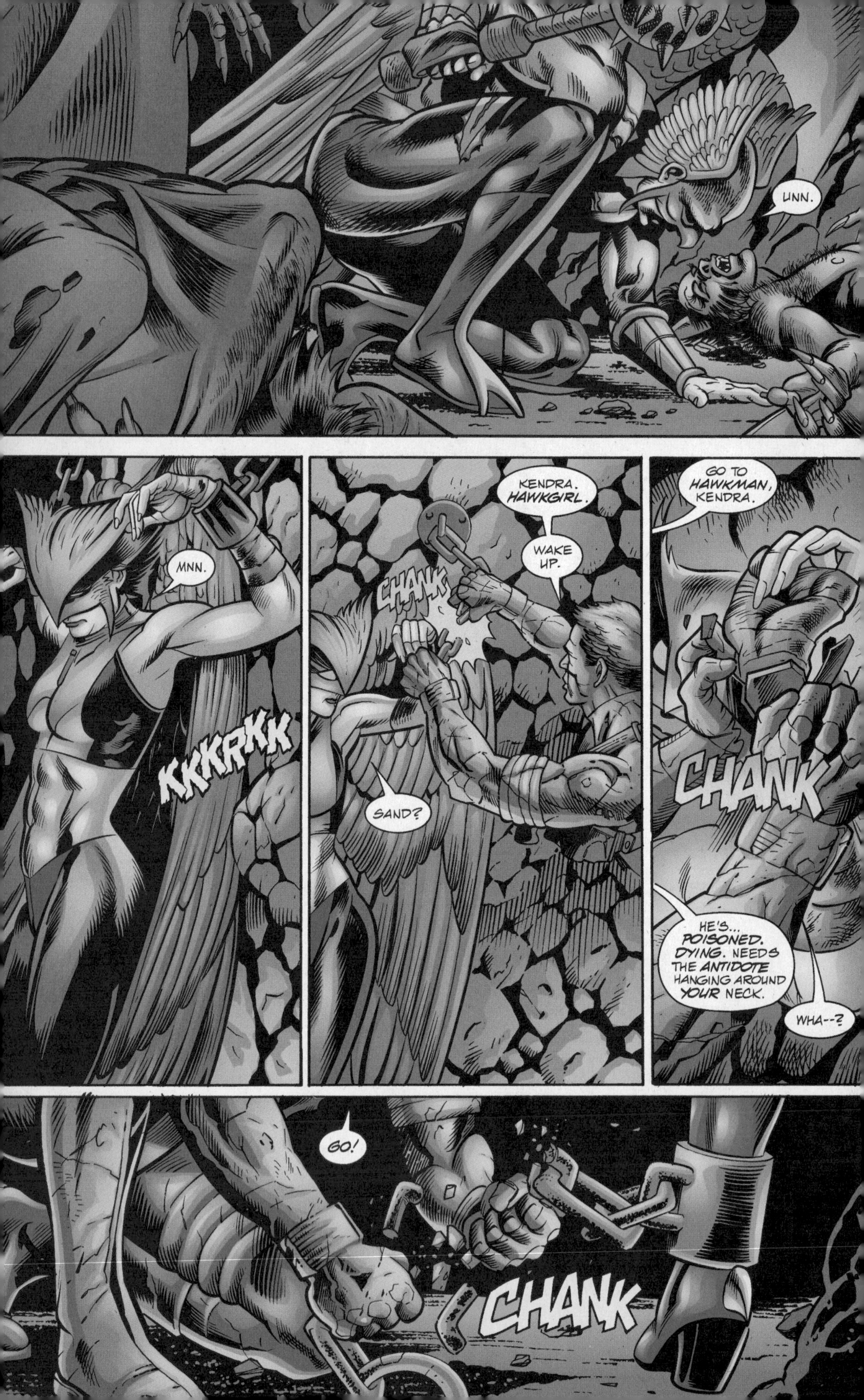
UNN.
MNN.
KKKRKK
KENDRA. HAWKGIRL.
WAKE UP.
CHANK
SAND?
GO TO HAWKMAN, KENDRA.
CHANK
HE'S... POISONED. DYING. NEEDS THE ANTIDOTE HANGING AROUND YOUR NECK.
WHA--?
GO!
CHANK

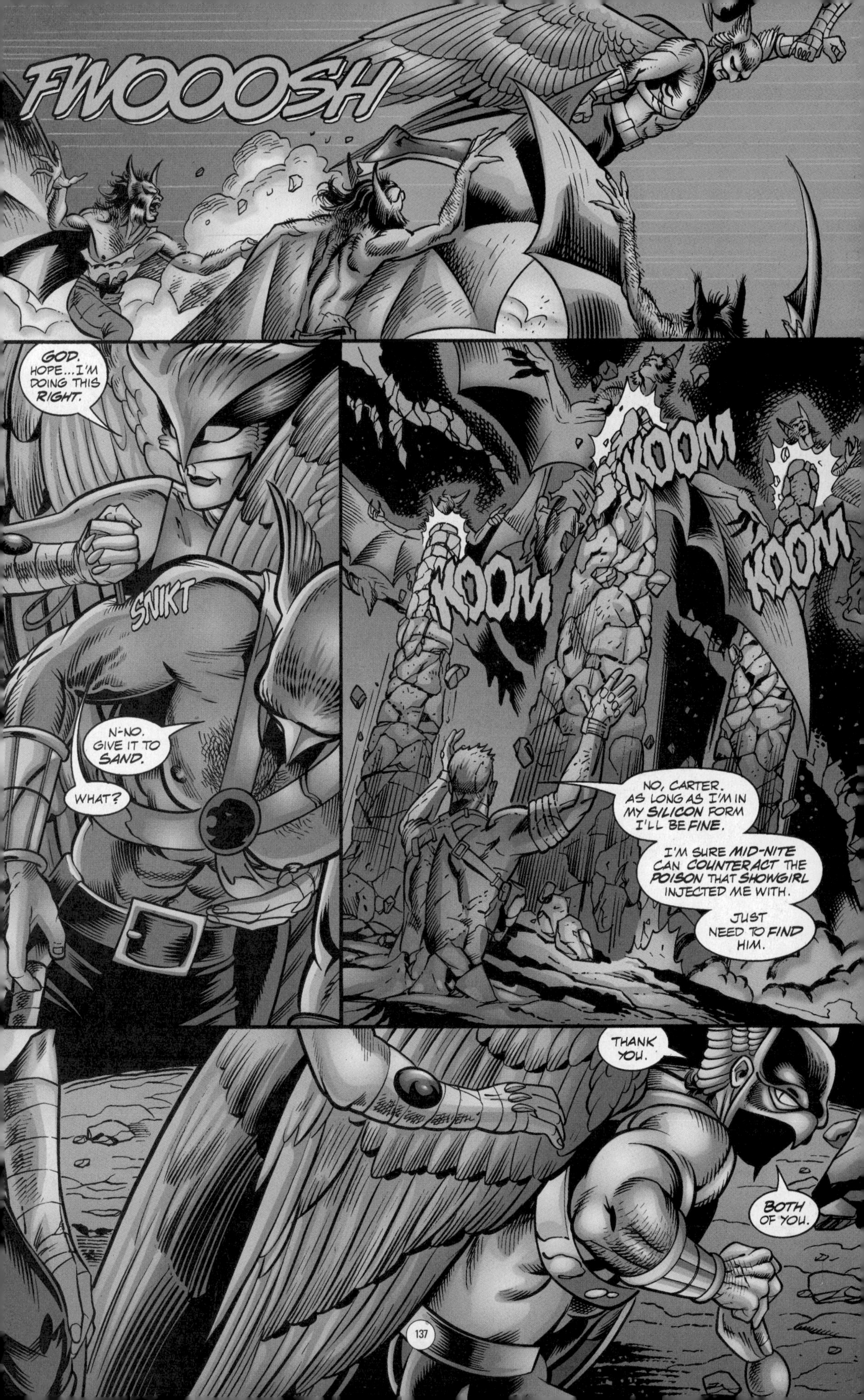
FWOOOSH
GOD. HOPE...I'M DOING THIS RIGHT.
SNIKT
N-NO. GIVE IT TO SAND.
WHAT?
KOOM
KOOM
KOOM
NO, CARTER. AS LONG AS I'M IN MY SILICON FORM I'LL BE FINE.
I'M SURE MID-NITE CAN COUNTERACT THE POISON THAT SHOWGIRL INJECTED ME WITH.
JUST NEED TO FIND HIM.
THANK YOU.
BOTH OF YOU.

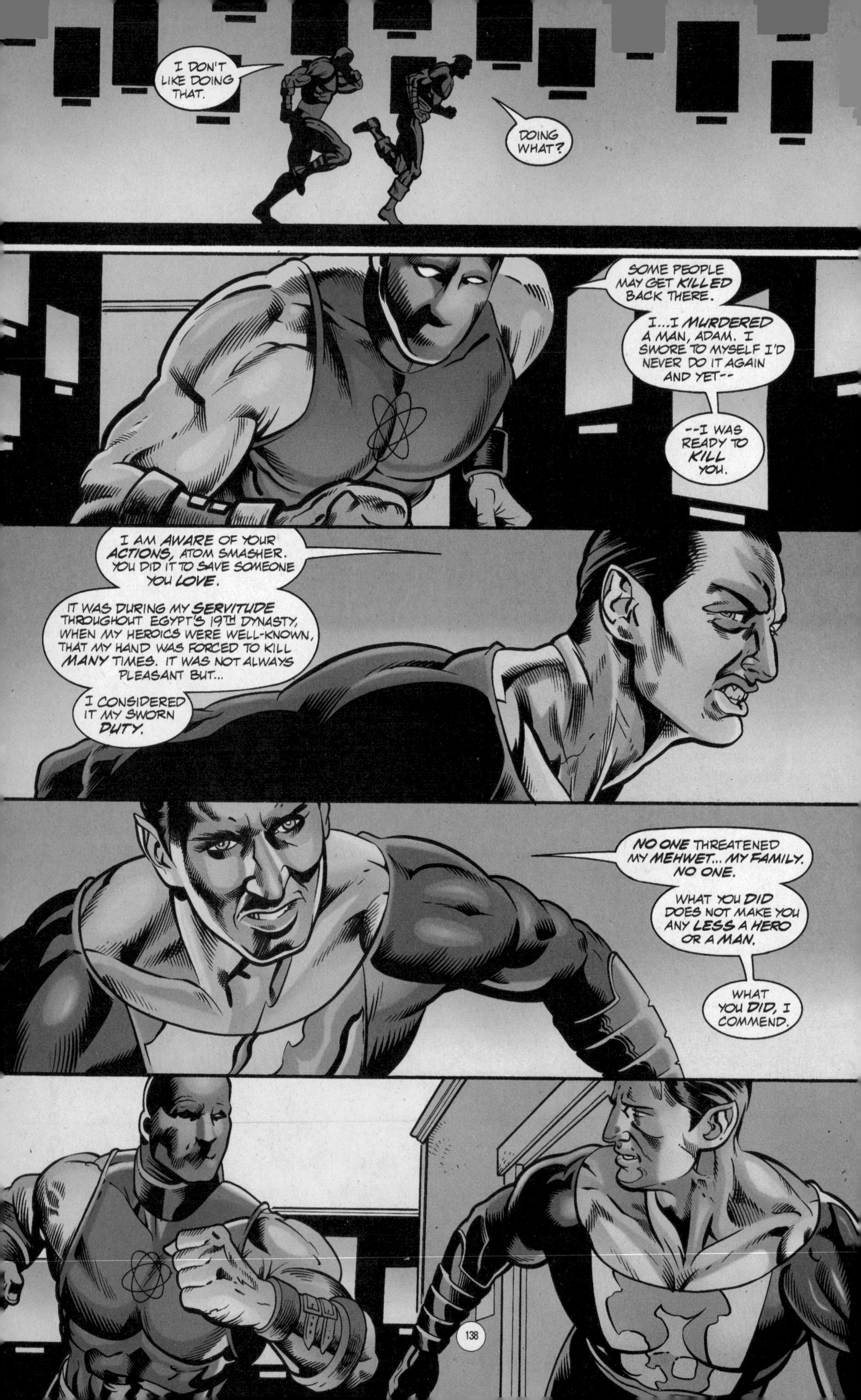

I DON'T LIKE DOING THAT.
DOING WHAT?
SOME PEOPLE MAY GET KILLED BACK THERE.
I...I MURDERED A MAN, ADAM. I SWORE TO MYSELF I'D NEVER DO IT AGAIN AND YET--
--I WAS READY TO KILL YOU.
I AM AWARE OF YOUR ACTIONS, ATOM SMASHER. YOU DID IT TO SAVE SOMEONE YOU LOVE.
IT WAS DURING MY SERVITUDE THROUGHOUT EGYPT'S 19TH DYNASTY, WHEN MY HEROICS WERE WELL-KNOWN, THAT MY HAND WAS FORCED TO KILL MANY TIMES. IT WAS NOT ALWAYS PLEASANT BUT...
I CONSIDERED IT MY SWORN DUTY.
NO ONE THREATENED MY MEHWET... MY FAMILY. NO ONE.
WHAT YOU DID DOES NOT MAKE YOU ANY LESS A HERO OR A MAN.
WHAT YOU DID, I COMMEND.

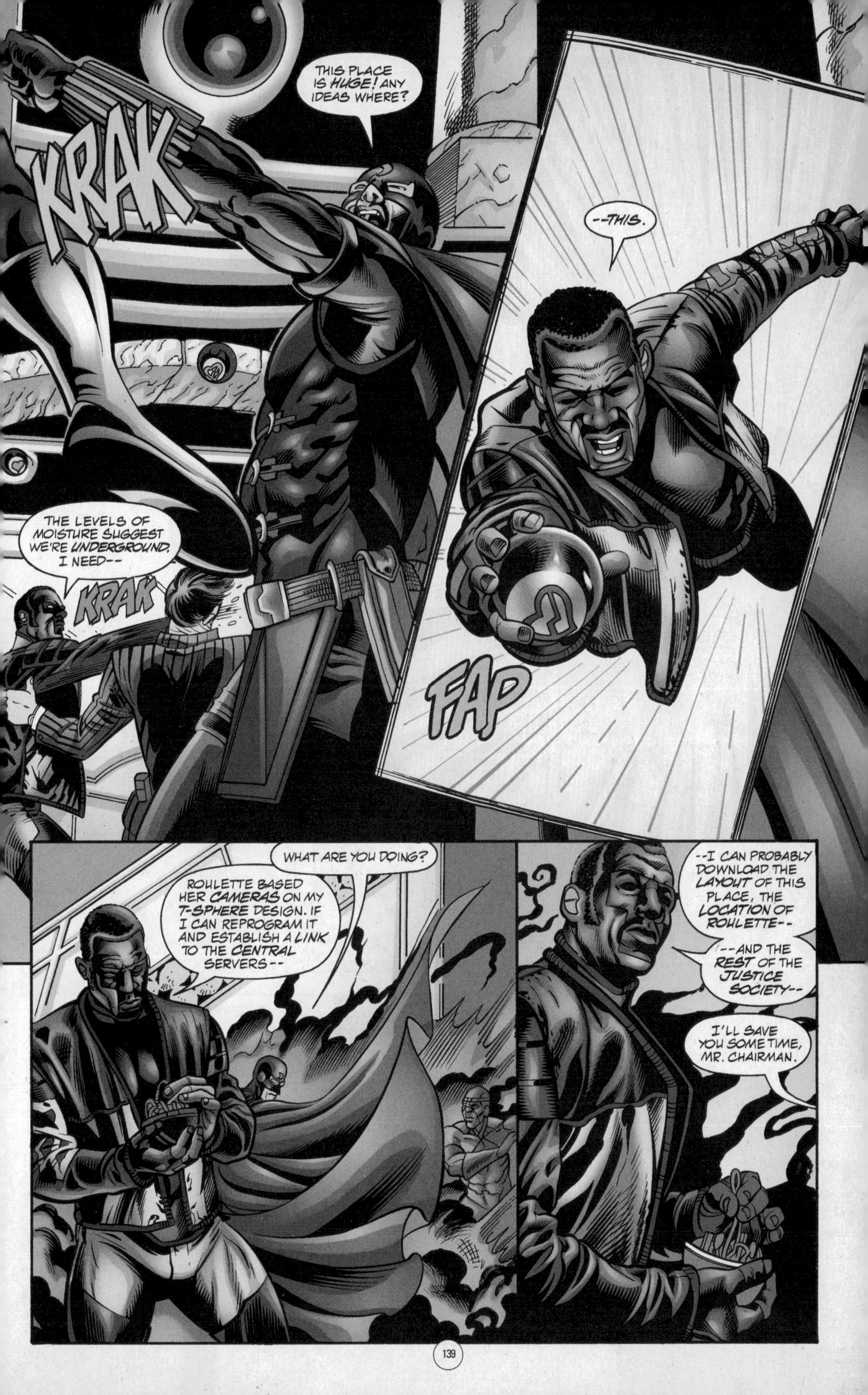
THIS PLACE IS HUGE! ANY IDEAS WHERE?
KRAK
THE LEVELS OF MOISTURE SUGGEST WE'RE UNDERGROUND. I NEED--
KRAK
--THIS.
FAP
WHAT ARE YOU DOING?
ROULETTE BASED HER CAMERAS ON MY T-SPHERE DESIGN. IF I CAN REPROGRAM IT AND ESTABLISH A LINK TO THE CENTRAL SERVERS--
--I CAN PROBABLY DOWNLOAD THE LAYOUT OF THIS PLACE, THE LOCATION OF ROULETTE--
--AND THE REST OF THE JUSTICE SOCIETY--
I'LL SAVE YOU SOME TIME, MR. CHAIRMAN.

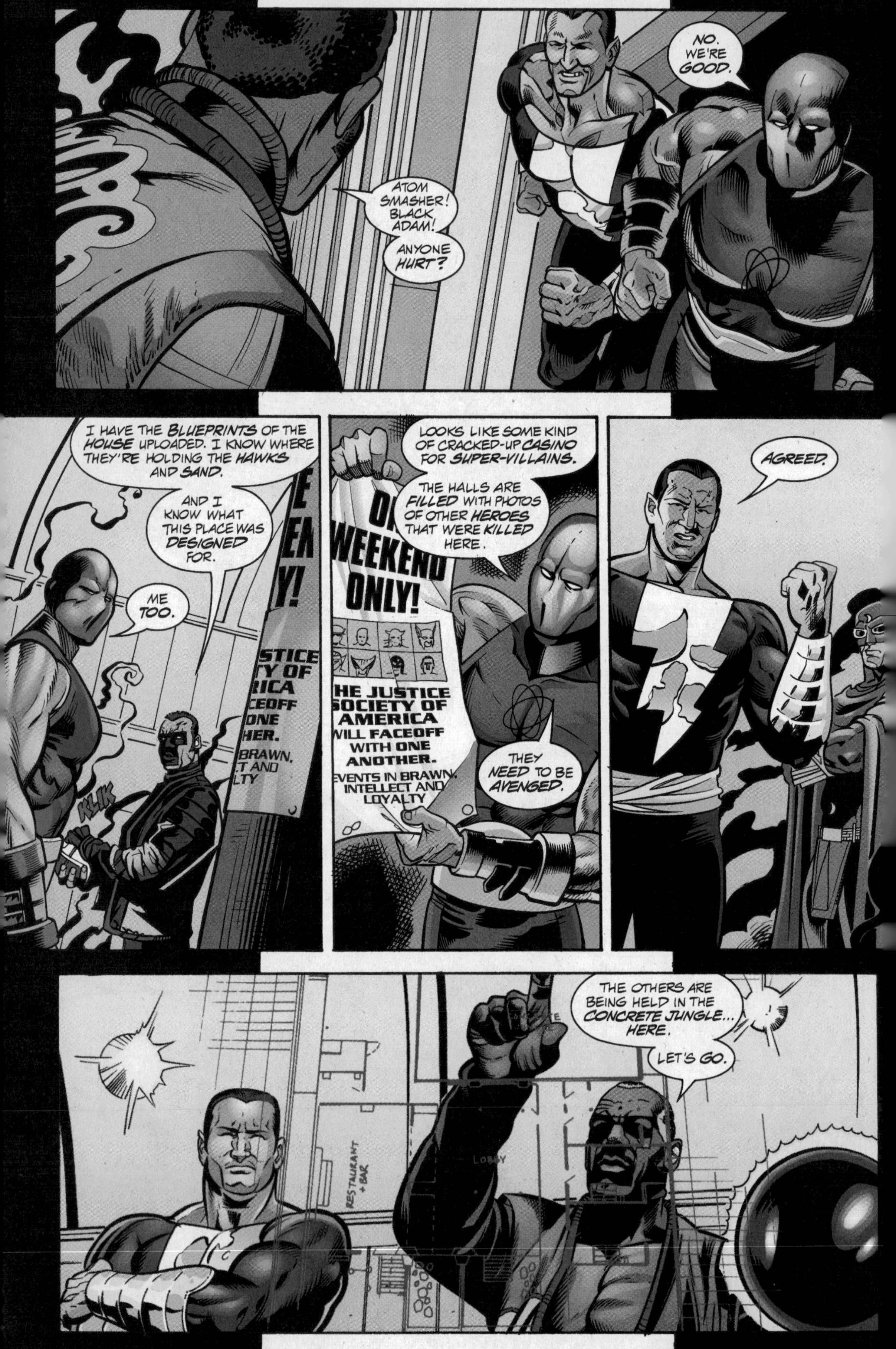
ATOM SMASHER! BLACK ADAM!
ANYONE HURT?
NO. WE'RE GOOD.
I HAVE THE BLUEPRINTS OF THE HOUSE UPLOADED. I KNOW WHERE THEY'RE HOLDING THE HAWKS AND SAND.
AND I KNOW WHAT THIS PLACE WAS DESIGNED FOR.
ME TOO.
KLIK
LOOKS LIKE SOME KIND OF CRACKED-UP CASINO FOR SUPER-VILLAINS.
THE HALLS ARE FILLED WITH PHOTOS OF OTHER HEROES THAT WERE KILLED HERE.
WEEKEND ONLY!
THE JUSTICE SOCIETY OF AMERICA WILL FACEOFF WITH ONE ANOTHER.
EVENTS IN BRAWN, INTELLECT AND LOYALTY
THEY NEED TO BE AVENGED.
AGREED.
THE OTHERS ARE BEING HELD IN THE CONCRETE JUNGLE... HERE.
LET'S GO.
RESTAURANT + BAR
LOBBY

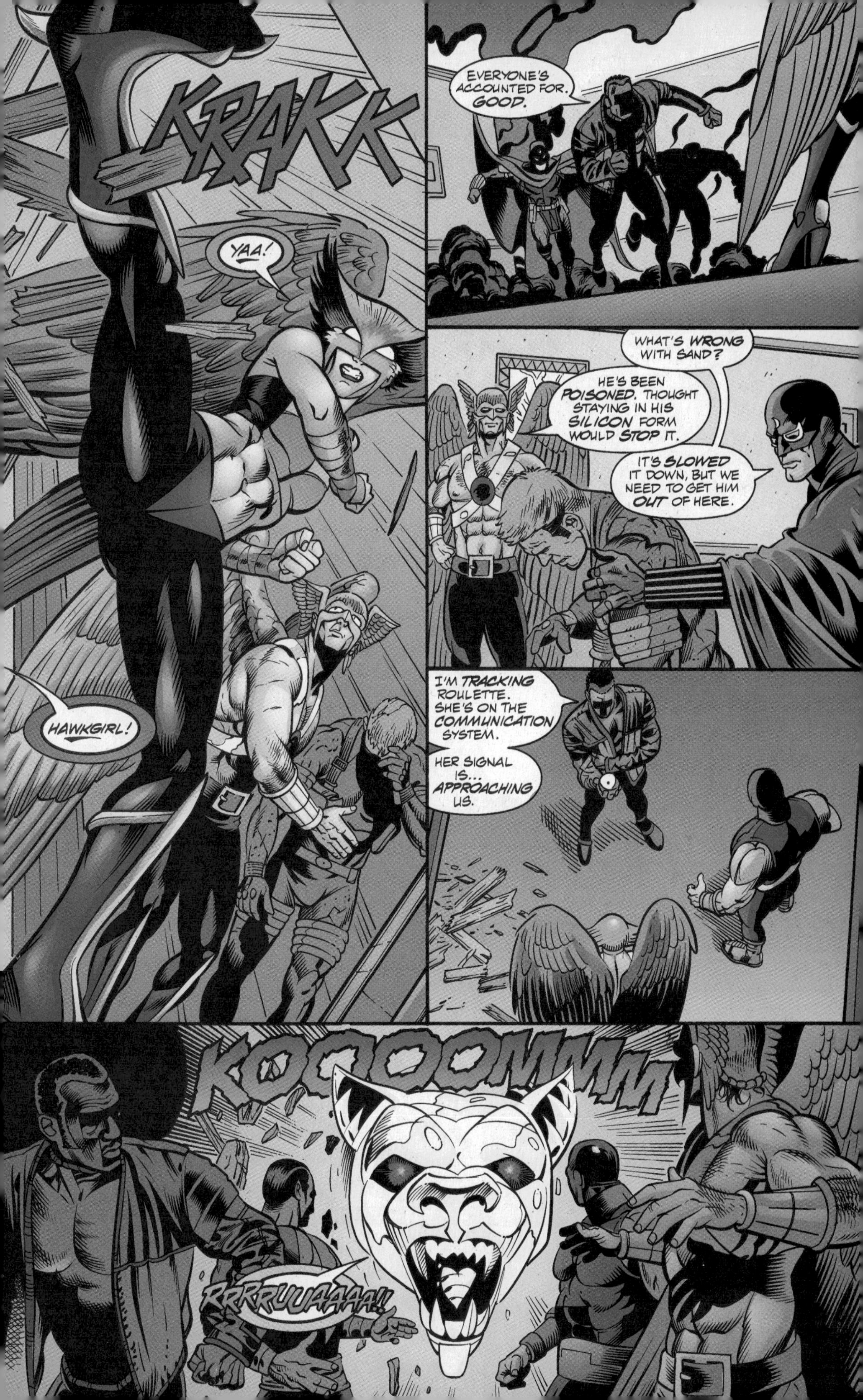
KRAKK
YAA!
HAWKGIRL!
EVERYONE'S ACCOUNTED FOR. GOOD.
WHAT'S WRONG WITH SAND?
HE'S BEEN POISONED. THOUGHT STAYING IN HIS SILICON FORM WOULD STOP IT.
IT'S SLOWED IT DOWN, BUT WE NEED TO GET HIM OUT OF HERE.
I'M TRACKING ROULETTE. SHE'S ON THE COMMUNICATION SYSTEM.
HER SIGNAL IS... APPROACHING US.
KOOOOMMM
RRRRUUAAAA!!

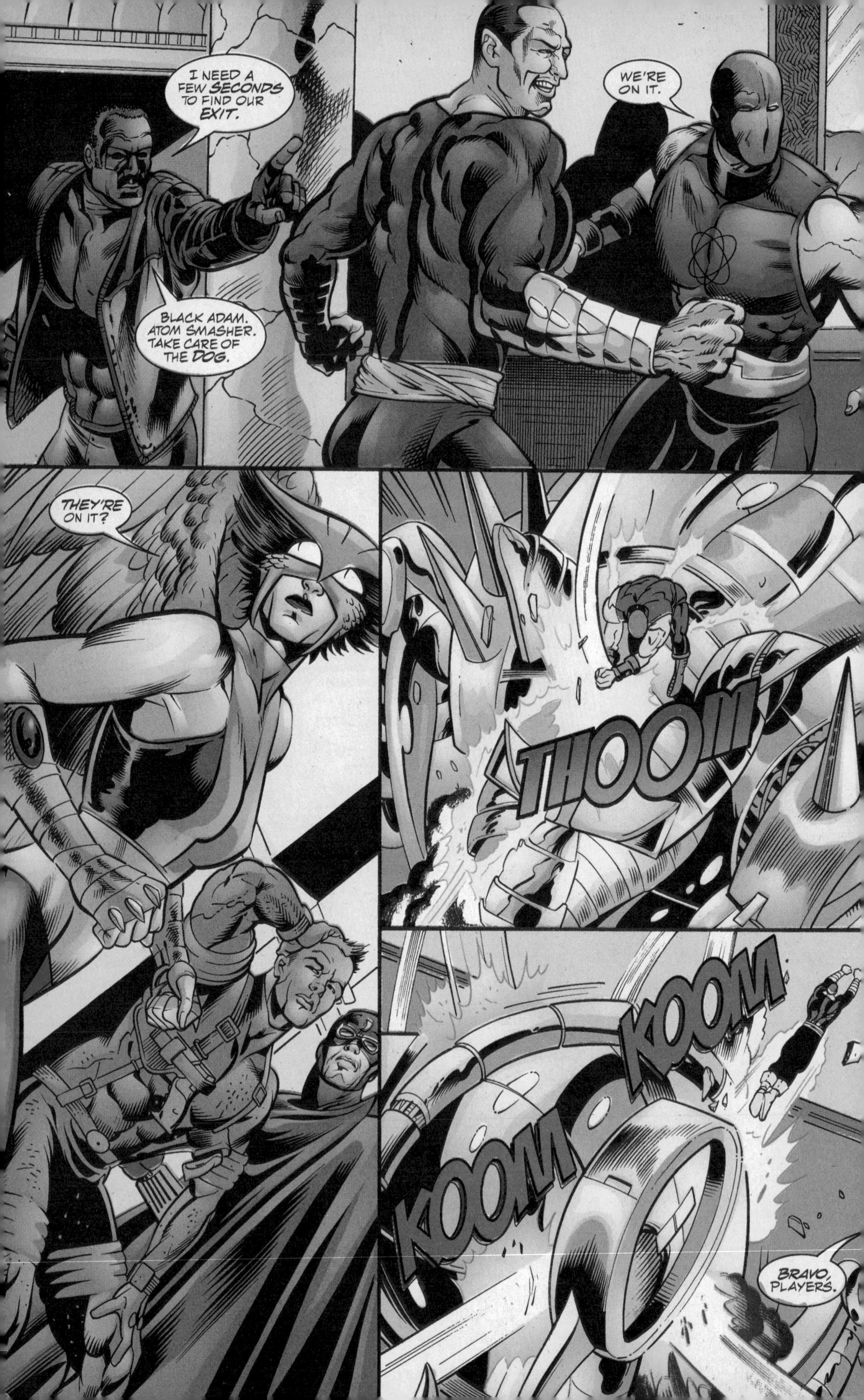
I NEED A FEW SECONDS TO FIND OUR EXIT.
BLACK ADAM. ATOM SMASHER. TAKE CARE OF THE DOG.
WE'RE ON IT.
THEY'RE ON IT?
THOOM
KOOM KOOM
BRAVO, PLAYERS.

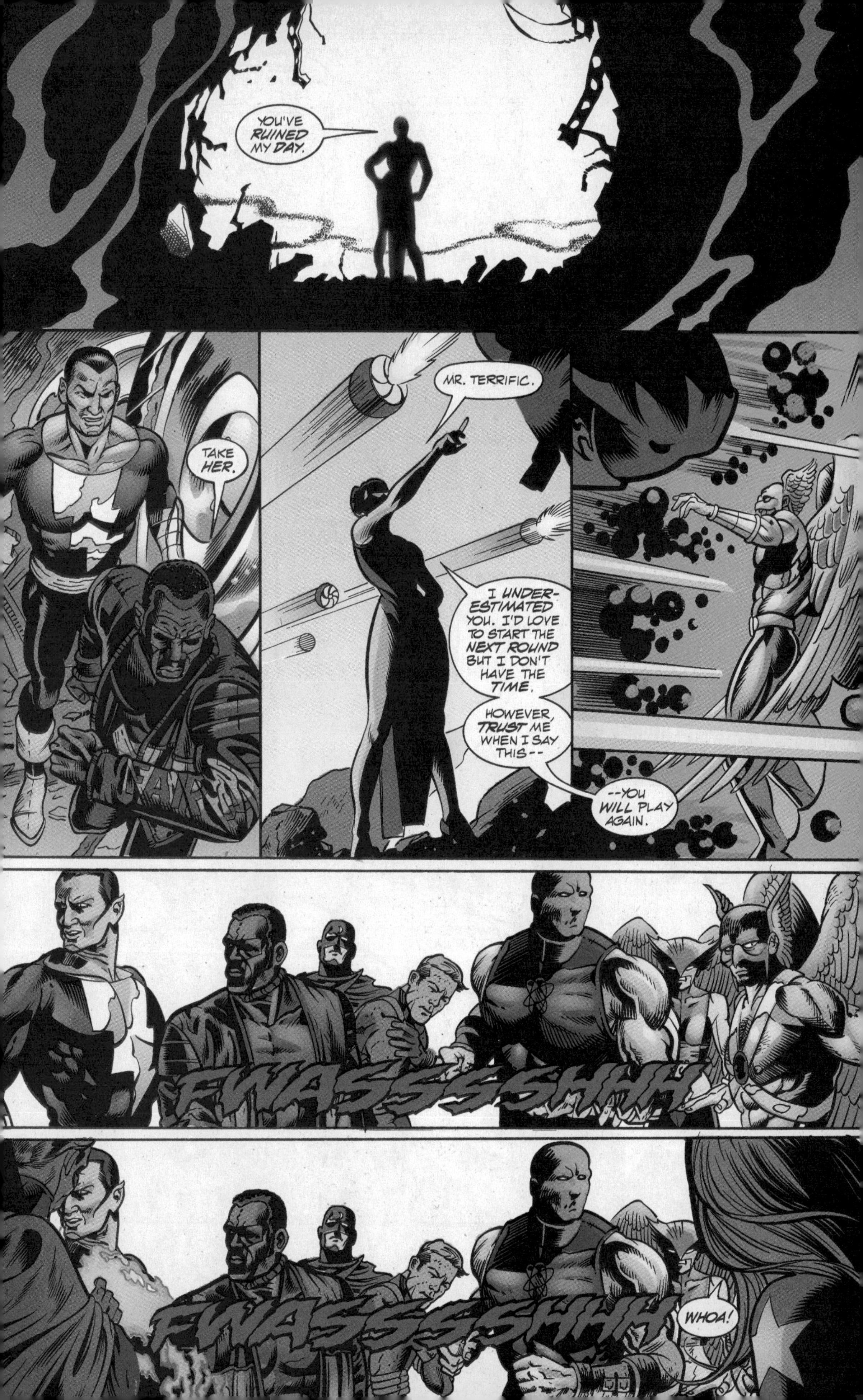
YOU'VE RUINED MY DAY.
TAKE HER.
MR. TERRIFIC.
I UNDER-ESTIMATED YOU. I'D LOVE TO START THE NEXT ROUND BUT I DON'T HAVE THE TIME.
HOWEVER, TRUST ME WHEN I SAY THIS--
--YOU WILL PLAY AGAIN.
FWASSSSHHH
FWASSSSSHHH
WHOA!

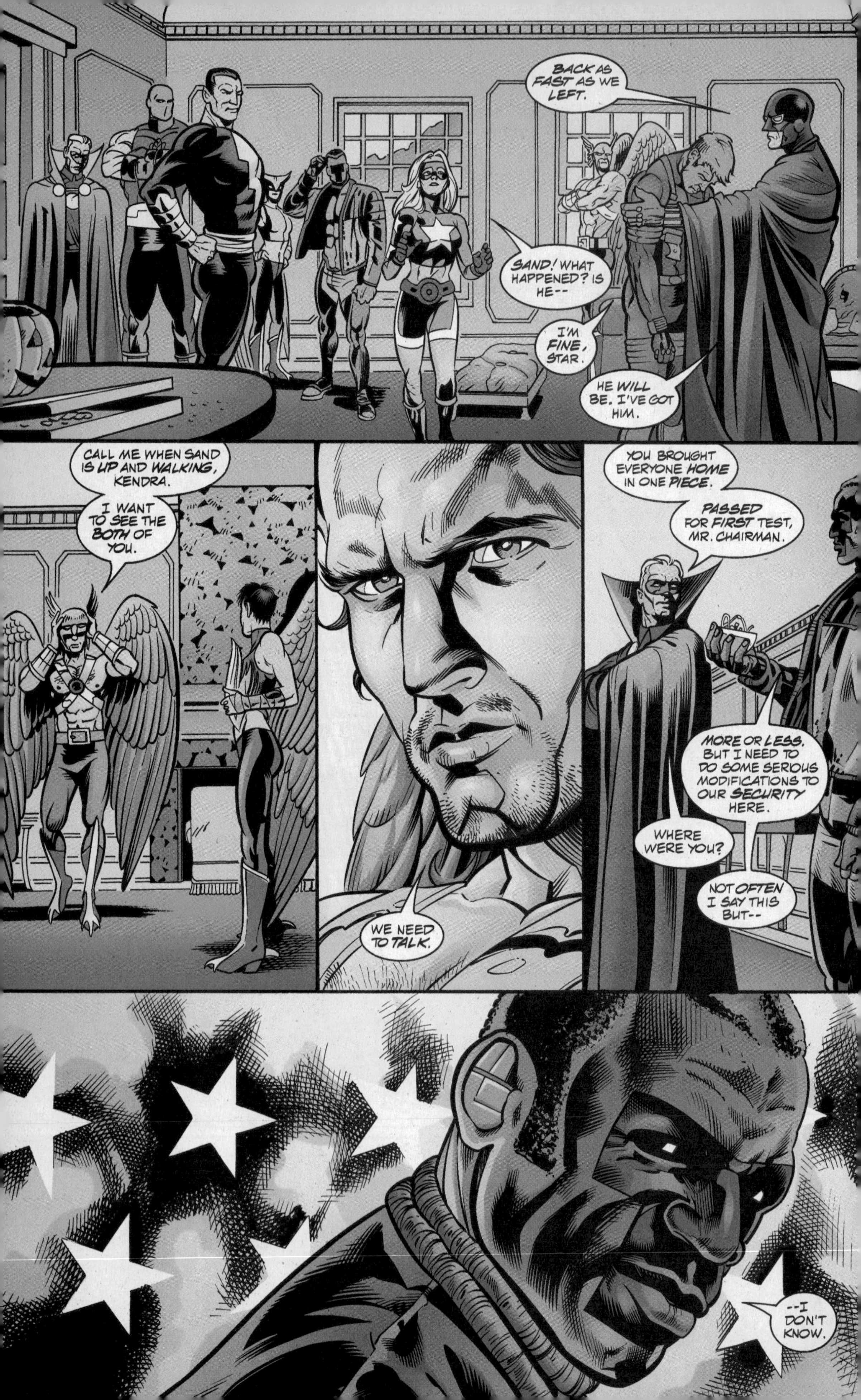
BACK AS FAST AS WE LEFT.
SAND! WHAT HAPPENED? IS HE--
I'M FINE, STAR.
HE WILL BE. I'VE GOT HIM.
CALL ME WHEN SAND IS UP AND WALKING, KENDRA.
I WANT TO SEE THE BOTH OF YOU.
WE NEED TO TALK.
YOU BROUGHT EVERYONE HOME IN ONE PIECE.
PASSED FOR FIRST TEST, MR. CHAIRMAN.
MORE OR LESS. BUT I NEED TO DO SOME SERIOUS MODIFICATIONS TO OUR SECURITY HERE.
WHERE WERE YOU?
NOT OFTEN I SAY THIS BUT--
--I DON'T KNOW.

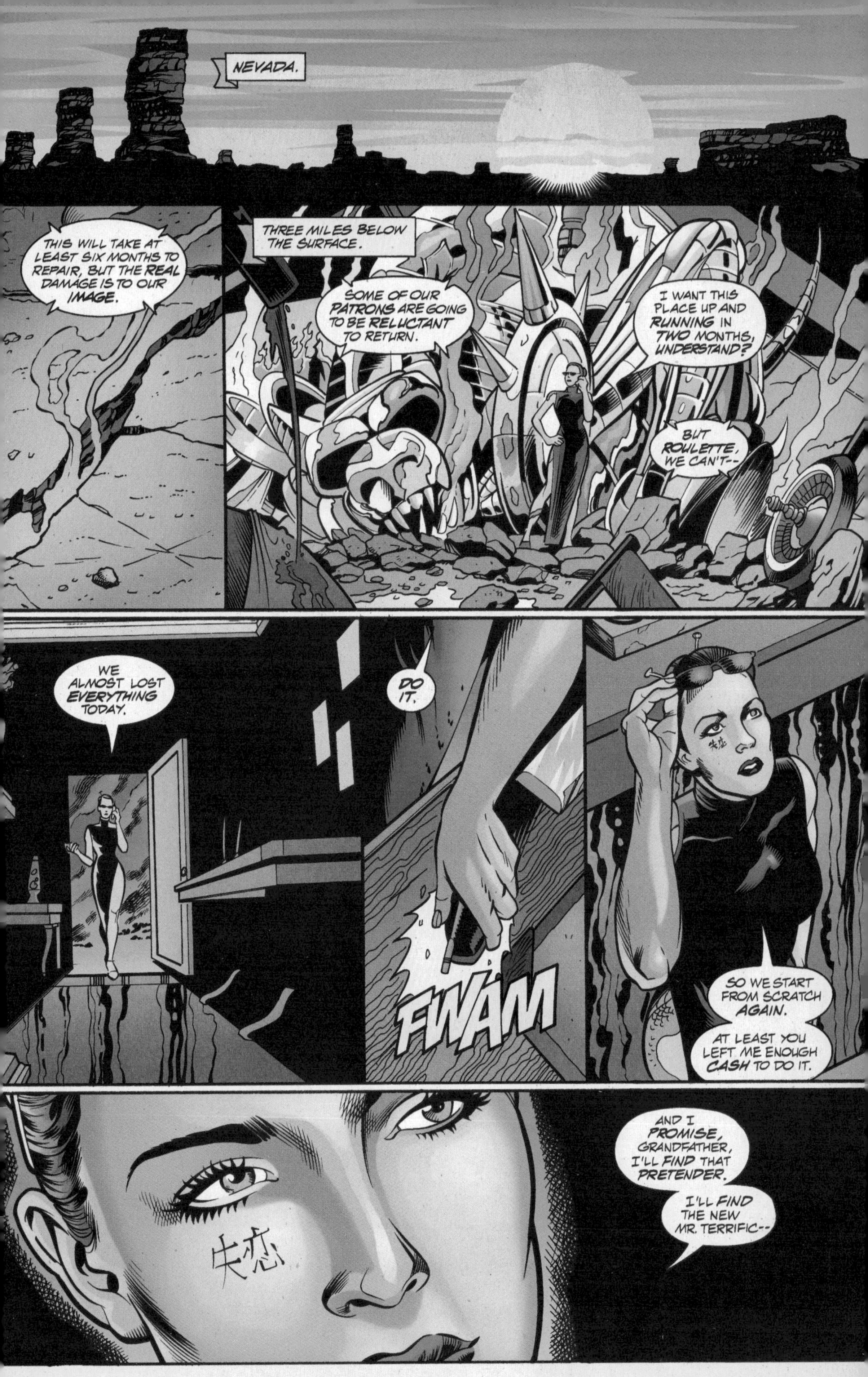
NEVADA.
THIS WILL TAKE AT LEAST SIX MONTHS TO REPAIR, BUT THE REAL DAMAGE IS TO OUR IMAGE.
THREE MILES BELOW THE SURFACE.
SOME OF OUR PATRONS ARE GOING TO BE RELUCTANT TO RETURN.
I WANT THIS PLACE UP AND RUNNING IN TWO MONTHS, UNDERSTAND?
BUT ROULETTE, WE CAN'T--
WE ALMOST LOST EVERYTHING TODAY.
DO IT.
FWAM
SO WE START FROM SCRATCH AGAIN.
AT LEAST YOU LEFT ME ENOUGH CASH TO DO IT.
AND I PROMISE, GRANDFATHER, I'LL FIND THAT PRETENDER.
I'LL FIND THE NEW MR. TERRIFIC--

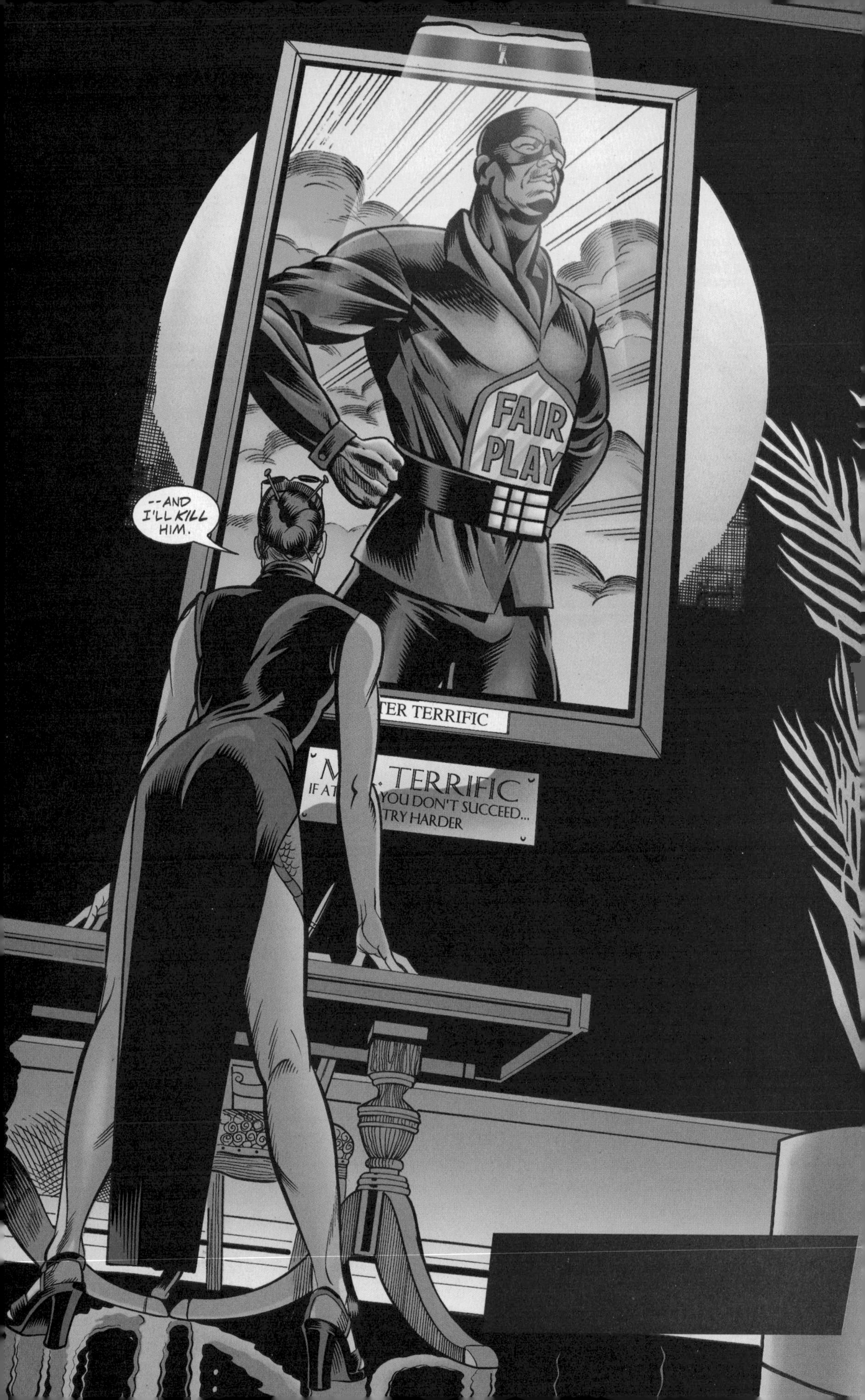
--AND I'LL KILL HIM.
FAIR PLAY
TERRIFIC
TERRIFIC
YOU DON'T SUCCEED...
TRY HARDER

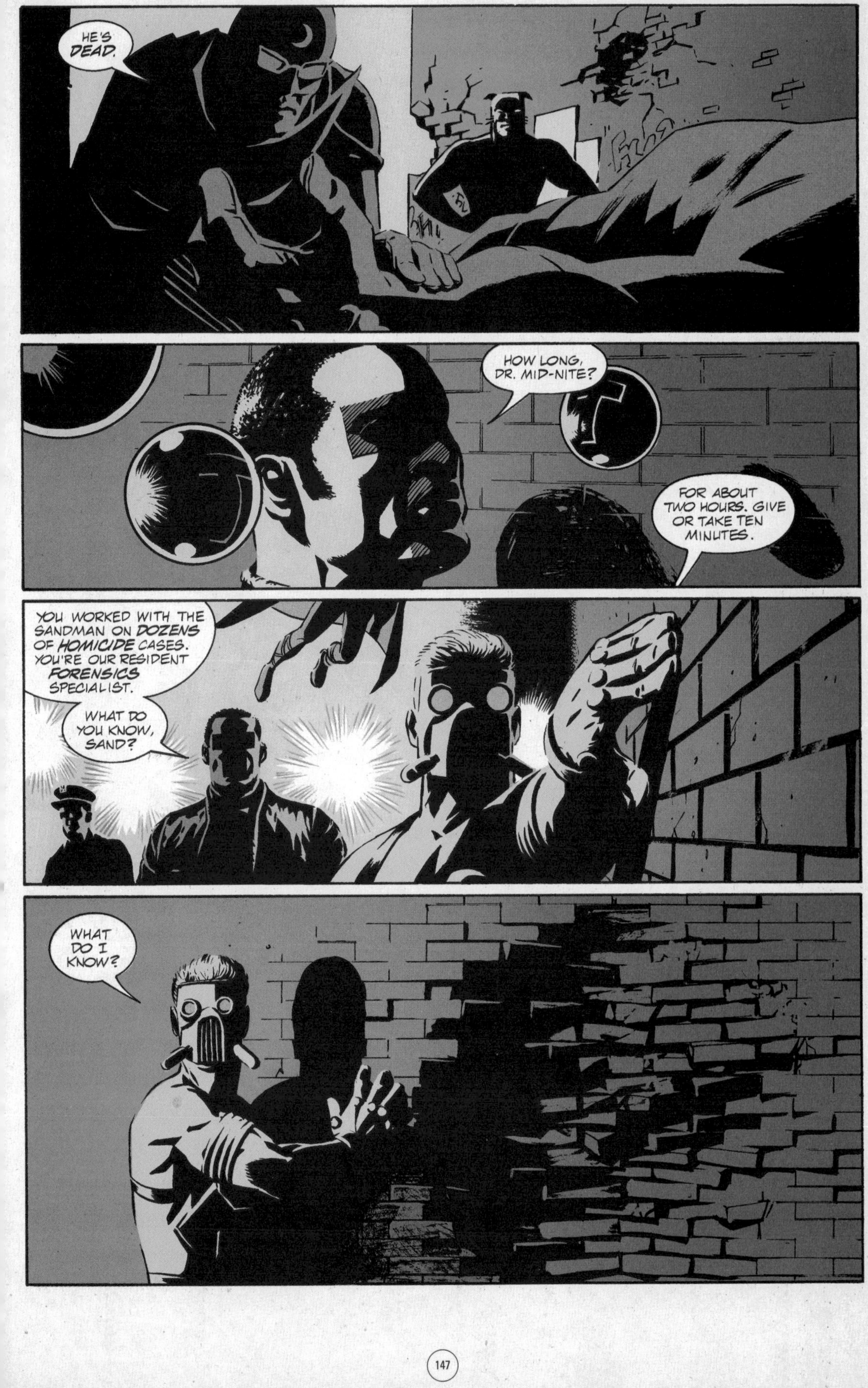
HE'S DEAD.
HOW LONG, DR. MID-NITE?
FOR ABOUT TWO HOURS. GIVE OR TAKE TEN MINUTES.
YOU WORKED WITH THE SANDMAN ON DOZENS OF HOMICIDE CASES. YOU'RE OUR RESIDENT FORENSICS SPECIALIST.
WHAT DO YOU KNOW, SAND?
WHAT DO I KNOW?

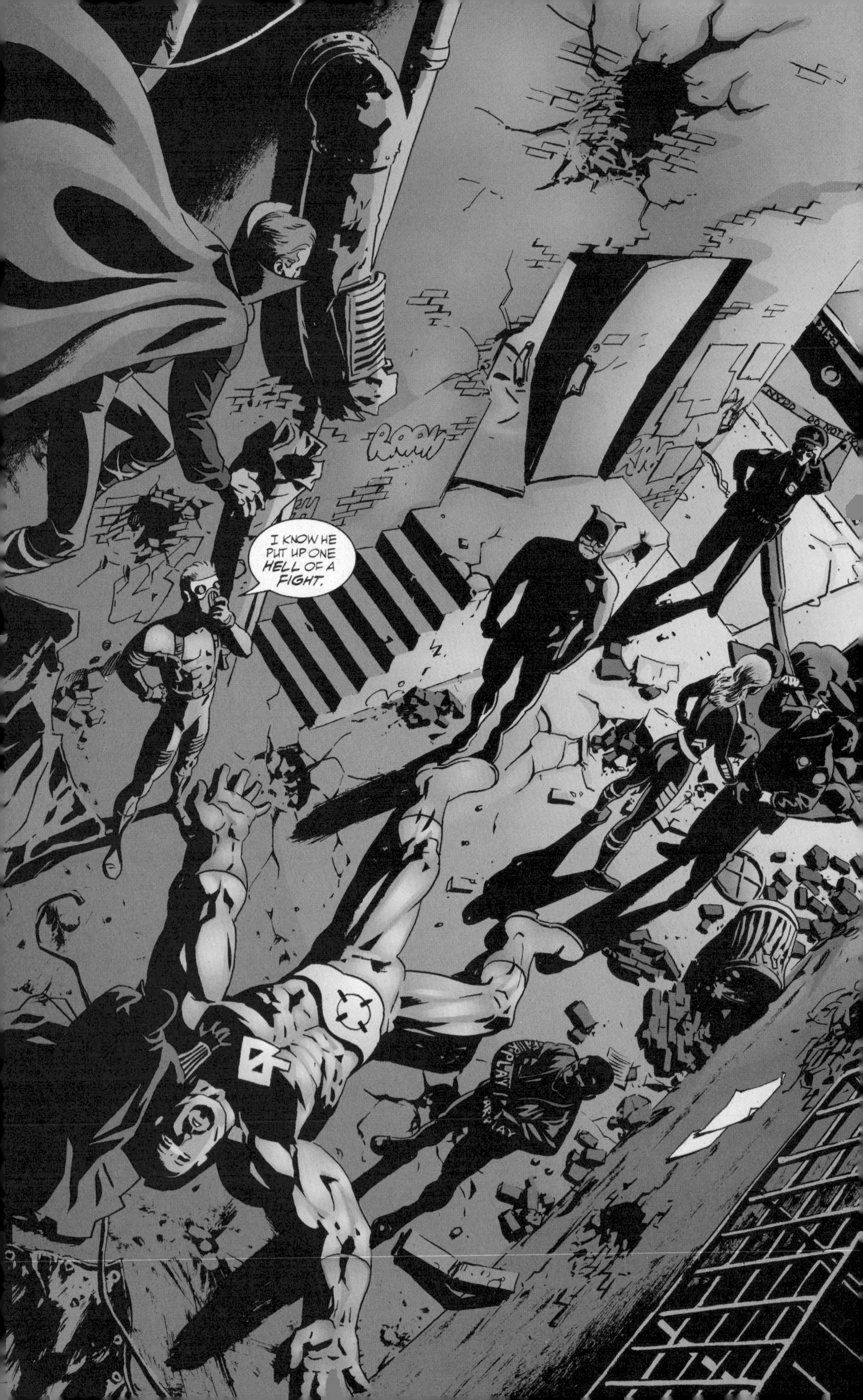
I KNOW HE PUT UP ONE HELL OF A FIGHT.

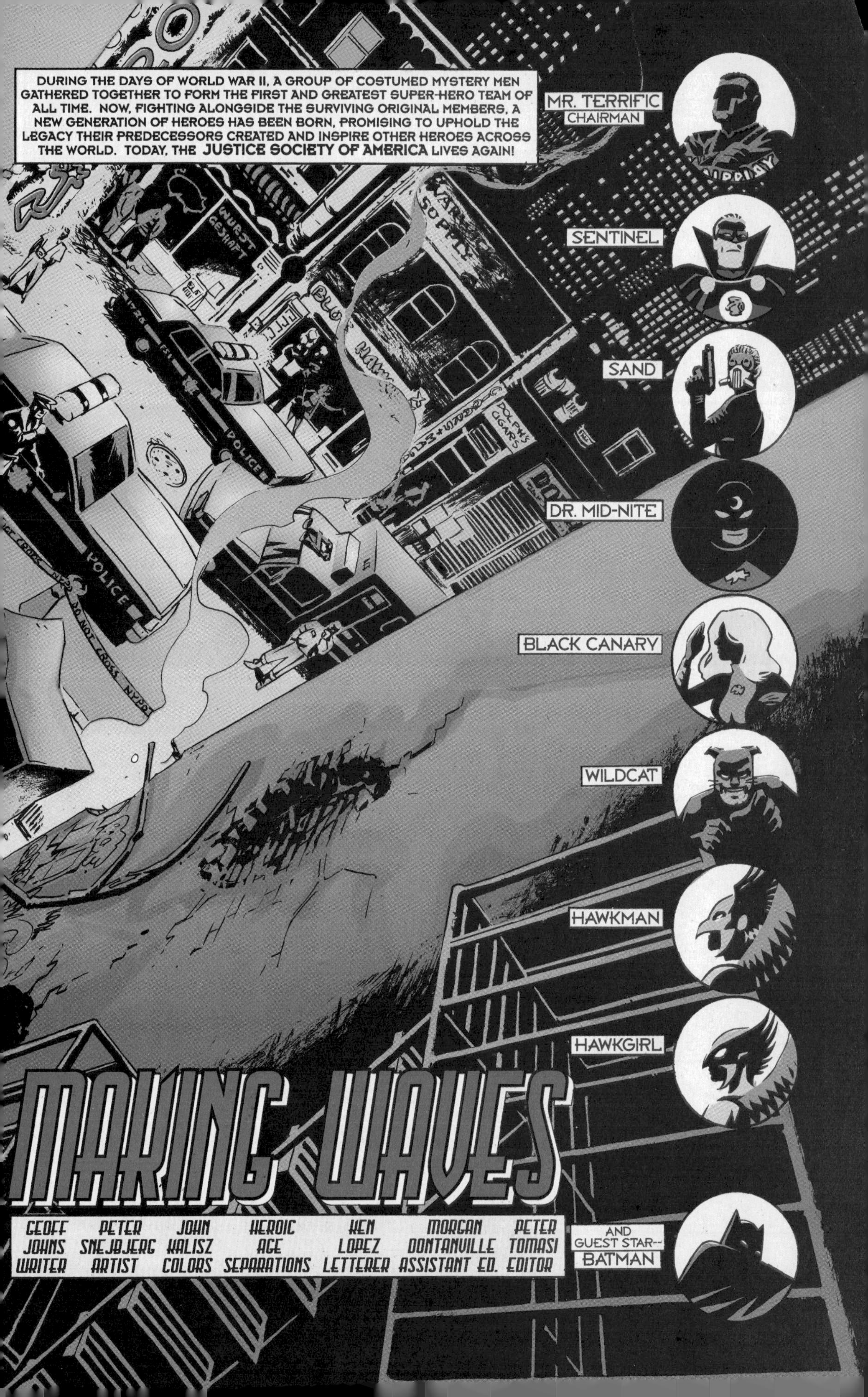

DURING THE DAYS OF WORLD WAR II, A GROUP OF COSTUMED MYSTERY MEN GATHERED TOGETHER TO FORM THE FIRST AND GREATEST SUPER-HERO TEAM OF ALL TIME. NOW, FIGHTING ALONGSIDE THE SURVIVING ORIGINAL MEMBERS, A NEW GENERATION OF HEROES HAS BEEN BORN, PROMISING TO UPHOLD THE LEGACY THEIR PREDECESSORS CREATED AND INSPIRE OTHER HEROES ACROSS THE WORLD. TODAY, THE JUSTICE SOCIETY OF AMERICA LIVES AGAIN!
MR. TERRIFIC CHAIRMAN
SENTINEL
SAND
DR. MID-NITE
BLACK CANARY
WILDCAT
HAWKMAN
HAWKGIRL
AND GUEST STAR-- BATMAN
WURST GESHAFT
POLICE
POLICE
DOLPH'S CIGARS
DO NOT CROSS NYPD
MAKING WAVES
GEOFF JOHNS WRITER
PETER SNEJBJERG ARTIST
JOHN KALISZ COLORS
HEROIC AGE SEPARATIONS
KEN LOPEZ LETTERER
MORGAN DONTANVILLE ASSISTANT ED.
PETER TOMASI EDITOR

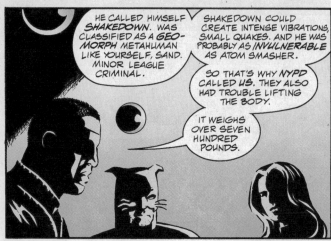

HE CALLED HIMSELF *SHAKEDOWN*. WAS CLASSIFIED AS A *GEO-MORPH* METAHUMAN LIKE YOURSELF, SAND. MINOR LEAGUE CRIMINAL.

SHAKEDOWN COULD CREATE INTENSE VIBRATIONS, SMALL QUAKES. AND HE WAS PROBABLY AS *INVULNERABLE* AS ATOM SMASHER.

SO THAT'S WHY *NYPD* CALLED *US*. THEY ALSO HAD TROUBLE LIFTING THE BODY.

IT WEIGHS OVER SEVEN HUNDRED POUNDS.

LOOK AT THOSE *ARMS*. WHOEVER MANAGED TO *OFF* THIS *PALOOKA* MUST HAVE BEEN ONE *TOUGH* HOMBRE.

NOT *NECESSARILY*, WILDCAT.

THERE MAY HAVE BEEN A PHYSICAL BATTLE HERE, BUT SHAKEDOWN WASN'T *BEATEN* TO DEATH--

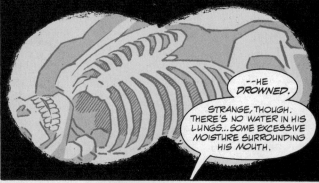

--HE *DROWNED*.

STRANGE, THOUGH. THERE'S NO WATER IN HIS LUNGS...SOME EXCESSIVE MOISTURE SURROUNDING HIS MOUTH.

THEN HE DIED FROM LARYNGOSPASM. *DRY DROWNING*. A MASSIVE AMOUNT OF LIQUID INTRODUCED INTO HIS THROAT PROBABLY FORCED HIS AIRWAY CLOSED.

HOW IS THAT POSSIBLE?

IN AN ALLEY IN MANHATTAN? TO A GUY LIKE THIS?

MAN, I'M NOT SURE.

YOU OKAY, CANARY? YOU HAVEN'T SPOKEN TO ME ALL NIGHT.

YEAH, MID-NITE... *THROAT* JUST HURTS THINKING ABOUT THIS.

DO YOU WANT ME TO--

NO.

I'M *FINE*.

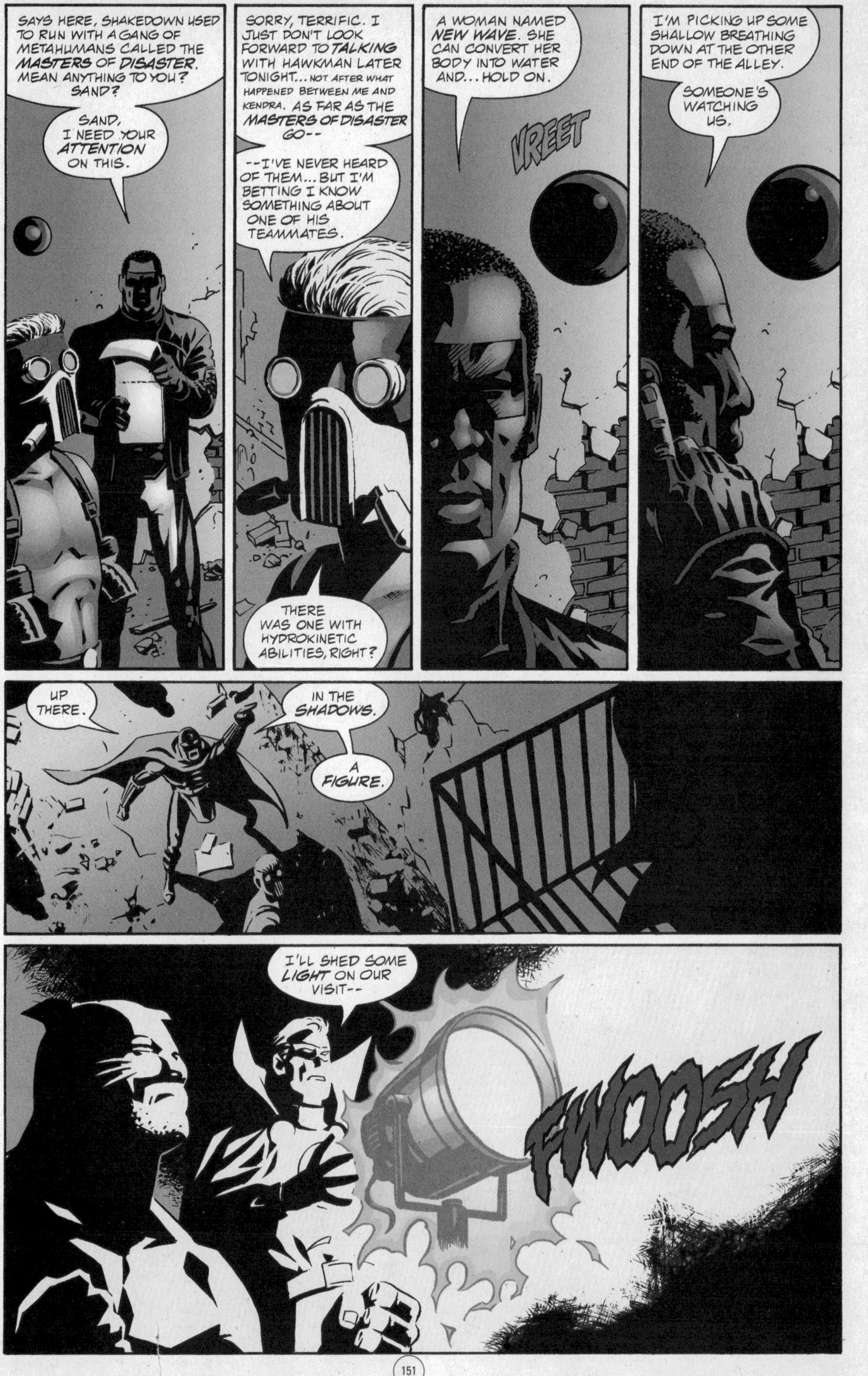

SAYS HERE, SHAKEDOWN USED TO RUN WITH A GANG OF METAHUMANS CALLED THE MASTERS OF DISASTER. MEAN ANYTHING TO YOU? SAND?
SAND, I NEED YOUR ATTENTION ON THIS.
SORRY, TERRIFIC. I JUST DON'T LOOK FORWARD TO TALKING WITH HAWKMAN LATER TONIGHT... NOT AFTER WHAT HAPPENED BETWEEN ME AND KENDRA. AS FAR AS THE MASTERS OF DISASTER GO--
--I'VE NEVER HEARD OF THEM... BUT I'M BETTING I KNOW SOMETHING ABOUT ONE OF HIS TEAMMATES.
THERE WAS ONE WITH HYDROKINETIC ABILITIES, RIGHT?
A WOMAN NAMED NEW WAVE. SHE CAN CONVERT HER BODY INTO WATER AND... HOLD ON.
VREET
I'M PICKING UP SOME SHALLOW BREATHING DOWN AT THE OTHER END OF THE ALLEY.
SOMEONE'S WATCHING US.
UP THERE.
IN THE SHADOWS.
A FIGURE.
I'LL SHED SOME LIGHT ON OUR VISIT--
FWOOSH

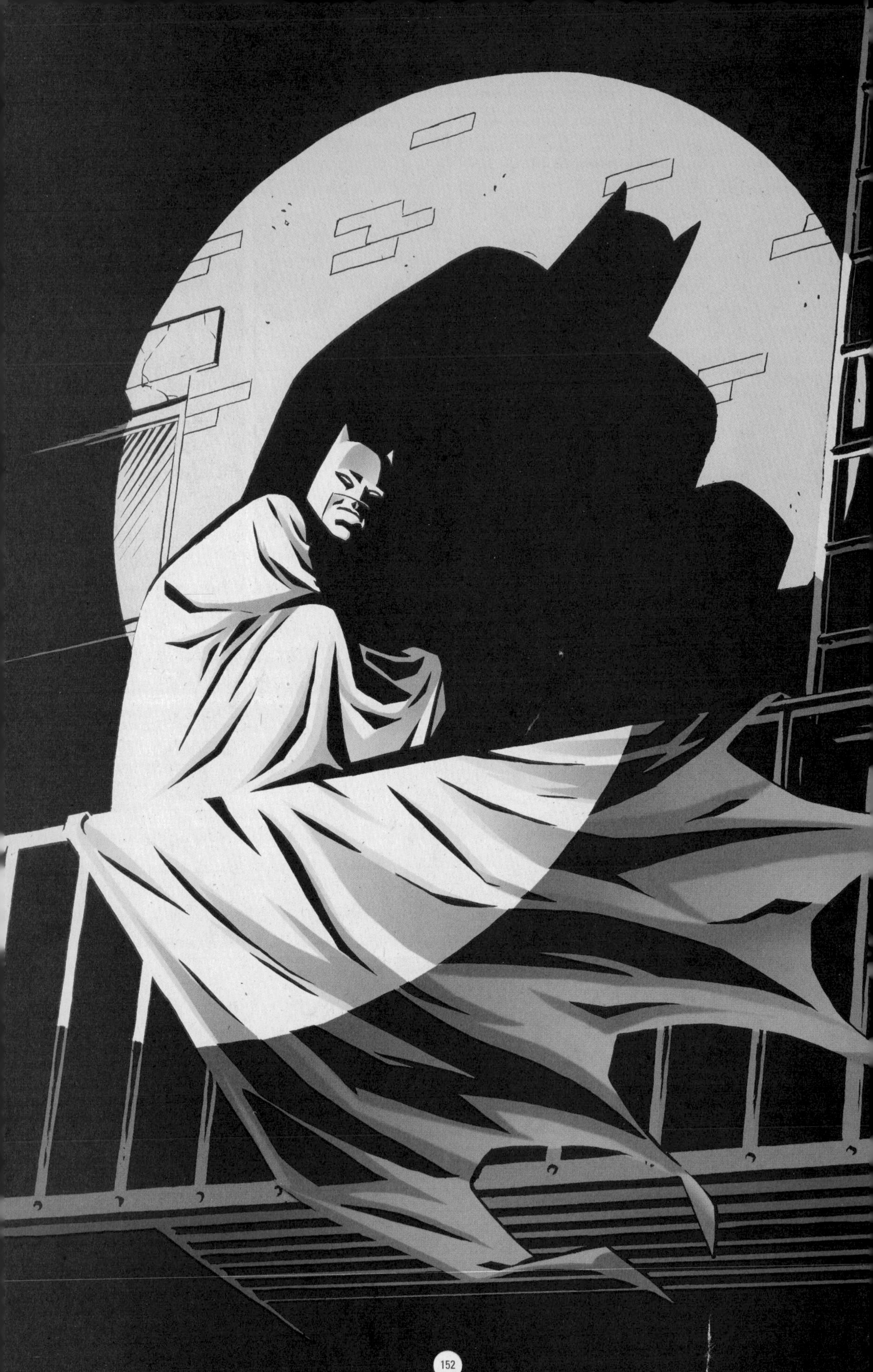

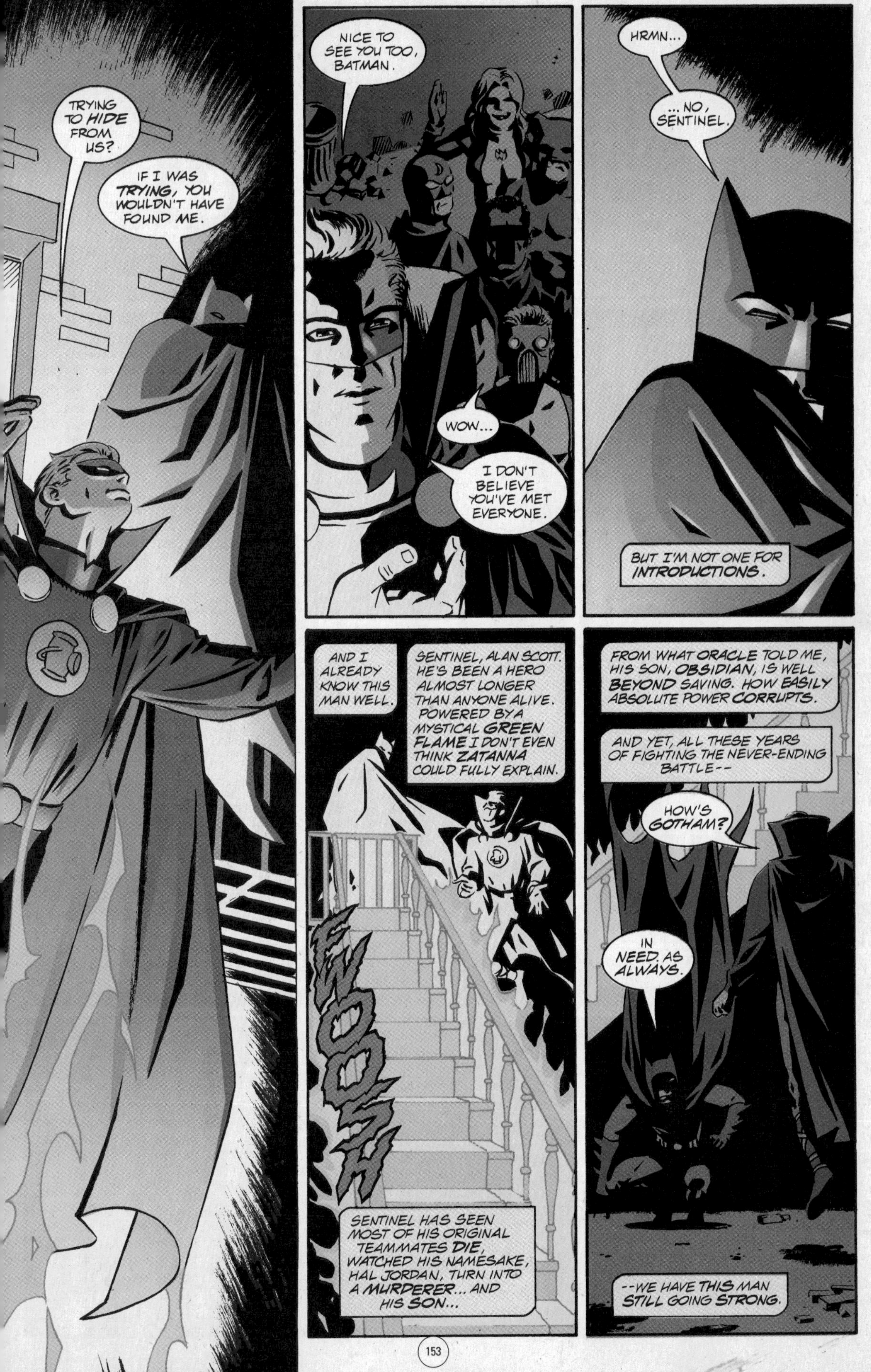
TRYING TO HIDE FROM US?
IF I WAS TRYING, YOU WOULDN'T HAVE FOUND ME.
NICE TO SEE YOU TOO, BATMAN.
WOW...
I DON'T BELIEVE YOU'VE MET EVERYONE.
HRMN...
...NO, SENTINEL.
BUT I'M NOT ONE FOR INTRODUCTIONS.
AND I ALREADY KNOW THIS MAN WELL.
SENTINEL, ALAN SCOTT. HE'S BEEN A HERO ALMOST LONGER THAN ANYONE ALIVE. POWERED BY A MYSTICAL GREEN FLAME I DON'T EVEN THINK ZATANNA COULD FULLY EXPLAIN.
WHOOSH
SENTINEL HAS SEEN MOST OF HIS ORIGINAL TEAMMATES DIE, WATCHED HIS NAMESAKE, HAL JORDAN, TURN INTO A MURDERER... AND HIS SON...
FROM WHAT ORACLE TOLD ME, HIS SON, OBSIDIAN, IS WELL BEYOND SAVING. HOW EASILY ABSOLUTE POWER CORRUPTS.
AND YET, ALL THESE YEARS OF FIGHTING THE NEVER-ENDING BATTLE--
HOW'S GOTHAM?
IN NEED. AS ALWAYS.
--WE HAVE THIS MAN STILL GOING STRONG.

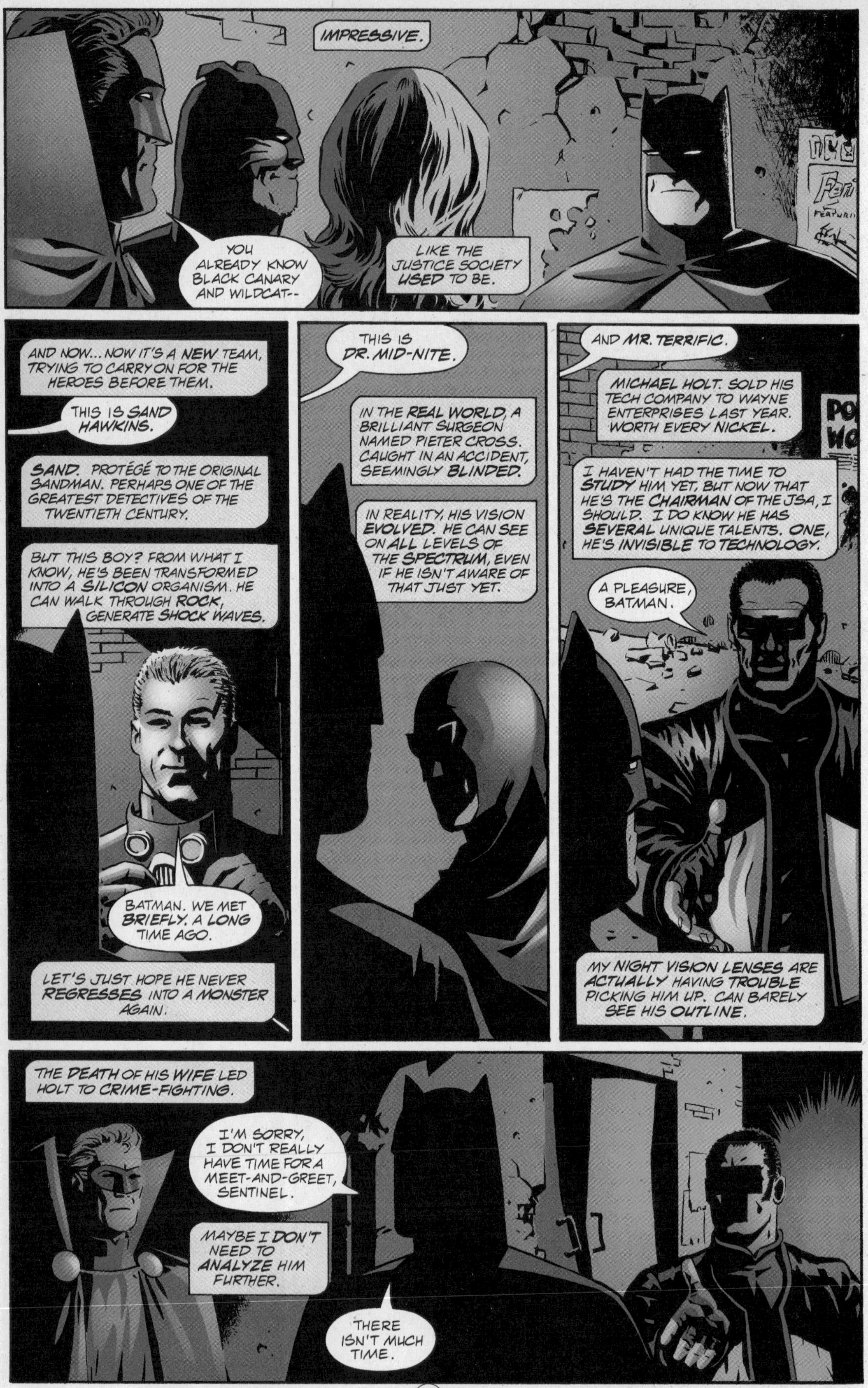
IMPRESSIVE.
YOU ALREADY KNOW BLACK CANARY AND WILDCAT--
LIKE THE JUSTICE SOCIETY USED TO BE.
AND NOW... NOW IT'S A NEW TEAM, TRYING TO CARRY ON FOR THE HEROES BEFORE THEM.
THIS IS SAND HAWKINS.
SAND. PROTÉGÉ TO THE ORIGINAL SANDMAN. PERHAPS ONE OF THE GREATEST DETECTIVES OF THE TWENTIETH CENTURY.
BUT THIS BOY? FROM WHAT I KNOW, HE'S BEEN TRANSFORMED INTO A SILICON ORGANISM. HE CAN WALK THROUGH ROCK, GENERATE SHOCK WAVES.
BATMAN. WE MET BRIEFLY. A LONG TIME AGO.
LET'S JUST HOPE HE NEVER REGRESSES INTO A MONSTER AGAIN.
THIS IS DR. MID-NITE.
IN THE REAL WORLD, A BRILLIANT SURGEON NAMED PIETER CROSS. CAUGHT IN AN ACCIDENT, SEEMINGLY BLINDED.
IN REALITY, HIS VISION EVOLVED. HE CAN SEE ON ALL LEVELS OF THE SPECTRUM, EVEN IF HE ISN'T AWARE OF THAT JUST YET.
AND MR. TERRIFIC.
MICHAEL HOLT. SOLD HIS TECH COMPANY TO WAYNE ENTERPRISES LAST YEAR. WORTH EVERY NICKEL.
I HAVEN'T HAD THE TIME TO STUDY HIM YET, BUT NOW THAT HE'S THE CHAIRMAN OF THE JSA, I SHOULD. I DO KNOW HE HAS SEVERAL UNIQUE TALENTS. ONE, HE'S INVISIBLE TO TECHNOLOGY.
A PLEASURE, BATMAN.
MY NIGHT VISION LENSES ARE ACTUALLY HAVING TROUBLE PICKING HIM UP. CAN BARELY SEE HIS OUTLINE.
THE DEATH OF HIS WIFE LED HOLT TO CRIME-FIGHTING.
I'M SORRY, I DON'T REALLY HAVE TIME FOR A MEET-AND-GREET, SENTINEL.
MAYBE I DON'T NEED TO ANALYZE HIM FURTHER.
THERE ISN'T MUCH TIME.

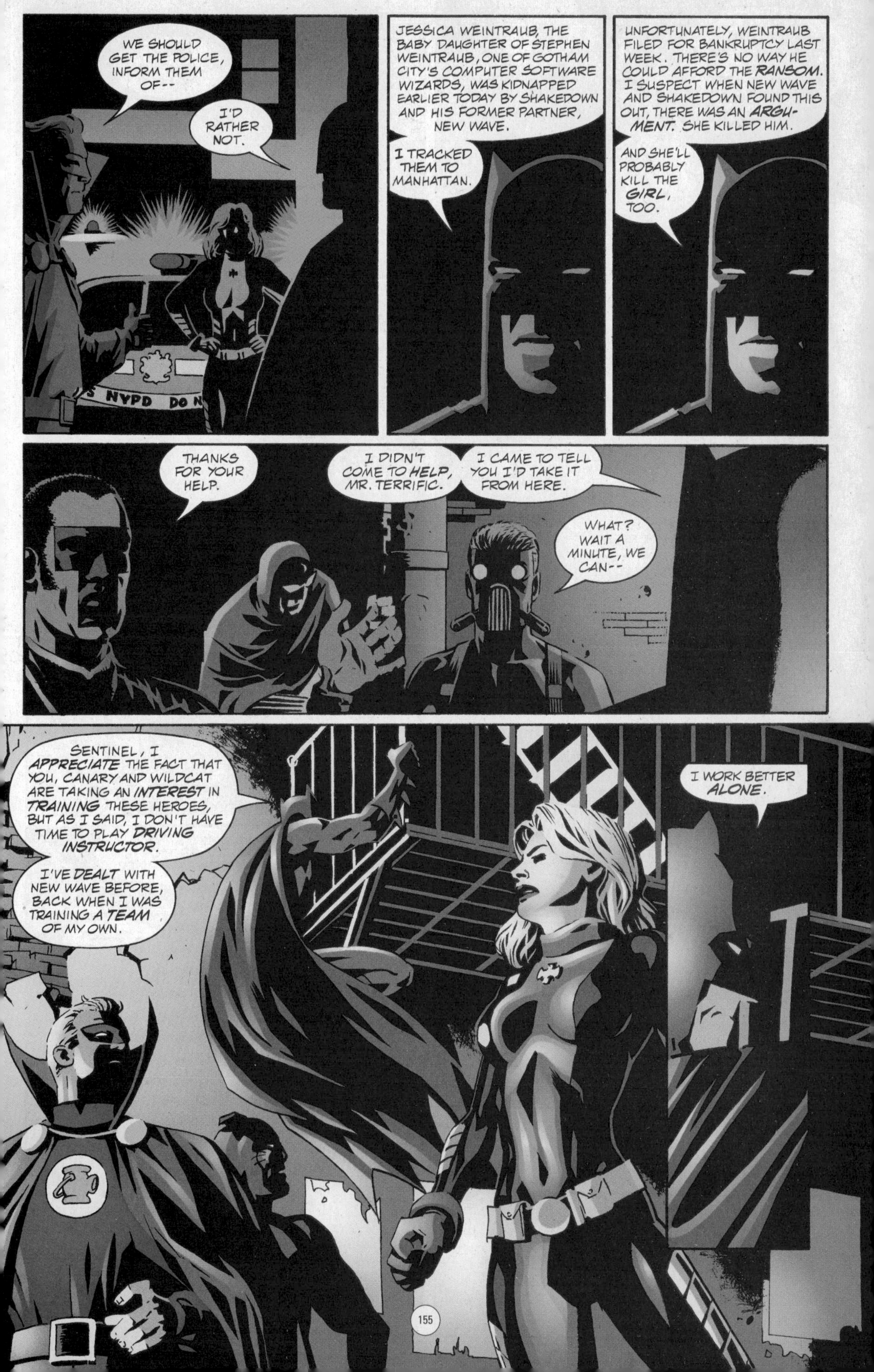

WE SHOULD GET THE POLICE, INFORM THEM OF--
I'D RATHER NOT.
NYPD DO N
JESSICA WEINTRAUB, THE BABY DAUGHTER OF STEPHEN WEINTRAUB, ONE OF GOTHAM CITY'S COMPUTER SOFTWARE WIZARDS, WAS KIDNAPPED EARLIER TODAY BY SHAKEDOWN AND HIS FORMER PARTNER, NEW WAVE.
I TRACKED THEM TO MANHATTAN.
UNFORTUNATELY, WEINTRAUB FILED FOR BANKRUPTCY LAST WEEK. THERE'S NO WAY HE COULD AFFORD THE RANSOM. I SUSPECT WHEN NEW WAVE AND SHAKEDOWN FOUND THIS OUT, THERE WAS AN ARGUMENT. SHE KILLED HIM.
AND SHE'LL PROBABLY KILL THE GIRL, TOO.
THANKS FOR YOUR HELP.
I DIDN'T COME TO HELP, MR. TERRIFIC.
I CAME TO TELL YOU I'D TAKE IT FROM HERE.
WHAT? WAIT A MINUTE, WE CAN--
SENTINEL, I APPRECIATE THE FACT THAT YOU, CANARY AND WILDCAT ARE TAKING AN INTEREST IN TRAINING THESE HEROES, BUT AS I SAID, I DON'T HAVE TIME TO PLAY DRIVING INSTRUCTOR.
I'VE DEALT WITH NEW WAVE BEFORE, BACK WHEN I WAS TRAINING A TEAM OF MY OWN.
I WORK BETTER ALONE.

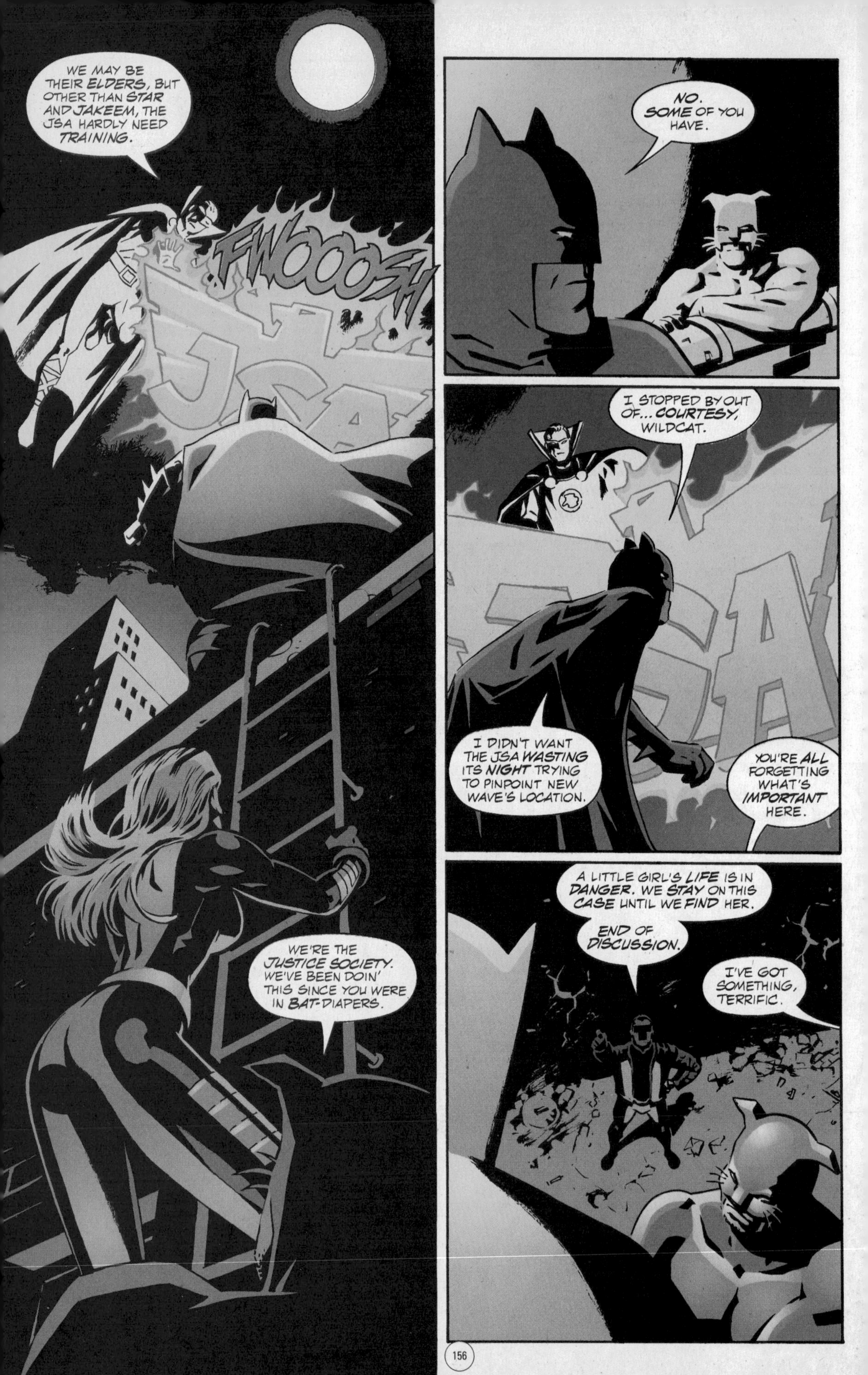
WE MAY BE THEIR ELDERS, BUT OTHER THAN STAR AND JAKEEM, THE JSA HARDLY NEED TRAINING.
FWOOOSH
JSA
WE'RE THE JUSTICE SOCIETY. WE'VE BEEN DOIN' THIS SINCE YOU WERE IN BAT-DIAPERS.
NO. SOME OF YOU HAVE.
I STOPPED BY OUT OF... COURTESY, WILDCAT.
I DIDN'T WANT THE JSA WASTING ITS NIGHT TRYING TO PINPOINT NEW WAVE'S LOCATION.
YOU'RE ALL FORGETTING WHAT'S IMPORTANT HERE.
A LITTLE GIRL'S LIFE IS IN DANGER. WE STAY ON THIS CASE UNTIL WE FIND HER.
END OF DISCUSSION.
I'VE GOT SOMETHING, TERRIFIC.

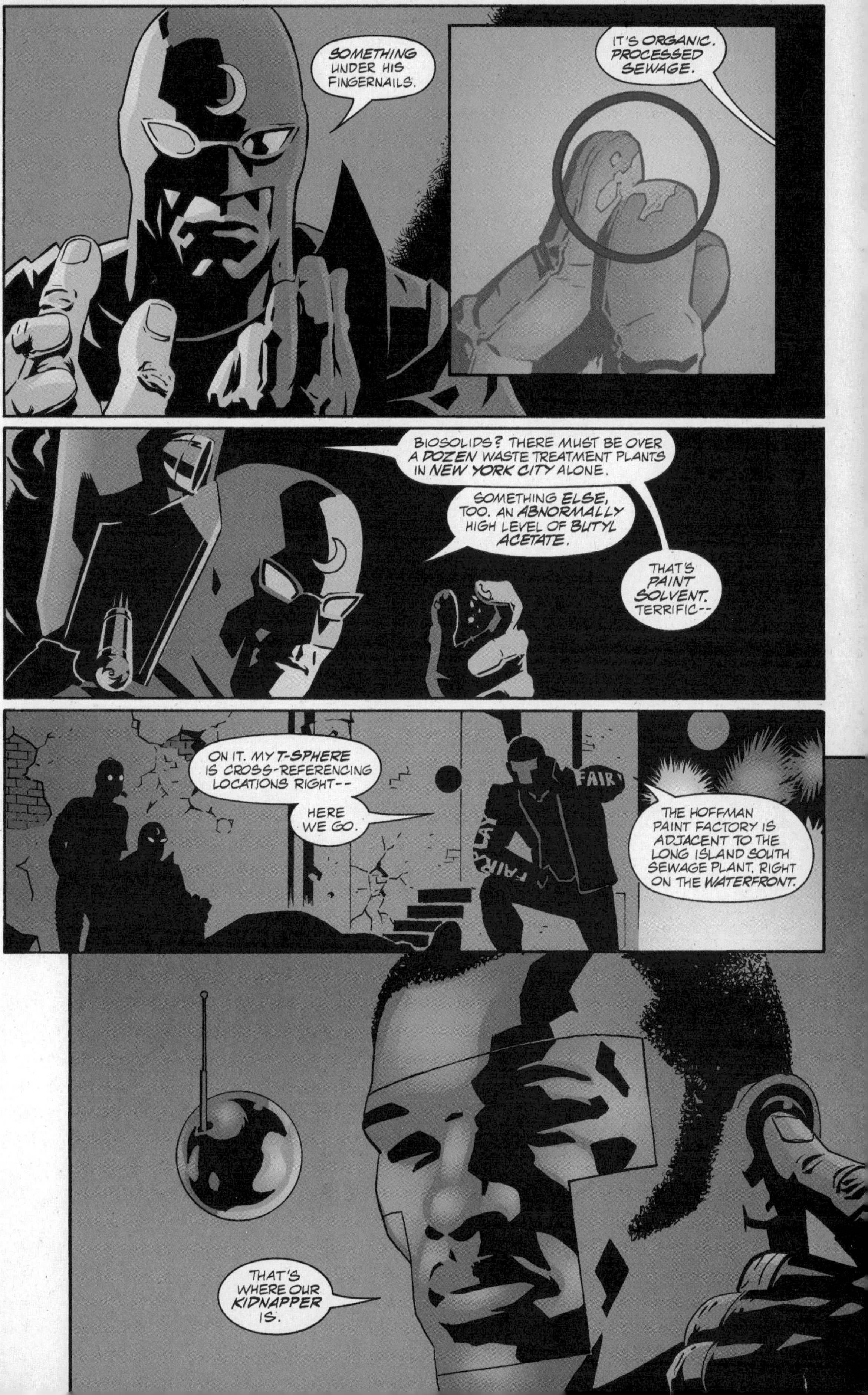
SOMETHING UNDER HIS FINGERNAILS.
IT'S ORGANIC. PROCESSED SEWAGE.
BIOSOLIDS? THERE MUST BE OVER A DOZEN WASTE TREATMENT PLANTS IN NEW YORK CITY ALONE.
SOMETHING ELSE, TOO. AN ABNORMALLY HIGH LEVEL OF BUTYL ACETATE.
THAT'S PAINT SOLVENT. TERRIFIC--
ON IT. MY T-SPHERE IS CROSS-REFERENCING LOCATIONS RIGHT--
HERE WE GO.
FAIR
FAIR PLAY
THE HOFFMAN PAINT FACTORY IS ADJACENT TO THE LONG ISLAND SOUTH SEWAGE PLANT, RIGHT ON THE WATERFRONT.
THAT'S WHERE OUR KIDNAPPER IS.

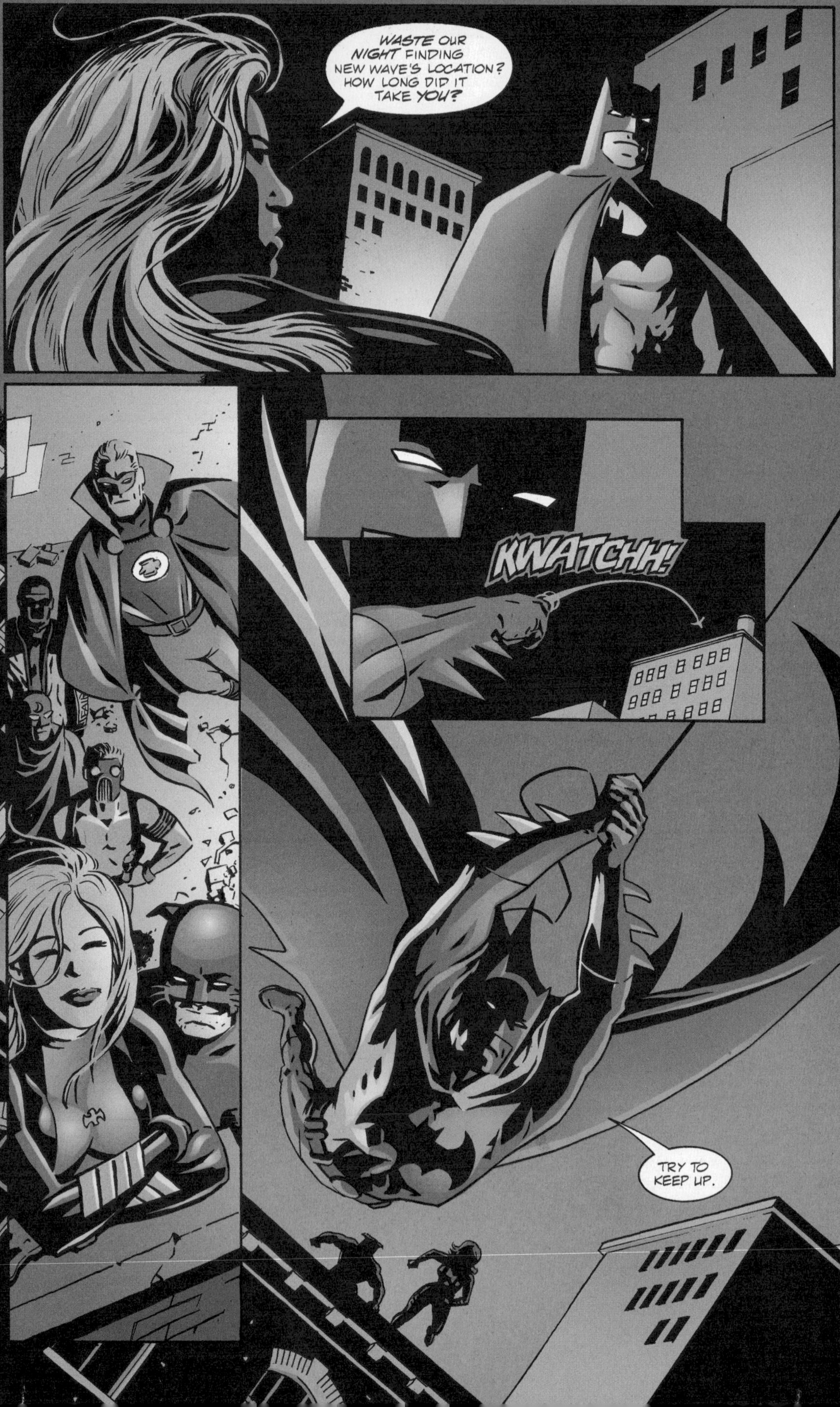
WASTE OUR NIGHT FINDING NEW WAVE'S LOCATION? HOW LONG DID IT TAKE YOU?
KWATCHH!
TRY TO KEEP UP.

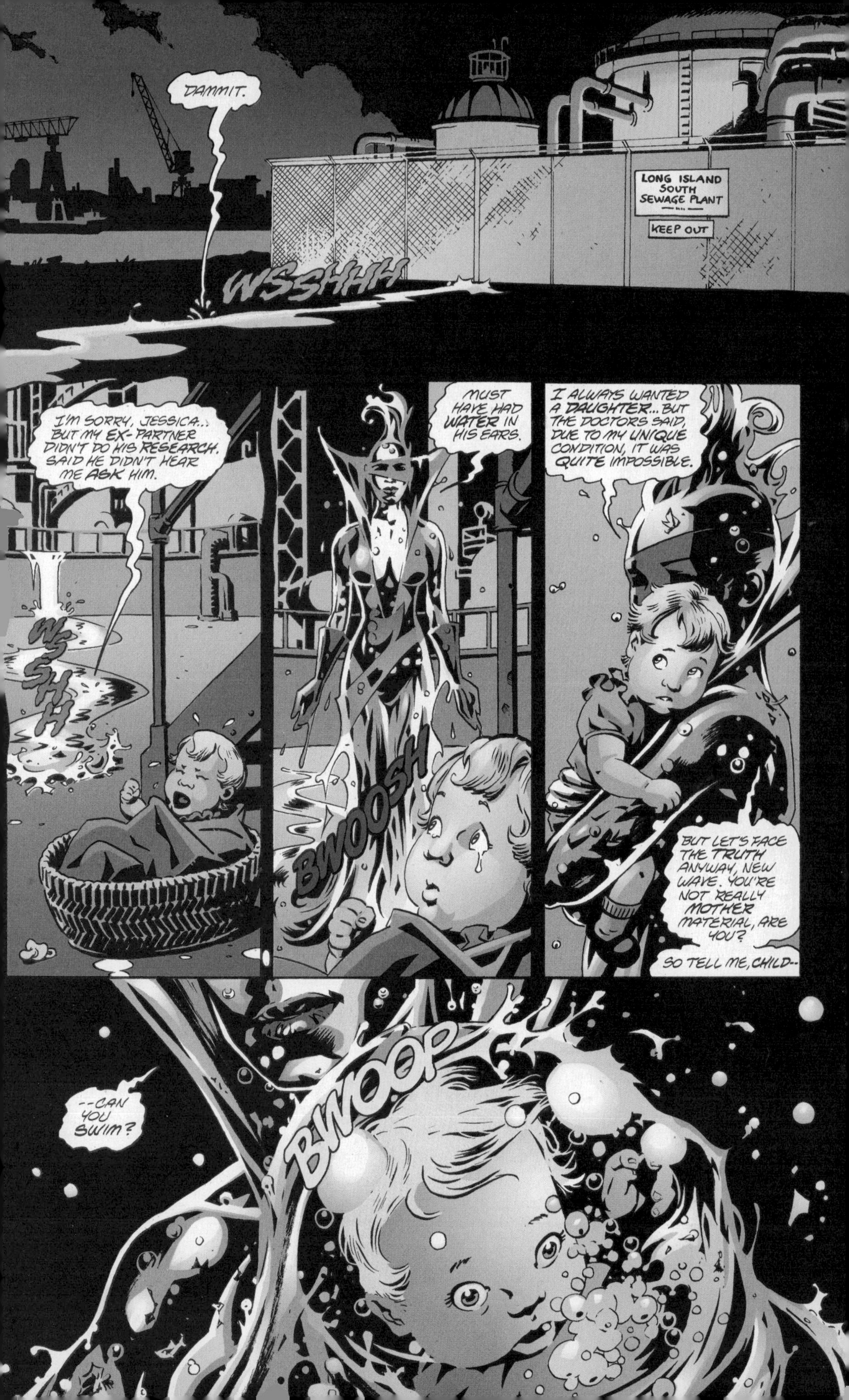
DAMMIT.
LONG ISLAND SOUTH SEWAGE PLANT
KEEP OUT
WSSHHH
I'M SORRY, JESSICA... BUT MY EX-PARTNER DIDN'T DO HIS RESEARCH. SAID HE DIDN'T HEAR ME ASK HIM.
WSSHH
MUST HAVE HAD WATER IN HIS EARS.
BWOOSH
I ALWAYS WANTED A DAUGHTER... BUT THE DOCTORS SAID, DUE TO MY UNIQUE CONDITION, IT WAS QUITE IMPOSSIBLE.
BUT LET'S FACE THE TRUTH ANYWAY, NEW WAVE. YOU'RE NOT REALLY MOTHER MATERIAL, ARE YOU?
SO TELL ME, CHILD--
--CAN YOU SWIM?
BWOOP

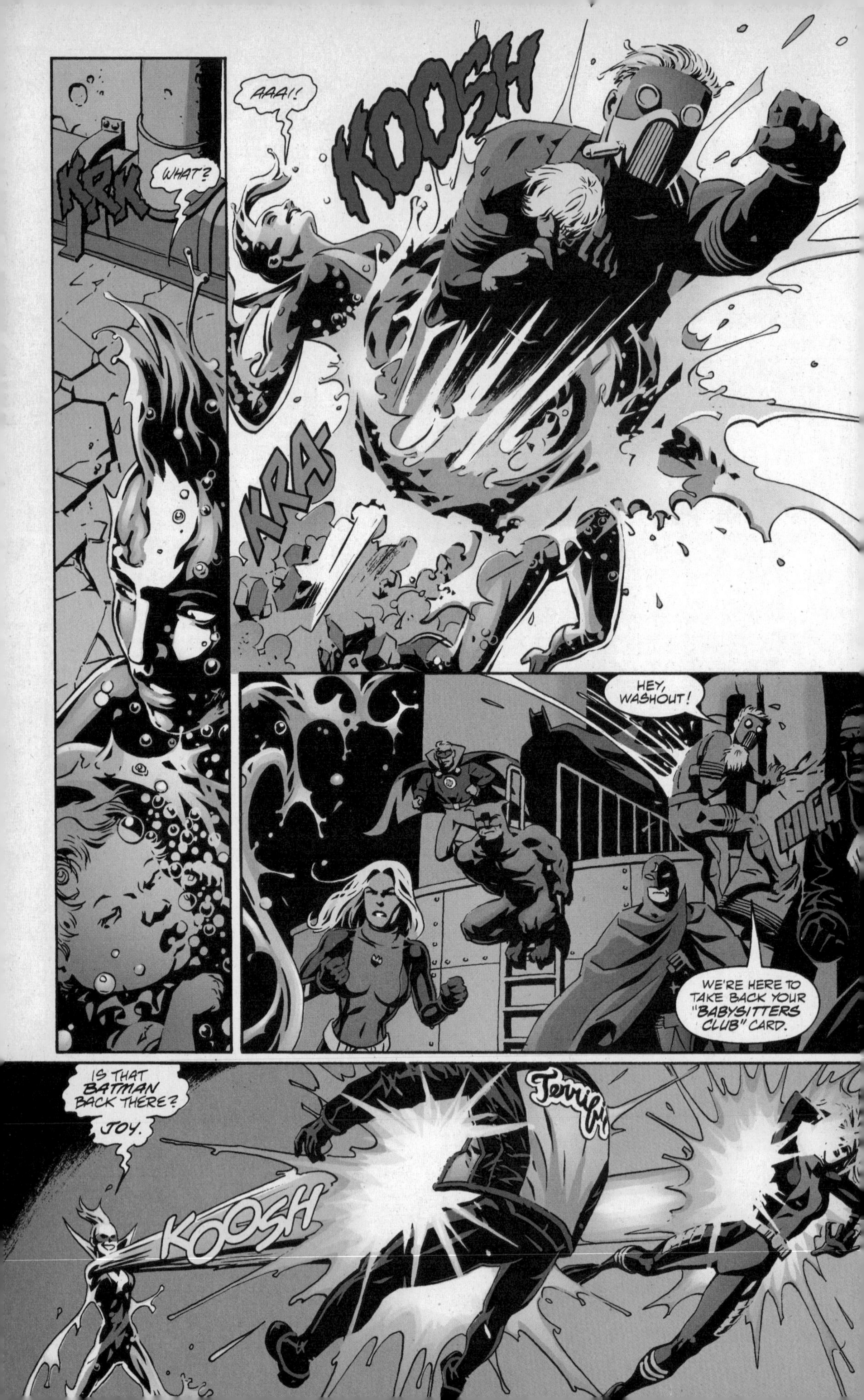
AAA!!
KOOSH
KRK
WHAT?
KRA
HEY, WASHOUT!
WE'RE HERE TO TAKE BACK YOUR "BABYSITTERS CLUB" CARD.
IS THAT BATMAN BACK THERE?
JOY.
KOOSH

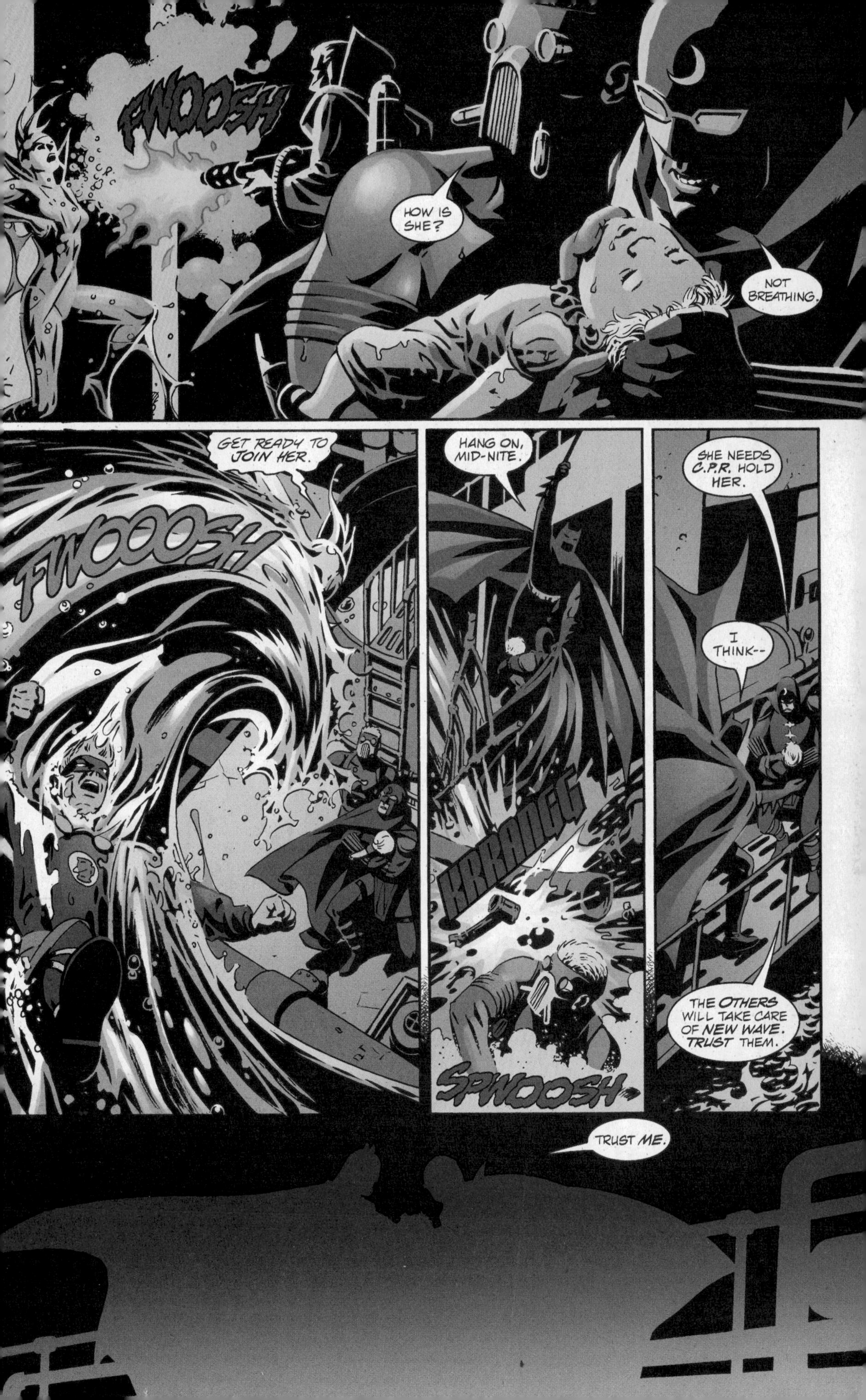
FWOOSH
HOW IS SHE?
NOT BREATHING.
GET READY TO JOIN HER.
FWOOOSH
HANG ON, MID-NITE.
KRRANGG
SPWOOSH
SHE NEEDS C.P.R. HOLD HER.
I THINK--
THE OTHERS WILL TAKE CARE OF NEW WAVE. TRUST THEM.
TRUST ME.

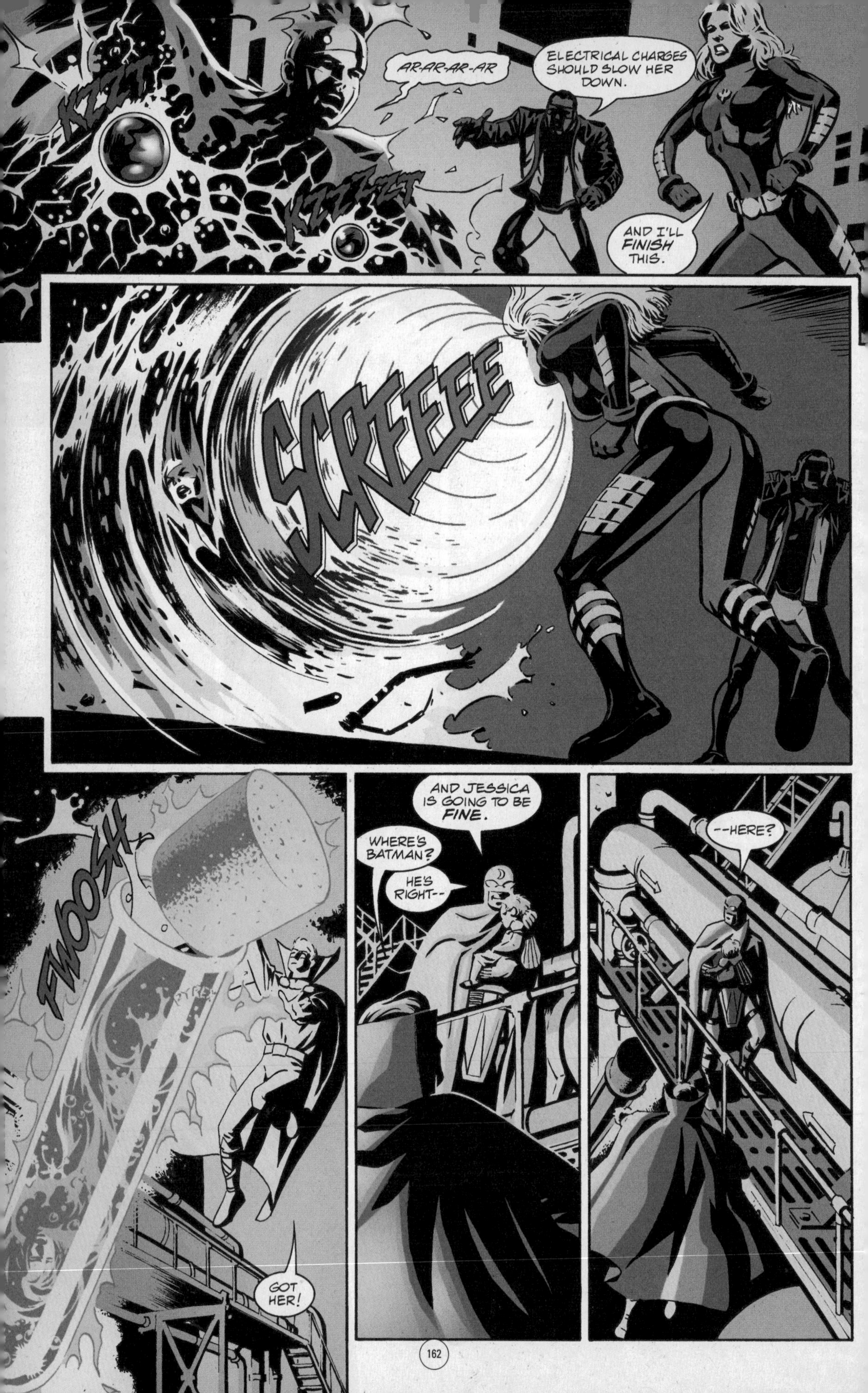

KZZZT
AR-AR-AR-AR
ELECTRICAL CHARGES SHOULD SLOW HER DOWN.
KZZZZZZT
AND I'LL FINISH THIS.
SCREEEE
FWOOSH
GOT HER!
AND JESSICA IS GOING TO BE FINE.
WHERE'S BATMAN?
HE'S RIGHT--
--HERE?

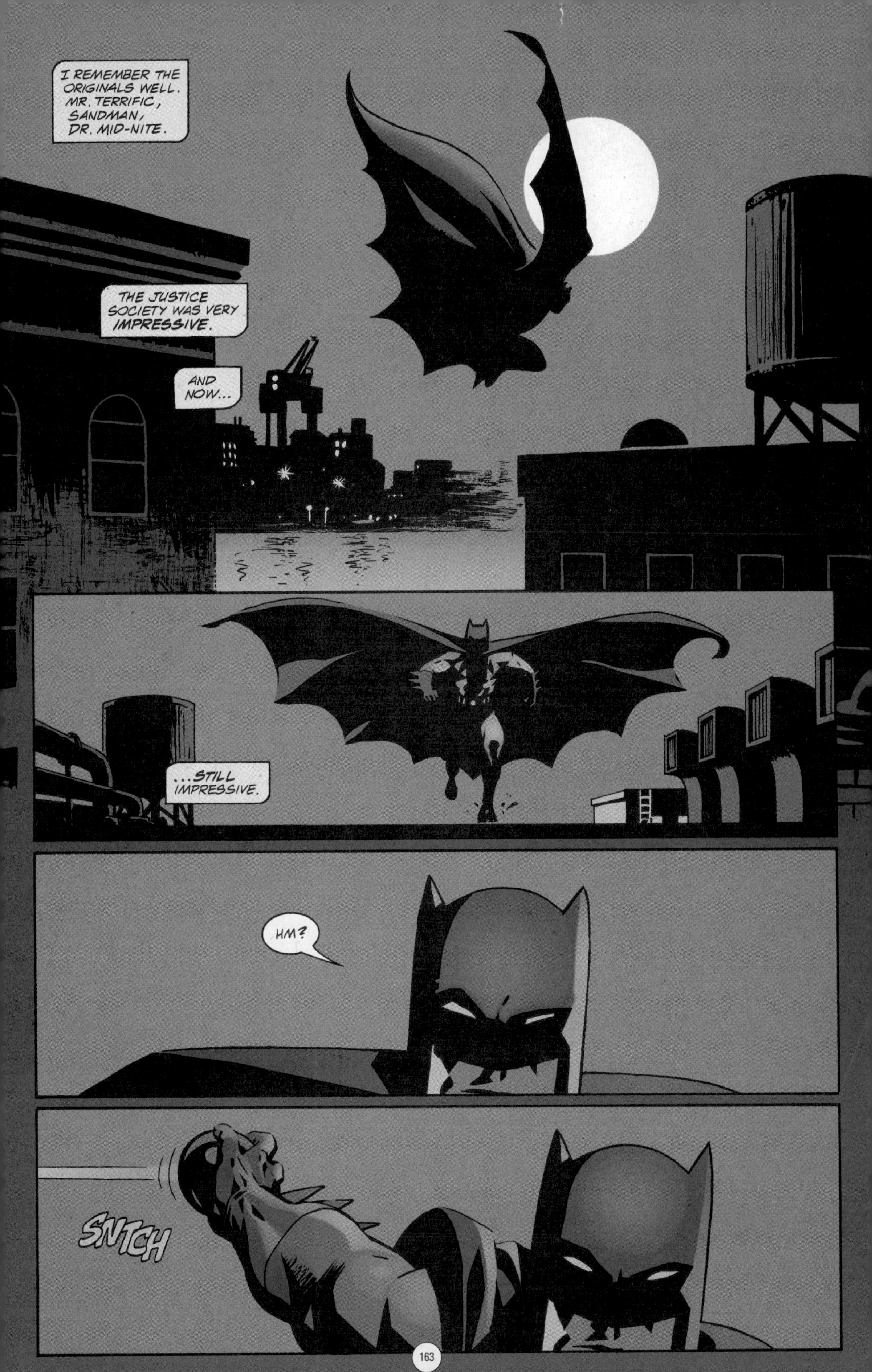

I REMEMBER THE ORIGINALS WELL. MR. TERRIFIC, SANDMAN, DR. MID-NITE.
THE JUSTICE SOCIETY WAS VERY IMPRESSIVE.
AND NOW...
...STILL IMPRESSIVE.
HM?
SNTCH

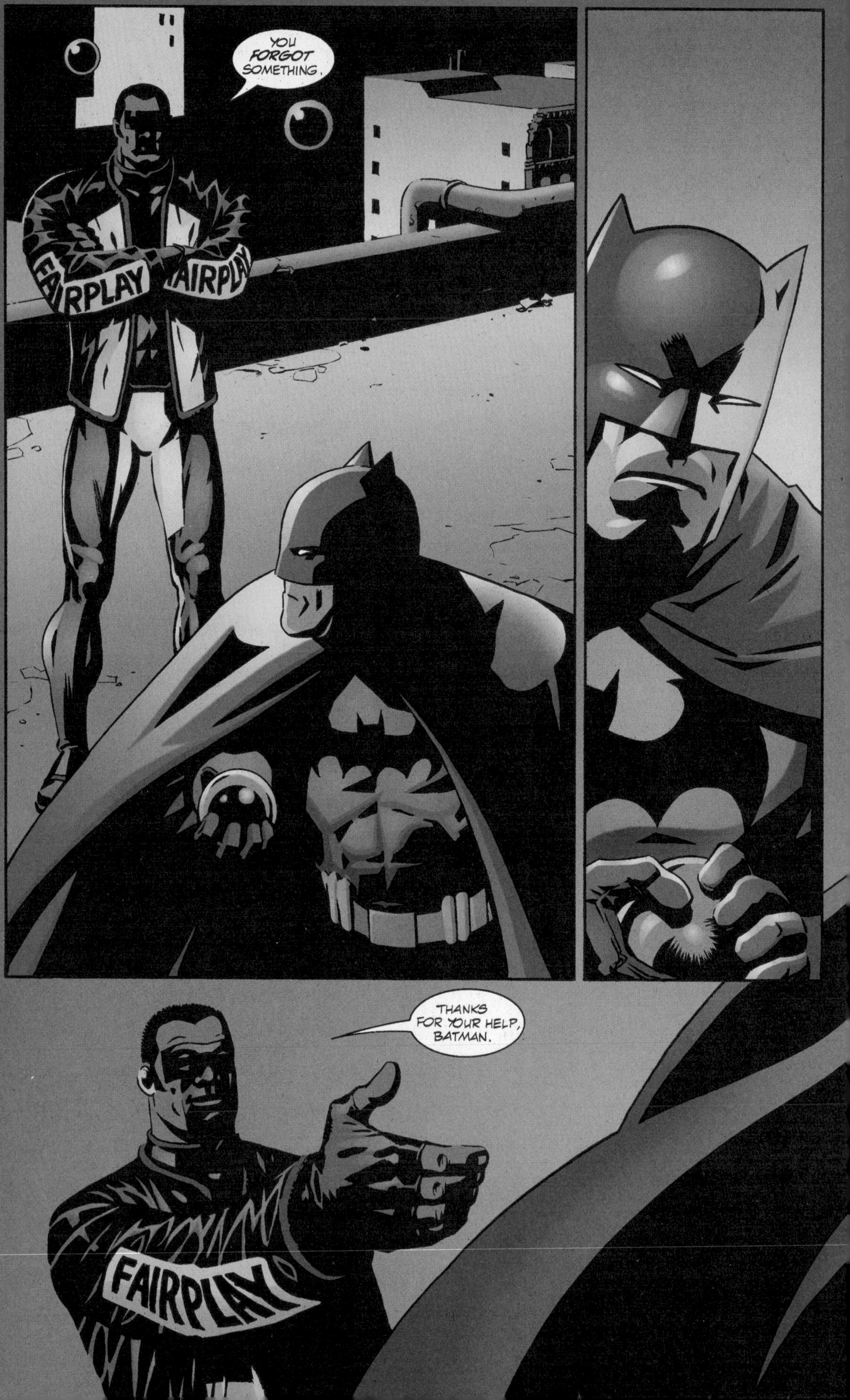
YOU FORGOT SOMETHING.
FAIRPLAY
FAIRPLAY
THANKS FOR YOUR HELP, BATMAN.
FAIRPLAY

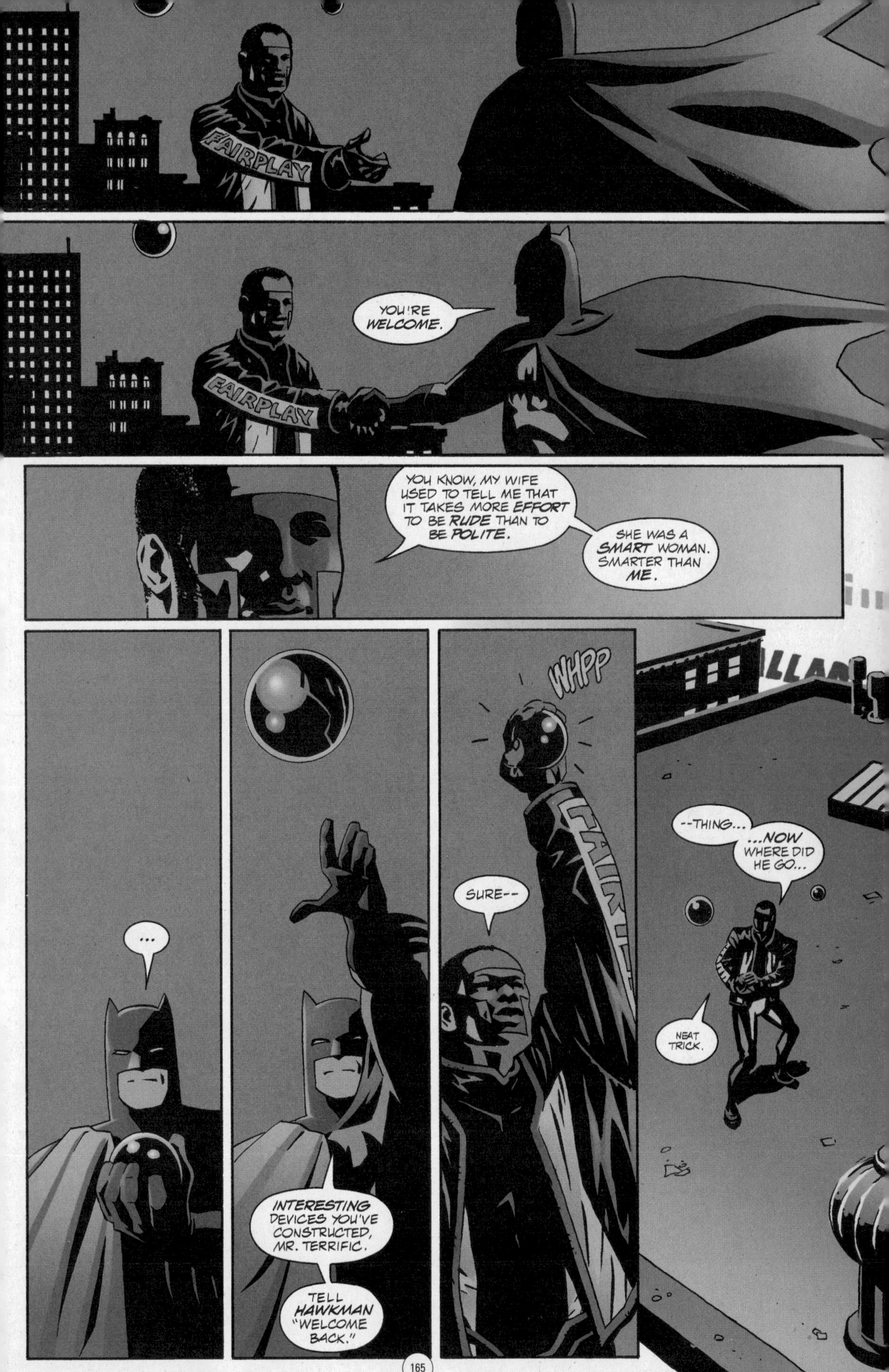
FAIRPLAY
YOU'RE WELCOME.
FAIRPLAY
YOU KNOW, MY WIFE USED TO TELL ME THAT IT TAKES MORE EFFORT TO BE RUDE THAN TO BE POLITE.
SHE WAS A SMART WOMAN. SMARTER THAN ME.
...
INTERESTING DEVICES YOU'VE CONSTRUCTED, MR. TERRIFIC.
TELL HAWKMAN "WELCOME BACK."
WHPP
SURE--
--THING...
...NOW WHERE DID HE GO...
NEAT TRICK.

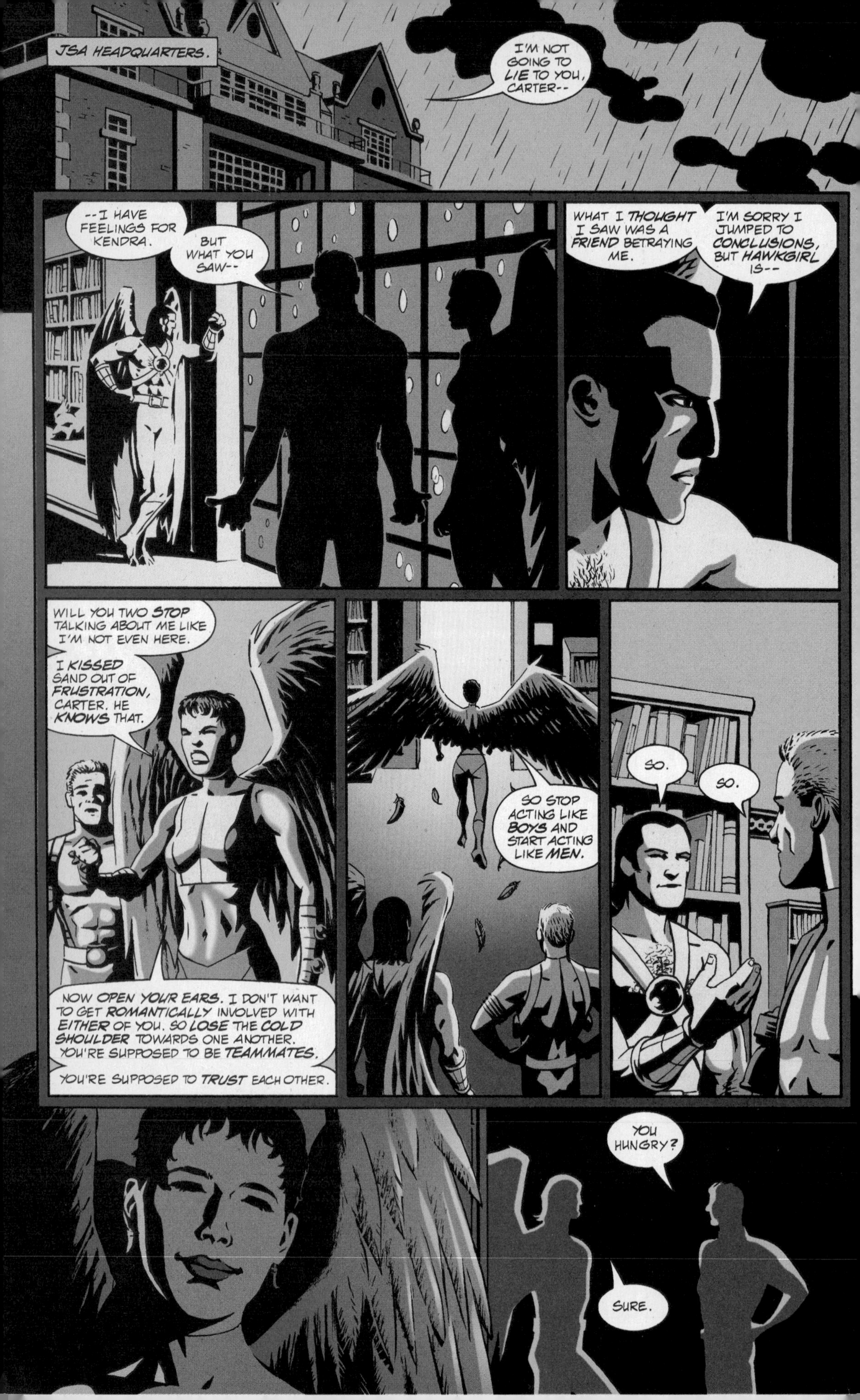
JSA HEADQUARTERS.
I'M NOT GOING TO LIE TO YOU, CARTER--
--I HAVE FEELINGS FOR KENDRA.
BUT WHAT YOU SAW--
WHAT I THOUGHT I SAW WAS A FRIEND BETRAYING ME.
I'M SORRY I JUMPED TO CONCLUSIONS, BUT HAWKGIRL IS--
WILL YOU TWO STOP TALKING ABOUT ME LIKE I'M NOT EVEN HERE.
I KISSED SAND OUT OF FRUSTRATION, CARTER. HE KNOWS THAT.
NOW OPEN YOUR EARS. I DON'T WANT TO GET ROMANTICALLY INVOLVED WITH EITHER OF YOU. SO LOSE THE COLD SHOULDER TOWARDS ONE ANOTHER. YOU'RE SUPPOSED TO BE TEAMMATES.
YOU'RE SUPPOSED TO TRUST EACH OTHER.
SO STOP ACTING LIKE BOYS AND START ACTING LIKE MEN.
SO.
SO.
YOU HUNGRY?
SURE.

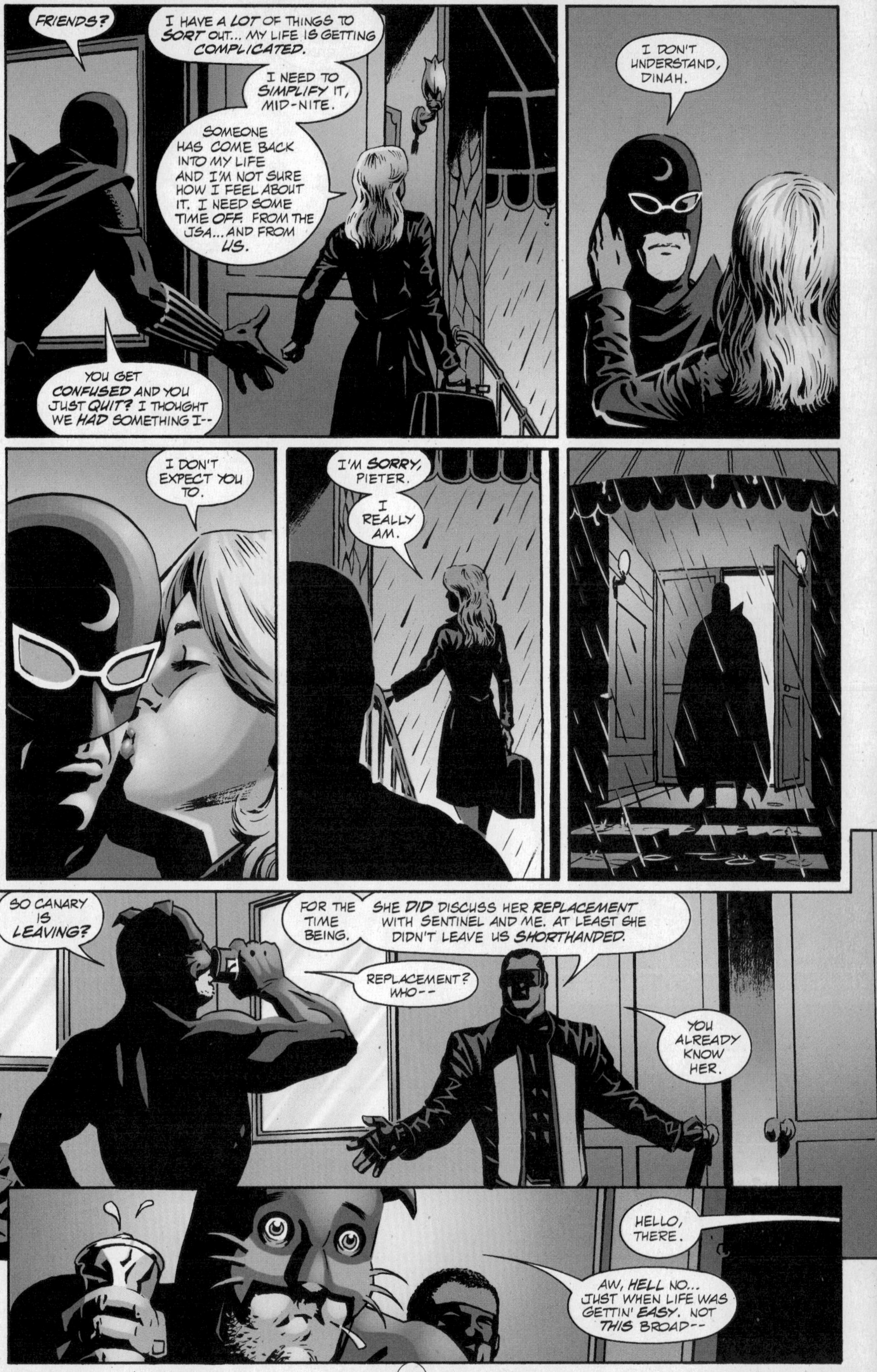
FRIENDS?
I HAVE A LOT OF THINGS TO SORT OUT... MY LIFE IS GETTING COMPLICATED.
I NEED TO SIMPLIFY IT, MID-NITE.
SOMEONE HAS COME BACK INTO MY LIFE AND I'M NOT SURE HOW I FEEL ABOUT IT. I NEED SOME TIME OFF. FROM THE JSA... AND FROM US.
YOU GET CONFUSED AND YOU JUST QUIT? I THOUGHT WE HAD SOMETHING I--
I DON'T UNDERSTAND, DINAH.
I DON'T EXPECT YOU TO.
I'M SORRY, PIETER.
I REALLY AM.
SO CANARY IS LEAVING?
FOR THE TIME BEING.
SHE DID DISCUSS HER REPLACEMENT WITH SENTINEL AND ME. AT LEAST SHE DIDN'T LEAVE US SHORTHANDED.
REPLACEMENT? WHO--
YOU ALREADY KNOW HER.
HELLO, THERE.
AW, HELL NO... JUST WHEN LIFE WAS GETTIN' EASY. NOT THIS BROAD--

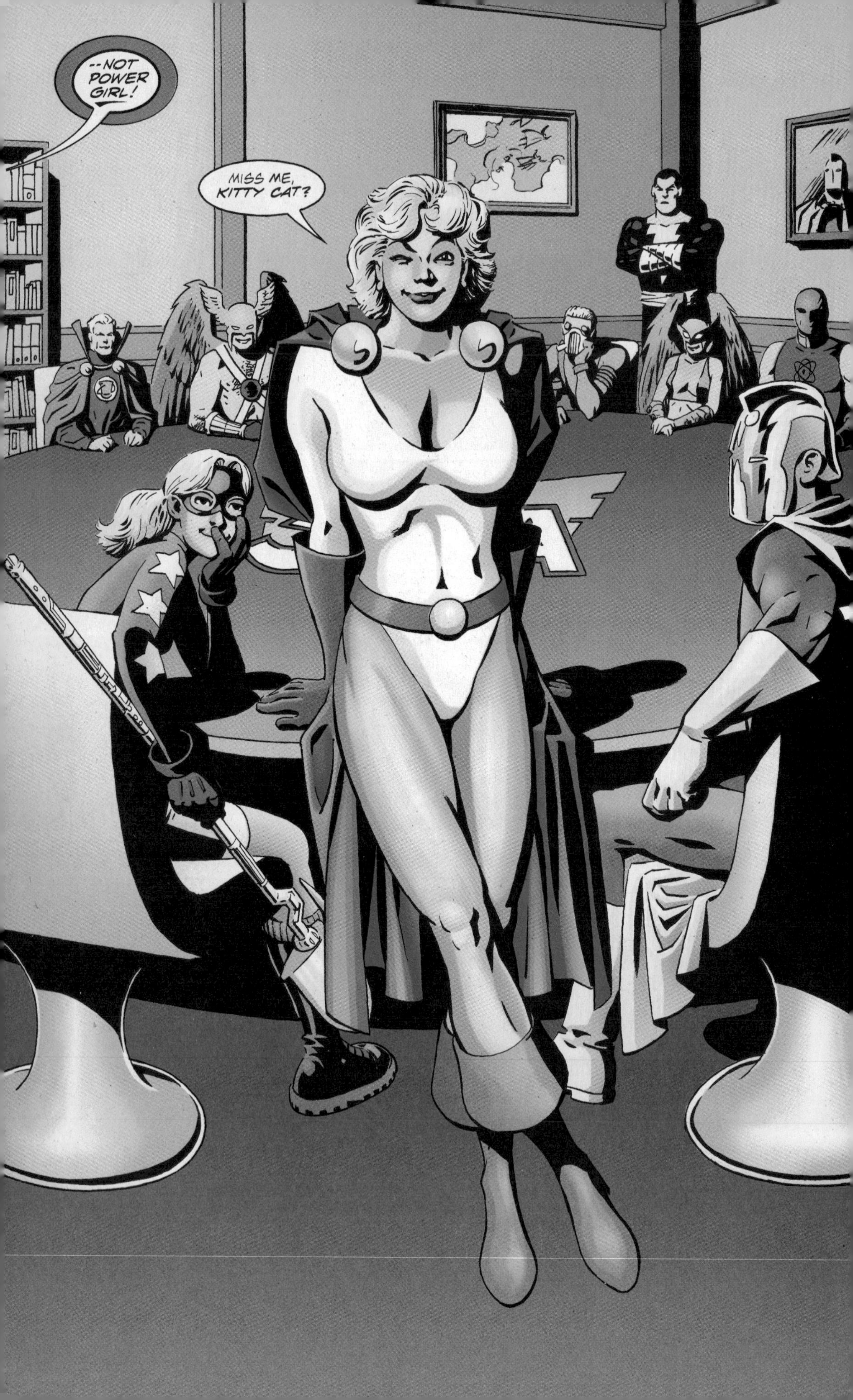
--NOT POWER GIRL!
MISS ME, KITTY CAT?

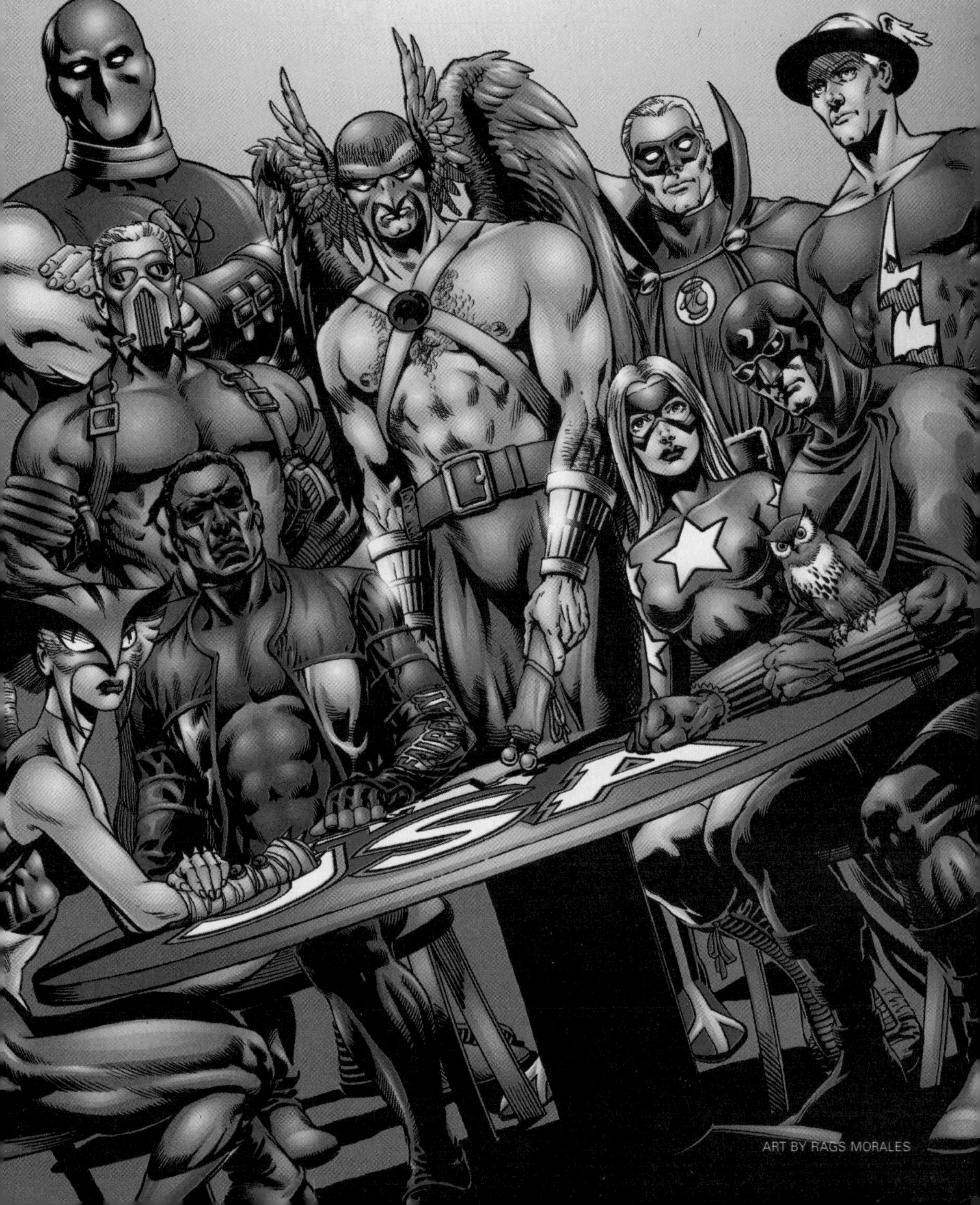
JSA

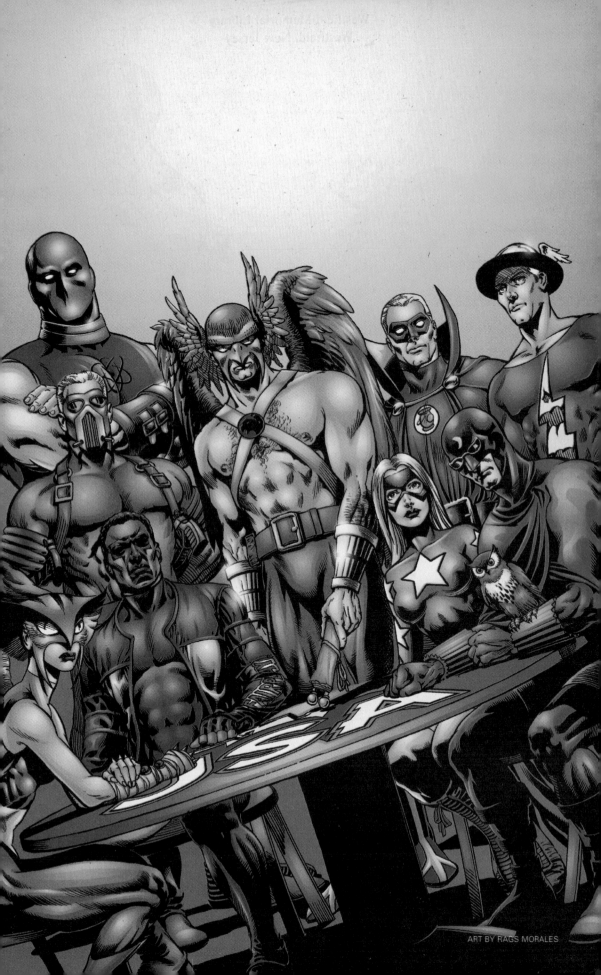

ART BY RAGS MORALES

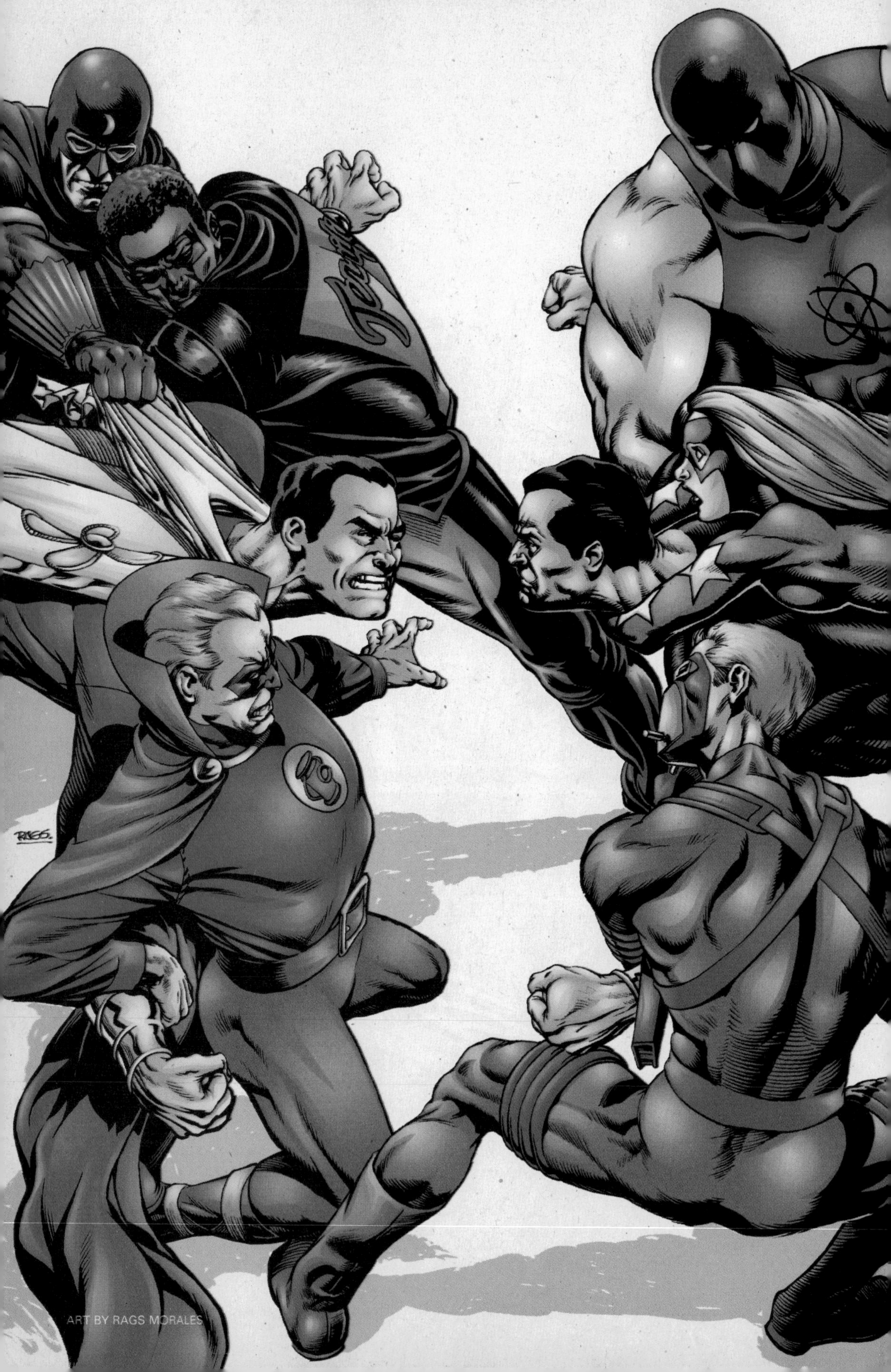
RAGS.

ART BY RAGS MORALES

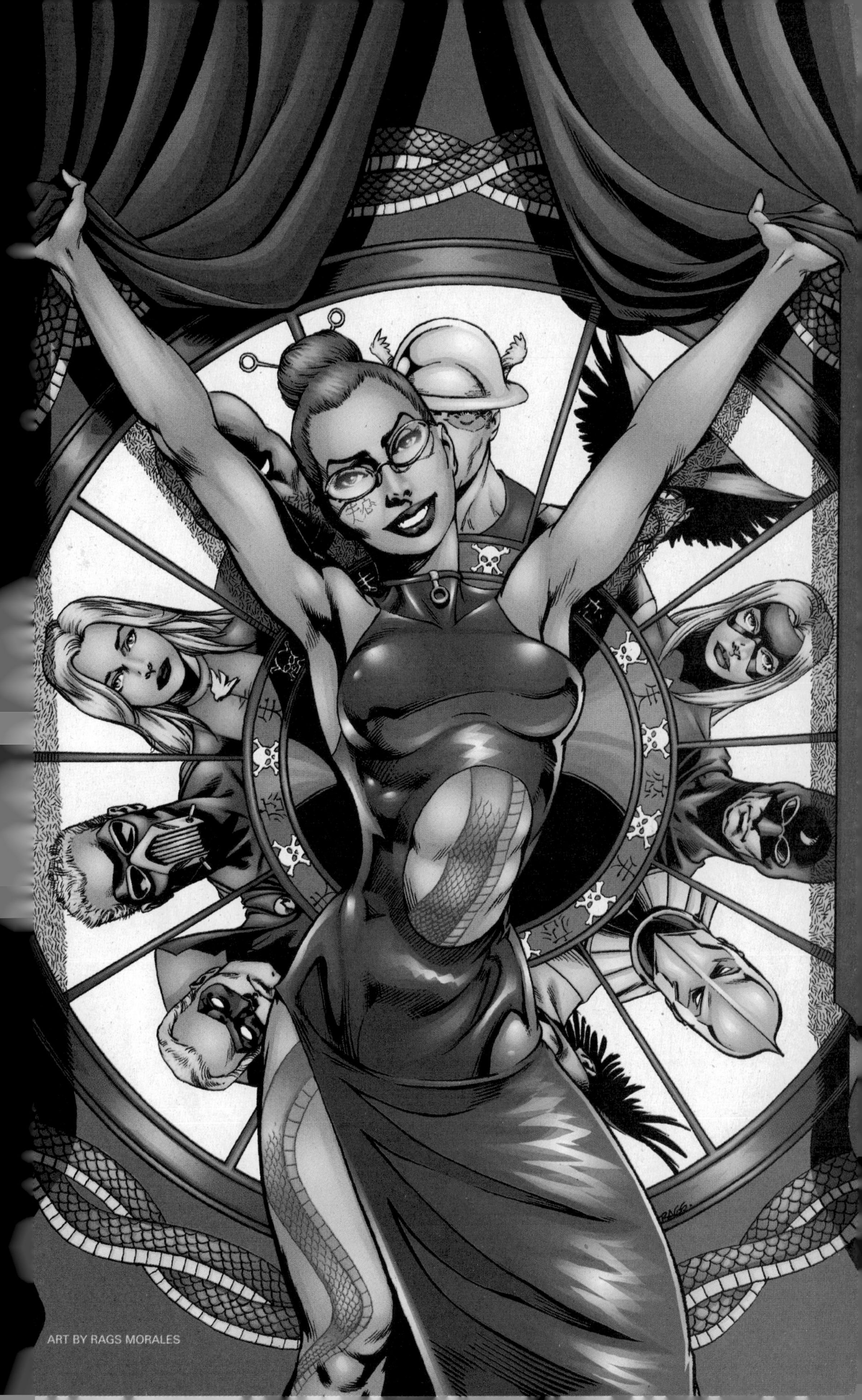

ART BY RAGS MORALES

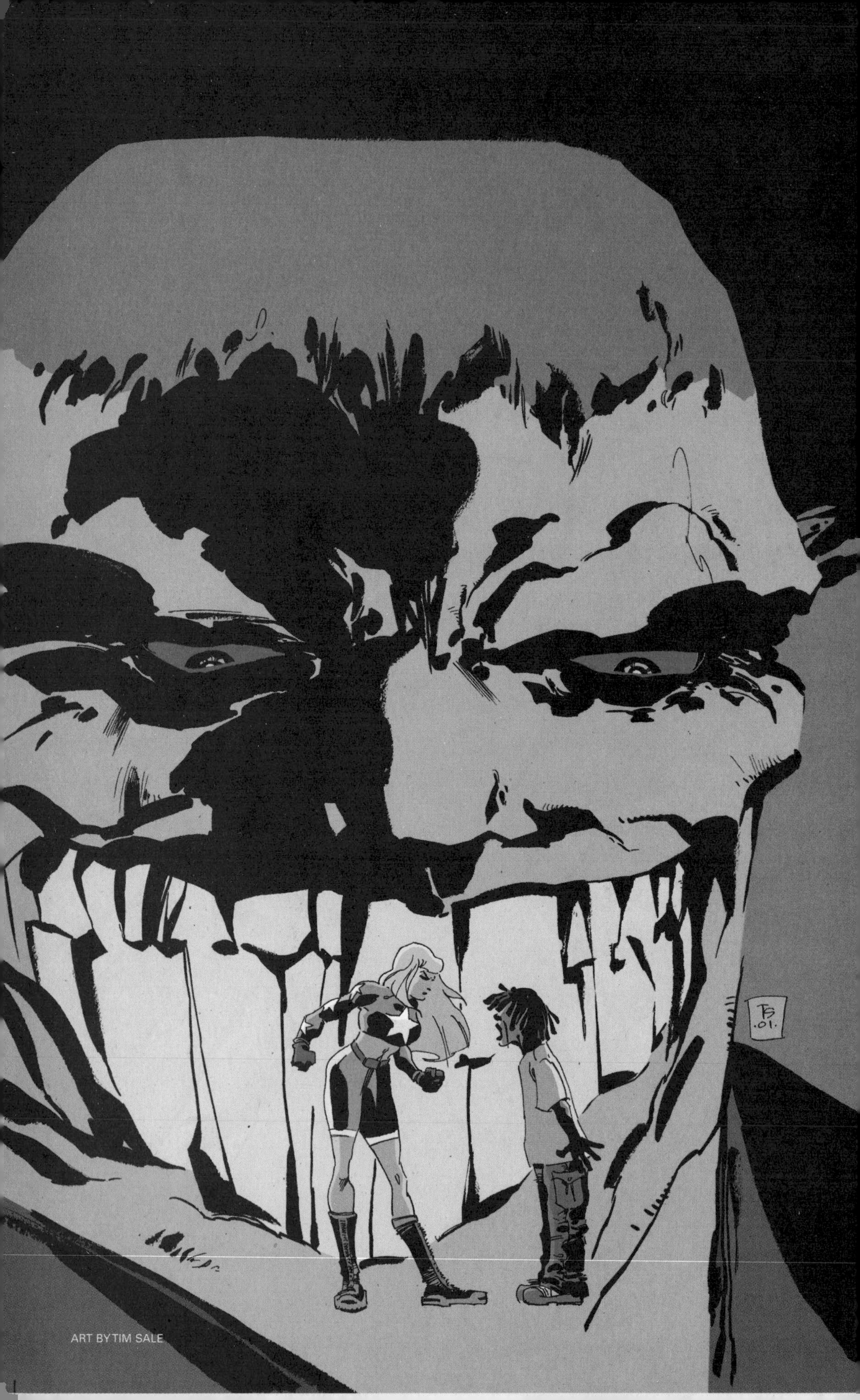

ART BY TIM SALE

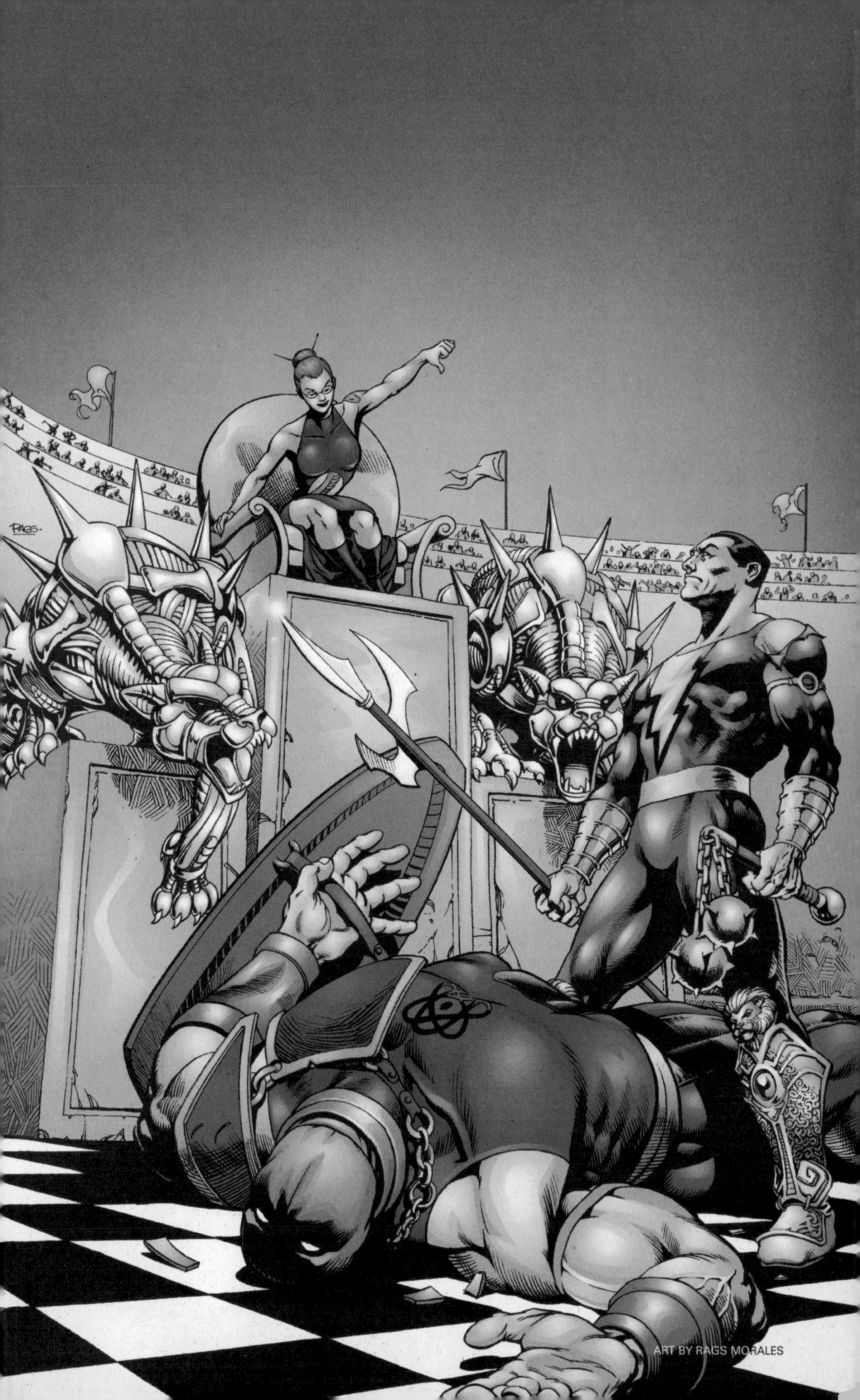
RAGS.
ART BY RAGS MORALES

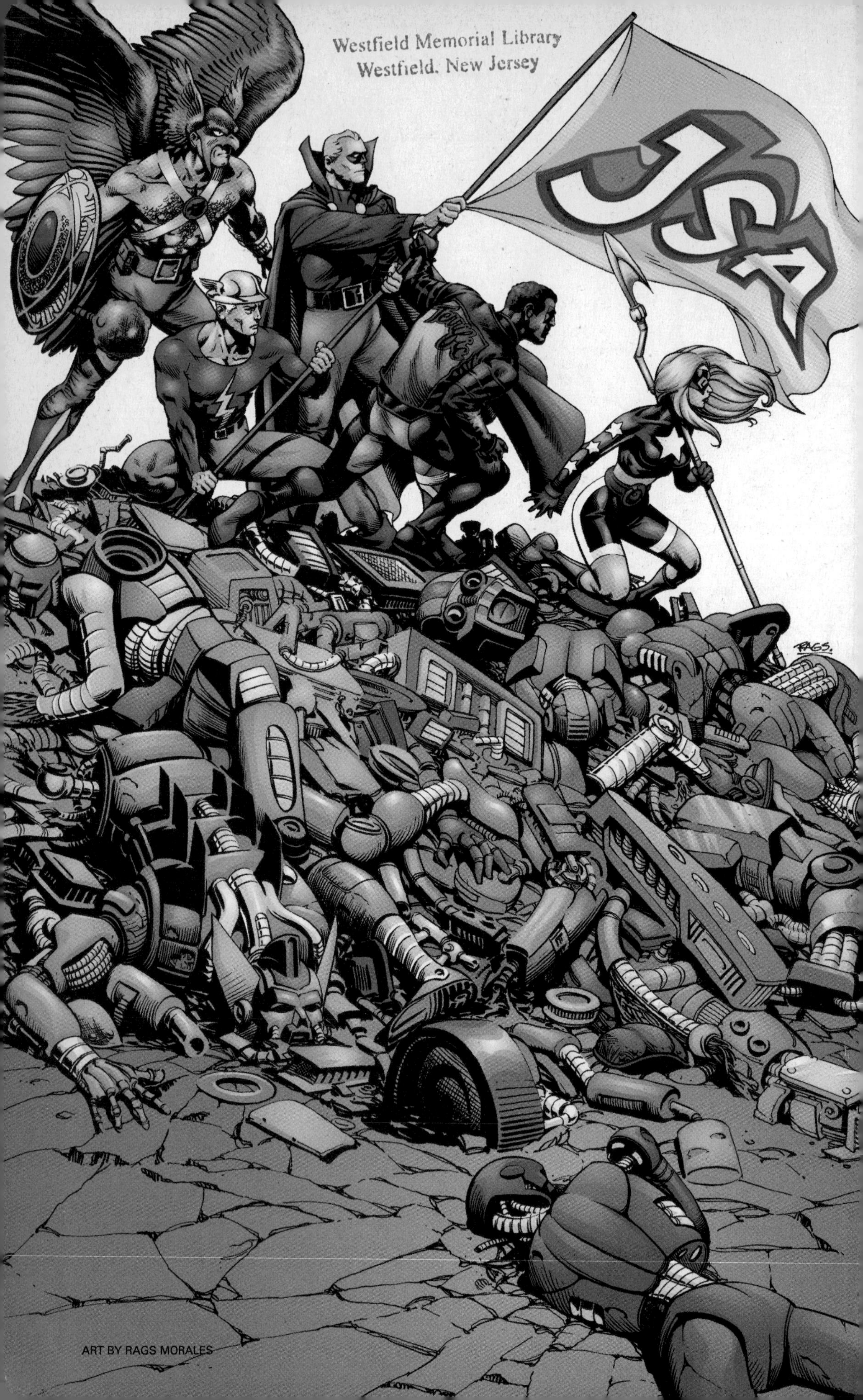
JSA
RAGS.

ART BY RAGS MORALES

S U P E R M A N
THE NEVER-ENDING BATTLE CONTINUES IN
THESE BOOKS FROM DC COMICS:

**FOR READERS OF
ALL AGES**

**SUPERMAN: ADVENTURES OF
THE MAN OF STEEL**
P. Dini/S. McCloud/R. Burchett/
B. Blevins

SUPERMAN: PEACE ON EARTH
Paul Dini/Alex Ross

**BATMAN & SUPERMAN
ADVENTURES: WORLD'S FINEST**
Paul Dini/Joe Staton/Terry Beatty

GRAPHIC NOVELS

SON OF SUPERMAN
H. Chaykin/D. Tischman/
J.H. Williams III/M. Gray

SUPERMAN: END OF THE CENTURY
Stuart Immonen/José Marzan Jr.

COLLECTIONS

THE KENTS
J. Ostrander/T. Truman/
T. Mandrake/M. Bair

**THE DEATH OF SUPERMAN
Trilogy**
THE DEATH OF SUPERMAN
WORLD WITHOUT A SUPERMAN
THE RETURN OF SUPERMAN
Various writers and artists

SUPERMAN: THE MAN OF STEEL
John Byrne/Dick Giordano

**SUPERMAN/DOOMSDAY:
HUNTER/PREY**
Dan Jurgens/Brett Breeding

SUPERMAN: THE DARK SIDE
J.F. Moore/Kieron Dwyer/
Hilary Barta

**SUPERMAN: THE DEATH OF
CLARK KENT**
Various writers and artists

**SUPERMAN:
THE DOOMSDAY WARS**
Dan Jurgens/Norm Rapmund

SUPERMAN: EXILE
Various writers and artists

SUPERMAN FOR ALL SEASONS
Jeph Loeb/Tim Sale

**SUPERMAN: KRISIS OF THE
KRIMSON KRYPTONITE**
Various writers and artists

SUPERMAN: PANIC IN THE SKY
Various writers and artists

SUPERMAN TRANSFORMED!
Various writers and artists

**SUPERMAN: THE TRIAL OF
SUPERMAN**
Various writers and artists

**SUPERMAN: THE WEDDING
AND BEYOND**
Various writers and artists

**SUPERMAN: THEY SAVED
LUTHOR'S BRAIN**
R. Stern/J. Byrne/B. McLeod/
J. Guice/K. Dwyer/various

**SUPERMAN VS. THE REVENGE
SQUAD**
Various writers and artists

**SUPERMAN: WHATEVER
HAPPENED TO THE MAN OF
TOMORROW?**
A. Moore/C. Swan/G. Pérez/
K. Schaffenberger

SUPERMAN: THE DAILIES
Jerry Siegel/Joe Shuster

**SUPERMAN: THE SUNDAY
CLASSICS**
Jerry Siegel/Joe Shuster

SUPERMAN IN THE SIXTIES
Various writers and artists

**THE GREATEST SUPERMAN
STORIES EVER TOLD**
Various writers and artists

**LOIS & CLARK: THE NEW
ADVENTURES OF SUPERMAN**
Various writers and artists

STEEL: THE FORGING OF A HERO
Various writers and artists

SUPERGIRL
P. David/G. Frank/T. Dodson/
C. Smith/K. Story

KINGDOM COME
Mark Waid/Alex Ross

**LEGENDS OF THE WORLD'S
FINEST**
Walter Simonson/Dan Brereton

**SUPERMAN/BATMAN:
ALTERNATE HISTORIES**
Various writers and artists

ARCHIVE EDITIONS

SUPERMAN ARCHIVES Vol. 1
(SUPERMAN 1-4)
SUPERMAN ARCHIVES Vol. 2
(SUPERMAN 5-8)
SUPERMAN ARCHIVES Vol. 3
(SUPERMAN 9-12)
SUPERMAN ARCHIVES Vol. 4
(SUPERMAN 13-16)
All by Jerry Siegel/Joe Shuster

**SUPERMAN: THE ACTION
COMICS ARCHIVES Vol. 1**
(ACTION COMICS 1, 7-20)
**SUPERMAN: THE ACTION
COMICS ARCHIVES Vol. 2**
(ACTION COMICS 21-36)
All by Jerry Siegel/Joe Shuster

**WORLD'S FINEST COMICS
ARCHIVES Vol. 1**
(SUPERMAN 76,
WORLD'S FINEST 71-85)
B. Finger/E. Hamilton/C. Swan/
various

TO FIND MORE COLLECTED EDITIONS AND MONTHLY COMIC BOOKS FROM DC COMICS,
CALL 1-888-COMIC BOOK FOR THE NEAREST COMICS SHOP
OR GO TO YOUR LOCAL BOOK STORE.

Visit us at www.dccomics.com

SM0011